The
Sir Thomas
More
CIRCLE

A program of ideas and their
impact on secular drama

BY PEARL HOGREFE

THE UNIVERSITY OF ILLINOIS PRESS, URBANA, 1959

A GRANT FROM THE FORD FOUNDATION HAS HELPED
TO DEFRAY THE COST OF PUBLISHING THIS WORK.

ACKNOWLEDGMENTS

For anything that may be worth while in this study I am deeply indebted to Charles Read Baskervill, who interested me in the More circle. Renaissance scholarship in general also owes him a debt which has not always been adequately acknowledged. His brief article, "John Rastell's Dramatic Activities," in *Modern Philology*, 1916, called attention to the drama connected with the More circle; the work of the 1920's and 1930's, both in England and in the United States, owed much to his pioneering.

Two other scholars urged and inspired me to go on to the completion of this work although they had had no personal connections with it. They are the late George R. Coffman, formerly Head of the Department of English at the University of North Carolina, and Hardin Craig, the generous friend of all students in the Renaissance.

I am grateful to many libraries and their librarians: Harper Library at the University of Chicago, the Newberry Library, the Henry E. Huntington Library, and the British Museum. But I owe the greatest debt to the Folger Shakespeare Library, a friendly, efficient research center where human and scholarly needs are anticipated. My special thanks are warmly extended to Louis B. Wright, Director, for other courtesies, for encouragement, and for constructive comment; I am grateful to the staff members and the many fellow readers who were good enough to listen or to read some of my chapters. I am especially indebted to Professor Kathrine Koller, Department of English, the University of Rochester, for reading the first versions of all my chapters. She promptly and generously gave suggestions which led me to eliminate faults and to add pertinent material. Her helpfulness was beyond the call of duty, either to friendship or scholarship.

Grants from three organizations have helped me to complete this book: a small grant many years ago from the American Council of Learned Societies, a fellowship from the Folger Shakespeare Library for the summer of 1951, and the Founders Fellowship from the American Association of University Women for 1952–53. The last grant made possible a year of uninterrupted study and writing. I acknowledge this assistance from individuals and from organizations with an appreciation which goes beyond mere words.

The frontispiece, a painting by Holbein, is copyright by the Frick Collection and used with permission.

PEARL HOGREFE
IOWA STATE UNIVERSITY
AMES, IOWA

CONTENTS

INTRODUCTION

Sir Thomas More and his friends were in close agreement on a body
of ideas which covered the important phases of human life. There
were several reasons for their tendency to express similar views.
First, any member of the More circle held ideas which were deeply
rooted in medieval soil—no matter how bitterly he opposed certain concepts or abuses in the centuries preceding him. Second, he
found his ideas in the classics and in the literature of the early
Christian church; when his views came from these sources, he
tended to agree with his friends, who were also engaged in making a synthesis of classical and Christian culture. Third, any member of the group was closely associated with the other members by
friendship and marriage, by legal and business ties, or by social
and educational interests; and thus he lived in a current of free-
flowing ideas. Fourth, instead of searching for individual ideas, each
man was looking for universal truth. Believing in divine revelation
and also in educated human reason—the power of every competent
educated man, Christian or pagan, to discover the law of nature—
he assumed that his truth would agree with the truth discovered
by his friends. Hence he accepted many ideas of classical writers;
and hence he sometimes spoke, as Erasmus did, of "Saint Socrates"
or "Saint Seneca," with no literal meaning but with a desire to
emphasize common truth.

To call these men a circle is not to imply any formal organization. But as they were closely associated, some term is convenient
for the group; and the term *humanist*, besides being somewhat
threadbare, tends to stir conflict, to produce a mental fog, and to
be too large or too limited. They were humanists according to the
definition of Gerald G. Walsh in *Medieval Humanism;* they believed that it is man's privilege to seek happiness in this life as a
human being, not an angel or a beast; and that worthy human
happiness is based on reason, conscience, and good taste, leading
men to truth, to right, justice, and goodness, and to permanent,
spiritual beauty. They were Christian humanists; they believed
that men best find these goals when they are helped by divine
revelation, divine commands, and divine grace.[1] But this large
definition may include some fathers of the early church—Abelard,
Thomas Aquinas, Dante, Petrarch—and even men of the twentieth
century. More and his friends had some of the interests named by
Hugh Watt when he classified humanists, but they do not fit neatly
into any one of his three groups: those who wished to practice all
the vices as well as the virtues of paganism; those who forsook an
incomplete, inaccurate Aristotle for Plato and the neo-Platonists;
and those who furthered a renaissance in religion based on a return
to the early fathers of the church and the New Testament.[2] None
of the More circle wished to adopt the vices of paganism; some
were interested in both Aristotle and Plato; and all or nearly all
were concerned with a renaissance in religion. A recent biographer
of Colet has said: "Colet's Christocentric Humanism showed itself
in a life altogether orientated towards God and Christ."[3] This
statement, with some allowance for differences in the degree of the
orientation and in the degree of emphasis upon the classics, might
be applied also to most of the men in the More circle. Their attitude
to the classics agreed with that of the early writers described by
Sir Richard C. Jebb: "Ancient Latin writers used the word *huma-
nitas* to denote the civilising and refining influence of polite letters
and of the liberal arts, as they also applied the epithet *humanus* to a

[1] Gerald Groveland Walsh, S.J., *Medieval Humanism* (New York, 1942), pp. 1–2.

[2] *Encyclopaedia of Religion and Ethics*, ed. by James Hastings, 12 vols. and index (New
York, 1913–1927), VI, 832, under "Humanists."

[3] Ernest William Hunt, *Dean Colet and his Theology* (London, 1956), p. 12.

character which had received that influence." [4] But all these definitions do not distinguish them from men of other centuries; and for
this study, they emphasize too much the concern with the classics.

Neither are the men of the More circle adequately described
by Roberto Weiss, precise as his definition may be for his study of
the fifteenth century. He defined *humanism* as a concern with
"the whole range of classical studies and activities as conceived
by the Italians from the days of Petrarch" and *humanist* as "the
scholar who studied the writings of ancient authors without fear
of supernatural anticiceronian warnings, searched for manuscripts
of lost or rare classical texts, collected the works of classical writers,
and attempted to learn Greek and write like the ancient authors
of Rome." [5] More and his friends did learn or try to learn Greek
and to use classic Latin, but they were not mere collectors or even
mere readers of manuscripts. They wished to edit and to print
Greek and Latin writings, both artistic and utilitarian, to make
them available for teachers and leaders first, and then to use them,
along with Christian literature, in a broad program of social reform.
They did not wish to revive classical antiquity, though discussions
about them sometimes imply that they cherished that aim. So it
seems better to avoid the terms *humanism* and *humanist,* whenever possible, because they put too much emphasis on the classics,
to consider More and his friends as a group of men working together in England, about 1500 to 1535, and to include Erasmus
and Vives, since each lived for some time in England.

To admit that many important ideas of the men in the More
circle were not original, when considered as separate ideas, may
save repetition later. Attacks on abuses in the church, combined
with piety and loyalty and with a serious desire to reform, can
be traced back to the early centuries of the church. Such attacks,
in either serious or satirical style, were common in fourteenth-century England, as G. R. Owst demonstrated in several chapters of
Literature and Pulpit in Medieval England. Pictures of clerical
vice presented with detachment or cynical amusement were char-

[4] *Cambridge Modern History,* 13 vols. and atlas (Cambridge, 1902), I, 538.
[5] Roberto Weiss, *Humanism in England during the Fifteenth Century,* 2nd ed. (Oxford, 1957), p. 1.

acteristic of medieval schwank and fabliau. Such pictures appeared in the *Decameron* and in the Shipman's and Pardoner's Tales; and Chaucer, too, drew his contrasting picture of the poor Parson. Defense of the secular classics by individuals may be found in almost any century of the Christian era. For example, Jerome (c. 340–420), though he once renounced the classics because of a fevered dream, taught them to boys, and owned and used himself a large collection of classical and Christian manuscripts. Origen, Basil, and Augustine were among those who approved at times modified use of the classics. Opposition to dialectic, usually implying approval of the grammatical method of interpretation, was not a discovery of sixteenth-century England. Jerome used the grammatical method. Augustine (354–430) sometimes used it, though he seems to have preferred the dialectic approach.[6] John of Salisbury (c. 1115–80) criticized the neglect of the grammatical method in his period, with the resulting loss of meaning and the decline of classical style and taste.[7] Petrarch said that the dialectical disputers liked to fight with subtle words, not to discover the truth. Lorenzo Valla (c. 1406–57), whose leadership Erasmus accepted, worked as a grammarian on classical or biblical material, using linguistic and rhetorical details, moral philosophy, and all legal, political, and historical information.

Opposition to the use of the Schoolmen as authorities appeared in England and elsewhere long before the sixteenth century. Roger Bacon (c. 1214–94) criticized the study of theology in his age because theologians gave too much attention to the *Sentences* and too little attention to the Bible. Standard biographies point out that Gerson (1363–1429) wished to banish scholastic subtleties and to return to a simpler theology founded on the scriptures; and that Richard Rolle of Hampole (c. 1290–1349), a mystic and individualist who remained entirely loyal to his church, stressed the love of God rather than the knowledge of God, exalted the spirit of religion over mere forms, and had a distaste for scholastic theology.

[6] Frederic W. Farrar, *Lives of the Fathers*, 2 vols. (New York, 1889), vol. I, Chapter VIII; vol. II, Chapters XIII, XVI, XVII.

[7] Sir John Edwin Sandys, *A History of Classical Scholarship*, 3rd ed.; 3 vols. (Cambridge, 1921), I, 673–74. No evidence appears that the second and third volumes were printed in this third edition.

In working as an editor of scripture and of the early fathers of the church, Erasmus was not an inventor of new methods. Jerome, whom Erasmus cited as authority for his work, tried to find the earliest texts of the earliest Christian writers, collated editions, made critical texts, and was proud of his efforts to use the three languages, Hebrew, Greek, and Latin. He refused to believe in a narrow, verbal inspiration, though he did not have the courage to defend his views consistently; and he sometimes let the rabbis who helped him with his Hebrew influence him toward the acceptance of *multiplex intelligentia*, or mysteries in the order of Hebrew words. Like Erasmus, Jerome met objections and abuse at times; he became unpopular in Rome when he revised the Latin text of the Bible at the command of Pope Damasus I. When he translated the Old Testament direct from the Hebrew, instead of following the Septuagint Greek version completed about the beginning of the Christian era, Augustine thought that his work was undesirable. But the arguments of Jerome convinced him and he withdrew his objections.[8] Roger Bacon stressed the need of knowing Greek, Arabic, and Hebrew grammar, adding that there were not four men in the Latin-Christian world who did have such knowledge and that the men who understood the languages did not understand the science in the classics they were trying to translate; he demanded translations of Aristotle from the original Greek; and if he had the power, he said, he would burn all the translations of Aristotle to keep men from wasting their time and multiplying errors. He also pointed out errors of translation in the Vulgate and errors made by those who had recently presumed to correct the text. With these and other comments he was laying the foundation for a sound textual editing of the scriptures.[9]

As for sermons adapted to the common people, stirring them to love God and to live like Christians, Fisher, Colet, Erasmus, and More were reviving an old tradition. Augustine, when he became Bishop of Hippo, began preaching short, plain sermons aimed to touch the hearts and lives of uneducated fishermen.[10] In medieval England, Owst concluded, "in a polite and official world of Latin

[8] Farrar, *Lives*, vol. II, Chapter XVI.
[9] Sandys, *A History*, I, 589–97.
[10] Farrar, *Lives*, II, 366–67.

and French, the pulpit alone had maintained a regular public use of the English tongue by educated men from the days of the Conquest." In the early thirteenth century the friars brought to England minds that had been educated in Continental learning; and when they were faithful to their calling they lived a life of evangelism among the common people.[11] But by 1500 preaching seems to have degenerated; it needed reform.[12]

The concern with the love of God rather than the knowledge of God only, the return to primitive Christianity and simplicity in the church, the emphasis upon the Bible instead of *Sentences* from the Schoolmen, the use of the grammatical instead of the dialectical method of reading and interpreting scripture, the fearless attacks upon vice even among monks and priests, and the education of schoolboys as a method of reform—all these had been taught in the fifteenth century by the Brothers and Sisters of the Common Life. Erasmus had been educated under their influences.[13]

The impact of More and his friends upon their contemporaries did not come from originality in individual ideas. It came perhaps from the contrast between their intellectual aliveness and the stagnation of the fifteenth century, from their united efforts to transform thought into action, and from their skill, oral and written, in expressing their ideas. The impact was deepened perhaps because Europe still held to a universal language and a universal religion and because these men belonged to almost the first generation who could spread their ideas through printed books. Perhaps their impact upon their contemporaries and upon us is lasting because they were mainly men of integrity, even when they lost property, native land, or life.

Part I of this study attempts to analyze and to document the main ideas which More and his friends wished to use for the reform of society: Chapter I, "Nature and the Law of Nature"; Chapter

---

[11] G. R. Owst, *Literature and Pulpit in Medieval England* (Cambridge, 1933), pp. 4–5.

[12] J. H. Lupton, *A Life of John Colet* (London, 1909), pp. 137–41; James Bass Mullinger, *The University of Cambridge . . . to . . . 1535* (Cambridge, 1873), pp. 437–41; T. S. K. Scott-Craig, "Thomas More's 1518 Letter to the University of Oxford," *Ren. News*, I, no. 2 (1948), 22.

[13] Albert Hyma, *The Youth of Erasmus* (Ann Arbor, Mich., 1930), Chapter III, and *passim;* Hyma, *The Christian Renaissance: A History of the "Devotio Moderna"* (Grand Rapids, Mich., 1924), Chapter III, sections III and IV.

II, "The Bases of True Nobility"; Chapter III, "Religious Reform"; Chapter IV, "Law and Government"; Chapter V, "Education in General"; Chapter VI, "Education of Women: Love, Marriage." Part II is concerned with the expression of these same ideas in the drama connected with the More circle either by printing or writing, and possibly by staging. Hence the six sections of Part II deal with the same ideas as Part I, in the same order.

The many scholars interested in theology will note, perhaps with some disappointment or disapproval, that this study does not include religious controversy about the fundamentals of the Catholic faith. The omission is a considered judgment and seems to have basic reasons: More and his friends (excepting John Rastell, in the last years of his life, and one or two other men) did not choose to change the basic theology of the Catholic church or to start controversy about it. Though More was finally drawn into debate by circumstances, he had told "Son Roper" that he would give his life if he might by so doing bring universal peace, settle well the king's marriage question, and eliminate the "many errors and heresees" with which the church was afflicted and bring a "perfecte vniformity" in religion.[14] But in dealing with their program of reform it seems necessary to deal with some ideas which were both theological tenets and the bases for secular views. Such an idea was freedom of the will. They took it for granted in all their thinking; they defined it more clearly in religious connotations. But it was *a* basis, perhaps even *the* basis, for their faith in education, including those phases of education which we might call secular. Hence it seems reasonable to cite their mention of it in religious works but to discuss it more fully in other connotations.

It is difficult to organize in six chapters or in any number of chapters the program of reform advocated by the men of the Sir Thomas More circle. But the task approaches possibility as one excludes the bitter controversy of the late 1520's and the 1530's. Though this controversy helped to block their hopes there is no evidence that it altered their basic beliefs about an ideal society based on the best classic and Christian principles.

[14] William Roper, *The Lyfe of Sir Thomas Moore, knighte*, ed. by Elsie Hitchcock, *EETS*, no. 197 (1935), 25–26.

PART I *Ideas: the program of reform*

CHAPTER I *Nature and the law of nature*

When the men of the More circle wrote about nature and the law of nature, between 1500 and 1535, they used the term nature with many different meanings.

First, in the phrase *the law of nature* (which they tended to use instead of *natural law*) they referred to the body of truths which they believed to be planted in the soul of every rational creature—Christian, Jew, or pagan. These innate truths were never wholly extinct in any man, though they might be dimmed by sin or remain undeveloped by lack of education. They were one form of revelation; the other form came from supernatural authority. Second, *nature* had another closely related meaning: the rational quality in man, his power to reason. Through this power, also innate, he could discover the law of nature. Third, *nature* sometimes meant the essential qualities of man in a generic sense, often uncorrupted man. As his power to reason was one of these essentials, this definition somewhat overlaps the preceding one. This meaning was also extended to other life; for example, birds or tigers live according to their nature. Fourth, *nature* meant also the individual quality, capacity, bent, direction, or inclination of a specific human being. Fifth, *nature* sometimes meant the whole physical world: "the world of sensible objects, its ordinary processes, and empirically known laws." Sixth, *nature* might be the agent of God, austere, benign, educative in function, the director of decay and creation in all things—inanimate, animate, and human. Seventh, *nature* was used to mean a norm of social organization or conduct, or a life adjusted to the views of the deity or his agent. So the Utopians lived a life according to nature. Eighth, *nature* as used occasionally, implied "the essence or Platonic idea, imperfectly realized in empirical reality." [1] Erasmus used it casually or lightly in this sense; Vives, more seriously at times.

Probably they sometimes used the word *nature* with other meanings, but only the eight definitions given above seem vital to the chapters of this work. The first, second, fifth, and seventh of these definitions are basic to this chapter; the third and fourth are important in Chapter V; nature as the agent of God will appear again in the discussion of certain plays. To provide full documentation for them here would be a needless repetition, it seems; instead they will be supported by quoted passages wherever they become important.

THE LAW OF NATURE

ORIGINS, CLASSICAL AND CHRISTIAN

The law of nature came from the two great traditions— classic and Christian. The classic or Greek view, held by the Stoics, assumed a fourfold division of the universe: first, a final cause; second, a causal agent, which might be spoken of as nature or personified as nature; third, primal matter; fourth, form, which is matter after it has been shaped by the causal agent according to the plan of the final cause, and which includes man, animal, plant, or any physical substance created by natural forces. The Stoics conceived of nature as the creative cosmic power, world-thought, or *logos,* and the human soul as a part of the divine world-thought. They believed harmony with nature to be a development of the essential nature of man in a morality which would coincide with genuine complete humanity and would also bring about an un-

---

[1] Arthur O. Lovejoy, *Essays in the History of Ideas* (Baltimore, 1948), " 'Nature' as Norm in Tertullian," pp. 308–38. Though the definitions were not applied to More and his friends, I am indebted for the ideas.

folding of the inmost germ of one's individual nature. Thus they
defined life according to nature as a duty which one fulfilled by
opposing the sensuous life; the demands of nature and reason were
identical and were opposed to those of the senses. They considered
duty to human society as a command of reason which only occasionally gave way to man's task of personal perfection; and the
basis of social duty was the fact that man's soul was one substance
with world-reason or world-thought. Thus they defined the ideal
state as a realm of reason, a universal empire, a spiritual unity of
knowledge and will. Those who held these principles of philosophy
were comparatively indifferent to the form of government, so long
as men practiced love and justice, even love for their slaves.

The Stoics believed that men have freedom of the will; they
based this belief upon an analysis of the differences between a
main cause, accessory causes or outer circumstances, and the assent
of personality. They removed any conflict in their ideas by simple
identification, or pantheism. The deity, to them, was the vital principle, the formative force unfolding itself in phenomena, a creating,
guiding reason, an all-ruling providence. Cicero's views, eclectic
but similar to those of the Stoics, included a tendency to personify
nature, with emphasis upon its benign, educative qualities. He
developed these views in his work *De natura deorum.*

The Christian tradition about nature may be traced to the beginning of the Christian era. In the works of some of the fathers of
the early church (the term includes apostolic literature and the
other main writers on Christianity to about the eighth century)
there were objections to the view that nature is God or *logos,* and
some objections to identifying God with either nature or reason.
But Abelard (1079–1142) identified conscience and the natural
moral law with the will of God. John of Salisbury (c. 1115–80)
insisted that a divine influence exists both in written revelation
and in man's reason, that the good man is also the man of knowledge, and that freedom and virtue are inseparable. Thomas Aquinas
(c. 1225–74) continued to identify reason and nature with God
when he "brought scholasticism to its highest development by
harmonizing Aristotelianism with the doctrines of the church."
In this identification, Aquinas, of course, reserved certain doctrines

as mysteries above reason and known only through faith. "The natural dictates of reason must certainly be quite true," he said; "it is impossible to think of their being otherwise." Of course, he added, the tenets of faith are true. "Since therefore falsehood alone is contrary to truth, it is impossible for the truth of faith to be contrary to principles known by natural reason." Assuming that God is the first cause, Aquinas said that all things owe their being to God; hence all have some likeness to God:

Thus also God gives to creatures all their perfections; and thereby He has with all creatures a likeness and an unlikeness at the same time . . . it is more proper to say that the creature is like God than that God is like the creature . . . that which is found to perfection in God is found in other beings by some manner of imperfect participation. . . .[2]

But though all created things have some likeness to God, only intelligent creatures are made in his image;[3] and they only are capable of growth toward perfectibility:

Now a thing's ultimate perfection consists in the attainment of its end. Therefore it belongs to the Divine goodness, as it brought things into existence, so to lead them to their end; and this is to govern. . . . Happiness is the attainment of the Perfect Good. . . . Now that man is capable of the Perfect Good is proved both because his intellect can apprehend the universal and perfect good and because his will can desire it. . . . Hence it is evident that none can attain true and perfect happiness in this life.[4]

Explaining freedom of the will, Aquinas said that human beings have an impulse toward the good, or an insatiable need of uniting themselves to that which is capable of perfecting them. This need is always present in human beings, and to the extent that it influences us, the will is determined. But we must often choose between things that have a partial goodness, and then our will is free: first, to act or to refuse to act—*libertas exercitationis;* second,

---

[2] Thomas Aquinas, *Summa contra Gentiles,* trans. by Joseph Rickaby as *Of God and his Creatures* (London, 1905), Book I, Chapter VII, p. 7; Chapter XXIX, pp. 22–23.

[3] Thomas Aquinas, *Summa theologica,* literally trans. by Fathers of the English Dominican Province, 3 vols. (New York, 1947), I, 21–23. Or see First Part, Question 4. This American version is cited instead of the 21-volume English set (London, 1912–1925) because it is accessible and easier to use. Both have papal authorization.

[4] *Summa theologica,* I, 505, 609, 610. Or see First Part, Question 103, and First Part of Second Part, Question 5.

to choose one of two things—*libertas specificationis.* Foreign elements, including education or the lack of it, either intensify or weaken the will. Anything which clarifies the understanding increases human liberty, and whatever dims intelligence decreases the degree of freedom. Implying man's freedom of choice, Thomas Aquinas also stated or restated a basis for the medieval debates between reason and sensuality: "Therefore it is clear that the universal reason directs the sensitive appetite, which is divided into concupiscible and irascible, and this appetite obeys it." [5]

Thomas Aquinas also stated the reasons for law and explained the kinds of law: "Irrational animals then have a sort of free determination or action but not a free judgment. . . . On the contrary, intelligent beings have not only free action but also free judgment, which is having free will. . . . The acts of irrational creatures . . . are guided by God according to a natural inclination consequent upon the nature of the species . . . there must be given to men something to guide them in their personal acts, and that we call law." [6]

He classified law as eternal, natural, divine, and human, the last three being manifestations of eternal law:

the world is ruled by Divine Providence . . . is governed by Divine Reason. Wherefore the very Idea of the government of things in God, the Ruler of the universe, has the nature of a law. And since the Divine Reason's conception of things is . . . eternal . . . this kind of law must be called eternal.

He also explained the law of nature or of reason:

the light of natural reason, whereby we discern what is good and what is evil, which is the function of the natural law, is nothing else than an imprint on us of the Divine light. It is therefore evident that the natural law is nothing else than the rational creature's participation of the eternal law. (Lex naturalis nihil aliud est quam participatio legis aeternae in rationali creatura.) [7]

---

[5] *Summa theologica,* I, 412, and *passim.* Or see First Part, Question 81, also Questions 82–83.

[6] *Summa contra Gentiles,* Book II, Chapter XLVIII, pp. 109–10; Book III, Chapter CXIV, p. 276.

[7] *Summa theologica,* I, 996, 997, and *passim.* Or First Part of Second Part, Questions 90–97, for extended discussion of law.

In connection with reason he explained the terms *synderesis* and *conscience*. Synderesis, he said, is a "habitus continens praecepta legis naturalis," a power to understand general principles; conscience is the ability to apply them to specific situations.[8] Reginald Pecock, about 1455, seemed to set the judgment of individual reason above all other authority, including the Bible, when he said that it is not the office of scripture to set forth any truth which man's reason may find, learn, or know.[9] But his heresies apparently had little impact. Summaries of canon law continued to repeat the ideas of Thomas Aquinas.[10] A contemporary of Sir Thomas More, Christopher Saint German, in explaining English common law, gave much the same definitions of synderesis, conscience, and reason that Thomas Aquinas had given, and explained the same relations of human law to divine law, the law of nature, and eternal law.[11] More thought him dangerous, probably because he reassured readers with the great body of orthodox thought but added ideas favoring the supremacy of temporal power.

These basic ideas about nature, reason, faith, freedom of the will, human perfectibility, the need of law, and the unity of all law—ideas which Thomas Aquinas organized in his *Summa*—were the foundation of orthodox thought in the early sixteenth century. To More, Erasmus, Vives, and to others who remained loyal to Catholic doctrine, these ideas had become "unconscious mental habits."

Because Thomas Aquinas had tried to harmonize much of Aristotle with Christian doctrine, and because the classical and Christian ideas of nature and the law of nature were similar, it would be difficult to determine (if that were the objective) how much the men of the early sixteenth century were influenced by the direct reading of the classics. But to look at some of the facts

---

[8] *Summa theologica*, I, 407–8. Or First Part, Question 79.

[9] Reginald Pecock, *The Repressor of Over Much Blaming of the Clergy*, ed. by Churchill Babington, 2 vols. (London, 1860), I, 10, 12–13, 25–26, and *passim*.

[10] See Angelus [Carletus] de Clavasio, *Summa Angelica* (1489), British Museum, for one example.

[11] Christopher Saint German, *Hereafter foloweth a dyaloge in Englysshe, betwyxt a doctoure of dyuynyte and a student in the lawes of Englande* (London, 1530), Chapters 13, 14, 15. The thought of these chapters remains the same in many early editions. The work is known to modern lawyers as *Doctor and Student*, from the title given to later editions.

leads to the conclusion that Stoic philosophy was inspiring More and Erasmus to new creation.

About 1500 to 1516 both men were concerned with a whole body of Greek literature and were especially interested in such Stoic philosophers as Plutarch, Cicero, and Seneca. In 1501 Erasmus published an edition of Cicero's *De officiis*, and in 1520 a second edition; in 1515 an edition of Seneca, followed by a second edition in 1529. In 1509 when he was writing *The Praise of Folly* at More's house, he was sufficiently concerned with the Stoics to make more than a half dozen references to them in general, besides his frequent mention of Cicero, Plutarch, and Seneca.[12] Between 1509 and 1514, when he spent most of his time in England, he was working on his edition of Seneca. On March 7, 1515, he dedicated this edition to Bishop Thomas Ruthall; after describing Jerome as "our only theological author whom we can put in the same rank with those of Greece," he added, "And Seneca was so esteemed by Jerome that he is the only non-Christian writer whom he deemed worthy to be read by Christians. Nothing is more holy than his precepts. . . ."[13]

About the same time, More was using his knowledge of Seneca and other Stoical writers, as well as a comprehensive view of the Greek classics, in writing *Utopia*. At the beginning of that work, when Peter Gilles was preparing to introduce More to Hythlodaye, he described the latter as "verye well lerned in the Latyne tonge" but "profounde and excellent in the greke tonge. . . ." He had applied himself to Greek because he had given himself wholly to philosophy, in which he knew that the Romans have left us nothing valuable except the work of Seneca and Cicero. As Hythlodaye named the Greek books he took on his fourth voyage, when he thought that he might not return, he included most of Plato's, more of Aristotle's, and Theophrastus *On Plants*. He added that the Utopians had come to value Plutarch highly and were charmed by the wit and grace of Lucian. They had the grammar of Lascaris, and dictionaries by Hesychius and Dioscorides; Aristophanes, Homer, Euripides, and Sophocles in an Aldine edition; the his-

---

[12] Erasmus, *The Praise of Folly*, ed. by Hoyt H. Hudson (Princeton, 1941), see index.
[13] F. M. Nichols, *The Epistles of Erasmus*, 3 vols. (London, 1901–1918), II, nos. 303, 316.

torians Thucydides, Herodotus, Herodian; and short medical works by Hippocrates as well as Galen's *Microtechne*.[14] Thus in Hythlodaye's account More emphasized natural science, medicine, history, and philosophy, as well as the *belles lettres*. Then, too, the praise of Cicero and Seneca, among Latin philosophers, and the recognition of Plutarch, not as historian but as philosopher, place a strong emphasis upon Stoical thought.

More's analysis of Utopian civilization, though it had many resemblances to the thought of Plato and though it was based upon the Christian principles of avoiding greed, strife, and pride, also furnishes many parallels with Senecan philosophy—parallels which illustrate the re-enforcement of ideas about the law of nature from classical sources. In the philosophy of Seneca reason was paramount: "reason . . . is nothing else than a portion of the divine spirit set in a human body." Hence man must cultivate wisdom by developing his mind, and only the good man can be truly wise. The wise man achieves a calm of spirit which is happiness: his reason directs him to reject sensuality, he exercises control over all his emotions whether they are sad or happy; and he does not seek for honor, wealth, or material possessions. He has also a duty as a citizen. Refuting an opponent who said that simplicity is not safe in a world of mad ambition, Seneca advised his wise man to find something in which he may be useful, even a minor role: "The service of a good citizen is never useless; by being heard and seen, by his expression, by his gesture, by his silent stubbornness, and by his very walk he helps." He suggested that the citizen measure his own powers, the work he undertakes, the men with whom he must work, and all other conditions before he begins action. Frequently he said that the wise man is a citizen of the whole world. The man of wisdom lives according to nature, or the will of the divine being; since nature is a rational force directing men and the universe, obedience to this force is his duty. By such obedience he can chart his course according to his destiny and his own satisfaction. He scorns the vicissitudes of fortune and does

---

[14] More, *Utopia*, trans. by Ralph Robinson and ed. by J. H. Lupton (Oxford, 1895), pp. 26–27, 214–17. This edition will be used throughout for references and quotations because it places side by side the Latin of the 1518 edition and the English of the first translation in 1551.

not blame fortune for his own errors. He faces death with equanimity; and his duty to live a life of inner calm may even compel him to suicide, if age or a painful but incurable illness prevents his use of his normal faculties or the commands of a tyrant force him to live a life not in harmony with nature.[15]

Some parallels of thought in Seneca and in *Utopia* are evident, though Seneca may not be the only source for some of these ideas. More and Hythlodaye, for example, debated the question of service to a prince, quoting both classic and Christian support. The Utopians defined virtue as a life according to nature, a life of reason and sober happiness; they gave citizens time to develop their minds; they valued mind and spirit above material possessions and placed service to the state above personal gain; they counted it cowardly to fear death, and when they had certain incurable diseases they might commit suicide with the consent of their priests.

So far as the law of nature is concerned, then, the classical as well as the Christian tradition had a possible influence on the creation of *Utopia* and on the ideas of Erasmus. The re-enforcement from the classics perhaps gave More and his friends the positive, dynamic quality with which they discussed human possibilities.

WRITINGS

The writings of More, Colet, Erasmus, and their friends are full of assumptions, conscious or unconscious, about the law of nature, man's reason, his freedom of choice, his dignity and perfectibility, and about the unity of all law—eternal, natural, divine, and human. When the ideas are most definitely stated, they tend to appear in theological dress; but the important ones have a habit of reappearing in secular garb. Often in the discussion of education and daily life, they are the unstated assumptions which a reader should not overlook.

John Colet mentioned man's ability to make choices in "A Ryght Fruitfull Monicion," a sermon of unknown date but be-

[15] Lucius Annaeus Seneca, *Ad Lucilium epistulae morales*, trans. by Richard M. Gummere, 3 vols. (London and New York, 1917–1925), II, "On the Proper Time to Slip the Cable," "On Taking One's Own Life," "On Philosophers and Kings," and others. See also *Moral Essays*, trans. by John W. Basore, 3 vols. (London and Cambridge, Mass., 1951), II, "On the Happy Life," "On Tranquillity of Mind," and others.

fore 1519, the year of his death. God, he said, made man "lyke to his owne similitude or ymage, hauynge regarde to thy memory, vnderstanding, and fre wyll"; and if the sensual appetite is not ordered by reason and grace, "thou arte worse ordred than a beest." [16] Bishop Fisher's sermon against Luther, in 1521, implied free will when he said that faith alone is insufficient and that love and good works are required also for justification.[17]

In his later works More defended the doctrine of free will against those who opposed the belief. In the *Dialogue concerning Heresies,* Book IV, Chapter 10, his heading announced this aim; in the heading of Chapter 12 he stated his purpose to attack the "secte of these Lutheranes, whiche ascribe our saluaycyon and damnacion and all our dedes to desteny." [18] In his letter to John Frith, More argued against what he called the great error of men, "some ascrybynge all thynge to destyny wythout any power of mannys free wyll at all. . . ." [19] In his *Apology,* Chapter VIII, he discussed his belief in man's freedom to use his will as a help in attaining faith. He had always held the belief, and he and his friends applied beliefs to all areas, spiritual and secular.

In his early poems, "The Twelve Weapons of Spiritual Battle," More gave the idea of perfectibility a strong religious coloring:

> Regarde, O man, thine excellent nature,
> Thou that with angell art made to bene egall,
> For very shame be not the deuils thrall.[20]

In his letter to Gonell, More applied the idea of perfectibility to the educational development of both men and women, without religious coloring. In letters to his household school about the study of astronomy he suggested perfectibility through education:

You tell me that Nicholas, who is so fond of you and so learned in astronomy, has begun again with you the system of the heavenly bodies. I am grateful to him and I congratulate you in your good fortune; for in the

---

[16] J. H. Lupton, *A Life of John Colet* (London, 1909), Appendix D, p. 306.

[17] *The English Works of John Fisher,* ed. by John E. B. Mayor, *EETS,* ex. ser., XXVII (1876, 1935), 325–26, and *passim.*

[18] More, *The workes . . . in the Englysh tonge* (London, 1557), pp. 261, 273.

[19] Elizabeth F. Rogers, *The Correspondence of Sir Thomas More* (Princeton, 1947), no. 190, p. 454.

[20] More, *The workes,* for the *Apology,* pp. 859–63; for the poems, p. 26.

space of one month, with only a slight labour, you will thus learn thoroughly these sublime wonders of the Eternal Workman. . . .[21]

In another letter he said:

Go forward, then, in that new and admirable science by which you ascend to the stars. But while you gaze on them assiduously, consider that this holy time of Lent warns you, and that beautiful and holy poem of Boetius keeps singing in your ears, to raise your mind also to heaven, lest the soul look downwards to the earth, after the manner of brutes, while the body looks upwards.[22]

In his letter to the University of Oxford in 1518, More said:

Moreover, there are some who through knowledge of things natural [i.e., rational] construct a ladder by which to rise to the contemplation of things supernatural; they build a path to Theology through Philosophy and the Liberal Arts, which this man condemns as secular. . . .[23]

Though the translator added the word *rational,* More's concept of the ladder of knowledge is perhaps made entirely clear by the word *natural.*

More's English letters written from the Tower to explain why he could not swear to the oath demanded of him are based on assumptions about the four kinds of law and the relation of human law to divine law. But these ideas, being even more closely related to law and government, will be discussed in Chapter IV.

Erasmus has so many passages on freedom of the will, human dignity, perfectibility by education, and the relation of eternal, divine, and natural law that pages might be spent quoting him, but a few examples will serve. Speaking of certain temporary laws in the Old Testament, he said, in a colloquy between a butcher and a salt-fishmonger: "I am of opinion that the law which nature has dictated, and therefore is perpetual and inviolable, ought to be counted the more obligatory, which never was, nor ever will be abrogated." In analyzing the difference between human and divine laws, Erasmus said: "he that transgresses a human law sins immediately against man (if you will allow me to use school terms)

---

[21] Rogers, *The Correspondence*, no. 106, p. 254, second paragraph; for translation, T. E. Bridgett, *Life* (London, 1891), pp. 136–37.

[22] Rogers, *The Correspondence*, no. 101; Bridgett, p. 133.

[23] Rogers, *The Correspondence*, no. 60; for translation, see T. S. K. Scott-Craig, "Thomas More's 1518 Letter to the University of Oxford," *Ren. News*, I, no. 2 (1948), 21.

but mediately against God; he that transgresses a divine law, *è contra*." Then he continued with a long discussion on immutable laws given by the church.[24]

Erasmus expressed his belief in man's perfectibility when he discussed education: "Nature, in giving you a son, presents you, let me say, a rude, unformed creature, which it is your part to fashion so that it may become indeed a man. If this fashioning be neglected you have but an animal still; if it be contrived earnestly and wisely, you have, I had almost said, what may prove a being not far from a God." [25] Faulty training might serve to explain human frailty, Erasmus thought, almost as well as the doctrine of original sin—true as the latter doctrine is, he added. His belief in freedom of the will as a theological doctrine is supported by his refutation of Luther, *De libero arbitrio*, printed by Froben, in September, 1524. It is usually considered a moderate, carefully reasoned work, citing Bible texts in support of man's freedom and arguing that repentance would be useless and punishment for sin would be unjust if men were not free to make choices. There is no reason to suppose that Erasmus did not hold this view consistently through his life.

Vives was explicit in many comments on the dignity, perfectibility, and the power of man to choose his own course of conduct: "The stoicke philosophers saye that ther be certayne fyeres or sedes . . . bredde by nature in us . . . that littell fyer, if it myght increase in us, it wolde brynge us up unto the perfection of vertue and blessed lyuynge." [26] In the Preface to his work *De*

---

[24] Erasmus, *The Colloquies*, 2 vols. (London, 1878), II, pp. 50, 70–71, and *passim*. In all quotations from the *Colloquies*, unmodern capitals will be changed to small letters, since the capitals add nothing to the thought of Erasmus.

[25] Erasmus, *De pueris instituendis*, as trans. by W. H. Woodward, *Desiderius Erasmus concerning the Aim and Method of Education* (Cambridge, 1904), pp. 187, 200. I have compared numerous passages from Woodward's translation with *Opera omnia* and with a so-called literal translation recently prepared as a dissertation. Comparison supports Woodward's statement: "Any compressions . . . are only by way of restraint of Erasmian redundancy." Hence Woodward will be cited for some general ideas in *De pueris instituendis* and in *De ratione studii*; and for more important details the Latin from *Opera omnia* will be quoted in footnotes.

[26] J. L. Vives, *A very frutefull and pleasant boke called the Instruction of a Christen woman*, trans. by Richard Hyrd [Herde] (London, 1529?), Book II, Chapter 11, M *verso*. In this title I have taken the liberty of expanding, without signs, a word with a long mark for one or more missing letters, as *woman* for *womā*, when the meaning is ob-

disciplinis he spoke of learning as that "by means of which we separate ourselves from the way of life and customs of animals and are restored to humanity and raised towards God himself. . . ." [27] In a part of that same work *De tradendis disciplinis* he said: "For we are not men because of our bodies, which we have in common with the brutes, but in consequence of the likeness of our mind to God and the angels . . . by the possession of reason we become most like to, and most united with, that divine Nature, which rules everything." [28]

In his work called "A Fable about Man," Vives summed up the philosophy of man's power to control his own destiny. At a birthday feast for Juno the gods were using the earth as a stage for plays: "they recognized in man himself a great resemblance to Jupiter, so that even the dullest of Gods might have known that man was born of Jupiter." Then they saw man, acting on the stage, become all things: "a plant . . . without any power of sensation . . . a moral satirist . . . the shapes of a thousand wild beasts. . . ." Then he became a man again, "prudent, just, faithful, human, kindly, and friendly, who . . . held the authority and obeyed in turn, cared for the public interest and welfare, and was finally in every way a political and social being." In this fable, Vives presented man as a creature who had received his power as a gift, and the climax of his power was his ability to become like his creator. His view differed from that of Francis Bacon, who thought that man would conquer the world through scientific knowledge. Vives wrote his fable in 1518, soon after he had met Erasmus. Though he added his own biblical implications, he is said to have based his idea on Giovanni Pico's concept of body and soul as equal parts of a human essence which is universal because it is undetermined. [29]

vious. The same liberty will be taken in titles and quotations throughout this work; the sign for *and* will be expanded into the word, and occasionally some basic punctuation will be added for clarity.

[27] Vives, *De disciplinis*, "Preface," trans. by Foster Watson, *Vives: On Education* (Cambridge, 1913), p. 6. Foster Watson's translation seems adequate for these ideas. In later chapters important terms will be checked with their Latin originals.

[28] Vives, *De tradendis disciplinis*, as cited above, pp. 86 and 250 for the quotations. See also pp. 250–52, 30, 40, and *passim*.

[29] See Cassirer, Kristeller, Randall, *The Renaissance Philosophy of Man* (Chicago, 1948), pp. 387–93, for Vives, "A Fable about Man," trans. by Nancy Lenkeith.

Other ideas of Pico della Mirandola illuminate the ideas of More and Vives, whether Pico influenced them directly or not. At least Pico expressed the ideas more completely. He compared man's learning to a ladder leading up to God. Man should, he said, begin with moral philosophy; to know himself, he must learn all nature thoroughly, since he is a part or a connecting link in nature; then he must proceed to theology. In studying natural philosophy, he accustoms his eyes to the first feeble rays of truth; gradually, as he learns the wonders of God in nature, he will be more inspired to love and worship the Creator. Like the Englishmen, Pico did not try to be original; his test of philosophic truth was its sameness. His ideas on man's freedom included a belief that each must find his own position in the realm of the spirit and that any compulsion in matters of faith is both wrong and futile.[30] (Thomas Aquinas had said that natural knowledge begins through the senses, that our senses cannot lead our intellect so far as to see the essence of God, but they can lead us to realize that God exists and that He causes the natural phenomena which we observe.) [31]

Pico della Mirandola's views on nature and the ladder of knowledge leading to God seem to be one form of *The Great Chain of Being*, which Arthur O. Lovejoy traced brilliantly in his early chapters from its Platonic origins through its medieval manifestations. It is the concept of the universe as an infinite number of links "ranging in hierarchical order from the meagerest kind of existents" up to the "highest possible kind of creature, between which and the Absolute Being the disparity was assumed to be infinite"; and every link differed from that one immediately below it by the "least possible degree of difference." It was assumed that difference in kind means difference in excellence and thus rank, in the hierarchy. The idea of the chain of being was sometimes used to justify "that worldly employment, the study of natural science"; but it was often assumed that the lower grades of being were to be quickly transcended.[32]

[30] *The Renaissance Philosophy of Man*, pp. 223–54, "Oration" of Pico della Mirandola, trans. by Elizabeth F. Forbes; Ernst Cassirer, "Giovanni Pico della Mirandola," *JHI*, III, no. 2 (1942), 123–44, and III, no. 3 (1942), 319–46.

[31] *Summa theologica*, Part I, Question 12, Article 12.

[32] Arthur O. Lovejoy, *The Great Chain of Being* (Cambridge, Mass., 1953), pp. 59, 64–65, 89, and *passim*.

Starkey's *Dialogue,* whether its ideas are really those of Pole or Lupset or not, shows what ideas were being discussed in the early sixteenth century; and the whole is permeated with comments on the dignity and perfectibility of man. Many of the comments were made by Pole, who said that the Turk, the Saracen, or the Jew thinks his religion is according to reason; and that man is ruler on earth: "man by nature far excelleth in dignity all other creatures in earth, where he is . . . set to govern and rule . . . none otherwise than God Himself doth in heaven govern and rule. . . ." Pole also said: "The goodness of God . . . hath made man of all creatures in earth most perfit, giving unto him a sparkle of his own divinity—that is to say, right reason—whereby he should govern himself in civil life and good policy according to his excellent nature and dignity." But because of his body, man has so many inclinations and vicious desires that "except man . . . resist . . . they over-run reason, this little sparkle," and thus bring man to the level of a beast.[33]

Lupset argued that man must come to his perfection "not compelled by fear of any pain or punishment, nor yet by any pleasure or profit allured thereto; but only of his free will and liberty." [34]

Sir Thomas Elyot implied man's freedom and perfectibility in many passages on education. In the *Governour,* Book III, Chapter iii, he made a non-theological comment not directly related to education: "And of that same mater and substaunce that his soule is of, be all other soules that nowe are, and haue ben, and euer shall be. . . . In semblable astate is his body, and of no better claye (as I mought frankely saye) is a gentilman made than a carter, and of libertie of wille as moche is gyuen of god to the poore herdeman, as to the great and mighty emperour." [35]

NATURE: THE PHYSICAL WORLD

ACTIVITY IN SCIENTIFIC AREAS

Some members of the More circle had a large interest in scientific subjects: medicine, mathematics, astronomy, and geography. In

[33] Thomas Starkey, *A Dialogue between Reginald Pole and Thomas Lupset,* ed. by Kathleen M. Burton (London, 1948), pp. 29, 152.
[34] Starkey, *A Dialogue,* p. 184.
[35] Sir Thomas Elyot, *The boke named the Gouernour* (London, 1531), Fol. 176 *verso.*

medicine, Linacre was outstanding. He received his medical degree at Padua about 1491, and according to Pace he did a brilliant piece of work in defending his thesis. When he returned to England he lectured on scientific subjects, but he was also famous for his knowledge of the classics in general. About 1509, or near that time, he became the king's physician; and during the years which followed, More, Erasmus, Colet, and Lily were sometimes his patients.

On September 23, 1518, Linacre, five other physicians, and Cardinal Wolsey were granted articles of incorporation for a college of physicians; in future no person could practice in London or within seven miles of it unless he had been admitted to membership in this college. Between 1517 and 1524 Linacre published six volumes of his own translations from Galen: *De sanitate tuenda*, 1517; *Methodus medendi*, 1519; *De temperamentis et de inaequali intemperie*, 1521; *De naturalibus facultatibus*, 1523; *De pulsuum usu*, 1523; and *De symptomatum differentiis et causis*, 1524.

When Linacre died in 1524 he had been licensed to found three lectureships in medicine, one at Cambridge and two at Oxford. Cuthbert Tunstal, his executor, assigned the Oxford lectureships to Merton College because more physicians studied there than at the other colleges. The Mercers' Company was also licensed to secure property, either from Linacre or from others, to support the projects, which were to be called "Linacre's Lectures."

Either Linacre alone or Linacre and More together probably exerted some influence on younger men of the group about the study of medicine. Richard Herde and John Clement, who had been tutors or students in More's household school and who were strongly attached to him, studied medicine, with Linacre, we might suppose, in the beginning. Herde had spoken of More in his preface to his translation of Vives' *Instruction of a Christian Woman* as "my singular good master and bringer-up . . . to whose judgment . . . I . . . submit whatsoever I do . . . that I set any store by. . . ." Herde was praised by Stephen Gardiner and Bishop Fox, with whom he was traveling as their physician, when he met his untimely death in 1528. John Clement became a distinguished court physician, and finally president of the College of Physicians in 1544.

Margaret Gigs, More's foster daughter, who married John Clement, had a reputation for a knowledge of medicine; but probably she gained it by reading for herself. According to Harpsfield, she had once diagnosed More's illness from her reading of Galen, and he says that a kinsman of hers had begun to teach her medicine.

When More's own daughter Margaret seemed hopelessly ill, according to Harpsfield, More suggested to the doctors the use of a glister. They tried the remedy, "much meruailing" that they had not thought of it sooner, and she began to improve at once. Harpsfield implies that prayer brought the idea into More's mind; but a reader is likely to think also of More's reading on medicine. More hoped that Margaret would study medicine after she had first given more time to humane letters. As he sent greetings to his son, Roper, in the same letter with this suggestion, he must have made it after her marriage. With medicine and also sacred literature, he told her she would be prepared for "the whole scope of human life . . . a healthy soul in a healthy body, and I know that you have already laid the foundation of these studies. . . ."

Erasmus, too, wrote a *Declamatio in laudem nobilissimae artis medicinae,* and an English translation was printed by Robert Redman. He emphasized the union of mind and body, saying that the diseases of the body "either do let or else do utterly quench the strength and power of the soul." Granting that only a few could have a perfect knowledge of the whole science, he suggested that no person should remain in ignorance of "that part of physik which appertaineth to the governance and preservation of the health." The *Declamatio* was printed by Froben in 1518, and in March of that year Erasmus sent a copy with a letter to his friend, Henricus Afinius, a distinguished physician in Antwerp. He said that the work had been "composed by me some time ago, when there was no subject which I did not attempt."

Sir Thomas Elyot, friend of More and student of the classics, also became interested enough in medicine to write *The Castle of Health,* which appeared in 1539. Apparently he was attacked by doctors for presuming to write such a book when he was not a physician; in his second edition, 1541, he defended himself by explaining that he did not intend his book to take the place of a doctor but only to help a sick person manage his diet and report his symptoms more accurately to his own doctor. He also named books of medicine which he had read with "a worshipfull phisition, and one of the moste renouined at that tyme in England." It seems most probable that his physician was Linacre. The public apparently found Elyot's book useful, for fifteen or more editions appeared before 1600.

John Rastell and More himself had a considerable interest in astronomy. Astronomy was an important subject in More's school, one for which he employed Nicholas Kratzer, the king's astronomer. (It is even possible that he introduced Kratzer to the English court.) He discussed astronomy in his letters to the young people in his school, suggesting the philosophy of studying nature as a means of ascending to God. Probably More tried to teach his wife astronomy, if we accept as autobiographical an example he used in the second part of the *Confutation of Tyndale's Answer;* but though the husband "longed sore" to make the gentlewoman understand the treatise of the sphere, she merely answered him with a counterillustration of her maid and her spinning wheel which showed her inability to grasp his ideas.

More also talked astronomy with Henry VIII, but with him he probably had better luck in communication. Roper told us that the king often sent for More to come to his "trauers" or his "leades" at night, "therefor to consider with him the diuersities, courses, motions, and operacions of the starres and planetes. . . ." More's pleasant disposition and his knowledge, Roper suggested, caused the king to summon him.

John Rastell used his interest in astronomy for designs in various pageants, dramatic performances, and settings for banquets, which will be mentioned under drama: the pageant at Coventry, which was perhaps his; some work at the Field of the Cloth of Gold, in 1520; a pageant at the Little Conduit in Cheap, 1522; and work with Nicholas Kratzer for the roof of the great banquet hall in 1527, with the twelve signs of the zodiac and the seven planets.

Rastell also showed an interest in astronomy and cosmography when he selected a printer's device representing the earth, air, clouds, fire, with two mermaids or persons who extend through clouds and fire into a starry heaven, with sun, moon, and planets.

Linacre was concerned with astronomy and geography, when he translated *Proclus de sphaera* from Greek into Latin and allowed Aldus to publish it in 1499 as a part of his series *Astronomici veteres*. Linacre also helped More at some time in his reading of the *Meteorologica* of Aristotle, as More told us in his letter to Dorp.

More and his friends had an interest in mathematics; Stapleton told us that its teaching was emphasized in the household school. Tunstal wrote one of the few books on mathematics published by an Englishman in the early sixteenth century, *De arte supputandi*, in 1522. When Tunstal was named Bishop of London, he thought of destroying the rough notes for this book; but instead he decided to publish it and to dedicate the work to More, since More had to examine accounts in the king's treasury and since he might pass the book on to his children. He added, "by nothing are the abilities of young folk more invigorated than by the study of mathematics."

More, Rastell, and their sons, John Rastell and John More, had some interest in geography. One might expect them to have some concern, since they lived through a period of such profound changes as the discovery of new lands, the development of globes and of new wall maps, changes in textbooks, or at least a need for change, and the faint beginnings of a shift from Ptolemaic to Copernican theories of the universe. But actually Englishmen were still clinging to Ptolemy in the textbooks of the seventeenth century; little literature on the new-found lands existed in England until after 1550; and London sailors were reluctant to go on voyages of exploration and discovery. The new geographical knowledge moved slowly into all human minds; and in the reign of Henry VIII it moved more slowly into English minds. The statement holds true not only of actual exploring but also of adopting globes, new maps and textbooks, and the Copernican theory.

Against this background John Rastell's active interest in geography stands out. In the spring of 1517 he set off on an actual voyage to the New Found Lands. But his voyage, partly financed by his father-in-law, Sir John More, failed because of a mutiny; he lost both ship and cargo and found himself in Ireland. John Rastell also tried to teach geography, not original theories but bare facts for the common man, in his play, *The Nature of the Four Elements*. Rastell's practical concern with geography does not seem to have been equalled, at least so far as printed records indicate, by that of any other Englishman in his day.

More's interest in geography was largely philosophical and theoretical rather than practical. Voyages like those of Vespucci became his springboard into an estimate of civilizations, in *Utopia*, and perhaps his mission to Bruges in 1515 gave him stimulus in this direction. It has been pointed out, also, that More differed from Pliny and Waldseemüller in working out his own theory of climatic symmetry; instead of assuming that every zone of the earth differed in climate from every other zone, he made his own deductions about the tropical and south-temperate zones.

Young John More, the son of Sir Thomas, and young John Rastell were the only other members of the More circle who were concerned with the new geography of exploration. Young More translated into English a work by Damian à Goes, a Portuguese scholar who had met Erasmus on the Continent and had given him a copy of his book. He called his translation *The legacy or embassate of prester John unto Emanuell, Kynge of Portyngale*. Young John Rastell tried a voyage of practical exploration to the New Found Lands, in 1536, when he was a student at one of the Inns of Court. He actually reached Labrador; but according to Hakluyt's account of this voyage, the men were on the verge of starvation and some of them resorted to cannibalism; they finally saved their lives by capturing the supplies of a French ship and sailing back to England.

Of course the members of the More circle who wrote on theories of education, Erasmus and Vives, for example, made comments on the teaching of geography. But only Sir Thomas More, John Rastell, and their sons showed any interest in the geographical activity which led to the discovery of new worlds.

This scientific activity in the More circle is in strong contrast to the inactivity in the period before 1500. In the medieval period Robert Grosseteste (c. 1175–1253) was interested in mathematics and the physical sciences and won the praise of Roger Bacon for his scientific knowledge. Bacon himself recognized the need of studying science in the original Greek; he studied astronomy, mathematics, botany, medicine, and chemistry or alchemy. He abhorred occult practices, explained the scientific method as no one else had done since Aristotle, and practiced experimental science. Both men saw that mathematics was the basis of progress in science.[36] But after Bacon there was little original science in Oxford, or for that matter, in all England. As R. T. Gunther said, there was no experimenting, and without the study of nature there was no progress. In discussing the history of chemistry Gunther passed from Roger Bacon to the seventeenth century, pausing only to name a certain Nicholas Hill and two Magdalen College alchemists. The decay of science is part of the general decay of learning, when through money and influence, degrees at Oxford were conferred on wicked drunkards and low-grade morons; when old formulas were losing their authority and old methods of scholastic dispute were losing their appeal.[37] The weakness of Henry VI and the long Wars of the Roses did nothing to improve these conditions. The influence of such men as Robert Flemmyng, William Grey, John Free, John Gunthorpe, John Tiptoft, and William Sellyng was hardly apparent before the last decade of the fifteenth century or before 1500.

Of fifteenth-century mathematics Gunther commented that there is little to be said. Of Cuthbert Tunstal in the sixteenth century he said: "His arithmetic *De arte supputandi* was the best of its time and is particularly valuable as containing illustrations of the medieval processes of computation." He considered Tunstal and Robert Recorde as "the founders at Cambridge of what has been the most brilliantly successful mathematical school in the

[36] Sir Charles Edward Mallet, *A History of the University of Oxford,* 3 vols. (London, 1924–1927), I; Sir John Edwin Sandys, *A History of Classical Scholarship,* 3rd ed.; 3 vols. (Cambridge, 1921), I; R. T. Gunther, *Early Science in Oxford,* 14 vols. (Oxford, 1923–1945), I. See indexes.

[37] Gunther, I, 7–8; Mallet, I, 338–43.

world." [38] In discussing medicine Gunther mentioned Linacre as the most important man in either the fifteenth or the first half of the sixteenth century; he praised him for the activities which have already been mentioned and for being, in all probability, the first Englishman to read Galen and Aristotle in the original Greek.[39]

It is not possible to say that the men of the More circle added to the knowledge of astronomy or geography.

WRITINGS: OPPOSITION TO MAGIC

More and his friends expressed a strong opposition to magic and to astrology, defined as foretelling the future by the stars; and they distrusted or disbelieved in the Christian cabala. Again, their views were like those of Giovanni Pico della Mirandola, whether they were influenced by him or not. True magic, he said, is not supernatural; the true magician knows and directs the forces of nature; he is not concerned with the fantasies of astrology but with the empirical and causal explanations of nature. Pico considered astrology unsound because it confuses the spiritual and the physical. It was, he said, neither an art nor a science; it was not founded on reason, experiment, or the work of Plato and Aristotle; it was not accepted by such philosophers as Pythagoras, Democritus, Seneca, and Cicero; and even Avicenna and Averroes condemned it.[40] Though attacks on magic and astrology were not new, the early fathers of the church had tended to condemn them because they were impious and heretical, not because they were unreasonable and unproved by experiment.

Though More, Colet, Erasmus, and Vives perhaps did not state so completely the reasons for their opposition to magic and astrology, their denunciations were definite. More's personal attitude is confirmed by eleven of his Latin epigrams. Two of them make satiric comments on the astrologer who looks at the stars and sees

[38] Gunther, I, 99–100. As Part II of vol. I was once issued under its own separate paging, some reprintings of the book seem to retain this paging but to disregard it in the table of contents and the index.

[39] Gunther, III (Oxford, 1925), 33–35.

[40] Ernst Cassirer, "Giovanni Pico della Mirandola," *JHI*, III, no. 3 (1942), 339–40; Cassirer, Kristeller, Randall, *The Renaissance Philosophy of Man*, pp. 246–49.

what has already happened. Six are concerned with an astrologer who consulted the stars about his wife's character; the stars did not inform him, but while he was busy with the heavens, she, on earth, used her chance to be unfaithful to him. All the epigrams on astrology confirm More's complete disbelief in such a method of foretelling the future.[41]

More approved of his Utopians for their serious study of nature and for the fact that they did not accept astrology and other magic: "But as for the amityes and dissentyons of the planettes, and all that deceytefull diuynatyon by the starres, they neuer asmuch as dreamed therof." In another passage from *Utopia* he said: "They vtterly despise and mocke sothe sayinges and diuinacions of thinges to come by the flighte or voyces of birdes, and all other diuinations of vayne superstition, which in other countreys be in great obseruation." [42]

More expressed an aversion to magic in his preface to three dialogues of Lucian in 1506. The preface was addressed to Thomas Ruthall, secretary to the king at the time. The *Necromantia*, he said, wittily attacks the deceitful tricks of magicians, the inane fictions of poets, and the uncertain arguing of philosophers on all sorts of subjects. The *Philopseudes*, he continued, teaches us not to put faith in the illusions of magic or the superstitions which creep in under the pretense of religion.[43]

Colet's comment on Reuchlin's *Cabalistica* is characteristic of the tendency to distrust theories not subject to testing by reason. Writing to Erasmus, he said:

I do not venture to give any judgment about it; and I acknowledge my own ignorance, having no insight in matters so remote, or in the resources of so great a man. And yet, as I read it, I did sometimes think that the wonders were rather verbal than real; for he gives us to understand that there is some mystery in the characters and combinations used to express Hebrew words.

Ah, Erasmus, of books and of knowledge there is no end; but there is nothing better for this short term of ours than that we should live a pure

[41] Leicester Bradner and Charles A. Lynch, *The Latin Epigrams of Thomas More* (Chicago, 1953), nos. 42–47, 49, 100, 151, 164.

[42] More, *Utopia*, pp. 186–87, 279.

[43] Rogers, *The Correspondence*, no. 5, p. 12.

and holy life . . . and so to realize that which is promised by those
Pythagorean and Cabalistical ideas of Reuchlin, but will in my judgment
never be attained but by the ardent love and imitation of Jesus.[44]

Erasmus usually attacked superstition with vigor, as he did in
his colloquies "The Exorcism or Apparition," and "The Alchymist,"
where he pictured the credulity of Balbinus, who was wheedled
out of his money, and the folly of those who think that base
metals can be transmuted into gold.[45] In a letter to Peter Zutpenius
he said seriously that many mortals do seek the causes of happiness
or unhappiness in celestial bodies; but as for himself, he will look
to the earth, which yields us good or bad fortune. In a letter to
Nicholas Cannius he made a statement which seems humorously
satirical, though it has been taken solemnly: "How great is the
happiness of astrologers, my dearest Nicholas, who know how to
choose from the stars their fortunate days and hours!"[46] Many
passages in many different works testify to his belief in man's
dignity and freedom of choice and his approach to problems by a
reasoning attitude which is hostile to astrology or magic.

Vives, a Spaniard by birth, a pupil of Erasmus, a friend of
More and other Englishmen, expressed strong opposition to all
kinds of magic: "suche craftes must therfore be shonned that fyght
ageynste vertue: all craftes that worke by vayne coniectures, as
palmestrie, pyromancie, nicromancye, hydromancie, astrologie,
wherin moche pestilent vanytie lieth hydde, inuented of the deuyll
. . . for they intreate and professe those thynges which god hathe
reserued unto hym selfe alone, that is to saye, the knowlege of
thinges to come."[47]

WRITINGS: INTEREST IN SCIENCE AND THE PHYSICAL WORLD

More and his friends expressed an interest in science and the physical world almost as strong as their distaste for magic and pseudo-

[44] Nichols, *The Epistles*, II, no. 586, also no. 568. Where dates of letters to or from
Erasmus are given, they are the dates given by P. S. Allen, *Opus epistolarum* (see footnote
46 below). He had more facts and hence more accuracy.

[45] Erasmus, *The Colloquies*, I, 391–401 and 402–11. See also the recent translations by
Craig R. Thompson, *Ten Colloquies of Erasmus* (New York, 1957), nos. IV, V.

[46] P. S. Allen, *Opus epistolarum Des. Erasmi Roterdami*, 12 vols. (Oxford, 1906–1958),
IV, 1005; VII, 1832.

[47] Vives, *An Introdvction to wysedome*, trans. by Rycharde Morysine (London, 1540),
leaf Diii *verso; also De tradendis disciplinis*, pp. 21–22, 30–32.

science. Bishop Fisher was enough interested in the study of nature to use it as a comparison in "A Sermon on the Passion":

Meruayling was the cause why that the Philosophers came to so greate knowledge as they had. They behelde and sawe many wonderfull thynges and effectes in thys worlde, as the marueylous earthquakes, Thunders, lightnings, Snow, Rayne, and Frostes, blasinng [sic] Starres, the Eclipses of the Sunne and of the Moone, and suche other effectes. And those marueylous wonders moued them to search for the causes of the same. And so, by dyligent searche and inquisition, they came to great knowledge and cunning, which cunnyng, men call Philosophie naturall. But there is another higher Philosophie which is aboue nature, which is also gotten with marueyling. And this is the verye Philosophie of Christian people.[48]

Colet showed no particular interest in the study of the inanimate world that we call nature, as far as the present evidence goes, just as he usually emphasized the dignity, perfectibility, and free will of man, through the grace of God. But he also had little to say on secular subjects as compared with More and Erasmus.

More expressed many times his interest in natural science. For example, his Utopians not only opposed astrology but they also made a positive approach to the study of nature and drew conclusions from what they observed:

Raynes, windes, and other courses of tempestes they knowe before by certein tokens, which they haue learned by long vse and obseruation. But of the causes of all thies thinges, of the ebbinge, flowinge, and saltenes of the sea, and fynallye of the orygynall begynnyng and nature of heuen and of the wordle [sic], they holde partelye the same opynyons that our olde philosophers holde; and . . . whiles they bringe new reasons of thynges, doo disagree from all them, and yet emonge themselfes in all poyntes they doo not accorde.

His Utopians also connected nature study with religion:

They thinke that the contemplacion of nature, and the prayse thereof cumminge, is to God a very acceptable honour.[49]

More's letter to Dorp in 1515 showed his interest in whatever facts the Greeks knew about science. When he was studying Aristotle's *Meteorology* with Linacre, he said, he discovered from his own knowledge of Greek that the accepted translation of it merely

---

[48] Mayor, *The English Works of John Fisher*, pp. 388–89.
[49] More, *Utopia*, pp. 186–87, 279–80.

confused him but the original Greek was perfectly clear. Albert the Great, who professed to clarify Aristotle in Latin, he added, sometimes gave a meaning which contradicted him; and he cited other incorrect translations. More's letter to the University of Oxford also reminded the "Trojans" that "not half of Greek learning has yet been made available to the West . . ." and here, too, More had science in mind.[50]

In the preceding passages from More and Fisher, both men assumed that the study of nature is a search that proceeds from the observation of specific events to conclusions about causes and effects, not an acceptance of tradition.

When Erasmus talked of nature study he was often not scientific in his attitudes. At times he accepted "unnatural" natural history, as he seemed to do when he thought that pupils should learn the nature and habits of the dragon, especially of the "large Indian variety." At times he tended to express fear lest minds should be led away from moral philosophy by natural philosophy. When his learned butcher, in disputing with the salt-fishmonger, said that he had recently seen the whole world described in a map, he had been interested only in the fact that a large part of the world is not Christian. Often Erasmus stressed the study of geography and the knowledge of trees, plants, animals, and precious stones, as if facts about them were mere servants to the study of classic historians and poets. At times he seemed to follow Aristotle without questioning; at other times he recommended the study of nature from nature first and then from the reading of such men as Pliny and Aristotle. When he wrote his praise of the art of medicine he considered the study of nature for the healing of human bodies almost divine.[51]

Roger Ascham, writing much later but agreeing with members of the More group on many other ideas, differed from them somewhat on scientific study, as if he foresaw the danger of over-

[50] Rogers, *The Correspondence,* no. 15, pp. 65–66, and no. 60. For a translation of no. 60, see footnote 23 above.

[51] Erasmus, *The Colloquies,* I, 156–201; II, 300–315, 316–25, *passim;* II, 52. See also *De ratione studii,* p. 167, and *De pueris instituendis,* pp. 189–90, as cited above; Nichols, *The Epistles,* III, no. 764, for the letter to Henry Aufinius about the praise of medicine; Allen, *Opus epistolarum,* III, 799.

specialization: "Some wittes, moderate enough by nature, be many tymes marde by ouer moch studie and vse of some sciences, namelie Musicke, Arithmetick, and Geometrie. Thies sciences, as they sharpen mens wittes ouer moch, so they change mens maners ouer sore, if they be not moderatlie mingled and wiselie applied to som good vse of life. Marke all Mathematicall heades, which be onely and wholy bent to those sciences, how solitarie they be themselues, how vnfit to liue with others, and how vnapte to serue in the world." [52]

Vives probably had more to say about the study of science and the study of nature than any other man in the More circle. For nature study, he said, the teacher should put together from the authors he had named the material to serve as a foundation for future study:

First . . . the four material elements . . . perception . . . the phenomena engendred in the air . . . then stones, then on all which has life, on life itself; on metals and all mineral bodies; on herbs, fruits, trees, quadrupeds, birds, fish, insects, and on man's body. The teacher will not expound by means of narrative . . . but rather seek to investigate causes, whence things are derived, how they exist, develop, continue, act, and discharge their own functions. . . .

In explaining his use of the term knowledge, Vives said:

But I only call that knowledge which we receive when the senses are properly brought to observe things and in a methodical way to which clear reason leads us on, reason so closely connected with the nature of our mind that there is no one who does not accept its lead. . . .

Again Vives said:

First we must consider the easiest kinds of knowledge, viz., those things that are evident to the senses. For the senses open up the way to all knowledge. There should be, in the first place, a general explanation . . . or, as it were, a picture of the whole of nature, of the heavens, the elements, and those things that are in the heavens and in the elements, in fire, air, water, and earth, so that a full representation . . . of the whole earth is included as in a picture. [53]

Observation of nature, Vives said, is not only a means to pleasure and recreation but a source of knowledge. No disputing is neces-

---

[52] Roger Ascham, *The Scholemaster* (London, 1570), First book, leaf 5 *verso*.
[53] Vives, *De tradendis disciplinis*, pp. 213, 22, 168.

sary but only careful observing of the heavens, weather, plains, mountains, and forests; then conclusions may be drawn only when the facts lead to sound conclusions. He wished the learner to use the experience of others as well as to observe: "Let him have recourse . . . to gardeners, husbandmen, shepherds, and hunters, for this is what Pliny and other great authors undoubtedly did." Again Vives said: "For not easily will any other pleasure of the senses be found which can compare with this in magnitude or in permanence, since it stimulates the desire of knowledge, which for every human mind is the keenest of all pleasures." [54]

Vives' concern with physical as well as philosophical ideas about life is shown by his discussion of a healthful location for the site of a school and the need for wholesome food for its pupils.[55] He also spent a number of pages on the qualifications, the training, and duties of a good physician.[56]

Vives' philosophy of nature study, like that of Pico and More, was a belief in using nature as an approach to God. Sometimes he said that the study of nature might be unnecessary or harmful "unless it serves the useful arts of life or raises us from a knowledge of His works to a knowledge, admiration, and love of the Author of these works." [57] But at times he enjoyed the beauty of nature without drawing philosophical conclusions about it. Most often, perhaps, he expressed with individual feeling his belief in fresh observation and the search for reasons and causes; in examining Aristotle, rejecting, and building only upon his truth, instead of following him blindly. In the preface to his work *De tradendis disciplinis*, he said:

I shall show that the old writers were mistaken, not through the limitations of the human intellect . . . but by their own fault. Therefore I have produced my reasons from nature, not out of divine oracles, so that I should not leap across from philosophy to theology. . . . Moreover it is far more profitable to learning to form a critical judgment on the writings of the great authors than to merely acquiesce in their authority. . . . Nature is not yet so effete and exhausted as to be unable to bring forth, in our times, results comparable to those of earlier ages. . . . Further, what was the

[54] *De tradendis disciplinis*, pp. 169, 170, 171.
[55] *De tradendis disciplinis*, pp. 53–54, 57.
[56] *De tradendis disciplinis*, pp. 219–26.
[57] *De tradendis disciplinis*, p. 167.

method of Aristotle himself? Did he not dare to pluck up by the root the received opinion of his predecessors? Is it, then, to be forbidden us to at least investigate and to form our own opinions? . . . Truth stands open to all.[58]

WRITINGS: COMELINESS OF BODY, BEAUTY OF NATURE

Since the men of the More circle were human beings, it is natural that some of them would express an interest in the beauty of the human body. But when they described people so as to correlate character and physique, assuming that a sound mind and a noble character live in a sound and beautiful body, there is a probability of influence from the classics. In the *History of Richard III*, probably written by More but influenced by the partisanship of Cardinal Morton, there is also a political bias. The author of the history described Edward thus: "He was a goodly parsonage and very Princely to behold, of hearte couragious, politique in counsaile, in aduersitie nothynge abashed . . . in peace iuste and mercifull, in warre sharpe and fyerce. . . . He was of visage louelye, of bodye myghtie, stronge and cleane made; howe bee it in his latter dayes, wyth ouer liberall dyet, sommewhat corpulente and nathelesse not uncomelye. . . ." But Richard was "little of stature, ill fetured of limmes, croke backed, his left shoulder much higher than his right, hard fauoured of visage . . . he was malicious, wrathfull, enuious, and from afore his birth euer frowarde." Though he won some friends by material gifts, he won these gifts first by plundering and looting; and thus he won as many enemies. He was "close and secrete, a deepe dissimuler . . . arrogant of heart . . . where his aduauntage grew, he spared no mans deathe whose life withstoode his purpose." [59]

In one of More's early epigrams, when he and Lily were writing in friendly rivalry, he produced this comment: "Your mind is as lame as your leg, and your external condition gives sure sign of your inner state." [60] But More, who considered pity for unfortunates or for animals as a chief quality which lifts man above animals, pictured his Utopians as kind toward deformed or crippled people. They considered it both stupid and cruel to taunt a cripple,

[58] *De tradendis disciplinis*, "Preface," pp. 7–9.
[59] More, *The workes*, pp. 35–36, 37.
[60] Bradner and Lynch, *The Latin Epigrams*, no. 11, p. 133.

since he could not help his deformity. The Utopians also thought it not right to neglect natural beauty but even worse to use artificial means, such as painting the face, to increase physical attractiveness—an idea that More stated seriously, in his letter to Gonell, about his own daughters. The Utopians knew, too, More said, that a man values his wife more for obedience and beauty of character than for mere physical beauty.[61] More also applied reason, imagination, and perhaps experience to the idea of physical beauty in marriage, warning his contemporaries that one custom of the Utopians might seem to them very foolish: "For a sad and an honest matrone sheweth the woman, be she maide or widdowe, naked to the wower. And lykewise, a sage and discrete man exhibyteth the wowere naked to the woman. . . . For all men be not so wyse as to haue respecte to the vertuous condicions of the partie; and the endowmentes of the bodye cause the vertues of the mynde more to be estemed and regarded, yea, euen in the mariages of wyse men." [62]

The Utopians recognized two special kinds of bodily pleasure. The first of these comes from food and drink, or "when we doo our naturall easemente, or when we be doynge the acte of generatyon, or when the ytchynge of annye parte is eased with rubbynge or stratchinge." Sometimes, too, we feel a pleasure that stirs our senses with "a certein secrete efficacy," like the pleasure from hearing music. The second kind of bodily pleasure comes from a state of health, a sense of well-being. The Utopians also appreciated the pleasures received "by the eares, the iyes, and the nose; which nature willeth to be proper and peculiar to man (for no other kind of liuing beastes doth behold the fayrenes and the bewtie of the worlde, or is moued with anny respect of sauours. . . ." They thought it madness for a man to despise the comeliness of beauty, to waste his physical energy, to make himself weak with fasting, or to punish himself physically—unless he was merely neglecting his own physical welfare while he labored for the good of the commonweal.[63]

[61] More, *Utopia*, p. 232.
[62] *Utopia*, pp. 225–27.
[63] *Utopia*, pp. 202–10.

Colet, who was not interested in physical beauty unless perhaps the beauty of style in sacred literature, provided for a headmaster at St. Paul's who should be "hoole in body, honest, and vertuouse, and learnyd," either married or single, and for an undermaster who was also to be "hoole in body." But probably Colet meant by the term "hoole," only hale, healthy, free from sickness, not comely and not free from blemish.[64]

Erasmus had something to say about bodily comeliness, about the use of the senses, and even about practical sanitation. He said that the pious who neglect all material things and the vulgar who value nothing except the material are like the figures in Plato's myth of the cave: each must think the other mad. Of the senses he said: "although all the senses have alliance with the body, certain of them are grosser, such as touch, hearing, sight, smell, taste; while certain ones are less closely tied up with the body, as the memory, intellect, and will. To whichever one the soul applies itself, that one grows strong. Forasmuch as every energy of the devout soul strives toward objects which are at farthest remove from the grosser senses, these grow numb, as it were . . . while the multitude . . . consider that without them life does not exist." [65]

Where Erasmus talked of bodily comeliness, as in the *Colloquies,* he never went beyond subdued reason. In "The Conflict between Thalia and Barbarism," he let Thalia say that a deformed mind usually accompanies a deformed body. In "The Unequal Marriage" he sympathized with the physical shrinking of the attractive young girl whose parents arranged her marriage to a diseased old man with a title. In "Diversoria" he also discussed sanitation in a modern way—the need of laws against the common drinking cup and laws to compel inns to furnish clean sheets for each new guest; he advised people to give up the custom of saluting with a kiss. Gabriel, a character in "The Unequal Marriage," said that the constitution of the body has a great influence on the mind; another character supported him with this statement: "Although the principal qualifications of princes are wisdom and integrity, yet it is

[64] Lupton, *A Life of John Colet,* Appendix A.
[65] Erasmus, *The Praise of Folly,* p. 121.

of some considerable moment what the form of his person is that governs others." [66]

Starkey, in reporting his *Dialogue* between Pole and Lupset, represented Pole as having the same sort of view on bodily comeliness. After discussing the practical need for health of body, Pole added, "to the which also must be coupled, of necessity, strength and beauty." For if the body is deformed, "if the parts be not proportionable, one agreeing to another according to the order of nature, they be not so acceptable nor pleasant, nor the body hath not his perfit state and virtue." Lupset disagreed somewhat with Pole, but Pole continued to defend his view: "forasmuch as the body is one part of man, he hath never most high felicity nor most perfit state in the highest degree, except the body with the mind flourish also with his virtues, and all things necessary for the maintenance of the same." [67]

Elyot implied in his *Governour* that he was concerned with the courtly appearance of one who is a skillful dancer.[68] In his *Image of Governance* he described the successful ruler in this way: "He was of visage fayre, and well proporcioned in body, large and goodly of personage, and therwith was stronge and durable to susteyne peynes, as he that knewe his owne strength, and in the preseruyng therof was not founde negligente. Therto he was amiable, and towarde euery man gentyl, and easy to be spoken unto. Also there was in hym . . . much humanitie and beneuolence. . . ." [69]

Roger Ascham, who agreed with Elyot in his concern about physical exercise, also declared his interest in comeliness of the body: "Nature it selfe taught men to ioyne alwayes welfauourednesse with profytablenesse. As in man, that ioynt or pece which is by anye chaunce depriued of hys cumlynesse, the same is also debarred of hys use and profytablenesse. . . . As he that is gogle eyde and lokes a squinte hath both hys countenaunce clene marred and hys sight sore blemmyshed, and so in all other members

---

[66] Erasmus, *The Colloquies*, II, 349, 155–56, 159, and *passim;* see also I, 286–93.
[67] Starkey, *A Dialogue*, pp. 47–52.
[68] *The Gouernour*, Book I, Chapters xix–xxii.
[69] Elyot, *The Image of Governance* (London, 1541), Chapter II, leaf 3.

lyke." [70] Ascham's view about physical beauty and character reached its climax when he said that virtue itself is nothing but comeliness.

Some members of the More group indicated their appreciation of beauty in the natural world, unconnected with the desire to teach virtue or piety; in this attitude they were not original and they were not philosophers. But Erasmus tended to unite piety with a vague appreciation of the beauty of nature. This comment is perhaps characteristic: "Nature is not dumb, but talkative enough, and speaks to the instruction of a man that has but a good will and a capacity to learn. What does the beautiful face of the Spring do but proclaim the equal wisdom and goodness of the Creator?" [71]

Vives surpassed the others in his enjoyment of nature, or at least in his expression of that enjoyment, just as he was more definite in his comments about the empirical study of nature. The best evidence is in the *Dialogues,* written for schoolboys. In "Garrientes" the boys are speaking of the nightingale's song:

B. Ah! Listen to that nightingale.

G. Where is she?

B. Don't you see her sitting on that bough? Notice how ardently she sings, and she never ceases.

N. Philomela laments for monstrous deeds.

G. Isn't it strange that she sings so sweetly, as if she were in Greece? There even the waves of the sea are dashing upon the shore in rhythm. [72]

In "Iter and equus" the boys are chatting about the landscape:

M. . . . See how softly the river flows, with its crystal water, over the golden rocks. What a delightful murmur! Do you hear the nightingale and the goldfinch? Really this country around Paris is most delightful. [73]

[70] Roger Ascham, *Toxophilus* (London, 1545), Book B, leaves 27 *verso*-28. A copy of this edition at the Folger Shakespeare Library has Ascham's holograph letter of presentation to William Parr, Earl of Essex, brother of Queen Catherine Parr.

[71] Erasmus, *The Colloquies,* I, 158. "The Religious Treat" has much general discussion of nature.

[72] W. H. D. Rouse, *Ludovicus Vives: Scenes of School and College Life in Latin Dialogues* (Oxford, 1931), p. 31. See Foster Watson, *Tudor School-Boy Life* (London, 1908), p. 45, for a translation, but it is neither literal nor euphonious.

[73] Rouse, p. 40, or see "Iter et equus," *passim.*

In other dialogues there are details for the training of pupils in using their senses—sight, sound, touch, taste, and smell—for the appreciation of natural beauty. For example, they are told to listen to the birds and to try imitating the sounds; to notice the sweet scent from the meadows, the crops, and even the fallow lands.

SUMMARY

In their ideas about nature, meaning the physical world with its objects which are perceptible to the senses, More and his friends expressed no completely new ideas. But as compared with the fifteenth century in England there were new emphases in the frequent mention of bodily comeliness as an index to character and its importance in marriage as a part of the good life—an idea not appearing in Christian doctrine—and the concept of virtue as life according to nature, a norm which is approved by the agent of God and is possible for uncorrupted man. Even the concern of Erasmus with practical sanitation and the emphasis of Vives upon good food and a healthful location for the site of a school were somewhat fresh approaches to life and education.

Linacre gave a new impetus to the study of medicine. Tunstal contributed to the founding of a great school of mathematics at Cambridge. Vives stressed the direct observation of nature both for pleasure and recreation and for discovering the causes of natural phenomena; he made sharp criticisms of Aristotle; he separated experiment in science from authority in religion. If the universities of England had applied his ideas, the development of inductive science might have come much sooner.

In their concepts about the law of nature, human reason, freedom of the will, and human perfectibility, More, Erasmus, Vives, and their friends were merely using their intellectual heritage. But as they read the classics sharply, with the accurate detail of better translations than their ancestors had, as they found likenesses between Stoic philosophers and Christian writers, they seemed to find new faith in human possibilities. Thus they found and expressed dynamic ideas.

CHAPTER II *The bases of true nobility*

The men of the More circle, being concerned with the question of true nobility, rejected the aristocratic view that it is based upon ancestry or wealth alone or is connected with titles, crests, and coats of arms. Such outer trappings were mere shells, like the practice of ritual without the inner attitudes of a true Christian. True nobility, they believed, is an inner reality, based upon piety, virtue, and learning; it expresses itself in action for the common welfare; and every individual with desire and capacity for intellectual growth should have a chance to develop such qualities. Thus they rejected a fixed status and favored a growth, a becoming, which an individual might achieve without wealth or ancestry.

In the sixteenth century, it has been said, three different views on nobility were expressed: first, a conventional assumption that nobility is connected with lineage, titles, and perhaps wealth; second, a popular opinion based on the first assumption but adding the idea that nobility tends to express itself "in a tone of luxury and sport, an overbearing manner, and a quick temper"; and third, the view of the "alleged philosophers" that all men owe their origin to God, the center of the highest nobility, and so every one is noble as long as his life is free of vice and full of virtue. More and his friends would have been sympathetic with the third of these views, but they added other ideas to define true nobility. When Einstein, in *The Italian Renaissance in England,* mentioned the view of the alleged philosophers, he referred to Annibale Romei, whose work, first published about 1585, appeared in English in 1598. Late as this work is, it has some interest here because Romei knew exactly what he meant by his philosophers. An aristocrat in sympathies himself, he assumed that a nobleman should have virtue but that his ancestors must have been famous for riches, heroic deeds, or other acts that men praise; and even a virtuous man cannot be truly noble until he has "lost the memory of his ignobilitie, which memorie remaineth during the reuolution of three generations." He cited Aristotle to support his own position, and he mentioned Boethius, Seneca, and Socrates to disagree with them. He tried especially to refute the Stoics, naming Seneca as the principal one of the Stoics. When he called upon Aristotle to help him refute these views he said that the great philosopher showed by clear reasons that the relationship of master and servant was allotted by nature and that the rank of noblemen was thus not contrary to the law of nature.[1]

Romei was correct about support from Aristotle and about the views held by his opponents. Plato held it dishonorable to rest any claim to nobility on ancestry alone. Boethius (480–524), a Christian philosopher who limited himself to "natural philosophy" in only one work *De consolatione philosophiae,* declared himself in favor of virtue. Since this work had been translated into Anglo-Saxon by King Alfred, into English by Chaucer, had been printed by Caxton, and again changed into English verse by John Walton about 1410 and printed in 1525, Boethius had been known in some form for centuries. He said:

And if sometime, which is very seldom, good men be preferred to honours, what other thing can give contentment in them but the honesty of those which have them? So that virtues are not honored by dignities, but dignities by virtue. . . . And dignity bestowed upon wicked men doth not only not make them worthy but rather bewrayeth and discovereth their unworthiness.[2]

---

[1] Haniball Romei, *The Courtiers Academie* (London, 1598?), pp. 187–88, 194, and *passim.*

[2] Boethius, *The Consolation of Philosophy,* published with the *Theological Tractates,* ed. by H. F. Stewart and E. K. Rand (London, 1946), pp. 207, 211. For John Walton's translation see *EETS,* v. 170 (1925).

And Seneca had said:

Philosophy did not find Plato already a nobleman; it made him one. Why then should you despair of becoming able to rank with men like these? They are all your ancestors if you conduct yourself in a manner worthy of them; and you will do so if you convince yourself that no man outdoes you in real nobility. We have all had the same number of forefathers . . . Plato says, "Every king springs from a race of slaves, and every slave has had kings among his ancestors." Then who is wellborn? He who is by nature well fitted for virtue. . . . A hall full of smoke-begrimed busts does not make the nobleman. . . . The soul alone renders us noble, and it may rise superior to Fortune out of any earlier condition.

One who is not a knight but a freedman may happen to be the only free man in a throng of gentlemen. Seneca said: " 'How?' you ask. Simply by distinguishing between good things and bad things without patterning your opinion from the populace." [3]

Romei's view differed from that of Lawrence Humphrey, whose Latin work of 1560 appeared three years later in English. In the dedication to the queen, Humphrey said that he did not agree with the common people in thinking that nobility meant hawking, hunting, great retinues, mighty power, hastiness, vain boasting, riots, mischief, as well as rank and titles. He estimated nobility by the degree to which men rose above beasts, and by this test he expected nobles to excel other men. [4]

VIEWS ON NOBILITY BEFORE 1500

For many years before 1500 men had carried on a verbal war about true nobility, with sincere Christians repeating that all men are equal in the sight of God, with many writers defending aristocracy, and with some writers stating sometimes one view and sometimes another view.

The aristocratic view appeared in a poem "The Describing of Man's Members," about 1418; it contained the familiar comparison of classes in the state to the parts of the human body— the head to a king, the neck to a just judge, the shoulders and backbone to lords, the feet to ploughmen, and the toes to faithful

[3] Seneca, *Ad Lucilium epistulae morales*, trans. by Richard M. Gummere, 3 vols. (London and New York, 1917), I, 287-91, "On Philosophy and Pedigrees."
[4] Lawrence Humfrey, *The Nobles, or Of Nobilitye* (London, 1563), the dedication, Aiiii *verso*, and *passim*.

servants.[5] (Aristotle had been a source for a comparison of this
kind; John of Salisbury developed it in detail in 1159; it appeared
in various medieval treatises on government; Elyot used it and
quoted Aristotle as his authority; Starkey repeated the idea when
he discussed the views of Pole and Lupset.) Hoccleve and Lydgate
varied their observations about nobility, from the view that Fortune cast a man off her wheel because he was a churl by lineage, to
the clear-cut advice to consider no man gentle but only by his
deed. The aristocratic view appeared in that pseudo-Aristotle, a
version of the *Secreta Secretorum*,[6] which James Yonge about 1422
called *The Governance of Princes*. He said that churls love praise
and great heaps of money because their hearts are low and little,
but noblemen of high peerage and great virtue love lordship and
chivalry and desire strength and power, without cunning.[7] Caxton
tended to favor aristocracy; in his *Order of Chivalry* and other
books he stated that knights should be of noble birth and that his
book was not for common men but for noble gentlemen who by
their virtue intend to enter the noble order of chivalry.[8]

The aristocratic view was expressed with quaint individuality
by Dame Juliana Berners about 1486. She argued that churls were
descended from Cain, who slew his brother; and Seth became a
gentleman through his father's and mother's blessing. His offspring
were gentlemen. Even more startling was her statement that Christ
was a gentleman of his mother's behalf and bore coat armor of his
ancestors.[9]

[5] *Twenty-Six Political and Other Poems*, ed. by J. Kail, EETS, v. 124 (1904), pp. 64–69.
See Starkey, *A Dialogue between Reginald Pole and Thomas Lupset*, ed. by Kathleen M.
Burton (London, 1948), pp. 57, 64, for similar ideas.

[6] The *Secreta Secretorum* was sometimes used in experiments with magic. A certain William Stapleton, who had, he said, been a monk at St. Bennet's, wrote Thomas Cromwell,
19 Henry VIII, that he had been called before Sir Thomas More, Knt., and that he had
used the *Secreta* and *Thesaurus Spirituum* to call up spirits. His plate "made for the calling
of Oberion" and his instruments were still in More's hands. See *Norfolk Archaeology*, I
(1847), 57.

[7] *Three Prose Versions of the Secreta Secretorum*, ed. by Robert Steele, EETS, ex. ser.,
LXXIV (1898), 172.

[8] Caxton, *Book of the Ordre of Chyualry*, ed. by Alfred T. P. Byles, EETS, v. 168
(1925), 1–2, 58–60, 121. See also *The Prologues and Epilogues of Wm. Caxton*, ed. by
W. J. B. Crotch, EETS, v. 176 (1927).

[9] Dame Juliana Berners, *The Boke of St. Albans*, ed. by William Blades (London, 1881),
section headed "Incipit liber armorum," especially subsections "How Gentlemen Shall Be
Known from Churls," Ai, and "A Gentilman Spirituall," Bi.

The story of Eve's children, in Alexander Barclay's fifth eclogue, is a charming discussion of aristocracy. Eve once received a visit from God. Ashamed of her many children, she presented to God only the handsome ones. God gave them positions; one became an emperor; others, noblemen of varied degrees; others judges, burgesses, and merchants. Delighted, Eve brought out her ugly children from hiding in straw and refuse. God was troubled, but though he had the power to make a nobleman of a vile villain, he decided to leave these children to toil, suffer, and be tillers of the soil. However balanced the attitude seems in parts of the poem, it remains true that God refused to change the classes.[10] Edmund Dudley, writing *The Tree of Commonwealth* about 1509 or 1510, defended aristocracy even more firmly as a part of God's plan for degrees between angels and men, men and other men, and men and beasts. But he was conscious that the children of noblemen were badly educated in virtue and cunning, and thus the children of poor men and mean folk were getting the positions of authority.[11]

The laws to regulate apparel during the fourteenth, fifteenth, and sixteenth centuries, though their aim was the control of extravagance, probably lent some support to aristocracy. A great wave of these statutes came under Edward III, after the decay of feudalism; in the next hundred years there were few; but a new wave came in the first, sixth, seventh, and twenty-fourth years of Henry VIII. Many of these statutes emphasized the rights of nobility to wear certain apparel without being imitated by those of lower rank. The statute in the sixth year of the reign of Henry VIII is perhaps typical; it was also enacted near the time when More and his friends were discussing the bases of true nobility. It began with the provision that only the king, queen, and the king's mother, brothers or sisters, or children should wear cloth of gold or "purpure" color or silk of the same, with a penalty of twenty pounds for each violation by others. Many degrees of nobility were protected in similar ways, and many classes and occupations were included—servants in husbandry, shepherds, com-

[10] Alexander Barclay, *The Cytezen and Uplondyshman*, ed. by F. W. Fairholt for the Percy Society (London, 1847), pp. 10–15.

[11] Edmund Dudley, *The Tree of Commonwealth*, ed. by D. M. Brodie (Cambridge, 1948), pp. 31–32, 45–46, 90–91.

mon laborers; ambassadors, heralds of arms, minstrels; players of interludes (perhaps during a performance) and some others were exempt. There was a note of great assurance in one phrase: "And this Acte to endure forever." Each new statute seemed to have more specific additions; the one passed in the twenty-fourth year of Henry VIII complained of the growing excesses in clothing and the detriment to the commonweal; it provided for the clothing allowed to utter barristers and students of the Inns of Court.[12]

In the fourteenth and fifteenth centuries there were also expressions of the non-aristocratic view that rank alone is not worthy of praise. The slogan of the fourteenth-century revolt by the peasants was an attack on aristocracy. Early anonymous poems also celebrated the common origins of man and the duties of nobility.[13]

Chaucer, like Dante, Boccaccio, and the author of the *Roman de la Rose,* had much to say in favor of virtue and against rank alone. One example is the "Moral Balade of Gentilesse." Another concerns the situation in the Wife of Bath's Tale. When the knight explained to the wife he had won that he was unhappy because of her age, ugliness, and low rank, she reproved him by citing Dante, Valerius Maximus, Boethius, and Seneca, as well as Christ, and contended that a nobleman lost his true nobility when his own actions became sinful. The Franklin's Tale showed that a clerk, as well as a squire or a knight, could practice "gentilesse." As Chaucer had translated Boethius, that work was one obvious source of his non-aristocratic ideas; but his characters were also quoting Seneca a hundred years before the members of the More group began writing about true nobility.

Before 1500 in England, perhaps the most important defense of virtue and learning against rank and lack of character (for this discussion, at least) was the *Declamacyon de noblesse,* by John Tiptoft, Earl of Worcester. His work was a translation of a summary of the *Declamatio de vera nobilitate,* written in Florence by Buonaccorsi about 1428, and dedicated to Carlo Malatesta, Earl of

---

[12] *Statutes of the Realm,* ed. by A. Luders, T. E. Tomlins, J. Raithby, *et al.,* 11 vols. (London, 1810–1828), II, III; see the *Alphabetical Index* (1824), where all these statutes are listed under "Apparel," or see the index with individual volumes.

[13] Kail, *Twenty-Six Political and Other Poems,* p. 81.

Rimini. Caxton printed Tiptoft's translation in 1481. The problem of the story is whether Lucres should marry Publius Cornelius, who has rank, wealth, a taste for hunting and hawking, no morals, and no service to the commonweal except that of his ancestors; or Gayus Flaminius, who is of lowly stock with moderate means, but with virtue, good manners, a desire to increase his own philosophical and classical learning, and to serve the commonweal. We are told at the beginning of this work that the decision is to be given by the senate, but the story ends by asking the reader to decide which suitor will be chosen for her.[14] Tiptoft's translation was the source of Henry Medwall's play *Fulgens and Lucres,* which was probably performed in the palace of Cardinal Morton about 1497. Though the play will be discussed more fully in Part II, it may be said here that the ending is definite, that Gayus Flaminius is chosen, and that the choice, with some tactful apologies, is made by Lucres herself.

Such was the debate between the factions about true nobility before 1500. Probably Tudor developments made the non-aristocratic view more acceptable than it had been, for example, in the fourteenth century. Feudalism had fostered a static society; its disintegration led to the efforts of commoners to imitate their social superiors. But after the Wars of the Roses, with the need of a new nobility, leaders in both church and state were coming up from the middle class or occasionally from the lower class of society. When Wolsey's enemies were galled by his pride, they reminded themselves that he was a butcher's son. The Tudors themselves had some middle-class ancestry; and to use a new term for an old truth, their emotional patterns did not forget that fact. Economic conditions, as well as fifteenth-century wars, were creating freedom of movement from one class to another. In this active society small farmers and agricultural workers might find themselves homeless and unemployed. Craftsmen, tradesmen, venturers

---

[14] John Tiptoft, *Declamacyon de noblesse* (1481), printed by Caxton. *Tulle of Old Age* and *Tullius de amicicia* are bound in the same volume. See *A Census of Caxtons* by Seymour de Ricci, no. 31. I used the Caxton at the J. Pierpont Morgan Library. The *Tulle of Old Age* says that the qualities which cause a man to be a noble or a churl are the same ones that make old age sweet and patient, and Seneca said that the ability to rise above the fear of death is a sign of nobility.

in commerce, and landowners whose enclosures helped them grow more wool, gained in economic power. While these changes probably did not cause More and his friends to develop and express ideas on true nobility, they may have helped to produce a more interested audience.

VIEWS ON NOBILITY OF MORE AND HIS FRIENDS

The older men of the More group and some of the younger men had much to say about the elements of true nobility. One of the early expressions of the idea appeared in More's translation of the life of Giovanni Pico della Mirandola. The author of the life had given small space to Pico's ancestors and much space to his own learning and virtue: "For these be the thinges whiche we may accompt for our owne, of which euery man is more properly to be commended then of the noblenes of his auncesters, whose honour maketh us not honorable. For either they were themself verteouse or not; if not, then had thei none honour themself, had thei neuer so great possessions, for honour is the reward of vertue . . . if they be vertuouse and so . . . honorable, yet maye they not leaue theyr honour to us as inheritantes. . . . But rather the more worshipfull that our auncesters wer, the more vyle and shamefull be we, if we declyne from the steppes of theyr woorshipful liuing." [15]

In *Utopia* More condemned through Hythlodaye those who honor wealth or rank without character:

In so muche that a lumpyshe blockehedded churle, and whyche hathe no more wytte then an asse, yea, and as full of noughtenes and folyshenes, shall haue neuertheles many wyse and good men in subiectyon and bondage, onlye for thys, bycause he hathe a great heape of golde.

A passage on those who expect honor for fine clothing is followed by this comment:

And agayne is it not a lyke madnes to take a pride in vayne and vnprofitable honoures? For what naturall or trewe pleasure doest thou take of an other mans bare hede or bowed knees? Will thys ease the payne of thy knees, or remedye the phrensie of thy heade?

We do not reward people according to their real value:

Is not thys an vniust and an vnkynd publyque weale, whyche gyueth great

---

[15] More, *The workes* (London, 1557), pp. 1, 2.

fees and rewardes to gentelmen, as they call them, and to goldsmythes, and to suche other, whiche be other ydell persones or els onlye flatterers, and deuysers of vayne pleasures; and . . . maketh no gentle prouision for poore plowmen, coliars, laborers, carters, yronsmythes, and carpenters, without whome no commen wealth can continewe?

We fail to reward the labors of their youth, the passage continues, and then we leave them needy and miserable in old age, to die wretchedly. The ideas conclude thus:

Therfore when I consider and way in my mind all thies commen wealthes which now a dayes any where do florish, so god helpe me, I can perceaue nothing but a certein conspiracy of riche men, procuringe theire own commodities vnder the name and title of the commen wealth.[16]

In *The Manual of a Christian Knight,* dated by its dedication in 1501, Erasmus commented simply on character and rank: "In Adam we all are borne of lowe degre. In Christ we are all one thyng, neyther hygh ne lowe of degre one more than another. Very noblenesse is to dispyse this vayne noblenesse; very noblenesse is to be seruant to Christ. Thynke them to be thyne ancestours whose vertues thou bothe louest and countrefaytest. . . . It is a low degre and shamfull to serue fylthynesse. . . ."[17] The passage is an interesting example of a Christian "humanist's" writing when he put aside philosophy and the classics and wrote simply as a Christian.

In many later works Erasmus attacked false nobility in a secular way, appealing to reason, and sometimes citing the classics. In *The Praise of Folly* he said:

Who would not avow that the king is a rich and great lord? Yet let the king be unfurnished in goods of the spirit, let him find satisfaction in nothing, and you see in a trice that he is the poorest of men. Suppose that his soul is given over to vices; now he is a vile slave.

If a wise man who had dropped down from the sky were to inspect our system of rank, he would not approve:

Suppose him to address another who is glorying in his ancestry, and to call him low and base-born, because he is so far from virtue, the only true fount of nobility.

---

[16] More, *Utopia,* ed. by J. H. Lupton (Oxford, 1895), pp. 182, 196, 302–3.

[17] Erasmus, *A booke called . . . in englysshe the Manuell of the Christen knight,* trans. into English and printed for John Byddell (London, 1533), Miii.

In the same work he said:

Although I must hasten on, I cannot pass over in silence those who, while differing in no respect from the meanest tinker, flatter themselves beyond measure with the empty title of nobility. One will trace his family back to Aeneas, one to Brutus, and a third to King Arthur. In every room they display pictures and busts of their ancestors . . . while all the time they are not so different from senseless statues themselves. . . .[18]

The *Colloquies* also have a great amount of either direct attack or satire on nobility. In one called "Of Things and Words," Beatus says: "But if man is a rational animal, how contrary it is to reason that in the conveniencies . . . and in external things . . . we had rather have the thing itself than the name; and in the real goods of the mind we put more value upon the name than the thing itself." In this colloquy Beatus and his friend Boniface discuss various illustrations of the idea and finally come to the knight:

Beatus. . . . . But how came this title to have so great a prerogative?

Boniface. Some have it by descent, some purchase it with money, and some take it to themselves.

Beatus. And may anybody have it that will?

Boniface. Yes, he may, if his manners but be answerable to theirs.

Beatus. What are they?

Boniface. Never to be guilty of doing a good action, to go fine, wear a diamond ring, whore stoutly, game continually, spend his life in drinking and diversion. . . .

Beatus. Such knights as these deserve to be mounted upon the wooden horse: but there are a great many such knights in Gelderland.[19]

In "The Unequal Marriage," Erasmus attacks the folly of parents who marry a beautiful young daughter to an old, immoral spendthrift who is half dead with the pox because he has "the glorious title of a knight." Such a knight is "always bragging of his castles and fiefs" and wishes to set up his coat of arms everywhere. But with its "three golden elephants in a field gules," it indicates that he is "a knave, a fool, and a drunken sot."

---

[18] Erasmus, *The Praise of Folly*, ed. by Hoyt H. Hudson (Princeton, 1941), pp. 36, 37, 38, 59.

[19] Erasmus, *The Colloquies*, 2 vols. (London, 1878), II, 132–38. For quotations see pp. 134, 138.

"The False Knight," another colloquy, is an extended satire on false nobility. Nestor first suggests to Harpalus, a would-be knight, a serious concept: "strive by virtuous actions, that your nobility may derive its original from yourself." But when Harpalus rejects this method as too tedious, he gives him mocking directions:

And take care not to wear anything that's whole; but cut your hat and your doublet, your hose and your shoes, and your nails, too, if you can . . . you must counterfeit letters sent you from such and such great persons in which you must frequently be styled the *Illustrious Knight;* and there must be mention made of great affairs . . . estates, castles, huge revenues . . . great offices, rich matches. . . . Then you must furnish yourself with companions or servants who shall stand cap in hand to you and call you my young lord at every turn. . . . Unless you are an expert gamester at cards and dice, a rank whoremaster . . . and have got the French pox to boot, scarce any one will believe you to be a knight.[20]

Erasmus' satirical directions to "The False Knight" suggest that he is attacking the second, popular view of nobility mentioned at the beginning of the chapter.

In *The Instruction of a Christian Prince,* 1516, Erasmus spoke with serious firmness about nobility:

Teach the young prince that nobility, statues, wax masks, family trees, all the pomp of heralds . . . are only empty terms unless supported by deeds worth while.

Again he said:

useful occupation should be respected and sluggish indolence not graced with the title "nobility." I should not strip the well-born of their honors if they follow in the footsteps of their forefathers and excel in those qualities which first created nobility. But if we see so many today who are soft from indolence, effeminate through sensual pleasures, with no knowledge of any useful vocation . . . (I will not mention any of their obscene practices) why, I ask you, should this class of persons be placed on a higher level than the shoemaker or the farmer? In former times leisure from the baser activities was granted the best families . . . so that they might learn the principles of government.

In *The Instruction of a Christian Prince,* where Erasmus quoted Aristotle, Plato, and Seneca by name as his authorities for many specific ideas on government, he discussed views on nobility which

[20] *The Colloquies,* II, 153–66, 181–91.

seem to be close to those of Seneca: "There are three kinds of nobility: the first is derived from virtue and good actions; the second comes from acquaintance with the best of training; and the third from an array of family portraits and the genealogy or wealth. It by no means becomes a prince to swell with pride over this lowest degree of nobility, for it is so low that it is nothing at all, unless it has itself sprung from virtue. Neither must he neglect the first, which is so far the first that it alone can be considered in the strictest judgment." [21]

So Erasmus wrote on nobility from many points of view. He was serious or satirical in his method but always serious in his intention. He discussed nobility in order to improve personal standards of living or to influence a ruler and thus to change the world; he used religious ideas alone or he called on all the resources of his classic background in his treatise on government.

Bishop Fisher affirmed the non-aristocratic view of virtue and true nobility when he preached the memorial sermon at the "month's mind" mass for Lady Margaret, the mother of Henry VII. There are four kinds of nobility, he said: nobleness of blood, in those who are descended from men of great rank; nobleness of manners or character "withouten whiche the noblenes of bloode is moche defaced," for as Boethius says, if there is good in the nobleness of blood, it is that thereby "the noble men and women sholde be ashamed to go out of kynde from the vertuous maners of theyr auncetrye"; nobleness of nature, "wherby full often suche as come of ryght pore and vnnoble fader and moder haue grete abletees of nature, to noble dedes"; and nobleness increased "as by maryage and affynyte of more noble persons." [22] Of course he suggested that the Lady Margaret had many kinds of nobility; but considering the time and the occasion, it is interesting that he defined the potential nobility of those with "pore and vnnoble" parents.

Vives was not surpassed by any of the other men in the earnest-

---

[21] Erasmus, *The Education of a Christian Prince*, trans. by Lester K. Born (New York, 1936), pp. 148–49, 226, 151, and *passim*. It seems necessary to use the standard title *The Instruction of a Christian Prince* in the body of this work, but to use *Education of a Christian Prince* in citing Born's translation.

[22] *The English Works of John Fisher*, ed. by John E. B. Mayor, *EETS*, ex. ser., XXVII (1876, 1935), 290.

ness of his arguments about virtue as the basis of true nobility. In one of his dialogues "Educatio," Grympherantes, a boy who held false standards about young noblemen, discussed the problem with Flexibulus, an ideal teacher and an advocate of piety and sound learning. Grympherantes had formerly been taught only external manners: training the body for proper courtly action; preserving his own noble rank and honor by yielding to no one else, by fighting anyone who seemed to detract from his honor, by being lavish with money, and by refusing to give honor to others, especially to the "new men" who had seized upon wealth nd who "dared to vie with the old standing and honours of our ce." Flexibulus opposed his false views with these ideals: internal ling and love for others, rather than superficial manners; the ning of the mind so as to rise above beasts, for without this ing a nobleman is only a beast; real nobility of character, ding sincere modesty, benevolence, genuine goodness. Instead lth, he recommended wisdom, religion, piety (a right atti- God, country, parents, dependents), justice, temperance, y, magnanimity, equability of mind toward calamity in hu- irs, and bravery of mind in adversity. These qualities, he constitute true nobility.

ommended further the common people through the h Flexibulus gave, not only to those who have acquired d culture, but to those who do the common labor: nts themselves—how many of the secrets of nature Sailors, too, know of the course of day and night, winds, the position of lands and seas." Such people with the proud young nobleman who considers no he is; he asks this nobleman, "How canst thou be yet thou are not *good?*" All the instances cited a imply that people who are good have learned ighly or can do something well.[23]

Vives spoke frankly of the conviction that had obles that nothing is more mean or vile than to

1540),

School-Boy Life (London, 1908), no. xxiv. The book has com-
ues. See also Foster Watson, *Vives: On Education* (Cambridge,
dis disciplinis, pp. 211–12.

pursue knowledge in anything.[24] In *Satellitium* or *Symbola* Vives inquired: "Which horse is noble? Which dog? Is it not the best and so in other animals and stock? Then the noble man is none other than the best man in character."[25]

In his *Introduction to Wisdom* Vives summarized the origin of false and of true nobility:

What other thynge is nobylite nowe, but a chaunce to be borne of this or that gentyll bloud, and an opinion grafte uppon the foolishnes of rude and unlerned people, whiche oftentymes is gotten by robberie and lyke wayes.

True and perfect nobilite springeth of vertue, wherfor it is gret madnesse for any man to crake of his parentes, beinge naught him selfe, dishonourynge theyr noble actes with his lewed doinges. . . .

Honour, if it springe not of vertue, is falsly gyuen and wrongfully taken, neyther it can fully delyte the, where as thy conscience denyeth the to deserue it. . . . Honoure muste folowe welle doinge, and is not to be craued of the well doers.[26]

In Starkey's *Dialogue,* Pole and Lupset both emphasized education, virtue, and perfectibility; thus they implied ideas about true nobility. Pole, as quoted by Starkey, said that there were too many servants and too many of the religious classes for the good of the commonweal. Lupset, in his closing speech, defined true nobility in terms of service to the state: "but when men desire to bear office and to rule to the intent they may stablish . . . in their country this commonweal which you before have described, it is the highest virtue that is in any noble stomach, and is a certain argument of true nobility; for sluggish minds live in corners and content themselves with private life, whereas very noble hearts ever desire to govern and rule to the common weal of the whole multitude. And Pole closed the discussion by saying that at another time he would discuss the obligation of the wise man to serve the common weal and "what is very true nobility."[27] But if that discussion ever took place, it was not recorded for us.

[24] *Tudor School-Boy Life,* p. 69.
[25] Vives, *Opera,* 2 vols. (Basel, 1555), II, p. 99, no. 53. See also no. 52.
[26] Vives, *An Introduction to wysedome,* trans. by Rycharde Morysine (London, Bvii *verso,* Bviii.
[27] Starkey, *A Dialogue,* p. 191.

Such examples represent the non-aristocratic views of the older men, More, Colet, Bishop Fisher, and Erasmus, and of the younger men, Vives, Lupset, and even Reginald Pole, who had royal blood. These men expected virtue and usefulness from aristocrats, they reproved their vices, they disliked the outer signs without the inner attitudes of nobility, they honored the contributions of common workmen, and they praised men of poor and unnoble families who rose to virtue, piety, learning, and service to the commonweal.

By 1531 there was a change of attitude, even in the members of the More circle. Publishing his *Governour* in that year, Sir Thomas Elyot was concerned with the qualifications of a courtier. Three different opinions on that subject were held in the sixteenth century, as Einstein suggested: first, a courtier should be a gentleman born but he should have virtue; second, a courtier might be of low birth if he were outstanding in wisdom and virtue; third, the "eminently practical view," a courtier should be a gentleman born, for though a man of low birth might have wisdom and virtue, he would not command the same respect from the people. The other men of the group who have been quoted held basically the second opinion; but Elyot held the third or the "eminently practical view."

Just why Elyot expressed more aristocratic views is not easy to decide. Perhaps he realized that More and Erasmus had lost their long struggle to tame the lion. As Wolsey fell, Thomas Cromwell rose to power, the friends of Anne Boleyn won imposing titles, and Henry VIII used men like pawns to help him win his chess game against the Pope, perhaps Elyot wished to try more tactful methods of teaching virtue. Clearly he wished to teach virtue; and the man who wrote *Of the Knowledge Which Maketh a Wise Man* and who is generally believed to have written *Pasquil the Plain* had steel within his tactful deference. Perhaps Elyot was influenced also by Castiglione's *Courtier*. Though an English translation did not appear until 1561, an Italian copy was being read in England and was within reach of Elyot in 1530, a year before the *Governour* was published: in that year Edmund Bonner wrote to Thomas Cromwell reminding him that "ye willing to make me a good Ytalion" had promised to lend the Triumphs of Petrarch; now he asked him to send that book and "especially, if it please you, the boke called Cortigiano in Ytalion. . . ." By 1528, as H. H. S. Croft told us in the Introduction to his edition of the *Governour*, Elyot and Thomas Cromwell were beginning a friendly relationship which developed rapidly. In the *Courtier*, Castiglione had stressed virtue and his characters had debated the question of noble birth. For example, in the first book, when Count Lewis and Lord Gasper Pallavicin were crossing mental swords, the Count seemed to win an advantage for aristocracy when he granted that men of base degree may have the virtues of gentlemen but he still maintained that the ideal courtier should be of noble birth because of other reasons and because the common opinion favored noblemen. In the fourth book Lord Octavian seemed to take for granted noble-ness of birth; then he discussed music, pastimes, and sports as the flower of courtliness, but its fruit, as the service of the courtier in turning his prince from evil to virtue.[28]

At least Elyot was consistently deferential to aristocracy while he continued to stress virtue and learning. He began his *Governour* by defining the term *public weal* and hotly rejecting the term *commonweal*. He approved of degrees as the basis of order in government and as the provision of God: "Hath not he set degrees and astates in all his glorious warkes?" Usually governors would be chosen from the higher ranks: "And excepte excellent vertue and lernynge do inhabile a man of the base astate of the com-munaltie to be thought of all men worthy to be so moche auaunced, els suche gouernours wolde be chosen out of that astate of men whiche be called worshipfull, if amonge them may be founden a sufficient nombre ornate with vertue and wisdome, mete for suche purpose. . . ."[29] He gave a number of reasons: noblemen were not so likely to use office for financial gain as men of lower rank because they would already have larger revenues; a gentleman was

---

[28] Castiglione, *The Courtyer* (London, 1561), first book, *passim*; and fourth book, Mmiiii. For Cromwell's loan of the book, see Hogrefe, "Elyot and 'The Boke Called Cortigiano in Ytalion,'" *MP*, XXVII (1930), 303–9; also Sir Henry Ellis, *Original Letters*, 3rd ser., 4 vols. (London, 1846), II, 177–78.

[29] Elyot, *The boke named the Gouernour* (London, 1531), Fol. 14 *verso*. See also Book I, Chapters i, ii, iii *passim*.

likely to have more affability than a man of base estate; the rule of a nobleman was more tolerable to the people, who would murmur less at his orders; a nobleman with stable possessions and background was better equipped for training his own children to serve the commonweal.

Elyot's aristocratic bias also influenced his discussion of the nobleman's education in the arts and in music. A nobleman's son should be taught music, since it would help him understand the order of degrees and the harmony in the public weal; but a nobleman should use his musical skill in private life only: "the tutors office shall be to persuade hym to haue principally in remembrance his astate, whiche maketh hym exempt from the libertie of vsinge this science in euery tyme and place . . . and to shewe him that a gentilman plainge or singing in a commune audience appaireth his estimation. The people forgettinge reuerence whan they beholde him in the similitude of a common seruant or minstrell." [30] A gentleman might also learn to paint or carve if he had the inclination, but again he must be careful to maintain his status: "I intende nat by these examples to make of a prince or noble mannes sonne a commune painter or keruer, whiche shall present him selfe openly stained or embrued with sondry colours or poudered with the duste of stones that he cutteth, or perfumed with tedious sauours of the metalles by him yoten." [31]

In explaining nobility Elyot assumed that in the beginning people gave property and dignity to those who were virtuous and who labored for the common benefit. So they were called gentlemen because of their character and their deeds. Also it happened that their children were trained in virtue and thus they were able to keep the respect of the people: "And for the goodnesse that proceded of suche generation the state of them was called in greke *eugenia,* whiche signifiethe good kinde or lignage; but in a more briefe maner it was after called nobilitie, and the persones noble, whiche . . . containeth as well all that whiche is in gentilnesse, as also the honour or dignitie therfore receiued. . . ." [32] Again

---

[30] *The Gouernour,* Fol. 23 *verso*-24, or Book I, Chapter vii.

[31] *The Gouernour,* Fol. 27, or Book I, Chapter viii.

[32] *The Gouernour,* Fol. 1012 (but the numbers here shift from 109 to 1010, 1011, 1012), or Book II, Chapter iv.

Elyot said that an evil man descended from a noble ancestor earns reproach, that a man should not glory in a titled ancestor who was not virtuous in conduct, and that nobility is not solely in dignity, ancient lineage, nor great revenues, lands, or possessions. He used the example of Numa Pompilius, a husbandman who was elected king of the Romans because of his wisdom and virtue, which brought him to dignity. But he closed the discussion by assuming that nobility and virtue are likely to be the same and that nobility is "the prayse and surname of vertue, whiche the lenger it continueth in a name or lignage the more is nobilitie extolled and meruailed at." [33]

In his *Image of Governance*, 1541, Elyot continued to support class distinctions. He told of the commoners who came, when gentlemen were wrestling, and without any sign of reverence or asking permission, mingled with the gentlemen. Their emperor, Elyot said, was sad because base-born men had so much presumption; he delivered an oration setting forth the three estates or degrees, every one necessary for the public welfare, and declaring that the commoners should have no authority but should follow their occupations, be ready to obey all laws, and to serve in war. [34]

Ascham's view of nobility combined virtue and learning with a desire to see the aristocracy qualified for positions in the state:

The fault is in your selues, ye noble men sonnes, and therfore ye deserue the greater blame, that commonlie the meaner mens children cum to be the wisest councellours and greatest doers in the weightie affaires of this Realme. . . .

And God is a good God and wisest in all his doinges, that will place vertue and displace vice in those kingdomes where he doth gouerne. For he knoweth that Nobilitie, without vertue and wisedome, is bloud in deede, but bloud trewelie without bones and sinewes . . . verie weeke to beare the burden of weightie affaires. . . .

But Nobilitie, gouerned by learning and wisedome, is in deede, most like a faire shippe, hauyng tide and winde at will, vnder the reule of a skilfull master. . . . [35]

---

[33] *The Gouernour,* Fol. 1015 *verso,* misnumbered for 1014, or Book II, Chapter iv.
[34] Elyot, *The Image of Governance* (London, 1541), leaves 59 *verso*-60, and *passim.*
[35] Ascham, *The Scholemaster* (London, 1570), first book, leaves 13 *verso*-14.

Thus Ascham's views were less like those of More, Erasmus, and Vives and more like those of Sir Thomas Elyot. But being less sure than Elyot that noblemen were qualified for positions in the state, he scolded them for their shortcomings.

SUMMARY

More, Erasmus, and Vives, judged by their writings, were in almost complete agreement about the basis of true nobility; and perhaps through the impact of Castiglione's *Courtier* and perhaps through his own personal tact and integrity, Sir Thomas Elyot (and to a lesser degree Roger Ascham) expressed a more aristocratic view. The first three men refused to consider as truly noble those who had wealth, titles, or aristocratic ancestry if their lives were evil, useless, or non-productive. They made many attacks on false nobility, the outer shell without inner reality. They did consider as truly noble, regardless of rank or money, those who were virtuous, competent, trained in wisdom and goodness, and active for the common good. Thus they accepted the view of the "alleged philosophers" quoted at the beginning of the chapter and sometimes stated the religious principle of virtue as nobility in the sight of God. But they went further. Often they treated the question of true nobility from a secular point of view, supporting it by such classical authorities as Plato, the Stoics in general, or Seneca in particular; and though there may have been no completely new idea about nobility which they could express, after the popularity of Boethius in the Middle Ages and the Chaucer characters who quoted Dante and Seneca, they put a new emphasis upon the ability of the poor boy from common stock to rise to true nobility through character and education. Thus More and his friends emphasized a nobility which was a growth and a becoming, a future and not a past. Thus they seemed optimists at times, as they seemed in discussing other parts of their program, when they considered theories and possibilities.

Since they recommended education as a means to achieving or increasing genuine nobility, and since men who were truly noble were the worthy leaders—educators, governors, rulers, kings—of the commonweal, the discussion of nobility tended to show the integration of the entire program of social reform.

They used some new ways of expressing old ideas: the dialogues of Erasmus and Vives, with characters who agreed or who clashed to give sharp contrast to ideas, with serious or satirical methods; and the imaginative contrasts between civilizations in *Utopia*. Often there was a positive firmness in stating points of view on true nobility, instead of raising questions and leaving the reader to decide, as Tiptoft had done in his *Declamacyon de noblesse,* or apologizing for a decision, as Medwall did before 1500 in his *Fulgens and Lucres.*

CHAPTER **III** *Religious reform*

We are not concerned here with the basic theology of the men in the More circle. They were Catholics, of course; some of them remained loyal, even in exile and death. Those who remained loyal were sometimes suspected of heresy because of their boldness in attacking evil. For example, Colet was accused of heresy by his conservative bishop, but Archbishop Warham dismissed the charges. Erasmus, always a storm center, was attacked by Catholics because he went too far and by Protestant reformers because he did not go far enough to serve their cause. But he followed the rules of his church in securing the Pope's approval of his work on the New Testament and then he dedicated it to the Pope; he refused to admit the authorship of *Julius Exclusus* even to the end of his life because he feared excommunication; and in his published work he said that there was no salvation outside the church. Vives apparently held the view that he would not find salvation outside the church. But one of the strange ironies in the early sixteenth century is the fact that Erasmus and some of his English friends, by their carefully reasoned attacks on abuses, may have furnished reformers with ammunition never intended to destroy the church in England.

Some of the friends of More died too early to meet the test of loyalty to their church—Morton, Medwall, Grocyn, Linacre, Colet,

William Lily, Herde, and Lupset—but there is no reason to suppose that they would have swerved from their beliefs. Some who lived through the period of what might be called the loyalty oath to the king have left no definite record of their decisions. Two or three gave up their earlier faith: John Rastell, converted by Frith, gave active support to Thomas Cromwell and the king's cause; Sir Thomas Elyot finally satisfied Cromwell's mind about his belief in the royal supremacy; Croke aided Henry VIII. Pace escaped a real test by his mental illness, which seems to have developed about 1525 or 1526. Tunstal gave "passive obedience" to Henry VIII, served his own church again under Queen Mary, journeyed to London to persuade his goddaughter, Queen Elizabeth, not to give up the Catholic faith, and as a result, died in custody.

Others remained loyal in spite of sacrifices. William Roper, who stayed in England, was a loyal Catholic until his death in 1578. He met trouble when he was accused of giving others money to go into exile, but he gave bond for his future conduct and remained for many years clerk of the Court of King's Bench. John Clement, Margaret Gigs Clement, their daughter Winifred, her husband William Rastell, and John Heywood all died in exile. Heywood's course was a changing one: he was probably uneasy through More's imprisonment but he was in favor again after Anne Boleyn's execution; he was convicted of treason in the plot against Archbishop Cranmer, but he made a public confession, recanted at Paul's Cross, July 6, 1544, and was pardoned. Soon after Elizabeth became queen, he fled overseas and lived in Malines, Antwerp, and Louvain until his death in 1578 or later. So the end was loyalty. Reginald Pole escaped to the Continent, issued his manifesto in favor of the universal church against Henry, and lived to return as a cardinal under Queen Mary; but the king took revenge on his mother and brothers. No one doubts that Sir Thomas More and Bishop John Fisher were loyal to their church in 1535, when they gave their lives for that loyalty. Some non-Catholics think that More changed his attitude to the church; but it seems that circumstances, not More himself, changed. He might be compared with a man who had once reproached his mother for her faults but who finally gave his own life in an effort to save her from rapists and murderers.

ACTION FOR RELIGIOUS REFORM

The actions of the men in the More circle are a firm foundation on which to base judgments about their idea of reform. Colet, Grocyn, and More gave lectures which were public and gratis and were intended to further the interpretation of religious literature. The leader in this work was John Colet with his Oxford lectures, which he seems to have begun in Michaelmas term, 1497. These were the lectures which either helped Erasmus to decide his life work or recalled him to that work when he was hesitating. After hearing them he wrote to Colet, Oxford, 1499, declining to help in the great work at that time because he was not yet prepared; he said that theology "ought to be at the head of all literature," but "it is mainly studied by persons who from their dullness and lack of sense are scarcely fit for any literature," and that Colet had "undertaken a pious work as regards theology itself and a most wholesome one in the interest of all studies. . . ." In 1501 he wrote James Tutor that he sometimes thought of going to England for a month or two to pursue theological studies with Colet. Late in 1504 he wrote to Colet again that he still wished to devote himself to sacred literature, and for that reason he had for the past three years "been entirely taken up" with the study of Greek.[1]

Of Grocyn's theological lectures at Oxford in the 1480's we know little detail. But after his return from Italy, where he studied about 1488 to 1490, he gave Greek lectures gratis; then probably through Colet's work, he became more and more interested in theology. One of Colet's recent biographers, J. A. R. Marriott, says of Grocyn that "he struck the keynote of the Oxford Renaissance, insisting on the interdependence of exact scholarship, Biblical exegesis, and sound religious teaching." It is a phrase which might be applied to most members of the More circle. Grocyn's lectures at St. Paul's, in London, were reported by More in his 1501 letter to John Holt. Grocyn had begun his lectures on "The Ecclesiastical Hierarchy of Dionysius," believing that the mystical account of primitive Christianity credited to a certain Dionysius had been

---

[1] P. S. Allen, *Opus epistolarum*, 12 vols. (Oxford, 1906–1958), I, 108, 159, 181; or see F. M. Nichols, *The Epistles of Erasmus*, 3 vols. (London, 1901–1918), I, nos. 108, 155, 180. The dates are those given by Allen.

written by Dionysius the Areopagite, a disciple of St. Paul. While
he was giving the series of talks, he discovered his error (his discovery had been anticipated by Valla) and made a public re-
traction.

More's own lectures at St. Lawrence Jewry, on St. Augustine's
Civitas dei, probably followed the pattern of interpretation established by Colet and Grocyn. The probability is supported by
More's interest in Grocyn's lectures, and by the fact that More,
in his letter of 1504 to Colet, called Grocyn his teacher and the
guide of his life in Colet's absence. The probability is further
strengthened by the fact that Grocyn was rector of St. Lawrence
Jewry, the parish church of the More family, when More delivered his expositions. But all that we know about the lectures by
More comes from Stapleton. He said that More drew great crowds,
that the talks were held in high esteem, and that his approach
was historical and philosophical, not theological.

The editorial work of Erasmus was, of course, a major effort to
exert an influence on religious literature. After he had given himself additional training in Greek and Hebrew, he began his critical
editions. In 1516 he published his first version of the New Testament, and in 1518, his revised edition. In 1516 also, besides some
other theological works, he published an edition of St. Jerome;
about 1520, St. Cyprian; in 1527, St. Ambrose; about 1528–29, St.
Augustine; in 1529, Lactantius; in 1530, St. Chrysostom; in 1532,
St. Basil, and in 1536, the works of Origen. These approximate dates
indicate his concern with such works throughout his mature life.

Many other men of the circle helped him in this editorial work.
As early as 1512 or 1513, after Lupset had entered the University
of Cambridge, Erasmus reported to his friends that Lupset was
assisting him on his New Testament and his St. Jerome. At times
Tunstal gave him competent help as an editor on his second edition
of the New Testament, from the summer or fall of 1516 until
July, 1517. Erasmus followed Tunstal from one place to another
—Bruges, Ghent, Brussels, wherever Tunstal's duties called him—
to make use of his assistance. Tunstal lent him a manuscript,
consulted other Greek manuscripts for him, suggested various
emendations, and at parting gave Erasmus fifty French crowns.

More defended the editorial work of Erasmus against Edward Lee, against Dorp, a theologian of Louvain who later withdrew his objections, and against an unknown monk. Pace and Lupset also defended Erasmus and tried to stop the attacks of Edward Lee on his work. In a letter to Erasmus, All Saints' Eve, 1516, More reported that William Latimer refused to help on the editing but praised the work:

He is delighted with your version of the New Testament, in which however, he thinks you have been more scrupulous than he would wish. He does not like your having left the word Sabbath, and some others of the kind, which you either did not think it expedient or did not venture to alter, whereas he does not admit any expression at all which would be strange to Roman ears. I approved his judgment so far as the Hebrew rites and practices would admit. . . . I advised him to send you a list of the words he would like to have differently translated, with his judgment about them, and this I think he will do.

More continued, saying that there are others who would be hostile, and "whose formidable intentions make me uneasy." Among these opponents was the great Franciscan theologian whom Erasmus had mentioned honorably in his edition of Jerome; he and other members of his order planned to attack Erasmus, More said, but he added facetiously that the attack was planned over their flagons of wine and next morning they cancelled the decree.[2]

More also wrote epigrams about the New Testament of Erasmus. In one addressed to the general reader he said that "the new law was first marred by the ancient translator and . . . damaged by the inaccurate copying of scribes. Jerome long ago may have removed errors, but his readings, excellent as they were, have been lost by long neglect. . . . Erasmus has not ostentatiously disputed the text word by word; he has considered inviolable whatever is merely acceptable." Thus, he said, a reader who skims the version may think that nothing important has been done, but if he reads closely, he will "decide that there is no greater or more helpful

---

[2] Allen, *Opus epistolarum*, II, 481. More said "Non placet et quod sabbati vocem reliqueris, et quaedam talia, quae tu mutanda aut non censuisti aut non es ausus. Sed ille nullum prorsus verbum admittit quod Romanis auribus fuerit insolens." See Nichols, *The Epistles*, II, no. 471, for translation. Latimer's view here seems the opposite of that expressed by Erasmus in *Ciceronianus* and of the usual view in the More circle.

work." More addressed to Wolsey another epigram to be included in the copy of the New Testament presented to him. In it he said (perhaps with the spirit in which Erasmus used the panegyric) that this law of Christ enabled Wolsey to render decisions which amazed people: "you resolve intricate differences in such a way that even the loser cannot complain." He addressed a third epigram to Archbishop Warham, who had been giving Erasmus a pension, saying that the two shared the honor of the work: "He provided the labor; you, kind bishop, provided the support." [3]

Colet and Fisher, who had been struggling to learn Greek themselves, wrote Erasmus with warm approval of his New Testament. Colet said: "I understand what you say about the New Testament. Your new edition is bought with avidity, and read everywhere here. There are many that approve and admire your studies, others that disapprove and find fault, and say the sort of things . . . in the letter addressed to you by Martinus Dorpius. For my part, I am so devoted to your studies and so charmed with your new edition that it produces in me a variety of emotions. . . . We are expecting your Jerome." [4]

Fisher wrote to Erasmus shortly after he received a copy of the work: "You have made me your debtor in a vast amount of thanks by presenting me with the New Testament translated by you out of the Greek. As soon as I received it and had seen the notes in several places, in which you extol your Maecenas of Canterbury with such ample praises, I went off to him myself and showed him those passages. When he had read them, he promised that he would do a great deal for you, and exhorted me . . . to persuade you to return." [5]

And Fisher wrote Erasmus in a letter dated June, 1517: "The New Testament, translated by you for the common benefit of all, cannot give offense to any wise person; when you have not only cleared up innumerable passages by your erudition, but have also supplied a very complete commentation of the whole work; so that it may now be read and understood by every one with much

[3] Bradner and Lynch, *The Latin Epigrams of Thomas More* (Chicago, 1953), nos. 239, 240, 241.

[4] Allen, *Opus epistolarum*, II, 423; Nichols, *The Epistles*, II, no. 411.

[5] *Opus epistolarum*, II, 432; *The Epistles*, II, no. 416.

more satisfaction and pleasure than it could before." [6] Fisher went on to say that the printer had sometimes been at fault; for "in practicing the rules you laid down, I have myself often found that Greek expressions and sometimes whole sentences are omitted. I have you to thank that I am able to some extent to guess where the Greek does not correspond with the Latin." There is nothing in the wording to suggest that he blamed Erasmus for taking any undue liberties with the text; Fisher's known candor operates against any such suspicion. Erasmus replied to Fisher in March, 1518, admitting that his first edition contained errors; he asked for further suggestions and added that he was taking a journey to be on the spot for the printing of the second edition.

It seems safe to say that Grocyn also approved the editorial work of Erasmus, though Grocyn left us little written evidence of his attitudes. But he was a beloved teacher of More, a lifelong friend and associate of Colet, Linacre, and Erasmus; and there is a persistent belief, without apparent documented evidence, that he lectured at St. Paul's through arrangements made by Colet after the latter became acting dean or dean at that place. Though his lectures, which More reported in 1501, seem to have preceded Colet's appointment as acting dean, Grocyn may have given there two series of lectures. Grocyn's library, listed by Linacre as his executor, shows a breadth of view which gives an indirect suggestion of his approval. He owned some works by Scotus and other Schoolmen, it is true, but also copies of Augustine and other fathers of the early church, the comedies of Plautus, much natural history, the comment of Ficinus on Plato, and much Stoical material, including the works of Seneca, the epistles of Cicero, the orations of Cicero, and another edition of his works. [7] If a recent biographer of Colet, Sir J. A. R. Marriott, is correct (though he does not give his source) Grocyn said: "To put the sacred Scriptures before the world in their original tongue, that was a divine work—a most arduous work—and one most worthy of a Christian man." If Grocyn made the statement, it is evidence of his support for the editorial work of Erasmus.

---

[6] *Opus epistolarum*, II, 592; III, 784; *The Epistles*, II, no. 568; III, no. 752.
[7] Montagu Burrows, *Collectanea*, sec. ser., O.H.S., v. 16 (Oxford, 1890), 319–23.

The men of the More circle encouraged effective preaching both for the leaders in church and state and for the masses. John Colet reformed preaching at St. Paul's when he became acting dean for Sherbourn about 1503 and when he formally assumed the deanship himself about 1505. In his letter to Colet, October, 1504, More paid tribute to the man and the sermons when he expressed his regret that Colet had not yet returned to London: "It has been my custom to rely upon your prudent advice . . . to be stirred up by your powerful sermons, to be edified by your life and example, to be guided, in fine, by even the slightest indications of your opinions. . . . By following your footsteps I had escaped from almost the very gates of hell, and now . . . I am falling back again into the gruesome darkness." In his biography of Colet Erasmus told us that the latter "restored the decayed discipline" and began preaching at every festival, and that "he would not take isolated texts . . . but would start with some connected subject and pursue it right to the end in a course of sermons: for example, St. Matthew's gospel, the creed, or the Lord's prayer. He used to have a crowded congregation, including most of the learned men both of the city and court." Colet also provided for other "learned preachers and expositors" at St. Paul's. His sermons were entirely different from the kind of sermon which had become conventional, a textarian, many-sided interpretation, full of logical subtleties and glosses by learned doctors. His three famous sermons might be discussed here, but since we have some remains of them as documents, they will be summarized in the next section of this chapter.

About this time John Fisher, with the help of the Lady Margaret, was reforming preaching by establishing the divinity readerships at Cambridge. By these readerships men were trained gratis and then were sent out to preach simple, eloquent sermons in London and in other parts of England. Both Fisher and Erasmus held one of these readerships for a time at Cambridge. A historian of the university, James Bass Mullinger, estimated this work of Fisher as one of the great ecclesiastical reforms of the century.

More showed his interest in preaching in his letter of rebuke to the University of Oxford in 1518, when he emphasized the need of good letters for any preacher who wished his sermons to reach the common man. Believing that an editor of the Bible needed an accurate knowledge of Hebrew, Greek, and Latin, Erasmus helped persuade Jerome Busleiden into founding the College of the Three Languages at Louvain—an action affecting England because he also tried to influence Englishmen to study or teach there.

Men of the More group, it seems, established the teaching of Greek at Oxford and Cambridge. From such writers as Sir John Edwin Sandys, *A History of Classical Scholarship,* Hastings Rashdall, *The Universities of Europe in the Middle Ages,* James Bass Mullinger, *The University of Cambridge . . . ,* Sir Charles Edward Mallet, *A History of the University of Oxford,* and Roberto Weiss, *Humanism in England during the Fifteenth Century,* one may conclude that there is little or no evidence of any systematic teaching of Greek at Oxford or Cambridge before 1490.

Much earlier, there had been scholars in England with a thorough knowledge of Greek. In the seventh century Theodore, Archbishop of Canterbury, founded a school for teaching that language and furthered its study in other ways; Aldhelm is said to have used Greek fluently in writing and speaking; Bede had some knowledge of it, though Aelfric and King Alfred did not. Robert Grosseteste brought Greek scholars to England and set them to translating new versions of Aristotle. Roger Bacon realized the need to study the original Greek texts both of the scriptures and of scientific writings. Bacon himself knew Arabic, Hebrew, and Greek; he said that language, not logic, was the means for clearing up thought on philosophical subjects; and he wished that he had the power to destroy all the existing translations of Aristotle, to keep men from spreading ignorance. On the Continent, Thomas Aquinas knew only a little if any Greek, and Abelard probably knew none at all. The Council of Vienne in 1311–12 and the efforts of Pope Clement V to establish teachers of Greek and other languages at Oxford and at other universities on the Continent were missionary efforts at converting the heathen instead of furthering secular learning; and though a few pence were collected in Winchester and Worcester for paying a master, there is no evidence that any master taught or any students learned Greek. About 1490 Grocyn returned from Italy, where he had acquired a sound knowledge of the language; and in 1491–93 he held rooms at Exeter College.[8] But though he was "one of the first to teach Greek" there, he apparently did not have any official appointment as a teacher of Greek. One or two Greeks who spent some time in Oxford in the late fifteenth century have been suggested as the first teacher of Greek, but the evidence is either conflicting or uncertain, and the teaching, if any, must have been sporadic.

Probably the first official establishment of Greek teaching at Oxford came in the sixteenth century, when Bishop Fox, using his own private funds, founded Corpus Christi College in 1517 and provided for Latin and Greek classics. The public lecturer on Greek was to speak to the entire university. "This readership," according to Thomas Fowler, in *The History of Corpus Christi College,* "appears to have been the first permanent office created in either university for the purpose of giving instruction in the Greek language." Fox suggested many Greek writers: Sophocles, Euripides, Aristophanes; also Hesiod, Demosthenes, Thucydides, Aristotle, and Plutarch; and he mentioned these Latin writers: Cicero, Sallust, Pliny, Livy, Virgil, Ovid, Lucan, and Terence. But the lists were suggestive, not prescriptive; and Fox made a gift to the college of other classics he himself had not named, including Herodotus, Homer, Horace, and Plato. The reader in theology was to lecture each working day, excepting ten weeks, through the college year; the authorities were not to be such ones as Nicholas of Lyra or Hugh of Vienne but "the holy and ancient Greek and Latin doctors, especially Jerome, Augustine, Ambrose, Origen, Hilary, Chrysostom, John of Damascus, and others of that kind." Lectures in logic were to be given to undergraduates, to explain Porphyry and Aristotle, in Latin and then in Greek. The reader in Latin was to eliminate from the "beehive," as Fox called his college, all "barbarism"—whatever he meant by the term. Probably he meant that the Latin should be free of extreme scholastic verbiage and the style fostered by medieval translations of Aristotle and should approach the style approved by contemporary Italian classicists.[9]

[8] *Collectanea,* pp. 336–37.
[9] Sir Charles Edward Mallet, *A History of the University of Oxford,* 3 vols. (London,

How much Fox had been influenced by members of the More circle is uncertain. As he had spent some time in Paris, it seems, when he was a young man, he may have had Continental influences. As early as 1506 Erasmus had dedicated to Fox a Latin translation of Lucian's *Toxaris*, or *Friendship*, and had made later efforts to get his favor. Fox did express great appreciation of Erasmus' New Testament, as we know from a letter of More to Erasmus, in December, 1516. Fox had been associated with Bishop Fisher, as both were executors for the Lady Margaret, though Fisher seems to have carried the major responsibility for the founding of St. John's College. In 1527 Fisher wrote Fox, dedicating to him his work *De veritate corpis et sanguinis Christe in eucharistia*, and saying that he did so because Fox had founded Corpus Christi College and because Fox, not the Lady Margaret, in recommending him to Henry VII for appointment as Bishop of Winchester, had been the cause of his own success.[10] But whatever their origin, the principles embodied in the statutes of Corpus Christi College might have been stated by More or Erasmus.

Probably John Clement became the first official teacher of Greek at Oxford, unless there was some short-time appointee about 1518 whose name has escaped notice. Clement began lectures at Oxford about 1518; and he was succeeded about 1520 by Thomas Lupset. In a letter to Erasmus, in 1520, More said: "Our Lupset lectures on Greek and Latin literature at Oxford before a large audience. . . . He has succeeded my John Clement, who has given himself up entirely to the study of medicine." [11] These facts also furnish a personal background for More's letter to the University of Oxford in 1518, rebuking those who were opposing the introduction

1924–1927), II, 20–26; Thomas Fowler, *The History of Corpus Christi College*, O.H.S., v. 25 (Oxford, 1893), Chapters I, II. He says that Reginald Pole was a fellow, Vives a Latin reader, and Nicholas Kratzer a teacher of mathematics there. Some authorities give 1515–16 as the date for the founding of Corpus Christi College.

[10] P. S. and H. M. Allen, *Letters of Richard Fox, 1486–1527* (Oxford, 1929), no. 88, p. 153. For Fox's appreciation of the New Testament see Allen, *Opus epistolarum*, II, 502, lines 19–24.

[11] For More's letter see: *Opus epistolarum*, IV, 1087, the closing part, p. 232: "Lupsetus noster magno auditorio summa cum laude sua, nec minore scholasticorum fruge, bonas literas in utraque lingua profitetur Oxoniae. Successit enim Ioanni Clementi meo; nam is se totum addixit rei medicae, nemini aliquando cessurus, nisi hominem (quod abominor) hominibus inuiderint Parcae." For Erasmus' letter about Croke, see *Opus epistolarum*, I, 227, lines 24–27. See also Fowler, *The History*, pp. 85–89.

of Greek. At Cambridge, about 1511, Erasmus began what seems to be the first unofficial teaching of Greek at that university, and in 1518 Richard Croke was appointed as, probably, the first official teacher of that language. Croke, it is said, learned his Greek from Grocyn (though if true, the place would have been London); probably Grocyn sent him to Paris to study; and there he was the pupil of Budé and Erasmus. In 1511 Erasmus wrote to Colet asking him to send money to help Croke; he described him as a former servant and disciple ("quondam ministro ac discipulo") of Grocyn, and added that at the time he was giving himself to the study of good letters in Paris. It also seems quite certain that More secured Croke's Cambridge appointment for him. There is no reasonable doubt that More had also arranged the appointment of John Clement, to whom he had been a "good master and bringer up," and of Thomas Lupset, at Oxford. It might be concluded, then, that the men of the More circle established Greek at the universities of Oxford and Cambridge, or if it had ever been taught at either place unofficially or for a short time, they at least established it on an official basis.

These actions underline the concern of More and his friends with the new interpretation of scripture, the editing of correct, authentic texts, the teaching of Greek (as well as Hebrew and Latin), and their desire to reach a whole population of leaders and common people with effective preaching.

IDEAS: WRITINGS

When Colet began his Oxford lectures, he broke some precedents and used some methods of interpretation which were new in England at that time. Besides making his lectures free to all, he lectured without degrees in theology (if Erasmus is correct) though he seems to have been granted status in 1497 or 1498 and in 1505;[12] he did not use the dialectic method—that is, he did not examine everything that had been said about a passage, by either Christian or non-Christian writers, and then reason out a meaning from all the comment; and he did not use the *Sentences*

[12] According to the *DNB*, Colet was ordained deacon December 17, 1497, and priest in March, 1497–98; and he "proceeded D.D. at Oxford in 1504."

of Peter Lombard or some other Schoolman as the basis of his discussion. Instead he based his comments directly on the New Testament; and he looked for the meaning of a whole unit, not an isolated text—a unit that had been written by a specific individual at a specific time, perhaps for a specific audience, and under special circumstances. He used the grammatical method; instead of reasoning about comments on the text he read the text, trying to discover with the help of grammatical knowledge what the original writer had meant to say.

Colet eliminated the use of the Schoolmen as authorities. In three important works he never quoted Aquinas, Scotus, or Abelard by name; he once quoted apologetically a phrase from "the Schoolmen," *by consequence*, because it happened to fit his meaning. In *An Exposition of St. Paul's Epistle to the Romans* he quoted by name Augustine twice, Chrysostom twice, the *Hierarchy* of Dionysius once, Jerome once, Origen once, Plato once, Plotinus once, Virgil's *Eclogues* once; he referred to Suetonius for historical background; he cited Pico della Mirandola at length; he quoted some two and a half pages from Ficino to support his view that it is a greater virtue to love God than merely to know God; and he discussed Paul's life as a means to understanding his work. Besides the references where he named the authorities just cited, there are many other ideas which the editor, J. H. Lupton, traces to them. The other two of his three main works, when examined, yield similar information about his use of authorities.[13]

Colet's material from "Platonist Marsilius Ficino," as he described him, included these sentences on the love of God:

But in this life the love of God far surpasses the knowledge of him, seeing that here no man truly knows God, nor indeed can do. But to love God is in his power . . . the searching out God . . . is exceeding painful and hard, and after all brings but small profit . . . while . . . the love of God gains much fruit in a very short space. . . . Hence of necessity love

---

[13] John Colet, *An Exposition of St. Paul's Epistle to the Romans,* ed. and trans. by J. H. Lupton (London, 1873). See the index, which carefully distinguishes the naming of these authorities in the text from the editor's footnotes tracing an idea to its source. The other two books are these: *An Exposition of St. Paul's First Epistle to the Corinthians* (London, 1874), and *Letters to Radulphus on the Mosaic Account of the Creation together with Other Treatises* (London, 1876). All are edited and translated by J. H. Lupton and all have the Latin version also.

is the more impetuous and efficacious, and swifter in attaining what is good than knowledge is in detecting what is true. Furthermore it is beyond doubt more pleasing to God himself to be loved by men than to be surveyed; and to be worshipped, than to be understood . . . and they who love God feel far more enjoyment than they who search him out; and men become at length far better men by loving than by inquiring into God.[14]

In the *Letters to Radulphus* he closed by citing Macrobius in support of his view that Moses was adapting ideas to the multitude when he gave an account of the creation. Early in Letter I he commented on the need for Hebrew (many years before he tried to master Greek with the help of John Clement): "It is a resource with which Origen and Jerome and all the most careful investigators of Holy Writ were well acquainted." In Letter III he divided the universe "as is done by the Platonist Mirandola in his *Hexameron,* into four worlds." [15]

Colet's three famous sermons, mentioned earlier, were pleas for reform. In 1512, when he preached to the convocation called to consider heresy, he denounced the sins of the clergy and called upon those high in office to renounce their pride of life, carnal concupiscence, covetousness, and interest in secular offices. They did not need new laws, he said—only lives in harmony with the laws they had; and if all the spirituality reformed themselves and led pure and holy lives, laymen would readily follow their good example.[16] On Good Friday, 1513, when England was ready to make war on France, Colet preached to king and court a sermon against all wars that are fought in hate or for ambition. (The text of the sermon is not extant, though, and neither is the report of the talk between him and the king after the sermon.) Again in 1515, when he preached the sermon for Wolsey's ordination as Cardinal, he exhorted that powerful prelate "to execute righteousness to rich and poor, and mercy with truth." In these three sermons he emphasized the reform of state and church as if the two were united.

[14] *An Exposition of St. Paul's Epistle to the Romans,* pp. 29–31.
[15] *Letters to Radulphus,* pp. 28, 3–4, 10.
[16] J. H. Lupton, *A Life of John Colet* (London, 1909), Appendix C, for the English version, probably written by Colet himself.

More's interest in the love of God, as well as the knowledge of God, was clearly indicated in his early writings. About the time he spent four years at the Charterhouse without vows, making a choice between the life of contemplation and the active life of wisdom and virtue, he chose to translate the life of Giovanni Pico della Mirandola, with this letter on prayer, which Pico had written to his nephew: "whan I stire thee to prayer, I stire thee not to the prayer that standeth in many wordes, but to that prayer which in the secret chaumber of the mynd, in the priuie closet of the soule, with very affect speaketh to god, and in the most lightsome darkenes of contemplacion not onelye presenteth the mind to the father but also unieth [sic] it with hym by unspeakeable wayes whiche onelye they knowe that haue assayed." [17]

About the same time More was also translating poems from the same Pico and writing some poems of his own called "The Twelve Properties or Conditions of a Lover." In these poems he transferred the feeling and even the language used in expressing the love of man for woman to the expression of religious feeling. The poems, whether his own or Pico's, leave no shadow of doubt about his concern with the love of God. A few lines selected here and there will indicate the tone of the group:

> To loue one alone and contempne al other for that one . . .
> To serue his loue, nothing thinking of any rewarde or profite . . .
> Graunt, I thee praie, suche heat into mine heart,
> That to this loue of thine may be egal . . .
> Graunt me, good lorde, and creatour of all,
> The flame to quenche of all sinnefull desire,
> And in thy loue sette all mine heart a fire.[18]

It seems unnecessary to give evidence that More also had a knowledge of God based on scripture, the early fathers of the church, canon law, Thomas Aquinas, church history, and other relevant material. His writings on religious controversy after he resigned the chancellorship are sufficient evidence.

More made many direct comments on abuses in the church, usually directing his darts at superstition and ignorance. These

[17] More, *The workes* (London, 1557), p. 13.
[18] *The workes*, pp. 27, 34.

comments were usually serious rather than satirical in style, with occasional satirical sentences—for example in his 1518 letter to the University of Oxford. Though he did not, it seems, use satire as the basic style for a whole work on religious reform, his early poem, "A Merry Jest how a Sergeant Would Learn to Play the Friar," has sometimes been discussed as if it were an attack on friars. The poem is only a bit of humorous advice pointed at lawyers, telling them not to pretend to be what they are not; it has been suggested that it was probably written for the feast when his father became a serjeant-at-law. The plot is this: "A serjeant has been trying to arrest a young spendthrift for debt; the spendthrift takes refuge in a friend's house and pretends illness; the serjeant, disguised as a friar, gets in and arrests his man. But the two start fighting; the wife and the maid of the household join in the fray; pulling the friar's hood over the face of the serjeant, they help beat him till he is glad to escape without his prisoner." The theme is explained in a long, didactic introduction; it is repeated in the close:

> In any wyse
> I would auyse
>   And counsayle euery man
> His owne crafte use,
> All new refuse
>   And lyghtly let them gone.
> Play not the frere.
> Now make good chere
>   And welcome euery chone.[19]

In his letter to a monk, written to defend Erasmus, More cited the incident of the friar he had once met in Coventry. Those who say daily the Psalter of the Blessed Virgin, the friar said, can never be lost. More and a wise parish priest both opposed him. The friar used a "Mariale" and such works as evidence; he was illogical, long-winded, and contentious, and his remarks were irrelevant. More was careful to say that all religious orders are cherished by every

---

[19] *The workes*, Ci, Cii.

good man; but he did attack the friar's ignorance and mere formalism. But his attack was straightforward, not satirical.[20]

In his letter to Dorp, in 1515, when he was again defending Erasmus, More related another incident of an ignorant monk he had met when he was dining with an Italian merchant, probably Antonio Bonvisi. The merchant, discovering that the monk knew his syllogisms better than he knew scripture, began to invent quotations in chapters of the Bible that did not exist. The monk refuted these imaginary passages without realizing the trick being played upon him; thus he proved his skill in scholastic subtleties but not his knowledge of the Bible.[21]

In *Utopia* More described a contentious friar at the house of Cardinal Morton, at a moment when the friar had been angered by a jester's comment:

"Whie" (quod the iester) "that is doon all redy. For mi lord him selfe set a very good ordre for yow, when he decreed that vagaboundes should be kept strayt, and set to worke; for yow be the greatest and veriest vagaboundes that be." [22]

The friar railed, quoted detached passages of scripture out of context as weapons, and threatened to use the Pope's bulls to excommunicate any who scorned him. But the Cardinal privately motioned the jester to leave and turned the talk to other things. The passage indicates that neither Morton nor More resented an attack on an ignorant, quarrelsome friar.

But if More did not himself use satire in a whole work when he attacked abuses such as these, he did defend Erasmus for attacking ecclesiastical abuses in *The Praise of Folly*. Erasmus had written this attack on human follies at More's house, dedicated it to him because he thought it would meet with his special favor; and thinking that it might need defense, he had asked More to defend it. More did so; but at the same time he made clear his own position as one who reverenced the church: "For god be thanked, I neuer had that mynde in my lyfe to haue holy saintes ymages or

[20] Elizabeth F. Rogers, *The Correspondence of Sir Thomas More* (Princeton, 1947), no. 83; for translation, T. E. Bridgett, *Life* (London, 1891), pp. 96–101.
[21] *The Correspondence*, no. 15; Bridgett, *Life*, pp. 90–91.
[22] More, *Utopia*, ed. by J. H. Lupton (Oxford, 1895), p. 75.

their holye relikes oute of reuerence. . . . Howbeit that boke of
Moria dothe in dede but iest uppon the abuses of such thinges,
after the maner of the disours [jester's] parte in a playe. . . ." [23]

As for making the Bible available in English, More, who was
supported by Erasmus and others, may speak for himself, in "The
Dialogue concerning Heresies":

Nor I neuer yet heard any reason layd why it were not conuenient to haue
the byble translated into the englishe tong, but al those reasons . . . myght
. . . for ought that I can see, as wel be layde against the holy writers that
wrote the scripture in the Hebrue tongue, and against the blessed
euangelistes that wrote the scripture in Greke, and against all those in
likewise that translated it oute of euery of those tonges into latine, as to
their charge that would well and faithfully translate it oute of latine into
our englishe tong.

More explained also that the English language was not barbarous
and that it had a vocabulary sufficient for a good translation of the
Bible. He added that a translation is difficult, if a translator succeeds so that he does not "minyshe eyther of the sentence or of the
grace that it bereth in the formar tong"; and that this fact is well
known to those who have already translated the scripture from
Greek to Latin or from Hebrew into one of the other tongues.
He added:

For scripture, as I said before, was not writen but in a vulgare tonge,
suche as the whole people understode, nor in no secrete cyphers, but such
common letters as almost euery man could rede. For neither was the hebrue,
nor the greke tong, nor the laten, neither any other speche than such as
all the peple spake. And therfore if we shold lay that it were euil done to
translate the scripture into our tong because it is vulgare and comen to euery
englishe man, than had it been as euill done to translate it into greke or into
latin, or to wryte the new testament first in greke or the old testament in
hebrew, because both those tonges wer as verye vulgare as ours.[24]

In letters to Dorp, to a monk, and to Edward Lee, about 1515
to 1520, when he was defending Erasmus, both as grammarian
and theologian, for his critical editions of Jerome and the New
Testament, More attacked theologians who spent time in scholastic

[23] More, *The workes*, "The Confutacion," p. 422.
[24] More, *The workes*, "A Dialogue concernynge heresyes," pp. 243–44 (243 being misnumbered 245).

subtleties and honored scripture and the writings of the early fathers of the church over the work of scholastic theologians. Writing to Dorp, and using simple realistic language, examples, and comparisons, he said:

To dance or to bend double like an acrobat is more difficult than to walk, and it is easier to masticate bread than to grind pot-sherds between the teeth, but what man would not prefer the common processes of nature to such empty feats? . . . I cannot hear it said that these minute questionings are more useful than the knowledge of the sacred writings . . . when you not only compare but prefer these kitchen-maids to the most holy Bible, the Queen of all books . . . I cannot refrain from saying . . . with Terence: *Abite hinc in malam rem cum istac magnificentia fugitiva: adeo putatis vos aut vestra facta ignorarier?*

He quite clearly separated the essentials from the non-essentials in the literature of religious teachings:

I do not think you will contest this with me, that whatever is necessary for salvation is communicated to us in the first place from the sacred Scriptures, then from the ancient interpreters, and by traditional customs handed down from the ancient Fathers from hand to hand, and in fine by the sacred definitions of the Church. If, in addition to all this, these acute disputants have curiously discovered anything, though I grant it may be convenient and useful, yet I think it belongs to the class of things without which it is possible to live.

In the same letter he united these ideas with the direct study of the classics, interest in a good Latin style, and concern about good preaching:

Theologians of this kind, who read nothing of the Fathers or of the Scriptures except in the Sentences, and the commentators on the Sentences, seem to me to act as if one were to set aside all the authors who have written in Latin, and, gathering the rules of grammar from Alexander, try to learn all else from the *Cornucopia* of Perottus and from Calepinus, being convinced that all Latin words will be found there. Well, most words will be found there. . . . Yet such a method will never make a good Latinist. And . . . though in your Summists and Masters of Sentences you will find many sayings of the ancients quoted as authorities, yet the study of these things alone will never make a good theologian, even though he is conversant with ten thousand thorny questions. . . .

Can such a theologian make a preacher? Why, as the people understand nothing of this kind of language, he must lay it aside and learn by heart a sermon from his *Veni mecum* or his *Dormi secure*, foolish in itself, and when it is declaimed by a man more foolish still, how dull and stupid the whole affair will be.[25]

With these desires for sound scholarship, More, it seems unnecessary to add, expressed the orthodox view of reason and faith when he said in his *Dialogue concerning Heresies*, in 1528, that "reason is seruant to fayth and not enemy, and must with faith and interpretacion of scripture nedes be concurrant." So he defended prayer to good men who are represented by images (not prayer to images), the judicious use of pilgrimages and relics, and the punishment of subversive heretics as lawful and necessary when they had been handled by charity with justice according to the common laws of Christ's Catholic church and the laws of the realm.[26] In his imprisonment, too, he searched his conscience according to the conventional analysis of the four laws; and he made his decision to accept death because a temporal ruler had no right to make a demand which violated the law of God.[27]

Erasmus explained and defended the work of the grammarian in a letter of 1505, as well as in other letters:

And yet if Nicolas Lyranus is listened to, while he plays the pedagogue to ancient Jerome, and pulls to pieces many things that have been consecrated by the consent of ages . . . what crime is it in Laurentius [Valla], if after collating some ancient and correct Greek copies, he has noted in the New Testament, which is derived from the Greek, some passages which either differ from our version, or seem to be inaptly rendered owing to a passing want of vigilance in the translator, or are expressed more significantly in the Greek; or finally if it appears that something in our text is corrupt? They will say perhaps that Valla being a grammarian has not the same privilege as Nicolas a theologian? I might answer that Laurentius has been counted by some great authorities as a philosopher and theologian. But after all, when Lyranus discusses a form of expression, is he acting as a theologian or as a grammarian? Indeed all this translating of scripture belongs to the grammarian's part; and it is not absurd to suppose Jethro to be in some things wiser than Moses. Neither do I think that Theology herself, the queen of all sciences, will hold it beneath her dignity to be attended and waited upon by her handmaid, Grammar. . . .

[25] Rogers, *The Correspondence*, no. 15; Bridgett, *Life*, pp. 92–94.
[26] More, *The workes*, "A Dialogue," First book, Chapter 23, p. 152; Fourth book, Chapters 13–15, pp. 274–80.
[27] Rogers, *The Correspondence*, no. 199; also nos. 200, 206, 216, pp. 558–59, and others.

If they reply that Theology is too great to be confined by the laws of grammar, and that all this work of interpretation depends upon the influence of the Holy Spirit, it is truly a new dignity for divines, if they are the only people who are privileged to speak incorrectly. . . . Again, what is the use of Jerome laying down rules for the translation of the sacred writings, if that faculty comes by inspiration? Lastly, why is Paul said to be more eloquent in Hebrew than in Greek? . . . Again, shall we ascribe to the Holy Spirit the errors which we ourselves make? Suppose the interpreters translated rightly, still what has been rightly translated may be perverted. Jerome emended, but what he emended is now again corrupted; unless it can be asserted that there is now less presumption among the half-learned, or more skill in languages, and not rather corruption made easier than ever by printing, which propagates a single error in a thousand copies at once.

But, say they, it is not right to make any change in the Holy Scriptures, in which even the points have some mysterious meaning. This only shows how wrong it is to corrupt them. . . .[28]

The conservative view on editing the Vulgate was stated by Dorp in his protest to Erasmus in 1514:

You are proposing to correct the Latin copies by the Greek. But if I show that the Latin version has no mixture of falsehood or mistake, will you not admit that such a work is unnecessary? But this is what I claim for the Vulgate, since it is unreasonable to suppose that the Universal Church has been in error for so many generations in her use of this edition, nor is it probable that so many holy Fathers have been mistaken, who in reliance upon it have defined the most arduous questions in General Councils, which, it is admitted by most theologians, as well as lawyers, are not subject to error in matters of faith.[29]

Erasmus' discussion of his work on Jerome helps in an understanding of the attitudes to critical texts, as he explained it in a letter to Cardinal Domenico Grimani in 1515:

I have . . . arranged in due order all his [Jerome's] works; especially his Epistles, which was the most laborious task; and in the next place I have with the help of old manuscripts and by my own ingenuity corrected the errors with which his language is defaced, or I might rather say effaced. We have added an analysis and such convenient annotations as will make

---

[28] Nichols, *The Epistles*, I, no. 182; Allen, *Opus epistolarum*, I (Oxford, 1906), 182.

[29] Nichols, *The Epistles*, II, no. 304. Whether capitals should be used for General Councils is a theological question; I have merely followed the editor whom I am quoting. See Allen, II, 304.

it possible that fairly educated persons may read this author without difficulty. For . . . we may see in St. Jerome a fresh and varied erudition combined with a sort of holy ostentation. The passages in Greek and Hebrew, which were either omitted altogether or inserted in such a fashion that they had better not have been put in at all, we have restored with the utmost care. The spurious additions, which make up a considerable part of the book, we have relegated to a separate volume. . . .[30]

Erasmus' *The Praise of Folly* is a good example of the satirical method used to attack abuses in the church. In dedicating it to More, Erasmus said:

Then I supposed that this exercise of wit would meet with special favor from you, because you are wont to enjoy to the full jokes of this kind, that is, those that are somewhat learned—perhaps I flatter myself—yet not at all heavy; and through our common course of mortality you move as a sort of Democritus. . . .

May you take in good will, then, this little declamation as a keepsake from a friend, and may you also undertake to defend it; dedicated to you, it is now yours and not mine. For probably contentious fellows will turn up who will cavil, on the one part saying that these trifles are more frivolous than befits a theologian, and on the other that they are more biting than befits a meek Christian; and they will cry that we are reviving the Old Comedy, or Lucian. . . . . .

Nothing is more puerile, certainly, than to treat serious matters triflingly; but nothing is more graceful than to handle light subjects in such a way that you seem to have been anything but trifling.[31]

Erasmus' attacks on ecclesiastical abuses in *The Praise of Folly* are at times satire, and at other times serious bitterness. But regardless of the method, he attacked extreme scholastic theologians with vigor:

They are protected by a wall of scholastic definitions, arguments, corollaries, implicit and explicit propositions; they have so many hideaways that they could not be caught even by the net of Vulcan; for they slip out on their distinctions, by which also they cut through all knots as easily as with a double-bitted axe from Tenedos; and they abound with newly-invented terms and prodigious vocables . . . they explain . . . the most arcane matters, such as by what method the world was founded and set in order, through what conduits original sin has been passed down along the genera-

---

[30] Nichols, *The Epistles*, II, no. 318, p. 187; Allen, II, 334.
[31] Erasmus, *The Praise of Folly*, trans. by Hoyt E. Hudson (Princeton, 1941), pp. 1-3.

tions, by what means, in what measure, and how long the perfect Christ was in the Virgin's womb, and how accidents subsist in the Eucharist without their subject.

But those are hackneyed. Here are questions worthy of the great and (as some call them) illuminated theologians. . . . Whether divine generation took place at a particular time? Whether there are several sonships in Christ? Whether this is a possible proposition: God the Father hates the Son? Whether God could have taken upon himself the likeness of a woman? Or of a devil? Of an ass? Of a gourd? Of a piece of flint? Then how would that gourd have preached, performed miracles, or been crucified? Also, what would Peter have consecrated if he had administered the sacrament while Christ's body hung upon the cross? . . .

. . . The methods our scholastics pursue only render more subtle these subtlest of subleties; for you will escape from a labyrinth more quickly than from the tangles of Realists, Nominalists, Thomists, Albertists, Occamists, Scotists—I have not named all, but the chief ones only. But in all these sects there is so much learning and so much difficulty that I should think the apostles themselves must needs have the help of some other spirit if they were to try disputing on these topics with our new generation of theologues.[32]

In *The Praise of Folly* Erasmus opposed mere formalism; he approved a union of inner piety with worthy action, and thus emphasized the orthodox teaching of the church:

And next to these come the folk who have arrived at the foolish but gratifying belief that if they gaze on a picture of Polyphemus-Christopher they will not die that day, or that whoever salutes in certain prescribed words an image of Barbara will come through a battle unharmed. . . . Then what shall I say of the people who so happily fool themselves with forged pardons for sins, measuring out time to be spent in purgatory as if with an hour-glass, and figuring its centuries, years, months, days, and hours, as if from a mathematical table, beyond possibility of error? . . .

I fancy that I see some merchant or soldier or judge laying down one small coin from his extensive booty and expecting that the whole cesspool of his life will be at once purified. He conceives that just so many perjuries, so many lustful acts . . . murders, frauds, lies . . . are bought off as by contract; and so bought off that with a clean slate he may start from scratch upon a new round of sins. And who are more foolish . . . than those who promise themselves something more than the highest

[32] *Praise of Folly*, pp. 78–79.

felicity if they daily recite those seven verses of the *Psalms?* . . . Things like that are so foolish . . . that I [Folly] am almost ashamed of them myself; yet they stand approved not only by the common people but even by teachers of religion.

Folly continued to speak:

Yet what do men ask of these saints except things that pertain to folly? . . . No one gives thanks for a recovery from being a fool. . . . Yet the whole life of Christian folk everywhere is full of fanaticisms of this kind. Our priests allow them . . . even foster them, being aware of how much money is wont to accrue from this source.

But suppose some wise man were to say what is quite true:

"You will not die badly if you live well. You get quit of your sins if you add to the money payment a hatred of evil-doing, add tears, watchings, prayers, fastings; and if you alter the whole basis of your life." [33]

The statement of such a truth as the preceding one, Erasmus added, would drive men into confusion. Folly, as conceived by Erasmus, spoke of pilgrimages:

This man leaves wife and children at home and sets out on a pilgrimage to Jerusalem, Rome, or the shrine of St. James, where he has no particular business.[34]

Folly attacked monkish ignorance:

For one thing, they [the monks] reckon it the highest degree of piety to have no contact with literature, and hence they see to it that they do not know how to read . . . when with asinine voices they bray out in church those psalms they have learned, by rote rather than by heart, they are convinced that they are anointing God's ears with the blandest of oil. . . .[35]

Folly also ridiculed ignorant and extreme use of mere forms:

they do everything by rule, employing . . . the methods of mathematics. . . . There must be just so many knots for each shoe and the shoe-string must be of a certain color; the habit must be decked with just so much trimming . . . and one must sleep just so many hours. Who does not see that all this equality is very unequal, in view of the great diversity of bodies and temperaments? . . . But Christ . . . will say ". . . I promised

[33] *Praise of Folly*, pp. 56–59.
[34] *Praise of Folly*, p. 70.
[35] *Praise of Folly*, p. 85.

the inheritance of my Father, not to cowls, orisons, or fasts, but to works of charity." [36]

Folly claimed for her own the highest officials of the church:

Our popes, cardinals, and bishops for some time now have earnestly copied the state and practice of princes, and come near to beating them at their own game. Let a bishop but consider what his alb, the white emblem of sincerity, should teach him, namely, a life in every way blameless. . . .

As to these Supreme Pontiffs who take the place of Christ, if they tried to emulate His life, I mean His poverty, labors, teaching, cross, and contempt for safety . . . who on earth would be more afflicted? . . . Were wisdom to descend upon them, how it would inconvenience them!

Then the mob of priests, forsooth, consider it a sacrilege to fall short of their prelates in holiness. O brave! They war on behalf of their right to tithe in the best military manner. . . . How keen-sighted they are, to elicit from the writings of the ancients something by which they can terrify the poor people and convince them that they owe more than their just tithes! [37]

Of course Erasmus often spoke of religion with complete seriousness, as he did in *The Instruction of a Christian Prince:* "Who is truly Christian? Not he who is baptized or anointed, or who attends church. It is rather the man who has embraced Christ in the innermost feelings of his heart and who emulates him by his pious deeds." [38]

The *Colloquies* of Erasmus give so much evidence of his tendency to attack abuses in a straightforward or a satirical manner and to advocate true piety that only a few need to be mentioned specifically. In the colloquy "Of Rash Vows," Cornelius had lightly undertaken a pilgrimage to Jerusalem, Rome, and Compostella; he had come home poorer and no more holy than he was before. But he consoled himself by the fact that so many had done the same thing and that he would have good stories to tell. Arnoldus admitted that Moria had once influenced him to do the same thing, though he left several children and an attractive wife at home without support. Both men poked a bit of satirical fun at the

[36] *Praise of Folly,* pp. 86, 88.

[37] *Praise of Folly,* pp. 97–101.

[38] Erasmus, *The Education of a Christian Prince,* trans. by Lester K. Born (New York, 1936), p. 153.

abuse of indulgences; Arnoldus added: "I don't speak slightingly of indulgencies themselves, but I laugh at the folly of my fuddling companion, who tho' he was the greatest trifler that ever was born, yet chose rather to venture the whole stress of his salvation upon a skin of parchment than upon the amendment of his life." [39]

"The Child's Piety," another colloquy by Erasmus, attacking priests who blab what they learn in confession and who "can't distinguish between a fault and a good deed, nor can neither teach, comfort, nor advise," is a serious exposition of religious views. Gaspar, the child who had been educated in the house of John Colet, salutes Christ and the saints, prays, acts in a worthy manner, confesses himself to Christ and then to a well-chosen priest, receives communion, follows the authority of his betters because he is a lad and a private person, and follows Christian custom wherever it does not oppose the scriptures. But he will not weaken himself by fasting while he is still growing; he will not, until he is twenty-eight, decide to become a monk or to follow any other way of life. In short, Gaspar is a model boy through whom Erasmus voiced his objection to abuses, his positive belief in worthy action and inner piety, and his loyalty to the Catholic church. [40]

In "The Virgin Averse to Matrimony" Erasmus attacked monkish immorality with bitterness. [41] In "The Religious Pilgrimage" he ridiculed those who reduce religion to the level of base superstition; his method is satirical dialogue: "and there was shewn us the middle joint of a man's finger; I kissed it and ask'd whose relick it was. He told me it was St. Peter's . . . I then took notice of the bigness of the joint. . . . Upon which, said I, Peter must needs have been a very lusty man." The pilgrims were shown linen rags which the Holy Man used to wipe the sweat and filth from his body, a shoe of St. Thomas, and so on. [42] The spirit of the colloquy is very similar to that of some passages in the plays of John Heywood, but also similar to many comments in the medieval period.

"The Exorcism or Apparition" centers around Faunus, an ig-

[39] Erasmus, *The Colloquies*, 2 vols. (London, 1878), I, 55; also 51–55 *passim*.
[40] *The Colloquies*, I, 86–99.
[41] *The Colloquies*, I, 225–36.
[42] *The Colloquies*, II, 11; also 1–37, *passim*.

norant, greedy, immoral priest. The satirical light touch is used here in dialogue with serious meaning.[43]

Another colloquy, a talk between a butcher and a salt-fish-monger, has innumerable examples combating formalism and emphasizing the spirit of the law with inner piety. The characters are a strangely learned pair; wherever they agree, as they often do, it seems safe to assume that they express ideas held by Erasmus. They discuss the four kinds of law: "Divine laws are immutable, unless such as . . . seem to be given only for a time . . . which the prophets foretold should end . . . and the apostles have taught us are to be omitted. . . ." Human laws, unlike divine ones, are "sometimes unjust, foolish, and hurtful. . . ." A human law "ceases of itself when the causes for which it was made cease . . ."; and a human law is not valid unless it is "approved by the consent of those who are to use it." Even the unjust laws of a bishop must be obeyed, though one may exclaim against them so long as he avoids sedition.

Both speakers, butcher and salt-fishmonger, agree that there is no salvation outside the church, and that the final authority for any tenet of the church is the decision of a general council, each of which is "a heavenly oracle, and is of equal authority with the gospel itself, or . . . near it." [44]

PROGRAM OF IDEAS ON RELIGIOUS REFORM

From the various activities and from the letters and treatises of the men in the More circle it is possible to summarize their ideas on religious reform and the religious life—not original ideas and not essential theological doctrine.

First, they believed in an emphasis on the essentials of the Christian religion—inner attitudes, a genuine love of God and man, and worthy action as a result. These essentials would be made more apparent, they thought, by a return to the gospels, the epistles, and the early patristic literature, "from the time of the apostles to the rise of scholasticism or the beginning of the middle ages." In the early texts they wished to find out what Christ had actually

[43] *The Colloquies*, I, 391–401.
[44] *The Colloquies*, II, 72–74, 53, 57; also the whole colloquy, 38–98.

said, not what a subtle reasoner a thousand years or more later deduced that he should have said. Thus they questioned, fixed at a lesser value, or discarded the accretions of intervening centuries, and with some exceptions they considered scholastic theologians less important. For example, Colet was irritated when Erasmus quoted even Thomas Aquinas as an authority; Erasmus reconsidered and lessened somewhat his admiration; but More cited him as a great and holy man.

Second, they preferred the grammatical method of studying scripture and other writings over the dialectic method. That is, they used all the resources of syntax, meaning of words, and rhetorical style to interpret meaning instead of comparing comments on a text and reasoning out what the writer *should* have said.

Third, they rejected the study of isolated texts without regard to the context and considered any book of scripture as a unit, written by a definite human being for a specific audience, at a fixed time and place, for a situation, and with a specific aim. They used all the available historical or literary background to understand the whole unit, just as they tried to understand a Greek or Latin play.

Fourth, in all scripture their first concern was literal, practical meaning which applied to action in daily life. They were less concerned about a tropical and an allegorical meaning; they were usually repelled by extremes of an anagogical or a mystical interpretation.

Fifth, they believed the work of the editor to be important. The job of a good editor was to find the authentic text and to make a critical edition by removing ignorant emendations and scribal errors, in the Old Testament, the gospels, the epistles, and patristic literature. For this work an editor needed a thorough knowledge of Hebrew, Greek, and Latin. He must not be hampered by a belief in plenary inspiration, or in mere wording as sacred; such a belief would prevent new translations and the removal of errors from manuscripts. Of course they believed that the thought of scripture was inspired, but not the words of translators or scribes. They opposed the assumption that scientific truth might be proved by a text of scripture and that all knowledge, sacred and secular, might be united in one *summa*. So they were ready for inductive study of the modern world, since a principle not established by authority was free for examination. (Their study of scientific subjects, described in Chapter I above, is evidence for this attitude.)

Sixth, they were concerned about good preaching, simple, clear, interesting talks, to persuade people—common people and leaders in state and church—to love God and to act like true Christians in their daily lives.

Seventh, they opposed mere formalism, as a natural corollary of their stress on inner attitudes, love of God and man, with a resulting worthy action. They believed that rites and ceremonies alone neither purify a man's spirit nor justify his life.

Eighth, they valued the love of God even more than the knowledge of God, though it could scarcely be said that they underrated the knowledge.

Ninth, like many men before them, they separated the law of God into those parts that were temporary, because they were adapted to specific times, places, circumstances, or to hardness of heart and other imperfect development, and those parts that were permanent. Using this principle, they disposed of some Old Testament law, many scholastic glosses, and all comments by those churchmen whom they considered ignorant.

Tenth, they often made a many-sided approach to religion. They were emotional, with restraint, exalting the love of God; they were sometimes mystics, not in the sense of seeing visions but in realizing a communion with the infinite. They valued authority and revelation, but they knew where authority ended and critical thinking began. They had historical perspective and also perspective in estimating the sacred and the secular. Or it might be said of them that they considered the two as one, and that they applied the essentials of Christianity to all phases of life.

Eleventh, they were zealous about spreading religion, as well as secular knowledge, through printed books. The invention and spread of printing fostered this development, of course, and helped to differentiate them from fifteenth-century classicists. Besides the accurate, authentic versions of scripture and early patristic literature in Hebrew, Greek, and Latin, they wished vernacular versions of the Bible, approved by the bishops, as usual, for the common people.

Twelfth, like men in many centuries before them, they combined serious or satirical attacks on abuses in the church with piety and genuine loyalty.

METHODS OF EXPRESSION IN RELIGIOUS REFORM

Even though none of the ideas on religious reform are original when considered alone, Erasmus developed two methods of expression which are rare, at least, in the English literature about religion. The first of these was the use of dialogue, with one character who seems innocent or even completely ignorant of the ideas to be discussed—the wise fool. But his questions, beginning with apparent naïveté, gradually and deftly bring out Erasmus' point of view, and bring it out more powerfully than an ordinary debate could do. The second method is the use of imagination and fantasy to create a light touch with a serious intention. Both More and Erasmus had learned to appreciate or to use this style or had at least become more adept at it from their experience in translating Lucian.

To examine briefly part of a dialogue of Lucian, *Menippus, a Necromantic Experiment* (one which More translated and Rastell printed, with another metrical version which he may have written himself) and to place it beside a colloquy by Erasmus will bring out the likeness. The thought of the Lucian dialogue is serious and philosophical, with some emphasis upon concern for the commonweal. Menippus finds that the gods have not taught him how to live; their own conduct flatly contradicts the human laws against sedition, plundering, and adultery. Menippus asks the philosophers; but their philosophical terms make him weary, they do not agree with each other, and they do the opposite of what they advise. Finally he makes a trip to Hades to ask Tiresias, who finally tells him: "The life of the ordinary man is the best and most prudent choice; cease from the folly of metaphysical speculation . . . pursue one end alone—how you may do what your hands find to do, and go your way with ever a smile and never a passion." The general theme of *Menippus,* how to live a good life, was of course important to men interested in classical philosophy. But the style is the chief concern here—the dialogue is developed with a light touch, imagination, and fantasy against this seriousness; and the listener, Philonides, is the innocent whose questions lead to profound truth.

At the beginning Philonides is merely uninformed—conveniently so:

Men. All hail, my roof, my doors, my hearth and home!
     How sweet again to see the light and thee!

Phil. Menippus the cynic surely; even so, or there are visions about. Menippus, every inch of him. What has he been getting himself up like that for? sailor's cap, lyre, and lion-skin? However, here goes. —How are you, Menippus? where do *you* spring from? you have disappeared this long time.

Men. Death's lurking-place I leave, and those dark gates
     Where Hades dwells, a God apart from Gods.

Phil. Good gracious! has Menippus died, all on the quiet, and come to life for a second spell?

Men. Not so; a *living* guest in Hades I.

Phil. But what induced you to take this queer original journey?

Men. Youth drew me on—too bold, too little wise.

Phil. My good man, truce to your heroics; get off those iambic stilts and tell me in plain prose what this get-up means; what did you want with the lower regions? It is a journey that needs a motive to make it attractive.

Men. Dear friend, to Hades' realms I needs must go,
     To counsel with Tiresias of Thebes.

Phil. Man, you must be mad; or why string verses instead of talking like one friend with another?

Men. My dear fellow, you need not be so surprised. I have just been in Euripides's and Homer's company; I suppose I am full to the throat with verse, and the numbers come as soon as I open my mouth. But how are things going up here? what is Athens about?

Phil. Oh, nothing new; extortion, perjury, forty per cent., face-grinding.

Men. Poor misguided fools! They are not posted up in the latest lower-world legislation; the recent decrees against the rich will be too much for all their evasive ingenuity.

Phil. Do you mean to say the lower world has been making new regulations for *us?*

The light touch appears in various other places. For example, Menippus' guide, Mithrobarzanes, prepares him thus for his trip to Hades: "Taking me under his charge, he commenced with a new moon, and brought me down for twenty-nine successive mornings to the Euphrates, where he bathed me, apostrophizing the rising sun in a long formula, of which I never caught much; he gabbled indistinctly, like bad heralds at the Games. . . . This charm completed, he spat thrice upon my face, and I went home. . . ."

When the assembly finally passes the decree against the rich, "A snort from Brimo and a bark from Cerberus completed the proceedings according to the regular form." Then, after this comic bit, Menippus manages to talk with Tiresias and to get his advice on how to live.[45]

In Erasmus' colloquy, "The Religious Pilgrimage," Menedemus and Ogygius begin in much the same way:

Men. What novelty is this? Don't I see my old neighbour Ogygius, that nobody has set their eyes on this six months? There was a report he was dead. It is he, or I'm mightily mistaken. I'll go up to him and give him his welcome. Welcome, Ogygius.

Ogy. And well met, Menedemus.

Men. From what part of the world came you? For here was a melancholy report that you had taken a voyage to the Stygian Shades.

Ogy. Nay, I thank God, I never was better in all my life than I have been ever since I saw you last.

Men. And may you always live to confute such vain reports. But what strange dress is this? It is all over set off with shells scollop'd, full of images of lead and tin, and chains of straw-work, and the cuffs are adorned with snakes eggs instead of bracelets.

Ogy. I have been to pay a visit to St. James at Compostella.

As the colloquy progresses the satirical method increases and the listener becomes less innocent than he had at first seemed. Ogygius has seen a letter, he says, which was written by the Virgin Mary and which is being handed about:

Men. . . . But who did she write it to?

Ogy. The letter tells you the name.

[45] Lucian, *The Works of Lucian of Samosata*, trans. by H. W. Fowler and F. G. Fowler, 4 vols. (Oxford, 1939), I, 156–67, "Menippus: A Necromantic Experiment."

Men. Who did she send it by?

Ogy. An angel, no doubt, who laid it down in the pulpit, where the preacher to whom it was sent took it up. And to put the matter out of all doubt, you shall see the original letter.

Men. Do you know the angel's hand that is secretary to the Virgin Mary?

Ogy. Well enough.

Men. By what token?

Ogy. I have read St. Bede's epitaph that was engraven by the same angel, and the shape of the letters are exactly the same. . . .[46]

With the type of colloquy illustrated by "The Religious Pilgrimage," Erasmus, perhaps, made the outstanding contribution of the early sixteenth century to the form and style used for religious reform. His contribution centers in the wise fool—a speaker who seems at first either ignorant or naïve. By a kind of Socratic questioning he leads his opponent deftly to the conclusions he wishes him to draw. Both More and Erasmus also absorbed the spirit of Lucian enough to use effectively fantasy, imaginative creation, and the light touch with the serious intention.

What effect More and his friends might have had with their program of religious reform, as well as other reforms, if Henry VIII and the Pope had not reached an impasse in their political quarrel is only conjecture—usually biased by Catholic or non-Catholic beliefs. Here such conjecture would be unseemly. As More and Erasmus might have said, it would fail to observe a decorum.

[46] Erasmus, *The Colloquies*, II, 1–2, 4; also 1–37 *passim*.

CHAPTER IV *Law and government*

Whenever members of the More circle discussed government they seemed to assume that good government is applied Christianity. From the teachings of Christ they drew three basic principles for all social relationships, including law and government: all things, material property as well as ideas, are a trust to be used for the common welfare; wars of conquest violate the divine law against murder; gold, silver, and other conspicuous signs of wealth should be held in contempt. That is, greed, strife, and pride are un-christian, and law and government in so-called Christian civiliza-tion should be based on the teachings of Christ.

Among these men, too, the phrase which echoed most often when they spoke of political affairs was "the good of the com-monweal." They did not invent the term commonweal; there are isolated examples of its use as early as the fourteenth and fifteenth centuries. The term had developed two meanings: first, the common well-being, general good, or welfare of a group of people; second, the whole body politic, the state, community, or the common-wealth. More and his friends tended to combine the two mean-ings, and when they used the term they were usually concerned about government for the common welfare.

ACTION FOR THE COMMONWEAL

About 1500 to 1535 More and his friends were frequently taking action based on their belief in Christian principles and aimed at the good of the state. In *Utopia,* 1515–16, More analyzed basic problems of government but raised the vital question of action. In Part I, written after Part II, he and Hythlodaye analyzed the evils—economic, legal, social, and ecclesiastical—in England and other Christian nations and the basic causes of those evils. In Part II More presented through his imaginary Hythlodaye a creative picture of an ideal civilization developed by human reason without a knowledge of Christianity. Reason led the Utopians to discover the laws of nature, the universal innate truths which agree with the principles of Christianity; and thus reason led them to discover the Christian principles of avoiding greed, strife, and pride. It is interesting to note that Budé, writing to Lupset, mentioned these Christian principles, instead of the basis of reason, and hoped that the book would have an influence on many states.[1] Erasmus and other Continental friends made similar comments on the meaning and the importance of *Utopia.* The basic question about action, interwoven into the discussion of the two worlds, is this: can an educated man, a philosopher, by becoming a counselor to a ruler, do anything for the regeneration of a world which does not practice its Christian principles? Must he at least try to do what he can to improve such a world? About 1517 More gave his personal answer to these questions by accepting appointment to the King's Council.

More's whole life, before and after that date, indicates that he tried to practice, as far as his civilization permitted, the principles of reason and Christianity. His life was a record of public service, often at financial loss—service for the city of London, in the law courts, in the King's Council. He entered the Council as Master of Requests in the Court of Poor Men's Causes; he was under-treasurer, sometimes secretary to the king in the absence of Pace, Chancellor of the Duchy of Lancaster, and finally Lord Chancellor. In this last office he presided over the court which was

[1] More, *Utopia,* ed. by J. H. Lupton (Oxford, 1895), pp. lxxxvii, xcii.

called "the court of conscience," giving justice where rigid law would have denied it. He was a partner to diplomatic business, often with Pace or Tunstal, at Bruges in 1515, at Calais in 1517, at the Field of the Cloth of Gold in 1520, and again at Bruges in the same year; he helped settle affairs between Henry VIII and the Emperor in 1521 and affairs with France in 1525 and in 1527; again in 1529 he helped make peace at Cambrai.

Wherever we can trace him, he worked for justice and the public good. Roper, whose own training at Lincoln's Inn lends weight to his words, told of the judges' complaints about More's injunctions when he was chancellor. More invited the judges to dine, and discussed with them all the injunctions he had granted. They had to admit that he was right. Then he told them that the justices of every court were "in consciens bound" to "mitigate and reforme the rigour of the lawe themselves. . . ." [2] Thus More said to the judges that every court should be a court of conscience, based upon Christianity.

Even in his later controversial literature, from 1528 to 1533, More was concerned with the good of the state. Arthur E. Barker, Trinity College, Toronto, said recently, in material not yet published: "The controversies are not simply doctrinal dissertations; they are efforts at counsel by demonstration, about the realm and its laws and the increasing anarchy at home. . . ." He added that the *Confutation*, the earlier *Supplication of Souls*, the *Apology*, and its supporting *Debellacion* defended the laws of the realm and were efforts to warn Henry VIII against anarchy.

John Colet sincerely applied the same Christian principles to church and state. In his well-known sermon of 1512, when he preached to a convocation called to root out heresy, he did not emphasize the need for orthodox theology; instead he concerned himself with the need of churchmen to give up pride, greed, and worldly power. Thus he applied the same principles to the church. In 1513, when he preached to the king and court his powerful sermon against war, he was applying Christianity to the state. In 1515, when he preached at the installation of Wolsey as cardinal and recommended humility, justice for rich and poor, and mercy

[2] Roper, *The Lyfe*, ed. by Elsie V. Hitchcock, EETS, v. 197 (1935), pp. 44–45.

with truth, he applied Christianity to human life—both church and state. Wolsey did not become Lord Chancellor until later in the same year; but as a member of the King's Council, he was already exerting a large influence on the state.

Erasmus, though he felt himself called to edit texts, made some serious attempts to influence powerful rulers. He used the panegyric, he said, for this purpose, defining it as a "kind of writing . . . invented by men of great sagacity . . . that by having the image of virtue put before them bad princes might be made better, the good encouraged. . . ." For example, he presented a *Panegyricus* to Duke Philip on his safe return from Spain to Brabant in 1504; he tried to encourage Henry VIII in 1517 by sending him a letter and books, including a copy of Plutarch on the difference between a friend and a flatterer; and he wished to influence Wolsey in 1519, when he praised him for solving problems in law, making peace between noblemen, reforming monasteries and clergy, and supporting polite letters. In writing *Institutio principis Christiani* for the young man who became Charles V, Erasmus again was doing his best to influence that future ruler to be a philosopher and a Christian.

In 1509, when Henry VIII came to the throne, Erasmus and Blount—possibly More also—hoped that a government by philosopher-Christians would develop; and though the first flush of hope faded, Erasmus continued his efforts to put before rulers the image of virtue.

John Rastell made many efforts to serve the state, but his work can be better summarized in dealing with the prefaces to his law books and his other comments on law. It is possible that More's employment of him, as an assistant who checked first all cases coming before the Lord Chancellor, was related to his definite views about justice and the common man.

Vives made valiant efforts to serve both his adopted city of Bruges and also the English king, even at the risk of his readership and his pension from Henry VIII. His work, *De subventione pauperum*, about 1525 or 1526, has been called a practical discussion showing his love for his city and his civic responsibility. As for Henry VIII, De Vocht gives a record of several documents in which Vives made pleas to the king for peace. On March 12, 1525, he sent a memoir from Oxford, where he held a readership, asking the king to be magnanimous about the capture of Francis I, to reassure the French people, and to bring about peace. About October 8, 1525, he wrote from Bruges, thanking Henry for the courtesy shown him as a stranger in England but again expressing the hope that the king would use well his position as Defender of the Faith and his power to make peace. This letter dimmed his welcome, at least by Wolsey, on his third visit to England, and perhaps lost him his readership at Oxford. On July 13, 1527, he again wrote to Henry from Bruges, showing appreciation and wishing that Wolsey might meet success in his diplomatic journey to France, the success that would be worthy of a churchman. Thus he again implied his desire for world peace and perhaps his desire to see a just settlement of the marriage question. Some time in 1528 Vives was compelled by Wolsey to make a deposition about his communication with Queen Catherine; and in doing so, he was definite about his own admiration for the queen and his desire to see her receive justice. Probably the *libera custodia* in which he was placed resulted from his statements in this document. About this time he wrote his own frank opinion on the marriage of Henry VIII and Catherine. In November, 1528, he made his last trip to England, as a member of the queen's counsel; but he displeased her by advising her to give up any defense (a course she later adopted) and to rely entirely on her innocence. So he left the country under her displeasure.

On January 31, 1531, Vives wrote the king again, saying that he was sending the material he had written, at Wolsey's request, on the king's marriage. He pointed out the danger of the king's course of action, suggested an alternative in the marriage of his daughter if he wished an heir to the throne, restated his appreciation for kindness received in England, and emphasized his desire for peace among Christian nations. He said these things, between 1525 and 1531, at the risk of his readership, his pensions, and at times even his liberty. Always he was courteous but courageous.

Sir Thomas Elyot also made some courageous efforts to influence Henry VIII. *Pasquil the Plain,* generally attributed to Elyot but published without his name, developed the theme of a servant's duty to warn his master when the master is "resolved into wrath or affections dishonest." Elyot's acknowledged work *Of the Knowledge Which Maketh a Wise Man* pictured a tyrant who cast off his favorite philosopher for daring to disagree with him; it developed the Platonic theory "that virtue and knowledge are identical and that the man who knows what is right will always act in accordance with his knowledge."

These examples illustrate the fact that the men of the More circle were seriously concerned about law and government and that they tried to transform their concern into action.

IDEAS IN WRITINGS

It might be difficult to find any new ideas on political theory when Aristotle and Thomas Aquinas had apparently stated most of the basic ideas. Aristotle had said that by nature there is an impulse in all men toward political life; that the state which exists by nature may be further developed by art and that it exists for the good life; that law is the true ruler and kings are its servants, for "the law is wisdom without desire"; that there is a great difference between a lawful monarch and a tyrant with an arbitrary will; and that a good ruler is both wise and virtuous.[3]

And Thomas Aquinas, in making his synthesis of Aristotle and Christian thought, had explained clearly the aims of government and the four kinds of law; he had also restated the basic rights of the individual, much as they had been stated in previous periods of history. The individual within society is insufficient alone, Aquinas said; he needs the material, intellectual, and moral support of the group for his own happiness in this world. But the political organization, the collectivity, he said, "exists for the individual and not the individual for the collectivity." Thus he placed a high value on human personality, according to the principles of Christian teaching—the antithesis of fascism, naziism, or any form of totalitarianism. An individual, slave or free, rich or poor, ruler or ruled, has the right, Aquinas said, "to preserve his life, to marry

[3] Aristotle, *Politics*, trans. by H. Rackham (London, 1952), Book III, *passim*.

and bring up children, to develop his intelligence, to be instructed, to hold to the truth, to live in society." He said further that though the power of rulers comes from God, they are established in power not "that they may seek their own profit, but in order that they may ensure the common well being." Sovereignty comes to a ruler through the people, and though the people do not usually have a right to kill a tyrant, they do have the right to depose him. Free subjects, he said in Part I, Question 81, "though subject to the government of the ruler, have nevertheless something of their own by reason of which they can resist the orders of him who commands."

Explaining the four kinds of law—eternal, natural, divine, and human—Thomas Aquinas added other ideas to the definitions which were quoted in Chapter I. Divine law is necessary, he said, because man was ordained for eternal happiness, which is beyond his natural faculties, and because human law "could not sufficiently curb and direct interior acts." Human law must spring from the law of nature and ultimately from eternal law; if it disagrees with natural law, it is not a law but a corruption. But human law may vary in specific details, such as the amount of a fine and the length of a prison sentence, or it may be changed for the benefit of the commonweal. But unnecessary change is bad, since custom makes laws easier to enforce. However no custom can prevail over divine law or the law of nature. The end of all law is to make men good, but truly good or virtuous men act firmly and with pleasure; hence love is most conducive to good actions. Law is for reasonable creatures only, since they only have freedom of choice. All rulers and preferably all people in a state should be virtuous: "the common good of the state cannot flourish unless the citizens be virtuous, at least those whose business it is to govern." [4]

Through the centuries between the life of Thomas Aquinas and the sixteenth century, his ideas on law were "unconscious mental habits." But the phrase the *law of nature* (with implications or certain references to the other kinds of law) appeared in strange

---

[4] Thomas Aquinas, *Summa theologica*, trans. by Fathers of the English Dominican Province, 3 vols. (New York, 1947), I, 993–1025, on laws; or First Part of Second Part, Questions 90–97. See also *Summa contra Gentiles*, trans. by Joseph Rickaby as *Of God and His Creatures* (London, 1905), Book III, Chapters CXIV–CXVII, pp. 276–78.

garb and strange company. Clever lawyers twisted its philosophical meaning to help their clients. It was used to support claims to the throne. It was used by judges trained in the English common law, who resorted to "the law of nature, which is the ground of all law." It was discussed by Sir John Fortescue in his work *De laudibus legum Angliae* and in his other works on law. It was cited, along with references to human and divine law, by nearly every one who made any statement, pro or con, about the legal right of Henry VIII to separate from Catherine of Aragon. It was discussed at length by Christopher Saint German (trained at the Middle Temple but, like More, familiar with canon law); in the works known to be his or attributed to him he explained it and the other conventional ideas about conscience, synderesis, and the four kinds of law.

IDEAS: WRITINGS IN THE MORE CIRCLE

The men in the More circle expressed many ideas on law and government; and these ideas, whether they were expressed by Colet, More, Rastell, Erasmus, Vives, Lupset and Pole, Elyot, or even Ascham, had much in common and were usually based on medieval thought.

Colet had less to say about secular government than some of his friends, perhaps because he was a churchman and a theologian; but his remarks in a letter to Erasmus are typical:

You have done well in writing on the Instruction of a Christian Prince. How I wish Christian princes would follow good instructions! Everything is upset by their mad follies.[5]

Colet had firm comments on church law, based on his belief that the aim of all law or government is to help men in becoming good:

How I wish that the ministers of ecclesiastical affairs, and those who call themselves expounders of pontifical law, would understand that, without the grace of Christ, they in vain administer laws for Christ's people. . . . For the poor Christian folk who pay the penalties of the law, are made to feel its sanguinary force before they understand its meaning. But your Doctors of the law—as they like to be called, though they are the last to *teach* the law—have no pleasure in instruction of that kind. . . . Rather,

[5] F. M. Nichols, *The Epistles of Erasmus*, 3 vols. (London, 1901–1918), II, no. 411.

in sooth, should they be called Torturers and tormentors of men. For all that they heed is where they may punish . . . so as to drain the golden blood of the laity.

He went on to call them an atrocious race of men and to say that it would be better if these men "would forsake their craftiness and insatiable greed, and . . . first learn what they are to teach, and then teach what they have learnt: if they would keep the law themselves before punishing transgressors: if they would make men understand the law before punishing them for not being apprised of it. . . ." [6]

In attacking law, Colet began with church law, but he included the whole system of human law and the legal fraternity. Before the coming of Christ, he said, most men lived without grace "by the corrupt law called the *law of nature*—not the law of simple, holy, and inviolate nature (for that state of innocence was in paradise alone) but of a defiled and corrupted nature." Using the terms *common* and *civil* law to include all secular legislation, he said:

Under this term . . . the law of man's nature, I include alike the Law of Nations, Civil Law, Common Custom, human Statutes and Decrees, and the like. . . .

We may conclude then . . . that all systems of law may be reduced to two only: the *divine*, or perfect law, and the *human* or corrupt. . . . Human reason is the enemy and opponent of grace. . . . Among Christians, who are all sons of God, no other law is to be listened to than the divine law which comes through our Saviour Christ. This is the evangelical law, which is charity, the fulfilling and perfecting of all law.[7]

More had much to say about law and government. About 1505, when he translated the life of Giovanni Pico della Mirandola, he repeated comments of the Italian on church law. When Pico was fourteen he went to "Bononie" to study the laws of the church, but after two years he found that the faculty was concerned with mere traditions and ordinances and became dissatisfied with his

---

[6] Colet, *Letters to Radulphus and Other Treatises* (London, 1876), pp. 162–63. These comments on law are from the incomplete *Exposition of St. Paul's Epistle to the Romans*, a version intended for an individual, perhaps for Edmund Knevet, a relative of Colet's mother.

[7] *Letters to Radulphus*, pp. 135, 139–40, 144, and *passim*.

study. But he did not lose his time, for young as he was, he made "a *summe*" upon all the decretals in one small volume, a task which might have been difficult for a learned doctor.[8] Of course the translation does not of itself prove that More was in entire agreement with the idea, but at least he chose the life for translation.

More's epigrams contain ideas on kings and governments which were repeated in other connections by him or by other members of the circle. "A king who respects the law differs from dread tyrants thus: a tyrant thinks of his subjects as slaves; a king, as his own children." "A king who performs his duties properly will never lack children. He is father to the whole kingdom." "A kingdom in all its parts is like a man; it is held together by natural affection. The king is the head; the people form the other parts." "What is the good king? He is a watchdog, guardian of the flock. By his barking he keeps wolves from the sheep. What is the bad king? He is the wolf." In another epigram he said that a king is not protected by fear and guards, but he is made safe by his own good qualities. In another he emphasized the consent of the governed: "Any one man . . . ought to have command not one instant longer than his subjects wish. Since kings, not their own masters, rule on sufferance, why are they proud?" In another he commented on the lust for power: "Among many kings there will be scarcely one . . . who is satisfied to have one kingdom. Among many kings there will be scarcely one . . . who rules a single kingdom well." Epigram 182 is a debate on whether a senate or a king furnishes the best form of government. A senator elected by the people owes his power to a reasonable agreement; a king becomes powerful by blind chance. "It is a mistake to believe that a selfish king can be satisfied; such a leech never leaves flesh until it is drained." Epigram 1, with its implied criticism of Henry VII and its marvelous hopes for Henry VIII, raises the question whether More had in mind the panegyric, as Erasmus analyzed it, to influence leaders, or whether his praise was literal.[9]

[8] More, *The workes* (London, 1557), p. 3.

[9] Bradner and Lynch, *The Latin Epigrams of Thomas More* (Chicago, 1953), nos. 1, 91–94, 96, 97, 102, 103, 182, 227. See also nos. 14, 62, 124, 185, 211, 222.

More's *Utopia,* the outstanding analysis of law and government in sixteenth-century England, is a creation and a fusion of Christian and classical ideas. Its monastic elements, less important though they may be, were discussed by J. H. Hexter; its Platonic influences are generally accepted; the Senecan-Stoic influences were discussed in Chapter I of this work; the Christian principles were stated by Budé, Peter Gilles, and Jerome Busleiden, and accepted by More for publication in his third edition. At the time it was written More had known his Greek and Latin classics intimately for fifteen years or more. His Hythlodaye knew that Seneca and Cicero were the only valuable Latin philosophers; and for his fourth voyage, when he thought that he might not come back home, he took along much of Plato, more of Aristotle, and Theophrastus on plants; his Utopians valued Plutarch and Lucian; they had Aristophanes, Homer, Euripides, Sophocles, carefully selected historians, and medical works.[10] Thus *Utopia* did not come to birth because its author dug out ideas bit by bit from the classics and footnoted each source. It is a free play of mind over classical and Christian literature and over the realistic world of the sixteenth century.

Utopia has two major ideas, already mentioned in an earlier part of this chapter. First, in Part I, though it was written later, More analyzed the legal, social and economic evils of his own day. Second, he raised the question whether a philosopher as counselor to a king could do anything to bring about reforms for these evils and thus to aid the commonweal.

The analysis of evils included the severe punishment for theft, the failure to remove the causes which lead men to beg or steal, the maintenance of large standing armies, the enclosures which forced farm laborers off the land, the indulgence in wanton luxury even by farmers and tradesmen as well as nobility, the high prices which remained unchecked, the neglect of cattle breeding and other agricultural work which would benefit the commonweal, and the use of unjust means to raise money for the king. These unjust means included increasing the value of money when the king was ready to pay his debts, decreasing it when he was ready

<hr />

[10] More, *Utopia,* pp. 26–27, 215–17.

to collect revenues, raising money under a pretense of imminent war and then diverting the money to other uses, enforcing forgotten laws and collecting fines for their violation, forbidding certain things by law but permitting some people who paid large sums of money to do these things, and coercing judges to decide law cases in the king's favor. As a last evil More mentioned international strife connected with fraudulent treaties and wars of conquest. Since the discussions of J. H. Hexter and of other recent historians are available, it seems unnecessary to offer evidence that these evils were present in England.

In developing his second major idea, the duty and the power of a philosopher to lessen these evils, More used the first of several ironic contrasts. His negative speaker in the debate is Hythlodaye, the ideal philosopher, theoretical and practical: he knew the best of Greek, Roman, and Christian thought; in his travels he had learned the customs and the laws of many lands; and as a human being he did not desire either money or power. But with his perfect qualifications, he said that he could do nothing, that rulers, itching for wars of conquest, do not wish good advice but will listen only to counselors who express their own desires. A wise man can do nothing in a civilization based on hate and greed. He must remain silent or become an accessory to madness. Thus Hythlodaye personified More's doubts and his own reluctance to enter the king's service: he wished perfection.

More answered him and thus brought "the speculative philosophy of free talk among friends" down to solid earth. He said that Hythlodaye's qualifications made him the ideal counselor, that it is the duty of such a man to help guide his prince—even though he believes in a Christian point of view but lives in a land of greed: "yet for this cause yow must not leaue and forsake the common wealth; yow must not forsake the shippe in a tempeste bycause yowe can not rule and kepe downe the wyndes. . . . But you must with a crafty wile and a subtell trayne studye and endeuoure your selfe, asmuch as in yow lyethe, to handle the matter wyttelye and handsomelye for the purpose; and that whyche yowe can not turne to good, so to order it that it be not very badde." [11] At the

[11] *Utopia*, pp. 99–100.

time *Utopia* was published, Wolsey was bringing about economic reforms and was even pursuing briefly a policy of international peace. So the affirmative won in More's own life after he had first expressed it in his writing—not the idea of perfection or nothing.

Among the ironic contrasts in *Utopia* is the difference between two civilizations: the so-called Christian civilization with its burden of evils and a non-Christian civilization based on reason and philosophy. Again the ultimate ideal of Christian love, which led the early followers to hold all things in common, is in ironic contrast to a civilization based on greed, pride, and hate; and the life of intelligent love for fellow men is thrown into sharp relief against the lives of the ignorant, immoral friar, the harsh lawyer, and those who cause international strife. Because the Utopians are educated but uncorrupted, they have found truth by human reason. To argue seriously that More wished to practice communism is to miss the point and the power of these ironic contrasts; but it does seem certain that More wished to improve the behavior of so-called Christians.

᾿ The conclusion of *Utopia* has also a tongue-in-cheek irony, as Mr. Hexter may have meant to imply when he pointed out that the serious arguments against communal sharing were used early in the work, and the frivolous ones were used at the close. But the frivolous ones were used in anything but a frivolous manner. More said that a few things about the Utopians seemed absurd: "chieffely . . . in the communitie of theire liffe and liuinge, without anny occupieng of money; by the whyche thynge onelye all nobilitie, magnificence, wourship, honour, and maiestie, the true ornamentes and honoures, as the common opinion is, of a common wealth, vtterly be ouerthrowen and destroyed. . . ." [12] There is nothing that More and his friends held in contempt more than uncritical public opinion—unless it was a display of nobility, magnificence, and splendor, in the common meaning of these terms. They spent their lives opposing such concepts.

So *Utopia*, the great document of the More circle on law and government, begins with the realistic evils of the time, penetrates

[12] *Utopia*, pp. 307–8.

to the basic causes, and then raises the question what a practical philosopher can do without digging up by the roots a whole civilization.

Utopia contains further pertinent comment on the duty of a ruler and of a philosopher, regarding law and justice. Saying that the duty of every good man is to help the ruler, More added the opinion of Plato that commonwealths would become happy when kings were philosophers and asked how far this happiness might be achieved if philosophers aided kings with good counsel.[13] Hythlodaye echoed an idea from an epigram of More's when he said that he would urge a king to improve his inherited kingdom, to love his people and be loved by them, to govern them with gentleness, and to let other kingdoms alone, since his own land would be all he could manage or even more than he could govern well.[14] He echoed another idea of the epigrams when he asked what would happen if he should disagree, when others had spoken on how to raise money for a king—if he should suggest that people choose a ruler not to honor him but to make their own lives safe and comfortable; that a king should be more concerned with the happiness of his people than his own welfare, as a shepherd should care for his flock; that a king who enjoys his own pleasure while his people are unhappy is a jailer who does not know how to govern free men.[15]

More said much in *Utopia* also about law and justice. Some of these ideas are directly connected with the discussion about contemporary England, such as Hythlodaye's discussion with the lawyer in the house of Cardinal Morton:

God commaundeth vs that we shall not kyll. And be we then so hastie to kyll a man for takynge a lytle money? And yf annye man woulde vnderstande kyllynge, by this commaundement of God, to bee forbydden after no larger wyse then mans constitucions defyneth kyllynge to be lawfull, then why maye it not lykewyse, by mannes constitutions, be determyned after what sorte hooredome, fornication, and periurye maye be lawfull? [16]

---

[13] *Utopia*, p. 80.
[14] *Utopia*, p. 87.
[15] *Utopia*, pp. 92–94.
[16] *Utopia*, p. 61.

Another passage on law in *Utopia* stated firmly what More and his friends restated in other connections:

Thei haue but few lawes. For to people so instructe and institute very fewe do suffice. Yea, this thynge they chieflye reproue amonge other nations, that innumerable bokes of lawes and expositions vpon the same be not sufficient. But they thinke it against al right and iustice, that men shuld be bound to thoes lawes, whiche other be in numbre mo then be able to be readde, or els blinder and darker, then that any man can well vnderstande them. Furthermore they vtterly exclude and bannyshe all proctours and ser-geauntes at the lawe, which craftely handell matters, and subtelly dispute of the lawes.[17]

One passage analyzed justice and treaties between nations in a realistic way:

Wherfore it maye well be thought other that all iustice is but a basse and a lowe vertue, and whiche aualeth it self farre vnder the hyghe dignitie of kynges; or, at the least wyse, that there be two iustices; the one mete for the inferioure sorte of the people, goinge a fote and crepynge by lowe on the grounde, and bounde downe on euery side with many bandes, because it shall not run at rouers; the other a pryncely vertue . . . as to the whiche nothinge is vnlawful that it lusteth after.[18]

Another passage commented on the origin of good laws:

Wherfore their opinion is, that nat onlye couenauntes and bargaynes made amonge priuate men ought to be well and faythfullye fulfylled, obserued, and kept, but also commen lawes; whiche other a good prince hath iustly publyshed, or els the people, nother oppressed with tyranny, nother deceaued by fraude and gyell, hath by their common consent constitute and ratifyed, concernyng the particion of the commodities of lyfe. . . . Thies lawes not offendid, it is wysdome that thou looke to thyne owne wealthe. And to do the same for the common wealth is no lesse then thy duetie. . . .[19]

In *Utopia* More also went to the roots of his opposition to war— a belief that taking part in war is a form of corruption. The Utopians, More said, "define virtue as living according to nature." Nature, in this sense, as defined in Chapter I, means a development of the essential qualities of man, uncorrupted man; in Stoic or Senecan doctrine, harmony with nature means a development of

[17] *Utopia*, p. 234.
[18] *Utopia*, p. 240.
[19] *Utopia*, p. 193.

the essential nature of man, in a morality which coincides with genuine, complete humanity and also brings about an unfolding of the inmost germ of one's individual nature. In *Utopia,* More said, the bondmen do the slaughtering and cleaning of all fish, meat, and poultry—that is, the bondmen who are already past the possibility of education. The free citizens are not permitted to do such work because, the Utopians think, slaughtering destroys the sense of compassion, the quality that more than any other raises us above the beasts.[20] The Utopians also abhor hunting: "But if the hope of slaughter, and the expectation of tearynge in pieces the beaste dothe please the, thou shouldest rather be moued with pitie to see a seely innocent hare murdered of a dogge; the weake of the stronger. . . . Therefore all thys exercyse of huntynge, as a thynge unworthye to be vsed of free men, the Vtopians haue reiected to their bochers, to the whiche crafte . . . they appointe ther bondmen. For they counte huntyng the loweste, vyleste, and moste abiecte parte of bocherye. . . ."[21]

Considering nothing so inglorious as the glory won in war, the Utopians use mercenary soldiers when they must fight, for example the Zapolites, a rude, fierce people who are already corrupted, and who live by hunting and stealing, as if they were born for war; they know no way to make a living except by taking away the lives of others.[22]

In his conflict with Brixius, More used ridicule to make the glory won in war seem inglorious. In a sea fight, August 10, 1512, the English *Regent* came into collision with the French *Cordeliere.* Both ships, with most of their crews, were sunk, and both captains perished. Brixius, a French poet, wrote an epic-hero poem, giving extravagant praise to the French, especially Hervé, as if the French had clearly been victors. Brixius said:

Hervé . . . attacked the foe in great force: he smote some with a dart driven through the temples, another he pierced through the ribs with a sword, for another he cut open the groin, of some he cut off the head with

---

[20] *Utopia,* p. 158.

[21] *Utopia,* pp. 200–201.

[22] *Utopia,* pp. 252–53. The biography of More, by Antonio M. Graziani, Bishop of Amelia, which is said to stress the reform of law, might add to More's views on law, but I have not seen it. See R. J. Schoeck, "Another Renaissance Biography of Sir Thomas More," *English Studies* (Amsterdam, Bern, Copenhagen), XXXIV (1953), 115–17.

a stroke of his axe on the neck, of these the belly, of those the shoulders he pricked with his keen spear.

More replied to this effusion in an epigram:

This escapes comprehension, that one man should be fighting with so many weapons—and he has a shield weighing down one hand. The steadfast nature of things is repugnant to such fighting . . . perchance you overlooked the fact that the reader should have been informed that Hervé had five hands.

In another epigram More said:

You wonder that Hervé . . . thus goes on fighting. His right hand is weaponed with the cruel axe, while his dangerous left is furnished with a sword. Now the dart, and that which serves as a dart, the spear, he stoutly holds in his mouth, clamping his teeth on them. But since missiles are flying against his head thicker than hail in winter, he puts his shield on his head.[23]

More's last comments on law and government were made in his letters, most of them written from the Tower, about the accusations which led to his imprisonment and his death. These letters are available in *The Correspondence of Sir Thomas More*, by Elizabeth F. Rogers; the quotations which follow are from letters 199, 200, 206, and 216. In a letter to Cromwell, written about a month before his arrest, he recalled the time when the king "sodaynly . . . brake with me of his great mater, and shewed me that it was now perceived that his mariage was not onely agaynst the posytive lawis of the Chirch, and the written lawe of God, but also in such wise agaynst the lawe of nature, that it could in no wise by the Chirch be dispensable." In this talk with the king, More reported, he heard for the first time "that it shold be in such high degre agaynst the law of nature. . . ."

Five days after his arrest he wrote to Margaret about his examination at Lambeth Palace and his refusing the oath. He had refused to state his reasons unless he was promised immunity against the king's anger and the king's statute. He was told that the king's license, even by letters patent, could not protect him against any statute which he might be violating. "My Lord of Canterbury"

---

[23] Hoyt H. Hudson, *The Epigram in the English Renaissance* (Princeton, 1947), pp. 49–52; Bradner and Lynch, *The Latin Epigrams*, nos. 174, 175, also 176–79.

had said to him, he wrote Margaret, "you knowe for a certenty and a thinge without doubt, that you be bownden to obey your souerain lorde your Kyng. And therfore are ye bounden to leaue of the doute of your vnsure conscience. . . ." The argument seemed subtle, especially as it came from the mouth of a prelate. If he were merely putting his opinion against the opinion of Parliament, More answered, he would give up his opinion; but since he had on his side, he thought, "as great a counsail and a greater to, I am not than bounden to change my conscience, and conferme it to the counsail of one realme, against the generall counsail of Christendome."

In another letter written by Margaret Roper to Alice Alington, his daughter reported her lack of success in persuading him to take the oath. Every man, More had said, is obligated to obey the law of the land or pay a penalty; and sometimes he must obey human law or suffer God's displeasure; but no one is bound to swear that every law is well made or "to perfourme any such poynt of the law, as were in dede vnleafull." Laws made by "the generall counsell of the whole body of Christendome" would not prescribe anything that might not be lawfully performed: the spirit of God would never permit it, as Christ had made plain in scripture. Any human law made to do him harm would be unlawful. When he was told that he should obey the king because the king had been made head of the church by English law, he answered: "a man is not by a lawe of one realme so bounde in his conscience, where there is a lawe of the hole corpes of Christendome to the contrarie in mater towchinge belief. . . ."

Thus More declared it his duty to obey human law only when it did not violate divine law. Divine law had been given him by scripture and by the general councils of the church; and in doubtful cases he must follow his own informed and carefully examined conscience. But when king or parliament or churchman asked him to violate divine law, it was his duty to disobey. Here he seemed to assume the unity of all law—eternal, natural, divine, and human— though circumstances impelled him to speak more of human and divine law, and he mentioned the law of nature only in reporting the views of Henry VIII, not in explaining himself. Thus he assumed that divine law is superior to human law in cases of conflict. In the whole defense he seemed to be following the philosophy of medieval law as it was summarized by Thomas Aquinas.

Of all the men in the More circle, no one was more persistent in his comments about the commonweal than John Rastell. Usually, in his non-dramatic writing, he was concerned with the law. In his preface to his *Liber assisarum,* about 1513 or 1514, he discussed his philosophy of law. In all countries, he said, men are concerned about the public and commonweal (the "comen well") and those who augment the commonweal are praised and honored. Philosophers, poets, and other learned men debate what the commonweal is. Some say riches; some, power and strength, even by conquering other countries; some, honor and renown. Others say that the commonweal is a mixture of all these things. But it must be something which is of itself goodness, since God, who is the source of all goodness, has naturally given to every man a common and universal love and zeal for it, or else it would not be worthy to be called a common good thing or a common *well* but rather, a common *evil.* Wherefore it must needs be good of itself; and if good of itself, every man may use it freely without doing evil to any other person. But men cannot acquire riches, power and strength, honor and renown without causing others to suffer poverty, feebleness, and shame. The commonweal, then, does not consist in these things but in increasing good manners and conditions of men, in training them to honor and love God and to live in love and tranquillity with their neighbors. For attaining these things and virtuous living, good laws are needed, to direct and constrain men as the bridle and spur direct horses. These good laws come principally from God; for nature, which is the final instrument of divine providence, does not lead itself but is led by that same providence. And since that providence of God beholds, orders, and conserves all things that are necessary to the use of man—the elements, trees, herbs, fruits, fowl, and all other brute beasts—it follows clearly that the same providence beholds and conserves man himself by ordering reasonable laws, necessary to man's welfare; hence it follows that laws must be good. Then who can deny that to make good laws, to write them, to study, learn, and teach them, and to execute them truly and justly are worthy actions? In reason, then, the *commonweal* does not consist in riches, power and strength, and honor and renown, but in augmenting and preferring good laws.

Then Rastell praised the laws of England, said that Fortescue's work *De laudibus legum Angliae* had inspired him to this book of assizes, and promised later to augment the great Book of Abridgements, which Anthony Fitzherbert had made. Rastell showed his concern about bringing law within the reach of the common man in his concluding statement: since some men to whom the book would come might not be able to understand "the nombres of algorisme" in the beginning of the book, he had also made a "lityl tabil" which any man, without any other teacher, might use to understand them in an hour.[24]

In his Prologus to the *Tabula magni abbreviamenti* (his *Index* to Sir Anthony Fitzherbert's *Great Abridgement*) Rastell gave an exposition in Latin on law. God created a diversity of beings, he said, who need various kinds of law. Thus we have divine, human, and natural law. Divine law commands us to live in love and peace with our neighbors, and its reward is the highest happiness of eternal life. Human law, based upon reason, commands us not to harm our neighbors and not to take their property, and gives us the right to dispose of our own possessions. Natural law, which prompts men and animals to preserve their lives, avoid pain, and reproduce their kind, is not enough for men, who are made in God's image. Thus we have also human and divine law. The three kinds of law are not in conflict with each other. If anyone considers himself obligated to fight for his own fatherland, said Rastell in one of his more individual comments, then it is fitting that he should also study to conserve the laws of his country. "Et sicut quis pro patria propria pugnare tenetur, sic naturaliter pro sue patrie legis consueracione studere decet."[25]

---

[24] Rastell, *Liber assisarum* . . . (1514?), STC 9599. The only complete copy listed in the United States is in the Law Library, Harvard University. Through the courtesy of Mr. William Jackson I have a photostatic copy of the preface, which is in English.

[25] *Tabula prime partis magni abbreviamenti,* compiled by John Rastell and printed by him in 1517. See STC 10955, under Sir Anthony Fitzherbert. My source is photostat no. 1660, Library of Congress. This prefatory statement in Latin is headed "Prologus. Johis Rastell."

Rastell made interesting comments on law in the Prohemium to his *Expositiones terminorum legum Anglorum,* 1527. He said:

Lykewise as the vniuersall worlde can neuer haue hys continuance but onely by the order and law of Nature whyche compellyth euery thinge to do hys kynde. And because the nature of man is fragyle and prone and redy to vice, therfore there is no multitude of pepull in no Reame that can continue in vnyte and pease wythout they be thereto compellyd by some good order and law; wherfore a good law obseruyd causyth euer good people, and a good reasonable commyn lawe makith a gode commyn pease and a comynwelth among a grete commynalte of people, and one good gouernour whyche causyth one law to be obseruyd amonge dyuerse and moche peple bringeth dyuerse and moche peple to one good vnyte . . . for as euery man is varyaunt from other in vysage, so they be varyable in mynde and condicyon, therefore one law and one gouernour for one realme and for one peple is most necessary.

Rastell went on to say that lack of law causes many wrongs to be committed willingly; and lack of knowledge of the law causes many wrongs to be done by negligence. Then since law is necessary and "a vertuous and a good thyng," and since the law of England is made to further justice, to maintain quietness of the people, and "for the commyn welth of the same," therefore his purpose in this work is "to expown certeyn obscure and derke termys" and also "the nature of certeyn wryttes" to help beginners. After some conventional apologies and appeals to men of learning to correct, add, or diminish, as they shall see need, he closed with the statement that "the trew execution of the same law shall be gretly to the augmentation of the commyn welth of thys realme. . . ."[26]

Rastell was guided by the same concern for the common welfare in his Prologus to *The Pastime of People.*[27] Using his best critical judgment, he said, he had omitted most "feigned" stories but included an occasional one with outstanding examples of princes who governed their people with wisdom and virtue; such a story might be an example to contemporary princes.

After Rastell had been converted by John Frith, he continued

[26] Rastell, *Expositiones terminorum legum Anglorum* (London, 1527). The Prohemium, in English, is intact in a copy of this first edition in the law department of the Library of Congress, though it is missing from other copies I examined.

[27] Rastell, *The Pastyme of People* (London, 1529), Aii.

to work for the common good as he saw it. He wrote Cromwell some time between 1534 and 1536 that he would continue to serve him as long as he supported God's cause and the king's, in spite of his own loss of income: "Syr, I am an old man, I loke not to lyff long, and I regard ryches as much as I do chypps, save only to have a lyffyng to lyff out of det; and I care as mych for worldly honor as I care for the fleyng of a fethyr in the wynd." [28]

Rastell died in prison because he was opposing Cranmer about the collection of tithes from poor people; he defended his views by the laws of nature, of God, and of man. It was perhaps a logical but a sad conclusion of his life.

Erasmus expressed decidedly and frequently his views on kings and on government. In *The Praise of Folly,* for example, he said that one who considers carefully the life of a king would surely not desire sovereignty: "He will consider that one who grasps the helm of great affairs must further the public, not his private, interest and give his mind to nothing except as it concerns the general good; he must not deviate a finger's breadth from the laws of which he is author and executor; he must himself be warrant for the integrity of all officials and magistrates. . . . A prince . . . if he lapses ever so slightly from honesty, straightway a dangerous and vital infection spreads to many people." [29]

In his *Colloquies* Erasmus made so many comments on rulers and government that only a few representative passages can be cited. In "The Religious Treat," he discussed the handling of an unruly king and decided that the best method would be "to train him up from his childhood in the principles of piety and virtue and to form his will before he understands his power." In "The Fabulous Feast" he said that "a good prince is that to the body politick which the mind is to the body natural. What need was there to have said a good prince when a *bad* prince is no prince?" In "Of Things and Words" he said that "He is really a king who aims at the good of his people and not his own, governing them by law and justice." In "The Unequal Marriage" Gabriel argued that even an innocent person with the pox should be executed

---

[28] Sir Henry Ellis, *Original Letters*, 3rd series, 4 vols. (London, 1846), II, 311.
[29] Erasmus, *The Praise of Folly*, trans. by Hoyt H. Hudson (Princeton, 1941), p. 94.

for the good of the commonweal. In another colloquy, a butcher and a salt-fishmonger discussed the relation of human and divine laws, the binding nature of law, and asserted that a person breaking a good human law sins indirectly against God.[30]

In *The Instruction of a Christian Prince,* first published in 1516, Erasmus covered rather thoroughly his important ideas on law and government. The people in choosing a ruler and the prince in ruling should consider only "the public weal, free from all private interests." Where people have a hereditary ruler, the only hope is in education: "Then the seeds of morality must be sown in the virgin soil of his spirit, so that little by little they may grow and mature through age and experience, to remain firmly implanted throughout . . . life. Nothing remains so deeply and tenaciously rooted as those things learned in the first years. . . . You cannot be a prince if you are not a philosopher; you will be a tyrant. . . . To be a philosopher and to be a Christian is synonymous in fact." [31] A tyrant, he continued, is "interested in his own pursuits"; a true prince "is vitally concerned with the needs of his subjects." He has the same attitude to his subjects as a good father to his family. As to the type of government, he said, "it is the consensus of nearly all wise-thinking men that the best form is monarchy." Just so, God rules the world. But he added that monarchy is the best form only if the ruler is good; otherwise it is the worst form.[32]

If people are given a Christian education only a few laws will be needed. The prince should obey the laws himself and should punish severely those who are corrupt in administering them. These laws should be just, clear, made known to the public, based on equity and honesty, blameless in motive, and wisely adjusted to the public welfare. The decisions of a prince are not *ipso facto* law, but only the decisions made by a good and prudent prince who hates dishonesty and is concerned for the good of the state are truly law. Laws are not good merely because they are rooted in

[30] Erasmus, *The Colloquies,* 2 vols. (London, 1878), I, 171–72; I, 431–32; II, 133, 163, 59–73, and *passim.*

[31] Erasmus, *The Education of a Christian Prince,* trans. by Lester K. Born (New York, 1936), pp. 140, 150, and *passim.*

[32] *Education of a Christian Prince,* pp. 161, 173, 212–13.

long-standing custom; for habit is not a measure of justice, and the conditions which made a law necessary may have changed. The purpose of statutes is to deter from crime by appealing to reason more than punishment, since man, "the noblest of animals," should be induced by rewards, not driven by punishment. "Finally let the laws be set forth in clear language, with as few complexities as possible, so that there will be no urgent need for that most grasping type of man who calls himself 'jurisconsult' and 'advocate.' " [33]

Erasmus used the symbols of kingship to emphasize the essential qualities of a king: "What does the gold mean except outstanding wisdom? What significance has the sparkle of the gems except extraordinary virtues, as different as possible from the common run? What does the warm rich purple mean if not the essence of love for the state? And why the scepter, unless as a mark of a spirit clinging strongly to justice, turned aside by none of life's diversions?" [34]

Erasmus cited classic sources, of course, as authorities for his ideas. For example, Aristotle was his authority for the acceptance of hereditary rulers, the definitions of a prince and a tyrant, the king's great opportunity as a ruler, and his need of virtue. He called upon Plato to support his view that the masses have false opinions, that a king should be a philosopher, that a worthy ruler is reluctant to assume power, and that he needs the ability to rule himself before he can rule others well. He quoted Plutarch on the king's need of wisdom (but added also Aristotle, Plato, and biblical authority), on the beneficent prince as the living likeness of God, on bribery, and on distinguishing a friend from a flatterer. He quoted Seneca's views, not only on true nobility, but on the need for a prince's teacher to be blameless in character, to know the art of combining understanding, restraint, and praise, and to have the skill to uproot false ideas; on the good king's resemblance to a king bee without a sting; on the value of a good reputation to a king, and numerous other ideas. [35]

As his reading program for a boy who is to become a ruler

---

[33] *Education of a Christian Prince*, p. 234, for the quotation. But see section VI, pp. 221–34 entire.

[34] *Education of a Christian Prince*, p. 152.

[35] *Education of a Christian Prince*, see index.

Erasmus recommended these things in this order: the *Proverbs* of Solomon, *Ecclesiasticus,* and the *Book of Wisdom;* the Gospels; Plutarch's *Apophthegmata* and his *Morals,* "for nothing can be found purer than these works," his *Lives,* too, are to be preferred to those of anyone else; then Seneca, "whose writings are wonderfully stimulating and excite one to enthusiasm for moral integrity. . . ." The boy may cull passages from the *Politics* of Aristotle and the *Offices* of Cicero; and he may use Plato, "the most venerable source of such things—in my opinion, at least." [36]

In *The Complaint of Peace,* 1517, Erasmus attacked the bases of war, considering it a force which corrupts man. Nature, he said, teaches us peace and unites us to peace by many enticements and cords which we cast aside; only when we realize that use and custom take away the sense of evil can we believe that men who make war are really endowed with reason. Christ, as well as nature, teaches peace. If even wars waged at the command of God profane the men who fight, what will be the effect of wars waged in wrath and ambition? (Iam illud interim perpende, bellator, si profanant bella, Numinis jussu suscepta gestaque, quid facient quae suasit ambitio, quae ira, quae furor?) If it is wrong to spill heathen blood unjustly, what is the effect of spilling the blood of other Christians? Rulers use frivolous excuses for going to war: they revive an old or a corrupt title to lands; they complain that some small detail was omitted in long articles of confederation; they use personal grievances; or they secretly incite some one to start a war. Getting down to basic causes, Erasmus said that if we are going to stop wars we must purge human hearts of evil cupidities and desires. War might be justified, he thought, to "repel the violent incursions of the barbarians" and to "defend the public and common tranquility." But nearly any plan for peace, however bad, is better than any war. Decisions to wage war should never be made by young men, nor for the pleasure and lust of one or two people; they should come only from older and wiser men who have mercy and benevolence.[37]

[36] *Education of a Christian Prince,* pp. 200–201.
[37] Erasmus, *The Complaint of Peace,* ed. by William James Hirten (New York, 1946), pp. 12, 20, 30, 39, 40, 43. For the Latin quotation see *Opera omnia* (Lugduni Batavorum,

In his treatise on education Erasmus spoke also of the close connection between education and the good of the commonweal; he said that parents, statesmen, and churchmen alike must see that there are enough men who are qualified to teach the youth: "it is a public obligation in no way inferior, say, to the ordering of the army." [38]

Vives expressed views on law and government which are similar to those of the other men in the Sir Thomas More circle. In a dialogue called *Princeps puer* he discussed the education of a ruler, in a talk between Prince Philippus, Sophobulus, and Morobulus. Sophobulus explained to the prince that his good and wise teachers should change his uncultivated manners into the virtue and excellence of a man, not a slave but a free man and a true prince. Sophobulus invited the prince to take part in a game called *king* and drew from him the admission that he did not know how to play it; then he rebuked him for being willing to undertake the rule of many people and great kingdoms although he knew nothing except the silly trifles taught him by Morobulus, was ignorant of the conditions in which his subjects lived, and knew nothing about prudence or the principles of administering government. He explained the difficulties of ruling men who think evil and do evil deeds; he quoted Isocrates who used to say that the two greatest offices in life are those of prince and priest and that only the most prudent man in the kingdom can rule well. As preparation for the act of ruling, Sophobulus suggested learning languages and gaining experience in ruling from Plato, Aristotle, Cicero, Seneca, Livy, and Plutarch.[39]

The learned man, Vives believed, should desire to be of service to as wide a circle as he could; but if he should be offered a position in the state, "let him first observe diligently the minds of his fellow

1703–1706), IV, 630, C. Page references indicate the modernized version in the Hirten edition because the facsimile has little paging. This translation by Thomas Paynell was printed in 1559. Paynell's sister married Thomas Roper, son of William and Margaret More Roper.

[38] Erasmus, *De pueris instituendis*, as trans. by W. H. Woodward, *Desiderius Erasmus concerning the Aim and Method of Education* (Cambridge, 1904), pp. 209–10.

[39] W. H. D. Rouse, *Ludovicus Vives . . . Latin Dialogues* (Oxford, 1931), pp. 100–107. See Foster Watson, *Tudor School-Boy Life* (London, 1908), pp. 172–84, for a somewhat free translation of this and other dialogues.

citizens whether they are sound or curable, so that if by any means he may be able to be of use, he must not refuse to undertake the labour. . . ." His remarks about rulers seemed sometimes quite as blunt as those of Erasmus: "Princes are, for the most part, of hearts so corrupt, and so intoxicated by the magnitude of their good fortune, that by no art can they be reformed for the better. . . . We must transfer our solicitude to the people, who are more tractable . . . and are more responsive to one caring for them. This also did Christ, with Whom a Prince is not valued more highly than anyone of the people." [40]

Believing that men are "born for society and cannot live thoroughly without it," Vives deduced that goodness, sound judgment, wisdom, and practical experience (both from life and from books about the lives of others) are essentials for the leaders of the state. Like his English friends he deplored war and for much the same reasons: it was the antithesis of goodness and wisdom; it grew out of hate, not love. Law becomes necessary, said Vives, only when love ceases: "But where love is absent, the function of legal justice takes its place, and this should be neither complacent nor without the force of weapons behind it." [41]

Vives also expressed a great concern about law and legal reforms to enhance the commonweal, since law is a fundamental part of good government. Justice, he said, is the preserver, the soul, the unifying force of society; reason is the means of discovering true justice, and reason is "not the capricious pleasure of each" but is that which is prompted by nature and wisdom. The discoverers of justice are usually not those "who are confused by their passions, or who have sluggish judgments, or who are not stirred by any of the teachings of philosophy." Vives also explained the significance of legislation:

Those who are of higher grade, who are held in rare estimation amongst the people, turn the fountain, as it were, of justice into the right channels (suited to the places, times, and the minds of men) so that the present state of society may derive the greatest good from their actions. . . . The

---

[40] Vives, *De tradendis disciplinis,* trans. by Foster Watson, *Vives: On Education* (Cambridge, 1913), p. 278.

[41] *De tradendis disciplinis,* p. 258, and *passim.*

magistrate, who has authority to compel others to obey the law, is called a judge or *lex loquens*. Hence it is manifest that it is a part of the philosopher's task to treat of law, and to place law on a philosophical basis.

Natural law, said Vives, consists of the principles "agreed upon by the unanimous sense and judgment of all men" and hence it is a "settled norm." Vives explained the study of law in this way:

The practical side of the study of laws consists in the rationalizing of the *good* and the *just* in these laws.

And the function of jurisconsults is much more than to know what legislation has taken place:

But . . . if it is the function and office of a true and thorough jurisconsult to explain the sense and spirit of laws, so as to discover the justice that is present in each law, i.e., what its life-giving force is, what its preservative force to the community is, what laws are usefully maintained at each period of time, what are of old-standing, all this surely demands philosophical knowledge in a man; a considerable amount of natural philosophy, and also a . . . complete equipment in moral philosophy.[42]

Any interpreter of the law, Vives said, should know the common nature of mankind, and the views and customs of many people, but especially those of his own people.

In his comments on St. Augustine's *Civitas dei,* Vives sharply rebuked kings and rulers: "Set Iustice aside then, and what are kingdomes but faire theeuish purchases? because what are theeues purchases but little kingdomes. . . ."[43]

To make laws really useful for the community, Vives said, laws should be known to all, expressed in a few simple words in the vernacular, adapted to all types of men, based on love and harmony, planned to give youth the right training by punishments and rewards, approved by the people, and taught by careful public discussion.[44]

Education, Vives said, especially the skills of writing and speaking with eloquence, should be applied to the practical life, both public and private; then the scholars will become governors,

[42] *De tradendis disciplinis,* pp. 261, 263, 264, 270, 262. Or see Book V, Chapter IV, "The Study of Law."

[43] Saint Augustine, *Of the Citie of God,* with . . . comments of Io. Lodovicvs Vives (London, 1620), Book 4, Chapter 4, p. 150.

[44] *De tradendis disciplinis,* pp. 262–71.

founders of states, princes, judges, and men learned in the law.
Some scholars should also become theologians and preachers, ready
to help men become better and wiser in action. Again Vives said
that the fruit of all knowledge is to "turn it to usefulness, and
employ it for the common good." [45] With these principles the
major members of the More circle would agree.

In *Satellitium* Vives said that a prince must subordinate his
private interests and his personal desires to the welfare of his people and that it is his duty to be concerned with the welfare of each
individual.[46]

Vives' work *De subventione pauperum,* addressed to the officials
of Bruges, indicates that he felt a deep Christian sympathy for the
unfortunate and had specific ideas about improving the whole life of
a community. He wished to protect the healthy against com-
municable diseases, such as syphilis and the plague; to register all
the unfortunates who needed attention; to put to work all the able-
bodied, teaching trades to those of an age and ability to learn and
insuring work for them by state contracts for making those things
a state needs to buy; to educate the blind and to provide them with
suitable work; to arrange light work for aged people as a means
of keeping them from brooding; to examine the insane, and instead
of mocking or irritating them into worse insanity, to give treatment to those who might be helped by medicine and kindness; to
establish schools for giving a sound education to orphan boys and
girls. For 1526, and it is so dated by Vives' introductory letter to
the councilors and senators of Bruges, it seems a rather unusual
document.[47]

Starkey's *Dialogue* between Pole and Lupset restates many of
the main ideas which More, Erasmus, and Vives held about law
and government. In the opening pages, Lupset asked Pole why he

---

[45] *De tradendis disciplinis,* pp. 283, 289, and *passim.*

[46] Vives, *Opera,* 2 vols. (Basel, 1555), II, 103, nos. 120, 121.

[47] Vives, *De subventione pauperum* (Lyon, 1532). I have not examined directly Vives'
work. A translation, *Concerning the Relief of the Poor,* by Margaret M. Sherwood (New
York, 1917), condenses the reasons but develops the practical suggestions. She used the
1783 Valencia edition. In 1535 Vives published *De communione rerum.* J. Estelrich, in
Vives (Paris, 1941), says of this latter work: "Si son amour pour les pauvres lui inspire
des opinions qu' on dirait socialistes, on voit par contre dans le *De communione rerum* . . .
que sa doctrine s'oppose avec force au communisme." See p. 104.

was not serving the commonweal. Pole answered that he must first learn to rule himself, and that he was still unsure about his choosing between the life of action and the life of contemplation, in which one learns to know God, nature, and the works of nature. Lupset had a ready answer: learn to know God and nature and also lead a life of action.

During the debate on service to the commonweal, Lupset defined the aim of such service: "that the whole body of the commonalty may live in quietness and tranquillity, every part doing his office and duty, and so (as much as the nature of man will suffer) all to attain to their natural perfection." Lupset also defined the duty of every prudent and politic man: "first, to make himself perfit, with all virtues garnishing his mind, and then to commune the same perfection to other. . . . For all such gifts of God and nature must ever be applied to the common profit and utility; whereby man, as much as he may, shall ever follow the nature of God. . . . So that virtue and learning, not communed to other, is like unto riches heaped in corners, never applied to the use of other." The true civil life, according to Lupset is "living togidder in good and politic order, one ever ready to do good to another, and as it were, conspiring togidder in all virtue and honesty." [48]

Pole compared the true commonweal to the body and soul of man, saying that the body is the multitude of people, and the thing similar to the soul is "civil order and politic law . . . administered by good officers and wise rulers. . . ." Then he continued with a long, unoriginal comparison of the parts of the state to the parts of man's body.

The state is in good condition, Pole said, "so long as they which have authority and rule of the state look not to their own singular profit, nor to the private weal of any one part more than to the other, but refer all their counsel, acts, and deeds, to the common weal of the whole. . . ." [49]

Pole said that a prince should be elected: "that country cannot be long well governed nor maintained with good policy where all is ruled by the will of one not chosen by election but cometh to it by natural succession. . . ." A prince must have wisdom and virtue; he is above law only when his reason is perfectly used, and he has no liberty to break laws. England would be in trouble, Pole continued, since the prince is not elected, "if we had not a noble and wise prince which is ever content to submit himself to the order of his counsel, nothing abusing his authority." Pole also objected to the view that tyranny is God's punishment sent upon a people for their sins; one could not logically accept this idea unless he agreed that all evil comes from the fountain of goodness—a belief that is "plain wickedness and impiety." [50]

Pole stated and Lupset agreed that capital punishment is too severe for a little theft, especially when one steals from necessity, without killing anyone in connection with the theft: "at the first time specially, better it were to find some way how the man might be brought to better order and frame."

Laws differ in various countries; but in every country, it is assumed, laws direct people to the law of nature; and, Lupset suggested, those who keep their own laws—Jew, Saracen, Turk, and Moor—perhaps "shall not be damned." Since human law, when good, aids the law of nature, it performs an educational and a moral service for people. The end of all law is to induce men to do good for the love of good; its end is not the punishment of people. Laws made by men are binding on only those who have received or consented to them, and in such people obedience is a virtue. [51]

Pole, unlike More and Erasmus, recognized a need of training for war. Our nobility, he said, are "not exercised in feats of arms and chivalry" but give themselves to idle games like dicing and cardplaying; hence they must be compelled by law "to exercise themselves in all such . . . feats of arms as shall be for the defence of our ream necessary. . . ." Again he said that nobles must be trained to use their minds for public and private justice and to "exercise themselves in feats of the body and chivalry, no less ex-

---

[50] *A Dialogue*, pp. 99, 102, 154, for quotations.
[51] *A Dialogue*, pp. 114–15, 34–35, and *passim*.

pedient for time of war than the other exercises be for time of peace." [52]

Lupset expressed the idea that the "common law would ever be written in the common tongue, that every man that would, might understand the better such statutes and ordinances as he is bounden to observe." Pole promptly added that "the same also is in the law of the Church, which appeareth to me no less necessary to be put in our mother tongue than the other." Pole asked that all laws be simplified and then put into either Latin or English, instead of Old French.

In criticizing English common law, Pole deplored the tendency to remove cases by writ from the shire towns to London and the avarice of proctors and attorneys, "which commonly regard more their own lucre than the justice of their client's cause." Pole also said of the English common law:

This is no doubt, but that our law and order thereof is over-confuse. It is infinite, and without order or end. There is no stable ground therein, nor sure stay; but everyone that can colour reason maketh a stop to the best law that is before-time devised. The subtlety of one sergeant shall inert and destroy all the judgements of many wise men. . . . The judgements of years be infinite and full of much controversy, and . . . of small authority. The judges are not bounden . . . to follow them as a rule, but after their own liberty they have authority to judge . . . this causeth suits to be long in decision.

Pole suggested that Englishmen might use the remedy which Justinian had used for Roman law, to cut away the long laws and to state fewer laws in better language, in English or in Latin. They might also study the laws of the Romans, where they would find decisions made more according to the law of nature "than they be in this barbarous tongue, Old French. . . ." Finally he said: "if we might induce the heads of our country . . . to receive the civil law of the Romans, the which is now the common law almost of all Christian nations," all this difficulty would be removed.[53]

[52] *A Dialogue*, pp. 148, 170.

[53] *A Dialogue*, pp. 117, 172–74. See also pp. 129–30, where Pole is represented as arguing that divine service should also be put into English or some means provided by which all people might understand the Latin. This seems an extreme position for the future cardinal and may really have been Starkey's idea.

Some other members of the More group mentioned with approval the "reception" of the Roman law. Erasmus and Vives, Dutchman and Spaniard, were enthusiastic about the idea. In 1514 Erasmus wrote the German, Ulrich Zasi, approving his plan to illustrate the imperial law, saying that William Budé of Paris was doing something similar and that Cuthbert Tunstal had annotated various passages. Erasmus also exchanged approving letters with the Italian, Andrea Alciati, law teacher and scholar.[54] Vives said: "Of all written laws, now known to us, the most excellent seems to be the old Roman law." It is fitted for the common life of men, he added; it draws men together, promotes peace, deters men from evil; it is devised with learning and seriousness and expressed in clear, simple words.[55]

Englishmen who gave any support to the reception of Roman law had usually had law training or other education on the Continent. Tunstal, for example, had studied civil law at Padua. Pole, too, had been at Padua from 1521 to 1527; late in 1529 he went to the University of Paris; and after 1532 he was an exile on the Continent until the accession of Queen Mary. More, who had been trained in the English common law at Lincoln's Inn, and who wrote Erasmus at one time that he "had naturally the greatest abhorrence of litigation even when it brings me profit," expressed no desire to "receive" the civil law; and neither did John Rastell, who studied English common law at the Middle Temple. Thus the program of reform agreed upon by More and his friends included only the clarification of law, its expression in language that people could understand, its use with justice and conscience, and its harmony with divine law and the law of nature.

Though Sir Thomas Elyot had much to say about law and government, he did not make extreme statements about the faults of kings or the rights of common people. Instead, he spoke with tactful and courtly optimism about the *status quo*. His concern for his country and his faith in the power of education to bring about good government appear in his statement of purposes for both

---

[54] Nichols, *The Epistles*, II, no. 299; see index for other letters. Or see Allen, *Opus epistolarum*, index, under Alciati and Zasius.
[55] Vives, *De tradendis disciplinis*, p. 270.

the first and the second books of the *Governour*. But in Book I, the first three chapters, where he was concerned with the form of government, he rejected the term *commonweal* and defined his own term, public weal: "A publike weale is a body lyuyng, compacte or made of sondry astates and degrees of men, whiche is disposed by the ordre of equite and gouerned by the rule and moderation of reason." [56] As examples of degrees he mentioned the heavenly hierarchy, the four elements—fire, air, earth, and water—and the differences in plants and animals. In a well-governed state, he said, inferiors have their place: they are to be industrious and to revere and obey their rulers. The best and surest government, he believed, is that by one king or prince who rules only for the welfare of his people; and that form of government is oldest and most generally approved. By way of analogy he mentioned the rule of God, the one sun in heaven, one moon, and bees, which have, he said "one principall bee for theyr gouernour, who excelleth all other in greatnes, yet hath he no pricke or stinge, but in hym is more knowlege than in the residue." [57] Elyot used also the commonplace comparison to the human body, applying it to a ruler's helpers; a prince needs many inferior governors, "whiche be named of Aristotel his eien, eares, handes, and legges." [58] Noblemen, he thought, made usually the better rulers.[59]

Unlike More and Erasmus, Elyot accepted war and training for it as a part of a ruler's education. In Book I, Chapter xvii, he recommended wrestling, handling weapons, swimming, and riding horseback as being useful training for war. In Chapter xxvii, on archery, he discussed shooting the long bow as good for muscular development, and also "the moste excellent artillerie for warres, wherby this realme of Englande hath bene . . . best defended from outwarde hostilitie. . . ." [60] Elyot's views were again like those of Castiglione. His characters, in the *Courtier*, assumed that martial training and physical bravery were desirable but disliked the grim attitude of a courtier who had wedded his harness for a

[56] Elyot, *The boke named the Gouernour* (London, 1531), Fol. 1.
[57] *The Gouernour*, Fol. 7 *verso*.
[58] *The Gouernour*, Fol. 14 *verso*.
[59] *The Gouernour*, Fol. 14 *verso*.
[60] *The Gouernour*, Fol. 99 *verso*.

wife and who refused to enjoy music and dancing. But none of
these views approached the extremes of Machiavelli, who said that
a ruler should have no study but war and should use hunting to
train his men for war.

In Book I, Chapter xiv, Elyot was concerned with the reform
of law. Since the laws of England were expressed in a barbarous
language, without eloquence and without any other usefulness in
life, he wished to see them rewritten either in English, in Latin,
or in good French, in a "more clene and elegant stile," instead
of law French. (Elyot's idea of "barbarous" is perhaps clarified by
an even later example from the Salisbury assizes of a prisoner "que
puis son condemnation ject un brickbat a le dit justice que nar-
rowly mist.") [61] Then if young men were trained until twenty-
one years of age in philosophy, in eloquence, in Latin and Greek,
before they began the study of law, they would bring to it a
breadth of reason, instead of seeing law as separate bits not related
to life or to reason. Also they should learn, Elyot thought, to apply
to law pleadings all the parts of a formal oration, including the
exordium; and thus they would become truly eloquent. As a
background for English law, a young man should read the laws
expounded in the orations of Cicero, all the histories of the beginnings of laws and public weals, and should become familiar with
the diverse laws and governments explained in the works of Plato,
Xenophon, and Aristotle. Then English laws and the English public
weal would really be equal to those of Greece and Rome. Like the
other men of the More group, Elyot thought that the true purposes
of law were to bring an erring man back to virtue or to protect
others from his actions, not to give him severe punishment.

In spite of his tendency to courtliness, Elyot sometimes spoke
like a true philosopher when he discussed rulers in relation to other
men:

If thou be a gouernour, or haste ouer other soueraygnitie, knowe thy selfe.
That is to saye, knowe that thou arte verely a man compacte of soule and
body, and in that, all other men be equall vnto the. Also that euery man
taketh with the equall benefite of the spirite of life, nor thou haste any
more of the dewe of heuyn or the brightnes of the sonne than any other

[61] F. W. Maitland, *English Law and the Renaissance* (Cambridge, 1901), p. 18.

persone. Thy dignitie or autorite . . . is . . . but a weighty or heuy cloke.
. . . Therfore whiles thou wearest it knowe thy selfe, knowe that the name
of a soueraigne or ruler without actuall gouernaunce is but a shadowe . . .
that by example of gouernours men do rise or falle in vertue or vice. And
as it is said of Aristotell, rulers more greuously do sinne by example than
by their acte.[62]

Elyot's desire to aid the commonweal dominated much of his
other work. *The Image of Governance,* a compilation of the actions
and notable sayings of Alexander Severus, developed many other
ideas about government and also the theme that the philosopher
is the ideal man to hold office; but the better he is, the more reluctant he will be to undertake that dangerous race. In the closing
words of the book Elyot described the emperor as one "whose lyfe
maye worthily be a paterne to knyghtes, an example to iudges, a
myrrour to prynces, a beautifull ymage to all theym that are lyke
to be governours." [63] In *The Doctrinal of Princes,* a translation
from Isocrates, Elyot recommended philosophy for the study of
a ruler; for philosophy would tell him the ways or means to manage
his affairs and experience would enable him to carry out the ideas.[64]
In the Proheme to the 1541 edition of *The Castle of Health* Elyot
spoke of his "labours taken without hope of temporall rewarde,
onely for the feruent affectyon whiche I haue euer borne toward
the publike weale of my countary." [65] In the preface of his work
Of the Knowledge Which Maketh a Wise Man, Elyot said that he
had spent the greater part of his life "perusynge diligently euery
auncient warke that I mought come by, eyther greke or latine,
conteyninge any parte of philosophie necessary to the institution
of mans lyfe in vertue," and then he had tried to set forth any
part of his study that might be profitable to his country. But at
this time he complained that his labors were not always appreciated.
Some men, he said, winced like galled horses when he attacked an
idea which they held dear; others maliciously said that he was at-

---

[62] *The Gouernour,* Fol. 176 *verso*-177 or Book III, Chapter 3.

[63] Elyot, *The Image of Governance* (London, 1541), Chapter XXVI, leaves 86–87.

[64] Elyot, *The Doctrinall of Princis* (London, 1533? or 1534), leaf 9 *verso.* This is a
work of twelve leaves only.

[65] Elyot, *The Castel of Helth* (London, 1541), Aii. Elyot was answering the criticism
which, it seems, had been made about his 1539 edition because he was not a doctor.

tacking a certain individual, hoping to anger against him some man in authority; still others complained of his strange terms when he was only trying to augment the English tongue and to help men express better the things that were in their hearts.[66]

Elyot's mention of Erasmus in the *Governour* is one example of the fact that younger men in the More circle carried on an influence from the older men. When Elyot discussed an orator's training he said that unless one wished to be an "exquisite" orator, the little book of Erasmus "whiche he calleth *Copiam verborum et rerum*" should be sufficient for his training. He also mentioned more than once Erasmus' *Institutio principis Christiani*, calling it by his own title *The Institution of a Christian Prince*, and including it in the reading program for a young gentleman of seventeen. He continued the tradition of More and Erasmus in combining scripture and the classics for this program. First he named Aristotle's *Ethics*, Cicero's *De officiis*, Plato's works for judgment and the form of speaking that philosophers use, the works of Cicero in general, the *Proverbs* of Solomon, the books of *Ecclesiastes* and *Ecclesiasticus*, the historical parts of the Bible, all the Old Testament, the New Testament, and the *Institution of a Christian Prince* by Erasmus. Of this last work he said: "there was neuer boke written in latine that, in so lytle a portion, contayned of sentence, eloquence, and vertuous exhortation a more compendious abundaunce." Mentioning the same work again in speaking of the care that princes and governors should take in forming the opinions of people, he said that it cannot be "so moche praysed as it is worthy." [67]

Ascham was unable to write his treatise on archery, *Toxophilus*, without relating his ideas to the good of the commonweal. But he differed from the older men of the More circle in some of his ideas, which resembled those of Elyot; he stressed training for war as well as for peace; he tended at times to be courtly and aristocratic; he emphasized education and the commonweal more than other ideas about government. Ascham evaluated education in this way:

---

[66] Elyot, *Of the Knowledeg* [sic] *whiche maketh a wise man* (1533). The edition of 1534? has the subtitle *A Disputation Platonic.*

[67] Elyot, *The Gouernour*, Fol. 42 and 204 *verso* for quotes. See also I, xi, III, xi, and *passim.*

"For the foundation of youth well sette (as Plato doth saye), the whole bodye of the commune wealth shal floryshe therafter." Kings and emperors, he said, had often been expert in using the bow and arrow, and "the best commune wealthes that euer were, haue made goodlie actes and lawes for it." He commended Cheke for his training of Edward VI and for other services to the commonweal; he praised Sir Humphrey Wingfield for bringing up children in the book and the bow, the two things which best prepare people to rule and to defend the whole country both in peace and in war.[68] Toxophilus himself wished to eliminate all the "unthriftie" games which make the commonwealth sick and to punish all those who indulge in harmful games by making their action felony and treating them as falsifiers of the king's coin, since they falsify the commonwealth.[69] He said also: "Reason and Rulers beynge lyke in offyce (for the one ruleth the body of man, the other ruleth the bodye of the common wealthe) ought to be lyke of condicions, and oughte to be obeyed in all maner of matters. Obedience is nourysshed by feare and loue, Feare is kepte in by true iustice and equitie, Loue is gotten by wisdome ioyned with liberalitie. . . ."[70] A country needs perfection in leadership: "surely I perceyue that sentence of Plato to be true, which sayeth that there is nothyng better in any common wealthe than that there shoulde be alwayes one or other excellent passyng man, whose lyfe and vertue shoulde plucke forwarde the will, diligence, laboure, and hope of all other, that folowyng his footesteppes, they myght comme to the same ende wherevnto labour, lerning, and vertue had conueied him before."[71]

COMMUNITY PROPERTY

The members of the More circle were concerned with the idea of holding all things in common, though they were not in complete accord. Probably the study of primitive Christianity and the reading of Plato had brought the idea into sharp focus for them. Probably, too, they had no immediate desire to start a plan

[68] Ascham, *Toxophilus* (London, 1545), Book A, leaves 21, 6, 33–34; Book B, leaf 22.
[69] *Toxophilus*, Book A, leaf 23.
[70] *Toxophilus*, Book A, 25 *verso*.
[71] *Toxophilus*, Book A, 33 *verso*-34.

of sharing all property; but they used the absolute concept as a contrast to Christian civilization, with its hate, pride, and greed.

In *The Praise of Folly* Erasmus commented on an early age of simplicity when laws and government were unnecessary.[72] Colet made similar implications: "This law of a corrupter nature is the same as that *Law of Nations,* resorted to by nations all over the world: a law which brought in ideas of *meum* and *tuum*—of property, that is to say, and deprivation—ideas clean contrary to a good and unsophisticated nature, for that would have a community in all things." [73]

More used the holding of all things in common as the basis of his Utopian civilization—again, as an ironic contrast to the greed of so-called Christian people in his own time. The houses in that country were never locked; anyone who came was admitted freely; and every ten years houses were changed by a method of casting lots. In a working day of six hours the Utopians produced more than enough of the conveniences and necessities for all, but none of the luxuries for vain display. All supplies were stored in warehouses, one in each of the four quarters of a city; each householder might freely take from them for his needs. Since there was enough of everything, there was no fear and therefore no strife and no greed. In the Utopian society, also, birth and wealth meant nothing; only ability and the willingness to use that ability were important. The Utopians elected their rulers, including their prince. Each year thirty households chose a magistrate called a syphogrant or phylarch. The syphogrants, two hundred in number, chose the prince from a list of four men, one having been nominated from each quarter of the city. The prince, once chosen, held office for life unless he was suspected of trying to become a dictator.[74]

Vives emphasized a sharing that was more than material when he said: "The wise man will reflect that this world is, as it were, a certain State, of which he is a citizen, or as a certain great house, of which he is one of the family, and that it is not matter of

---

[72] Erasmus, *The Praise of Folly,* p. 44.

[73] John Colet, *Exposition of St. Paul's Epistle to the Romans,* the incomplete version published with *Letters to Radulphus and Other Treatises* (London, 1876), p. 134.

[74] More, *Utopia,* pp. 130, 142, 156–57, 135–38.

consequence by whom anything good is said, as long as it is said truly; that further, here in this State those treasures which are collected together are to be applied to public use; it is of no consequence by whom they were collected, the main point is, they are provided and they should be distributed." [75]

Elyot, often the aristocrat in his views, protested sharply, in the first chapter of Book I, against any idea of holding all things in common: "And they which do suppose it to be so called for that, that euery thinge shulde be to all men in commune without discrepance of any astate or condition be ther to moued more by sensualite than by any good reason or inclination to humanite." [76]

SUMMARY

In the popular treatises on government before 1500—such works as Hoccleve *Regiment of Princes,* Lydgate *Fall of Princes,* and versions of the *Secreta Secretorum*—writers tended to use personal threats or the promise of personal rewards as an incentive to good rule. God would deprive the unjust king of his kingdom or his wealth; the just king would have victory in battle or future fame. Such appeals to prudence and fear were usually dominant. The same treatises often advised rulers to govern according to the old customs of their countries. Instead, More and his friends used the positive approach, emphasizing virtue and goodness, the product of a sound classical and Christian education. They wished rulers to know the best ideas about goodness and justice in ruling, and to practice this knowledge because they had the inner urge to rule well, to act for the good of the whole country. They advocated a critical examination of all areas of life; and wherever improvements could be made, they recommended change. Political and economic conditions, to them, were not God's punishment for sin; and they were not "unchangeable embodiments of the divine will." They were conditions which men had created; therefore men could and should bring about changes.

More and some of his friends engaged in the free play of mind about an elected ruler, but they tended to believe that a monarchy

[75] Vives, *De tradendis disciplinis,* p. 289.
[76] Elyot, *The Gouernour,* Fol. 1 *verso.*

was desirable, acceptable, or inevitable. Like the Stoics, they considered the form of government unimportant if rulers gave justice and if rulers and ruled were motivated by love and goodness. Since they lived under hereditary monarchs, they were concerned with making good rulers from imperfect material, shaping them by an education in virtue, piety, and learning. A ruler should be subject to law; and his power, they often said, came from the people. If they said that his power came from God, they usually added that he should try to rule like God, with love, wisdom, and justice.

The common people, as well as the educated, competent men, had an obligation to further the common welfare. But they had rights as well as duties. More and Erasmus stressed the right to an education and thus the right to rise in church and state; they and John Rastell, as well as Vives, emphasized their right to economic conditions giving them employment, fair wages, and some provision for sickness and old age.

The real purpose of law was to give justice and peace and to make men good. All laws, canon, civil, or English common law, should be few, simple, clear, made known to all, and stated in the language of the people. Human laws should have the consent of the people who were expected to obey them. Vives said explicitly that law would not be needed if human beings were ruled by love, and probably More and Erasmus would have agreed.

War, according to More and Erasmus, corrupted men; and once corrupted, men were willing to wage war. Colet and Vives agreed with them in opposing war. Younger men, especially those with aristocratic leanings, recommended training for war as a part of education. It is doubtful whether More and Erasmus would have conceded that any war in their own times between Christian nations was justified; but they saw also that war would not cease as long as greed, hate, and strife ruled the hearts and minds of men. More, to quote his words from *Utopia,* summed up the problem thus: "But you must with a crafty wile and a subtell trayne studye and endeuoure your selfe, as moch as in yow lyethe, to handle the matter wyttelye and handsomelye for the purpose; and that whyche yow can not turne to good, so to order it that it be not very badde. For it is not possible for all thynges to be well, onles all men were good: which I thynke wil not be yet thys good many yeares." [77]

Each man in the group believed that an education in virtue, piety, and learning, in Christian and classical literature, was the best way to work toward a solution of the problems of law and government—and all other problems. Again the whole problem of law and government might be summed up by saying that More and his friends believed in applied Christianity.

[77] More, *Utopia*, p. 100.

CHAPTER V *Education in general*

Like other human changes, the developments in education fostered by members of the More circle about 1500 to 1535 did not spring suddenly from nothing. They grew partly from early concepts of the rights of man, including the right to education; and these concepts were restated by Thomas Aquinas. They evolved partly from the provision that every cathedral, monastery, collegiate church, and perhaps every chantry in medieval England should have its school. They resulted partly from a statute, in the seventh year of the reign of Henry IV, 1405–6, which is like a continental divide between the feudal right of a lord and the right of a parent to educate his child. Confirming other feudal rights, the statute exempted education: "Provided always, That every Man or Woman, of what Estate or Condition that he be, shall be free to set their Son or Daughter to take learning at any manner School that pleaseth them within the Realm." The law French includes the phrase "de mettre son fitz ou file dappendre lettereure." [1] One effect of this statute was to stop the fines which had been frequent in the fourteenth century for sending a son to school without "the lord's leave."

Even in the unsettled conditions of the fifteenth-century schools,

[1] A. Luders, T. E. Tomlins, J. Raithby, *et al.*, *Statutes of the Realm*, 11 vols. (London, 1810–1828), II, 157–58.

there were some interesting developments. First, guild schools, like the one in Stratford-on-Avon, were being established in other places. Second, lay masters were in charge of a few schools scattered over England, between 1432 and 1488. Third, laymen were occasionally the trustees in charge of a school; for example, a free school founded by John Abbott in 1443 was placed under his own group of mercers. Fourth, some of the schools really were free of tuition fees; St. Anthony's in London, where More and perhaps Colet had their education, was founded in 1441 to teach "all boys and others whatsoever wishing to learn and become scholars without cost to them." Fifth, Greek may possibly have been taught in one or two of these schools (perhaps by William Horman at Eton and Winchester, between 1485 and 1502), but the evidence is doubtful.[2] Sixth, one school, Bishop Thomas Langton's *domestica schola*, which Pace attended, probably about 1493–95, seems to have been based on principles which Erasmus and Vives were expressing later: the "literary humanities," encouragement of an individual bent, praise and rewards for excellence, the plan of having the boys repeat to the bishop in the evening what they had learned from the master so that each worthy boy might be given some reward, and kindness to dull pupils in the hope that "diligence might strive with nature."[3] Perhaps Pace, in writing about this school years later, idealized it, shaping it to patterns he had learned from More and Erasmus; or it is possible that the bishop had imported principles from Italy.

Seventh, Magdalen College School, founded by formal statutes in 1480, at the gates of Magdalen College, Oxford, was doing some interesting work in grammar teaching. The master and the ushers were to teach all comers freely without exacting a fee; there was a provision for thirty "demyes" or needy scholars; the pupils were to be trained well in grammar before they could go on to other subjects; two or three of the "demyes" were to work so hard at "grammar, poetry, and other humanist arts," that they might

[2] Arthur F. Leach, *The Schools of Medieval England* (New York, 1915), Chapter XII, 247; Chapter XIII, 280, 286; Foster Watson, *The English Grammar Schools to 1660* (Cambridge, 1908), Chapter XXX.

[3] Jervis Wegg, *Richard Pace: A Tudor Diplomatist* (London, 1932), pp. 4–5. No edition of *De Fructu* is available at present.

be prepared to teach others; and its early informators adapted grammar and vocabulary lists to contemporary life for the boys. John Holt and William Lily, friends of the young Thomas More, were pupils there; and Holt was its headmaster about 1494–95.[4]

Eighth, an important development in fifteenth-century England was a growing recognition of the need for Latin in secular life— the so-called classical Latin approved by Italian scholars—for diplomats, king's proctors at the papal court, and royal secretaries.

But in fifteenth-century England and earlier no books were written to explain the theories of a liberal education. There were courtesy books dealing with manners or with service in great houses, such as John Russell's *Book of Nurture* and John Lydgate's *Stans puer ad mensam;* there were manuals for princes, like *The Regiment of Princes* by Hoccleve and *Speculum principis* by Skelton. In Italy during the same period many educators and many books explained theories of education inspired by the classics: Vittorino had opened his school "La Casa Giocosa" for the children of Gianfresco Gonzago about 1423; and Aeneas Silvius, later Pope Pius II, had written about 1450 an educational treatise which contained most of the ideas expressed later by Erasmus and Vives.

The complete optimistic program of education developed by More, Erasmus, and Vives between 1500 and 1530 or 1535 certainly had some roots in the fifteenth century. It is not so easy to say why it suddenly burgeoned, nor to believe that anyone knows all the reasons. Certainly the education of Grocyn, Linacre, Lily, Latimer, and Colet in Italy in the last two decades of the fifteenth century had an influence; More received the impact of their education without a journey to Italy; Erasmus had a liberal training in some phases of his early education and in his early contact with England. Certainly, too, the belief of these men that they were getting the real ideas of the whole body of classics, for the first time, not mere summaries or bad translations—whether that belief was entirely true or not—acted like a tonic to thought. But whatever the causes, classic thought, as expressed by Plutarch,

<hr />

[4] John R. Bloxam, *A Register of . . . Saint Mary Magdalen College . . .* , 5 vols. (Oxford, 1863–1881), III, 1–26. See also Beatrice White, *The Vulgaria*, EETS, v. 187 (1932), xvi–xx; and Foster Watson, *The English Grammar Schools to 1660*, Chapter XXX. Wolsey had also been an informator at Magdalen College for about six months.

Pliny, Seneca, Cicero, and Quintilian, increased faith in the law of nature. The program of education was based on the law of nature, the freedom of man's will, and human perfectibility. Since the non-Christian philosophers had found many great truths, without the help of revelation, the secular phases of education were exalted without any loss of interest in Christian education—or it might be said again that More, Erasmus, and their friends never saw life as separate parts, some sacred, some secular, but as a Christian-classical whole. In this whole unit, education, like a magnet, drew together all other ideas on reforming human life —an education in virtue and piety for the service of the commonweal.

ACTION TO FURTHER EDUCATION

THOMAS MORE'S SCHOOL

More's first venture into action for general education seems to have been his contribution to the Latin grammar *Lac puerorum*, issued by his friend, John Holt, whom he may have known in Cardinal Morton's household or at Oxford. Since the book was dedicated to Morton, it was first issued before 1500, the year of Morton's death. It is possible that More wrote part of the book, since he said "Our door is new and easy for the young crowd." Tables of declensions were illustrated by rude woodcuts: one woodcut representing an outstretched hand with a finger and the thumb for each of five cases and with the ablative on the ball of the thumb; another, representing six candles with wicks at the top for the six cases and with the endings of the five different declensions printed on the candles.[5] More's epigrams in the volume praised Holt for expressing clearly the essentials of grammar in one small book and for offering boys a good diet of milk, not wild strawberries or heavy meat. For advanced work More and Holt recommended other grammars, especially that by Sulpicius.[6] In his

[5] J. H. Lupton, *A Life of John Colet* (London, 1909), pp. 23–24. I have not been able to examine a copy of Holt's grammar. See also William Nelson, "Thomas More, Grammarian and Orator," *PMLA*, LVIII (1943), 341, and *passim*.
[6] Bradner and Lynch, *The Latin Epigrams of Thomas More* (Chicago, 1953), Appendix II, nos. 2, 3, pp. 238–40.

letter of 1501 to Holt, More mentioned a comedy of Solomon as if he had helped to write it; and it seems reasonable to suppose that it had been written to help in the teaching of Latin.

More's next venture in practical education, so far as we know, was the establishment of a school in his household. It was probably started about 1510 or 1511, when Margaret was five or six years old; if so, it was carried on in the Bucklersbury house for ten or twelve years and continued in Chelsea. Students outside More's family were drawn into the school, besides his three daughters and his son: his stepdaughter, Alice Middleton; his foster daughter, Margaret Gigs; his son-in-law, William Roper; perhaps his niece, Frances Staverton; Margaret Abarrow, who became the second wife of Sir Thomas Elyot about 1522; and Anne Cresacre, who married young John More. Young men connected with the school include Master Drew, William Gonell, Nicholas Kratzer, Richard Herde, and John Clement. Nicholas Kratzer, who went to England in 1517 and became the king's astronomer in 1519, is mentioned in More's letters as a teacher of astronomy; he was probably well educated when he joined More's household. Little is known of Master Drew. Gonell was apparently an experienced teacher when he was sent to More by Erasmus, though More may be said to have educated him by sending him the long letter discussing the education of women; Herde and Clement, who apparently received their education through the direct help or the influence of More, may have been tutors in the school.

Since William Roper was silent on the household school we must depend on Harpsfield, Stapleton, and More's letters. From the letters cited in Chapter I to illustrate More's concern about astronomy as a part of the study of nature which leads to a knowledge of God, we had evidence of More's concern with virtue and piety as well as thorough knowledge. From the biographies and the letters we know that More created an atmosphere of happiness and used kindness and gentleness, with praise whenever it was deserved. He asked the tutors to discourage pride and arrogance, and to cultivate in the students modesty, humility, self-command, charity, and piety. He stressed purity and beauty in Latin style, using double translation as a means to this end and encouraging members of his school to write often to him in Latin. The subjects named by his biographers were Latin and Greek literature, rhetoric, poetry, philosophy and logic, and mathematics, with some formal disputing. Judging from his ironic barbs in *Utopia* on the extremes of dialectic, these disputings avoided verbiage and any placing of the desire to win above the desire to discover the truth. From a chance reference in a letter of Palsgrave to More we know that the daughters once disputed in philosophy before the king and that Palsgrave regretted not being there to hear them.

Always in the letters to his school he used love, kindness, praise; in one letter he teased the young people with gentle satire about their knowledge of astronomy and encouraged them seriously:

But I think you have no longer any need of Mr. Nicholas, since you have learnt whatever he had to teach you about astronomy. I hear you are so far advanced in that science that you can not only point out the polar-star or the dog-star, or any of the constellations, but are able also—which requires a skillful and profound astrologer—among all those leading heavenly bodies, to distinguish the sun from the moon! Go forward, then, in that new and admirable science by which you ascend to the stars. But . . . consider that this holy time of Lent warns you . . . to raise your mind also to heaven, lest the soul look downwards to the earth after the manner of brutes, while the body looks upward.

In one letter addressed to his own children and to Margaret Gigs he praised John for his efforts and for turning his own jokes back on himself "wittily . . . merrily . . . with due moderation" and with due respect for his father, whom he wished to please. In a letter to Margaret he expressed the hope that she would devote the rest of her life to medicine and to sacred literature (*literas sacras*). In another letter to Margaret he reported the high praise that the Bishop of Exeter had given her for Latin scholarship, when he showed the Bishop her letter to himself.[7] He also wrote her that a nobleman (Reginald Pole), to whom he showed one of her letters, had thought her scholarship almost miraculous.

More's deep appreciation for human development is perhaps shown best by an epigram which he was composing while he

[7] Elizabeth F. Rogers, *The Correspondence of Sir Thomas More* (Princeton, 1947), nos. 101, 107, 106, 108. For translations see T. E. Bridgett, *Life* (London, 1891), pp. 132–38; and Stapleton, *Life,* trans. by Philip E. Hallett (London, 1928), pp. 45–46, 115–16.

traveled on horseback over dangerously muddy roads, in the fall of 1517, toward Calais on an embassy. In the epigram, addressed to his children, he recalled to them how often he had kissed them and bought them little luxuries of food and dress, how seldom he had whipped them, habitually using a peacock's tail wielded gently, as he told them, "so that sorry welts might not disfigure your tender seats": "But at this moment my love has increased so much that it seems to me I used not to love you at all. This feeling of mine is produced by your adult manners, adult despite your tender years; by your instincts trained in noble principles which must be learned; by your pleasant way of speaking, fashioned for clarity; and by your very careful weighing of every word. These characteristics of yours so strangely tug at my heart, so closely bind me to you, my children, that my being your father . . . is hardly a reason at all for my love of you." [8]

COLET'S SCHOOL

John Colet's chief action to further education was the founding of his school at St. Paul's, using his patrimony for its endowment and putting it under the control of the Mercers' Company (the group with which his father and the Mores had been connected). On June 6, 1510, the king granted a license for the school; on November 4, 1511, Colet made a will for its endowment. It provided for 153 children from all nations, including a "pore Scholer," who was to sweep the school and keep it clean. Probably the number was determined by the number of seats the physical space provided, not by any mystic concept. To be admitted, a child must be able to read and write and must know the catechism. If a child, after being admitted, attended any other school he would not be admitted again; and if any child fell into "unthriftynesse and misbehauior" and continued in it after due warning, he was to be sent away and another chosen in his place.

As for subjects, Colet, of course, prescribed Latin literature, especially such works as joined the true Roman eloquence with wisdom and were written by Christian authors. Colet apparently had a fear of the secular, and he lacked knowledge of the Greek

[8] Bradner and Lynch, *The Latin Epigrams,* no. 248.

language and Greek literature. Of the authors he named, Lactantius, Proba, Sedulius, Juvencus, and Prudentius were fourth- and fifth-century writers who combined Christian material and an imitation of the classical Latin style. (Prudentius with his *Psychomachia* established the pattern of a war between the vices and the virtues.) Baptista Mantuan was a fifteenth-century friend of Giovanni Pico della Mirandola. Colet also prescribed by name the *Institutum Christiani hominis* and the *Copia verborum* by Erasmus.[9]

Whether Colet's curriculum remained narrow is a question for speculation. In sending him his treatise *De ratione studii,* Erasmus suggested that Colet would not approve of some things in it because he disliked method and art; and in the work Erasmus named an overwhelming list of Greek and Latin authors for the young students to master in getting a working knowledge of the two languages: Lucian, Demosthenes, Herodotus; the poets, Aristophanes, Homer, Euripides; among Latin writers, Terence, selected comedies of Plautus, Virgil, Horace, Cicero, Caesar, and Sallust.[10] But there is much indirect evidence that the broader curriculum triumphed. First, Colet answered Erasmus' suggestion that he might disapprove by writing to him: "What is there of Erasmus that I do not approve? I have run through that Epistle of yours about studies . . . and . . . I not only approve it all but I truly admire your genius, and art, and learning, and copiousness, and eloquence."[11] Second, Colet and Erasmus remained warm friends until Colet's death in 1519. Third, Colet made great efforts to learn Greek between this time and the time of his death. Fourth, Colet had provided for changes and had left many decisions to the headmaster and the mercers. Fifth, William Lily, one of the best classical scholars of his time, became the first headmaster and held the position until his own death in 1522.

Colet expressly provided in his statutes that there was to be no cockfighting, no "rydyng aboute of victory," and no disputing at St.

---

[9] Lupton, *A Life of John Colet,* Appendix A.

[10] Erasmus, *Opera omnia,* 10 vols. (Lugduni Batavorum, 1703–1706), I, 521, D, E. The passage is from *De ratione studii.* Or see W. H. Woodward, *Desiderius Erasmus concerning the Aim and Method of Education* (Cambridge, 1904), p. 164, where the same books are named in the translation in the same order.

[11] F. M. Nichols, *The Epistles of Erasmus,* 3 vols. (London, 1904), II, no. 223. See also no. 221, the letter of Erasmus to Colet.

Bartholomew's, which he described as foolish babbling and a waste of time.

He wished to adapt grammar to youthful minds, as John Holt and Thomas More had done in the plans for *Lac puerorum*. In his "proheme" to a grammar, reprinted in an edition of 1527, he said that he had tried to make everything clear and easy for the tenderness and the small capacity of little minds. He indicated that the pupil should learn the rules by reading Latin authors and poets, for Latin speech existed before the rules, not the rules before Latin speech.

Colet provided well for his headmaster, as Erasmus and Vives suggested in their treatises on education. He was to have a mark a week in salary, a livery gown of four nobles delivered in cloth, sick leave for not more than thirty days a year, a pension if he developed an incurable disease or became too old to teach, lodgings at the school, and a house in Stepney "to resort unto," the latter house to be maintained and kept in repair by the mercers. His mark a week, at the rates then current, was about thirty-five pounds a year, when the ten pounds a year paid at Stratford-on-Avon was considered an unusually good salary. In 1522, when a survey was made to find lodgings for the retinue of Charles V, his lodgings at the school were described thus: "Master Lily, schoolmaster, one hall, four chambers, four featherbeds, one kitchen, and other necessaries." [12] Pictures of the house in Stepney indicate that it was commodious.[13]

Friends who helped or praised the school included More, Erasmus, Linacre, and Pace. There was some opposition: Colet wrote Erasmus in 1512 that a bishop, "regarded as one of the wiser sort, in a great meeting of people, took our school to task, and said that I had founded a useless and indeed a mischievous thing . . . a house of idolatry. I believe that he said this because the Poets are read there." Erasmus promised to write verses for it; Colet asked him to do so with his "usual facility and sweetness." Besides sending *De ratione studii,* perhaps a brief version, to Colet in 1511, Erasmus dedicated *De copia verborum et rerum* to Colet and his school,

---

[12] H. B. Wheatley, *London Past and Present,* 3 vols. (London, 1891), III, 53.

[13] See *Gentleman's Magazine,* 88, Part 2 (1818), pp. 233–34, for a picture and a brief account of the house in Stepney, with a picture of the school and a list of its highmasters.

calling it a "small literary present to assist in the furniture of your school," and saying, "He is no friend to England that will not do his best to aid such an enterprise." Erasmus also wrote an oration *Concio de puero Jesu,* to be delivered before the school by one of the pupils, perhaps as J. H. Lupton suggested, for the formal dedication. Erasmus felt no call to be the headmaster himself, though Colet wished that he might do so, and at least that he might give some help, "if it is only in teaching our masters, when you come away from those Cambridge people." [14] But he tried at Cambridge to secure a headmaster for Colet, without success.

More supported Colet's school by writing him a letter of commendation—one of two extant letters between them—saying that his school was rousing envy because its scholars were showing up the ignorance of others.[15]

Various men aided Colet by writing grammars or revising them for his school. Linacre, apparently at Colet's request, had written a grammar, but Colet rejected it as too hard for the tender minds of his young boys. Probably this was *Rudimenta grammatices Latinae,* which he later adapted or provided for the Princess Mary. Lily, as the first headmaster, used his own *Syntax* or *Grammatices rudimenta* for which Colet had written a dedication dated August 1, 1509. In 1513 Lily published his *Construction of the Eight Parts of Speech,* a revision and a compilation, "the work of Colet and Lily, emended by Erasmus"—the grammar which with changes at intervals was used at Stratford Grammar School when Shakespeare was a boy and was, in some form, continued into the eighteenth century.[16]

Pace dedicated *De fructu,* published in 1517, to Colet and his school; he praised Colet's devotion to letters, his school, his headmaster, and his use of love and praise as incentives.

OTHER ACTION FOR EDUCATION

As every scholar in the More group seemed to consider himself an educator, it is difficult to select details to illustrate their action for education. Many defenses of points of view were educational

[14] Nichols, *The Epistles,* II, nos. 246, 248, 223, 231.
[15] Rogers, *The Correspondence,* no. 8.
[16] Beatrice White, *The Vulgaria,* p. xxxviii and *passim.*

efforts: More's letters to Edward Lee, to Dorp, and his 1518 letter to the University of Oxford rebuking ignorant attacks on good letters. When More and Pace acted as a joint force against an ignorant preacher who had attacked learning and the new interpreters of scripture, in a sermon at court, they were furthering education as well as defending the editorial work of Erasmus.

When Colet wished to learn Greek, More and Erasmus praised him and John Clement helped him. When Fisher developed the desire to learn Greek, More and Erasmus tried unsuccessfully to persuade William Latimer to help him; Latimer refused, saying that he had not been recently using the Greek used in scripture but he approved the idea and was glad to have a bishop set the example for such learning. Finally Erasmus gave Fisher help on his study.

Nearly all, perhaps all the books written or translated by any man of the group were parts of an educational program. Colet's works, for example, *An Exposition of St. Paul's Epistle to the Romans,* were written to emphasize points of view and were thus educational. All the books and critical editions prepared and written by Erasmus were an effort to educate the world; *De ratione studii, De pueris instituendis,* as well as the treatise by Vives *De tradendis disciplinis,* were written to help parents and teachers practice ideas on education. Pace's *De fructu* attempted a defense as well as a eulogy of classical learning.

John Rastell also had a strong desire to educate the general public and to serve the commonweal through his books. Evidence appears in the prefatory statements, discussed in Chapter IV, for his *Liber assisarum,* his *Abbreviations of the Statutes, The Exposiciones of the Termes of the Lawes of England,* and in the *Pastime of People.* The works of Sir Thomas Elyot alone are a large commentary on efforts to educate the public—books on government, education, health, the place and education of women, Christian living and dying, and general philosophy. Some of them are original works based on the classics and some are translations of classics. About the same time, from 1528 on to 1559, Thomas Paynell was translating Latin works into English, including works by Erasmus, Tunstal, and Vives. And since the members of the More circle did not live in a vacuum, other translations of the classics existed from the time of Caxton onward; about 1530 to 1550 the number of translations into English began to increase.

John Palsgrave took action to further language teaching, French instead of Latin, when he published *Lesclarcissement* in 1530. He attempted to explain French pronounciation, to state rules for French grammar, to give a detailed grammar or an English-French dictionary arranged by parts of speech; and he used phrases or whole sentences, first in English and then in French, to clarify the meaning of words.[17] In 1540, when he published *Acolastus*, a translation from Fullonius, he placed in the margin beside the English words Latin phrases to illustrate any manner of speaking which differed in the two languages and to help schoolboys understand the figures of speech and the meters.[18]

HELPING YOUNG MEN TO AN EDUCATION

When Erasmus gave Ulrich von Hutten an account of More's life and character in 1519, he said of him: "Whatever authority he derives from his rank, and whatever influence he enjoys by the favour of a powerful sovereign are employed in the service of the public, or in that of his friends . . . this disposition is more conspicuous than ever, now that his power of doing good is greater. Some he relieves with money, some he protects by his authority, some he promotes by his recommendation, while those whom he cannot otherwise assist are benefited by his advice." [19] There is much evidence that More did help many young men to an education or to some position for which an education fitted them; and often Colet, Erasmus, Grocyn, and Linacre were promoting the welfare of the same young men.

More probably furthered the education of Richard Herde before

---

[17] John Palsgrave, *Lesclarcissement de la langue Francoyse* (London, 1530), "Author's Epistell," Aii. In dedicating the work to the king he said that he had tutored the king's sister Mary in French, that she and her husband, the Duke of Suffolk, had examined the work and encouraged him in it. See *Letters and Papers . . . of the Reign of Henry VIII*, III, no. 3680, for indentures between Palsgrave and Pynson for the printing and sale of this work. Hereafter cited as *L. and P.*

[18] *The Comedy of Acolastus*, trans. from the Latin of Fullonius by John Palsgrave, ed. by P. L. Carver, *EETS*, v. 202 (1937).

[19] Nichols, *The Epistles*, III, no. 585 B, p. 397.

he employed him as a teacher in his household. In the preface to his translation of Vives' *Instruction of a Christian Woman* Herde described More as his singular good master and bringer up, the one to whose judgment and correction he still submitted whatever important work he undertook. More had meant, Herde reported, to do the translation himself but he was glad to have it done sooner than he could have managed; he added that he had asked More to read it over and correct it, and that he gladly did so. When allowance is made for the conventional wording of dedications, there is still no reason to doubt that Herde's statements had some basis of fact.

John Clement, who had begun his education in Colet's school, probably went to More's household through Colet's recommendation. In 1515 he went with More to Bruges and was represented as a listener when Hythlodaye talked of the Utopians. In his letter to Peter Gilles, More described him at that time as "my boye, who as yow knowe was there present with us, whome I suffer to be awaye from no talke, wherin may be anye profit or goodnes (for out of this yong bladed and new shotte up corne, whiche hath alredy begonne to sprynge up bothe in Latine and Greke learnynge, I looke for plentiful increase at length of goodly rype grayne)." By 1518 Clement was lecturing at Oxford; he settled for a short time in Corpus Christi College; he was appointed first as a rhetoric reader and then as a reader of Greek by Cardinal Wolsey. It would be difficult not to suppose that these appointments were helped by Sir Thomas More. Perhaps More felt that his hopes for Clement were realized at this time and later since Clement (who married Margaret Gigs, lived in the Bucklersbury house which had been More's home, and was More's host on the Sunday when his presence in London enabled officials to serve the summons which led to his imprisonment) became the king's physician, attended Bishop Fisher when the latter was a prisoner in the Tower, and had a distinguished career as a physician.

As both Herde and Clement studied medicine, they probably had the help of both More and Linacre in entering this profession. Probably Sir Thomas Elyot had the help of More, at least informally, in his Greek studies and again the help of More and Linacre in the study of medicine which he described in the preface to the second edition of *The Castle of Health*. There Elyot explained that before he was twenty years old one of the most renowned physicians in England had read unto him works of Galen, Johannicius, and Hippocrates. Later he had himself read many other books on medicine. There is no reason to doubt that he referred to Linacre.

More and several other friends took an interest in the career of Thomas Lupset, who had started his education as Colet's "boy" in his house, had been taught by William Lily in Colet's school, and when he was about thirteen, had been given a benefice in the diocese of Norwich, probably through the influence of Colet. About 1512 or 1513, when Lupset had become a student at Cambridge and was helping Erasmus edit his Jerome and his New Testament, Erasmus reported to More that Lupset had rejected all the "sophistical books" and had chosen Greek; he added, "When the occasion arises, spare no pains to act your part." About 1517 Erasmus was suggesting to Lupset that he become a professor in the College of Three Languages at Louvain. During the summer of 1517 Lupset saw through the press of Rube, in Paris, Linacre's translation of *De sanitate tuenda* and supervised the edition of More's *Utopia* which came from the press of Gilles de Gourmont. During this editorial work he met Budé, who wrote to Linacre praising his character and scholarship; and though the detail may be somewhat irrelevant, when he returned to France the next year he had in his charge a pair of greyhounds sent as a gift from More to Budé. In 1519 Lupset was named in Colet's will; he was to be remembered at the discretion of the executors and to have such books from Colet's library as he needed to complete his education.

In the spring of 1520 More wrote Erasmus that Lupset had succeeded Clement as a reader at Corpus Christi College; in 1522 Lupset was nominated by the king for a pension from the Abbot of St. Mary's in York. It would not be surprising if More had furthered both these appointments. In the 1520's Lupset spent some time as a tutor of Thomas Winter, Wolsey's natural son, probably but not certainly by More's suggestion. He also tutored other young men before his untimely death in 1530.

Richard Croke is said to have had the basis of his Greek education from Grocyn but if so, it was in London; and perhaps Grocyn helped finance his education in Paris. About 1511 when Grocyn was studying at Cambridge, Erasmus asked Colet to send money to help him, but Colet refused. Probably Croke had received some help from Bishop Fisher: when the university made its plan to honor Fisher on the anniversary of his death, whenever that should be, Croke objected; as a result he was denounced by Thomas Baker, a historian of St. John's College, as a wretch who had once eaten Fisher's bread and who lacked gratitude. About 1518 More was writing Croke a letter full of affection, telling him that both he and Pace had talked to the king about the position Croke wished to secure. About that time Croke was appointed as a Greek professor at Cambridge. Later Croke spent some time, in the 1520's, as a tutor to the Duke of Richmond, the natural son of Henry VIII. It is probable that More recommended him to this position.

John Palsgrave, schoolmaster to "my lady princess" (Mary, sister of Henry VIII), possibly a first cousin of Charles Brandon, and a relative of Sir Richard Wingfield, had some interesting connections with Sir Thomas More. Palsgrave's biographer states definitely that More presented Palsgrave to the living of Alderton in 1520; to a similar position in the village of Holbrook, near Ipswich, in 1523; and to the living of Keyston, Huntingdonshire, in 1524.[20] About 1525 Palsgrave became a tutor to the Duke of Richmond and a member of the Council of the North, with the young duke as its nominal head. Though we do not seem to have precise evidence that More recommended him for the position as tutor, we do know that he wrote More for support in carrying out principles of education which William Parr, Erasmus, More, and certain classical writers had agreed upon. He asked More to use his best manner and to confirm the king in the good opinion he already had to have the boy educated.

[20] *The Comedy of Acolastus*, Introduction, p. xviii.

Probably More helped John Heywood by introducing him to the court, as A. W. Reed suggested, in his *Early Tudor Drama*, Chapter II, "The Heywoods." It is probable that More had some influence on the king's letter in 1523, asking that Heywood be admitted to the Freedom of the City of London; on the appointment of Heywood, January 20, 1530, as measurer of linen cloth; and on his transfer from the Stationers' to the more important Mercers' Company. Later Heywood, as musician and dramatist, was associated with the children of St. Paul's and perhaps with the children of the Chapel Royal; in some of these positions he worked with John Redford. But about 1523 Heywood had married More's niece, Joan Rastell; and it is uncertain whether More was helping a deserving young scholar or aiding a member of his family, or doing both.

Sir Thomas More gave as generously of his time, means, and influence to help young Vives, the Spanish scholar, as he had given to any young Englishman. Vives was in England a half dozen times, from May, 1523, to about April, 1524; from October, 1524, through April, 1525; from February to May, 1526; from April to June, 1527; from October, 1527, to April, 1528; and in November, 1528, he returned as a member of the counsel to Queen Catherine.

More and Vives had met first at Bruges in the latter part of August, 1520. Cranevelt introduced the two, but Erasmus had already given More information about Vives; More wrote Erasmus from Canterbury, perhaps on the way home, that he had high hopes of something for Vives from the Cardinal. In August, 1521, More again met Vives on the Continent. By July 7, 1522, when Vives dated his dedication of the *Civitas dei* to Henry VIII, he had definite hopes of going to England to offer the king this work in person. He hoped, Henry de Vocht says, to be appointed a court scholar through the influence of Queen Catherine, Fisher, and More.

On Vives' first trip to England, More supplied his personal needs, gave him understanding and sympathy, and used his influence for him at court. On the second trip, Vives was More's guest for the month of April, 1525, on terms of intimate friendship. Vives did secure the Wolsey readership which More had earlier mentioned to Erasmus. The king and queen stopped to see Vives at Oxford late in 1523 and invited him to court for the Christmas holidays. He wrote books for the queen and the Princess Mary; he addressed a book on education to William Blount, Lord Mountjoy, for his son Charles. By 1524 his published work had given him a sound reputation; he had the friendship of Linacre, Tunstal, Latimer, and Fisher, as well as that of Erasmus, Blount, and More, the friendship of the king and queen, and he was on both the royal pension lists. Vives' relationship to More's family is emphasized by a chapter on salutations in his book on letter writing. Using More as one of several examples, he advised a reader to begin by greeting him and then his children but especially "my Margaret Roper whom . . . I loved no less than if she had been my own sister." [21]

Of course Vives lost royal favor later because he dared to befriend Catherine and to ask Henry to keep peace with other nations and not to separate from his wife. But his pensions, his friendships, and his readership, which he had secured by 1524, seem to have resulted from the influence used by Sir Thomas More for a young scholar and educator.

The record of More's help to young scholars includes two letters between Fisher and More, possibly in 1521. Fisher wrote asking More to remember his Cambridge scholars:

We have very few friends at Court who have the will and the power to commend our interests to the King's Majesty, and among them we reckon you the chief; for hitherto, even when you were of lower rank, you have always shown the greatest favour to us. We rejoice that now you are raised to the dignity of Knighthood and become so intimate with the King . . . for we know that you will continue to show us the same favour. Please now give your help to this young man, who is well versed in theology and a zealous preacher to the people. He puts his hopes in your influence with our noble King and in your willingness to accept my recommendation.

<hr />

[21] Henry de Vocht, *Monumenta humanistica Lovaniensia: Texts and Studies about Louvain Humanists* (Louvain, 1934), pp. 1–42. This work is the source for the three paragraphs on Vives' connections with England. For the comment on Margaret Roper see Vives, *De conscribendis epistolis* (Basel, 1536), leaf 40a.

More replied that he had so wrought with the king that he would probably raise no obstacle. He added: "Whatever influence I have with the King—it is very little, but such as it is—is as freely at your disposal for yourself or your scholar, as a house is to its owner." [22] The implication of the letters is that More helped many young scholars from Cambridge, whom we shall never know by name; and he must have helped also many others from Oxford.

CAMBRIDGE AND ST. JOHN'S COLLEGE

The ideas of Sir Thomas More and his friends and the ideas of Roger Ascham, in spite of a cleavage in religion, have much in common. One answer to the question whether there was any direct influence between the groups is found in the connections between Fisher and Erasmus and in the joint influence of three men— Erasmus, Fisher, and Metcalfe—upon Cambridge and upon St. John's College.[23]

Bishop John Fisher became vice-chancellor of Cambridge University in 1501 and chancellor in 1504. He was re-elected annually as chancellor for ten years and was then elected to the post for life. The university refused to have any other chancellor during his imprisonment, and he officially held the office until the day of his execution in 1535.

In spite of his rigid early training in Beverley, Yorkshire, and his university training at Michaelhouse, Cambridge ("one of the most monastic and conservative of our English colleges," according to Mullinger), he brought about great changes at Cambridge and had a widespread influence.

First, his position as chancellor gave him great power. It was his duty to summon the convocation of the regents or teachers; to convene both houses; to consider all affairs affecting the general interest of the university; to give assent to all graces or degrees

[22] Rogers, *The Correspondence*, nos. 104, 105. See the last main statement of More's letter: "non minus profecto libere quam sua cuique domus patebit." For translation see Stapleton, *Life*, pp. 47–48.

[23] James Bass Mullinger, *The University of Cambridge . . . to . . . 1535* (Cambridge, 1873); Thomas Baker, *History of the College of St. John the Evangelist*, ed. by John E. B. Mayor, 2 vols. (Cambridge, 1869). These well-indexed volumes contain most of the facts for the discussion which follows. For Baker, see index in vol. II.

before they could be proposed or passed; to preside in his own court, hearing and deciding all cases except atrocious acts or those against the public peace, in which a scholar was concerned; and to be present at the university "during the continuance of the reading of the masters."

Second, with the help of the Lady Margaret, he originated the divinity readerships and the plan of public preaching connected with the readerships. Thus he revived the idea of simple, earnest sermons aimed to affect the lives of listeners.

Third, having persuaded the Lady Margaret to found colleges and having helped her secure the consent of her son, Henry VII, to divert to this purpose funds she had intended for the Abbey of Westminster, Fisher established Christ's College for her. He planned the college, supervised its building, drew up its statutes, and became a "visitor" or supervisor for the term of his life. He provided for students of promise who intended to devote themselves to literature (the *bonas artes*) and the sacred profession; he arranged for lectures on dialectics, on logic, on philosophy, and on the poets and orators.

Fourth, Fisher established St. John's College for the Lady Margaret also, but without him that college would never have come into existence. She had provided in her will the funds for the college; but after her death, less than two months after the death of Henry VII, it was found that the codicil covering this particular gift had not been sealed. Fisher was one of several executors, but he was the "sole or principal agent in overcoming these difficulties." He waged and won a fight against the indifference or hostility of Henry VIII, the slowness of the Pope, and perhaps the opposition of Wolsey, who was interested in Oxford. He did lose part of the Lady Margaret's gift, but he secured funds from several other decayed foundations. Thus he brought to birth St. John's College; its charter was granted in 1511, and Fisher attended its formal opening in 1516.

Bishop Fisher drew up the statutes for St. John's College; they were "identical in tenor" with those of Christ's College and thus they included the emphasis upon the poets and orators, or the *bonas artes*. Fisher was a "visitor," making inspections at regular intervals, and had much to do with its later administration. He helped in selecting the first two masters, Robert Shorton and Alan Percy, whose terms together covered about two years. After Percy presented his resignation to Fisher on All Saints' Day, 1518, Nicholas Metcalfe "was constituted master by the Bishop of Rochester . . . and the rest of the executors." Metcalfe remained master of the college until 1537.

Like Fisher, Nicholas Metcalfe was from Yorkshire; he had been Fisher's chaplain for many years, probably from about 1500; and about 1513 or 1515, if not earlier, he had become the archdeacon to Fisher as bishop of Rochester. An archdeacon, the chief assistant to a bishop, is appointed by the bishop; he superintends the rural deans, holds the lowest ecclesiastical court, and has the power of spiritual censure. The two men had been associated about eighteen years or more when Fisher helped choose him as master of St. John's; and the subsequent glory of St. John's College came from their cooperative effort. The two men greatly increased the revenues of the college; as Baker says, they were both from "the same northern county" and thus they drew many gifts from Yorkshire.

The influence of Nicholas Metcalfe on St. John's College has been summarized by Thomas Baker, the historian of that college, and by Roger Ascham. Baker called Metcalfe a man of "sufficient abilities and tolerable acquirements in most sorts of learning . . ." and one who encouraged learning in others both readily and impartially. When he called scholars to his lodging to dispute, the best ones were encouraged and "if indigent, they had moneys conveyed to them into their studies, from unknown hands, but undoubtedly from his; of which Sir John Cheke was, I suppose, an instance." [24]

Roger Ascham gave Nicholas Metcalfe high praise for his impartial encouragement of learning, his attitude as "a father to euery one in that Colledge," and his supplying money to all needy students who had "wil to goodnes or wit to learning . . .": "I am witnes my selfe, that mony many tymes was brought into yong mens studies by strangers whom they knew not. . . . He

[24] Baker, I, 107–8.

was a Papist in deede, but would to God, amonges all vs Protestants, I might once see but one that would winne like praise in doing like good for the aduauncement of learning and vertue." [25]

Though Bishop Fisher's influence at Cambridge was outstanding, to determine the nature of that influence we need to examine the relationship between him and Erasmus. In 1505–6 Erasmus' name was listed in the University of Cambridge grace books for the degree of doctor of theology. Whether the degree was conferred or not, its proposal required the assent of the chancellor; hence Fisher must have known Erasmus and his work by that time. Erasmus became also the fourth divinity reader under the plan established by Fisher and the Lady Margaret, Fisher himself having been the first reader. Erasmus was residing at Cambridge much of the time from 1511 to 1514, the years when his letters were often written from Queen's College. In the years from 1511 to 1518 or 1520, letters passed between them frequently, the last one recorded by P. S. Allen being one from Erasmus to Fisher in September, 1524. The letters include Erasmus' accounts of his work on Isaiah and the New Testament, Fisher's desire to learn Greek and his partial success in doing so with the help of Erasmus, Fisher's criticisms but his real approval of the New Testament. The two wrote as intimate, intellectual friends, describing new books they were reading and giving news of mutual friends.

Most important to this discussion are the letters in which Fisher implied the value of Erasmus to Cambridge or his need of advice: "I look upon you as necessary to the university and will not suffer you to want as long as there is anything to spare out of my own poor means." Again he said: "When you start . . . to Basle do come our way, as I have need of your advice. . . ." In another letter Fisher said: ". . . and hasten your return to us, which will be welcome to everybody. . . ." [26]

With these direct contacts from 1511 to 1514, with visits and teaching Greek to Bishop Fisher, and with personal letters continuing into the 1520's, Erasmus exerted influence on Bishop Fisher and on Cambridge.

[25] Ascham, The Scholemaster (London, 1570), Second book, leaf 54.
[26] Nichols, The Epistles, II, nos. 255, 327, 416. See also nos. 400, 468, 568. In III, see nos. 625, 734, 742, and index.

First, Erasmus created a new interest in the interpretation of scripture and in preaching, partly at least through the divinity readership which he held. The evidence appears in letters some years later from Erasmus' friends at Cambridge.

Second, Erasmus taught Greek at Cambridge, probably with some pay secured for him by the university, but without taking fees from students and without being listed officially as a reader in Greek. He seems to have given Fisher an understanding of the need for Greek, a desire to learn it himself, and a willingness to further its teaching in the university. Evidence for this influence appears not only in the letters between Erasmus and Fisher but in letters written by Henry Bullock and other friends to Erasmus after he had left Cambridge. Probably the influence of Erasmus and Fisher is corroborated by More's 1518 letter of rebuke to the University of Oxford; More used Cambridge as a good example of zeal for Greek, saying that its scholars were raising funds to pay for such teaching, and that it was being welcomed, not attacked with hostility.

Third, Erasmus did leave a few friends or even disciples behind him at Cambridge—men who wrote him later praising him for his influence on the study of Greek or divinity. Among them were Henry Bullock, John Watson, Robert Aldrich, John Brian, William Gonell, John Vaughan, and John Fawne. Three of these special friends of Erasmus—Fawne, Watson, and Bullock—became Fisher's vice-chancellors at periods between 1512 and 1524.[27]

Fourth, it seems highly probable, according to Mullinger, that Fisher added the poets and orators, or the *bonas artes* to his curricula for Christ's College and for St. John's College, because he was influenced by Erasmus.

Certainly some great changes took place in Cambridge at this time. Fisher himself pointed out a loss of lethargy, in his oration of 1506 to the royal visitors. Erasmus, in a letter which Mullinger cited, gave the credit to Bishop Fisher for the peaceful introduction of Greek, for the theological influences, especially for the sincere preaching fostered by the Lady Margaret professorship, and

---

[27] Nichols, *The Epistles*, II, nos. 436, 441, 557; III, no. 781. For others see indexes of the three volumes.

for the golden mean which united traditional studies with the "good letters" of the classics.

In another letter, written to Henry Bullock from Fisher's episcopal palace at Rochester in 1516, Erasmus summed up the change from the old "dictates" of Aristotle and the questions of Scotus, to the study of good letters, mathematics, Greek, and a "renovated" Aristotle. Erasmus continued: "Now I ask, what has been the result to the university? It has become so flourishing that it may vie with the first schools of the age, and possesses men, compared with whom those old teachers appear mere shadows of theologians." [28]

When Mullinger said that Fisher included the *bonas artes* in his curricula through the influence of Erasmus, he added: "The various evidence . . . of their interchange of opinion on such subjects would seem to indicate that Erasmus' influence over Fisher, and through Fisher over Cambridge at large, was far greater and more enduring than their respective biographers would lead us to suppose." [29]

While Erasmus, Fisher, and Metcalfe were exerting their influence, the center of interest in "good letters" shifted to Cambridge. About 1490 to 1500 the center had been Oxford, with frequent mention of Magdalen College. Though Wolsey had imported scholars from Cambridge for his Oxford College and had done whatever he could in other ways to make it supreme, St. John's College became the great center of learning. About 1535 to 1537, when Fisher had been executed and Metcalfe was eased out by the new chancellor, Thomas Cromwell, St. John's changed from the Catholic to the Protestant point of view. But "good letters," with many ideas, remained.

The two famous teachers of classics in the mid-century, Sir John Cheke and Roger Ascham, studied at St. John's College during the mastership of Nicholas Metcalfe. Cheke received his B.A. degree there in 1529 or 1530. Ascham entered as a student about 1530, took degrees in 1533 and 1537, and was a fellow of the

---

[28] Nichols, *The Epistles*, II, no. 441, p. 331.
[29] Mullinger, *The University of Cambridge*, p. 497.

college from 1534 to 1554. Cheke became the tutor and also the secretary of state to Edward VI and is said also to have tutored the Princess Elizabeth. Ascham taught her before she became queen, and after she was on the throne, read Greek with her daily for some time, up to the date of his death. It is ironic that the children of Henry VIII had their education under men trained by Nicholas Metcalfe and Bishop Fisher.

William Cecil, later Lord Burghley, statesman, and patron of many literary men, entered St. John's College in May, 1535. Though Fisher was already in the Tower, Metcalfe remained the master until 1537. Cecil remained at St. John's about six years, became the friend of Cheke and Ascham, made an imprudent but apparently happy marriage to Mary, sister of John Cheke, and was recalled by his father before he had taken a degree. He is said to have carried with him always, to the day of his death, Cicero's *De officiis,* because he considered it "sufficient . . . to make both a scholar and an honest man." In his will he left a small endowment to St. John's College, "only as a memory" of the place where, he said, his happiest days had been spent.

Perhaps no action for education, taken by any members of the More circle, had a greater influence on the future of England than the founding of St. John's College, Cambridge.

IDEAS IN WRITINGS

MORE'S COMMENTS

More's ideas on education have necessarily been developed in the first section of this chapter because they were often directions or suggestions to his school. He wrote no treatises on education, unless his letter to Gonell could be called a treatise; and its substance belongs in the next chapter on the education of women. His views on the extremes of dialectic and the scholastic questions, too, were illustrated in Chapter III, since they had a vital relation to religious reform.

But one comment on dialectic in his letter to Dorp had larger implications. More was defending somewhat the English universities as compared with those of Paris and Louvain, which, he said, he had visited about seven years before, not long, but long enough to find out the subjects taught and the methods of teaching:

I will not . . . deny that our students owe much to James Lefèvre of Paris, who has been welcomed everywhere by the happier intellects and saner judgments among us, as the restorer of true Dialectic and true Philosophy, especially that founded upon Aristotle. . . . It is much to be wished that the students of Louvain and also of Paris would all accept the commentaries of Lefèvre upon Aristotle's Dialectic. Their teaching, if I am not mistaken, would be less controversial and more accurate.[30]

More made a satirical and secular comment on dialectic in the *Utopia* also:

But as they in all thynges be almoste equall to our olde auncyente clerkes, so our newe Logiciens in subtyll inuentyons haue farre passed and gone beyonde them. For they haue not deuysed one of all those rules of restryctyons, amplyfycatyons, and supposytyons, very wittilye inuented in the small Logycalles, whyche heare oure chyldren in euerye place do learne. Furthermore they were neuer yet able to fynde out the second intentyons; in so muche that none of them all coulde euer see man hymselfe in commen, as they call hym; thoughe he be (as yow knowe) bygger than euer was annye gyaunte. . . .[31]

Utopian education had some striking resemblances to the ideas which More, Erasmus, and Vives expressed elsewhere and to the practices in More's school. A few Utopians were freed of all other obligations and "appointed only to learninge"; these were the ones who, even from their childhood, had shown "a singuler towardnes, a fyne witte, and a minde apte to good learning. . . ." But all children were given an education and thus had a chance to prove their worth; and "the better parte of the people, bothe men and women, throughe owte all theire hole lyffe, doo bestowe in learninge" all the time left from their physical work (a Utopian day of six hours). More added that they were taught in their native tongue, which was copious, pleasant to the ear, and exact enough for expressing all the ideas of a man's mind. These phrases are

---

[30] Nichols, *The Epistles*, II, no. 350, gives a translation which includes this passage. See Rogers, *The Correspondence*, no. 15, p. 36, and the last sentence of the Latin, which reads: "Esset ea disciplina (ni fallor) et minus vtrisque rixosa, et paulo repurgatior."

[31] More, *Utopia*, ed. by J. H. Lupton (Oxford, 1895), pp. 184–86.

similar to the ones More used in defending the English translation of the Bible.

The curriculum seemed to parallel that of More's own school in many ways. The subjects were music, a modified logic (instead of the extremes satirized in the passage quoted above), astronomy, mathematics, nature study, medicine, and philosophy. They had cleverly devised instruments for the study of astronomy, but they avoided irrational astrology. In the study of nature they tried to discover the causes of all things, including "the orygynall begynnyng and nature of heuen and of the wordle [sic]"; in some things they held the opinion of the old philosophers and in others they had made new discoveries. Their philosophic ideas were systematic and rather complete, probably as complete, More seemed to imply, as uncorrupted people could develop without the Christian religion. Although the Utopians were very healthy people, they valued the study of medicine as perhaps the "mooste profytable" and the "goodlieste" part of philosophy. In this opinion they were like Linacre, Erasmus, Herde, Clement, and More himself. Because the Utopians lived outside the influences of Western Europe, they could not emphasize Latin; but they were beginning to attack the Greek language and literature with all its ideas.

The basis for the Utopian emphasis upon education was the concern with "the free liberty of the mind and garnisshing of the same. For herin they suppose the felicity of this liffe to consist." [32]

Some other general remarks on education in *Utopia* reveal serious ideas, not mere flights of fancy. Hythlodaye became eloquent when he discussed the lack of proper education in England as a cause of crime and deplored the tendency to make thieves and then punish them—even by severe penalties which violated the law of God. The Utopians avoided such errors; their children, while still young and pliant, learned opinions profitable for the commonweal. These ideas are completely secular, of course, as the whole of *Utopia* is secular, in contrast to the letters written to More's school, which are imbued with Christianity. But the fundamental ideas remained the same, whether adapted to family and school or to a Utopian kingdom.

[32] *Utopia*, pp. 183–87, 217, 152.

In his letter to the University of Oxford, 1518, cited in other connections, More's main purpose was to defend a liberal education and the study of Greek at Oxford. He made what might be called a double-barrelled attack: first, the sermon against Greek (which had led More to write the letter, probably with the king's full approval) was a degradation of the sacred office of preaching; and second, opposition to classical learning, coming from a man connected with the university, was a sign of ignorance and folly. More insisted that classical learning is helpful to lawyers, for whom "the wisdom that comes from the study of humane things is requisite"; and that it is vital to theologians, since the study of the classical poets, orators, and historians helps in preaching sermons to reach the common man. He summarized our debt to the Greeks when he said that we owe them "all our precision, in the liberal arts generally and in theology particularly. . . . Take philosophy, for example. If you leave out Cicero and Seneca, the Romans either wrote their philosophy in Greek or translated it from Greek." In spite of recent and better translations, he said, "not half of Greek learning has yet been made available to the West"; and no matter how good the translation, "the text of the original still remains a surer and more convincing presentation." [33]

THE YOUNG TEACHERS

The young teachers who had personal connections with More, Colet, and Erasmus seem, so far as they can be checked, to have stated the same general principles of education. Richard Croke, who had been helped in his own educational career by Grocyn, Pace, Fisher, Erasmus, and More, stated educational theories in his letters to the king and to Wolsey, while he was a tutor to the Duke of Richmond. Though some of these letters are concerned merely with the conflicts and the waste of supplies in the young duke's household, one or two emphasized sound training in Latin and in writing a good style, and a preference for liberal training above sports even for the son of a king.[34]

[33] T. S. K. Scott-Craig, "Thomas More's 1518 Letter to the University of Oxford," *Ren. News,* I, no. 2 (1948), p. 22, and *passim;* Rogers, *The Correspondence,* no. 60.

[34] *L. and P.,* IV, nos. 1948, 3135; also 1947, 1954. Croke was complaining also about Sir William Parr and his general conduct.

But the young teacher who had most to say about principles of education was John Palsgrave, a tutor to the Duke of Richmond. His letter "Devised to bee sente vnto Master More" was a plea for help in carrying out principles of education. Palsgrave reported that he had been teaching Latin and Greek together, after reading classic authors and Erasmus and asking advice from "Doctor Stevens," More, Horman, Gonell, and Rightwise; but since More had once shown him that a little Latin would serve, so that the boy might have French, he had been trying not to give the boy too much Latin. The boy had a "singular wytt," that is, a capacity which should be developed. But the "schavyn folk," even those in high positions, did not wish him to be learned; and callers enticed him to hunting with hawks and hounds and to other pastimes. Would More please confirm the king in his desire to have his son educated? Palsgrave reported that he did not create a fear of correction in the boy nor keep him at study so long that he was overcome by tediousness; he did use all possible allurements to learning, so that his officers "wott not whyther I lerne hym or playe with hym." Although he had managed to give the boy an understanding of Greek and Latin grammar, there had been one bad handicap, the "barbarus tong" of the one who taught him his matins, just as Quintilian and Erasmus had said. Palsgrave thought learning becoming to a nobleman, but the "hyghe schavyn" folk thought it nonsense for men of high rank. A short letter could not express better the theories of education accepted by the members of the More circle.[35]

Palsgrave also wrote about his educational problems with the Duke of Richmond to Lady Elizabeth Talboys, the boy's mother, and to Henry VIII. To the mother he reported that Henry VIII had asked him, in the presence of Parr and Page, to bring up his son in virtue and learning. Palsgrave's letter to the king repeated some of the things he had said to More but also spoke of having the boy's teeth looked after, to cure his lisp; he wished to have a painter as a help in teaching, and since he had heard that the king meant to use in another way the painter about whom Doctor Taite had "motioned" him, he asked permission to secure one through

[35] Rogers, *The Correspondence*, no. 168, for the letter to More.

members of the Privy Council: "it is a great furtherance in learning
to know the names of things by their pictures, and the want of a
painter 'causeth both him and me to stay.'" [36] From this request
for a painter, some scholars deduce that Palsgrave was far ahead
of his time; but he was merely repeating what Erasmas, Vives, and
other men recommended as standard practice.

ERASMUS AND VIVES

Since Erasmus and Vives wrote complete treatises on education,
were in substantial agreement on nearly all important ideas, and
represent, as teacher and student, the older and younger members
of the More circle, their views will first be summarized together.
Where they seem to disagree, Vives had sometimes made more use
of his practical experience in teaching, based his views on changing
conditions in the world, or had perhaps analyzed a practical idea
more shrewdly.

Both Erasmus and Vives believed that human beings can be
successfully educated because they have reason "innate in the soul
from its beginning" and also free will, to help them change from
rude, unformed creatures to men and to beings not far below God
himself, and because they have the power to discover and to use
knowledge and goodness. Concerned with the nature of human
beings, they used the term *nature* in two main ways; first, the
rational element in all human beings; second, the individual ability
of a particular man, including his natural bent or inclination. They
believed that a boy with the ability and the desire for a liberal
education should be given the chance to have such an education,
no matter how low his rank or how deep his poverty. They believed in some form of public responsibility for the education of
those who needed help but with slightly different approaches to a
solution of the problem. They deplored scolding, beating, and
any form of physical punishment as a means to compel learning,
except for a few extreme cases where all other methods failed.
They emphasized allurements to learning: kindness, praise, judicious
recreation; play and games as methods of teaching; stories, fables,
and jokes to spice uninteresting facts; and graphic devices of many

[36] *L. and P.*, IV, no. 5807, no. 5806 ii; also no. 5808.

kinds. They cautioned against the overcrowding of young minds, using vivid but not highly original figures of speech to drive home the idea. They discussed notebooks and paper books, and word lists that perhaps substituted for dictionaries.

Erasmus stressed three factors in education: *nature, training, practice;* or *natura, ratio,* and *exercitatio.*[37] Vives named four factors: *natural capacity, judgment, memory, application,* or *ingenio, iudicio, memoria,* and *studio.*[38] They stressed the importance of the early years for inculcating wisdom and virtue, for making general progress in learning instead of wasting time in idleness, and for teaching Latin and Greek grammar, with the correct pronunciation of Latin. They were in general agreement, with some differences, about teaching Latin and Greek together. Alike, they deplored idleness and the wasting of time in senseless or "naughty" pastimes.

They stressed the same subjects: Greek and Latin grammar as the gates to important knowledge; astronomy, arithmetic, geography, history, and nature study. They considered logic and rhetoric as rules of expression to be learned by writing and speaking, not as mere parts of grammar. They admitted value in the dialectic of Aristotle but deplored the verbiage that had collected around it; they wished to use logic as a means for testing the truth, not for silencing an opponent or displaying verbal skill. They made lists of books to be used as tools in learning or lists of preferred books for appreciating the literature of the Romans and Greeks. They differed in details when they discussed subjects of study, as they expressed small differences in other details of education. They considered formal teaching preferable to learning by experience, in acquiring skill and knowledge and in forming moral and Christian character.

[37] Erasmus, *Opera omnia,* I, 496 F-497 A: "Tota vero ratio felicitatis humanae tribus potissimum rebus constat, natura, ratione, & exercitatione. Naturam appello docilitatem ac propensionem penitus insitam ad res honestas. Rationem voco doctrinam, quae monitis constat & praeceptis. Exercitationem dico usum ejus habitus quem natura insevit, ratio provexit. Natura rationem desiderat, exercitatio nisi ratione gubernetur, multis periculis atque erroribus est obnoxia."

[38] J. L. Vives, *Opera* (Basel, 1555), I, 518. "Quator rebus constat eruditio: ingenio, iudicio, memoria, studio; tria prima, cedo unde habes, nunquid non ex Deo? Si qua est docti laus, de postremo petitur, quae res infima est omniū et leuissima. . . ." See also Foster Watson, *Vives: On Education,* p. 275.

They agreed in preferring the inductive method for much teaching of grammar, and they recommended some kind of double translation as a means of acquiring correctness and fluency in writing and speaking Latin.

They agreed, perhaps completely, about the importance of a good master and about his qualifications: sound learning; excellent character so that no word or gesture of his would influence a child to evil; and such pedagogical virtues as an understanding of the difference between children and adults and between individual children, and skill in using praise and creating a desire to learn— a master who could handle children like an ideal father who was also a teacher. They agreed on the need of adequate pay: Erasmus complained that men of wealth were willing to pay a groom or a cook more than they paid a philosopher-teacher; Vives suggested an amount, to be paid by the state, which a wicked man would scorn but a good man would desire. Both stressed the same aims of education: virtue, piety, knowledge and wisdom, personal satisfaction from knowing and doing good, and the ability and willingness to serve the commonweal.

These ideas expressed by Erasmus in two works *De ratione studii* and *De pueris instituendis* and by Vives in his work *De tradendis disciplinis* might be considered the core of the educational ideas held by the men of the More circle. No other man expressed all of them in complete detail since no other man wrote a comparable treatise on education. The actions of More, Colet, and others agreed with these fundamentals; and no person in the circle expressed disagreement with any important idea which Erasmus and Vives advocated.

ERASMUS

Erasmus phrased with unusual clarity some of the ideas on which he and Vives agreed. One example is his explanation of nature:

By the nature of man, we mean, as a rule, that which is common to man as such: the characteristic . . . of being guided by reason. But we may mean something less broad than this: the characteristic peculiar to each personality, which we call individuality. Thus one child may show a native bent to mathematics, another to divinity, another to rhetoric or poetry, another to war. So strongly disposed are certain types of mind to certain studies that they cannot be won to others; the very attempt . . . sets up a positive repulsion. . . . The master will be wise to observe such natural inclination, such individuality in the early stages . . . since we learn most easily the things which conform to it.[39]

He became eloquent in his diatribes against beating. He used many examples, one of his own punishment as a boy and one of a good boy who had committed no wrong but was whipped severely by a master who thought he must break his spirit. Men are freed from a servile state, he said, by humane control:

Do schoolmasters consider how many earnest, studious natures have been marred by treatment of this type—the hangman type—crushed into indifference? Masters who are conscious of their own incompetence are generally the worst floggers. . . . It is, indeed, the mark of the servile nature to be drilled by fear. . . . Teaching by beating, therefore, is not a liberal education. Nor should the schoolmaster indulge in too strong and too frequent *language* of blame. . . . You may quote against me the old proverb, "He that spareth the rod hateth his own son." . . . But I do not accept it as true for Christians today. . . . Lycon, the philosopher, sets forward these two spurs to industry: shame and desire for praise. . . . Let these, then, be the schoolmaster's weapons today.[40]

Not every classicist of the period agreed with the men of the More circle in their dislike for physical punishment, as Thomas Tusser indicated when he compared the methods of John Redford at St. Paul's School with the beatings given him by Nicholas Udall at Eton—fifty-three stripes for a small fault or no fault at all.[41] But Lupset agreed with Erasmus and others when he advised young men not to be scourgers, no matter who followed the practice, but to cast the rod into the fire.[42]

[39] Erasmus, *Opera omnia*, see footnote 37 above, also I, 499 C: "Jam quod de natura dictum est, non est simplex. Est enim natura speciei communis, velut hominis natura est, ratione uti. Sed est natura huic aut illi peculiaris, veluti quosdam Mathematicis disciplinis, alios Theologiae, hos Rhetoricae, aut Poeticae, illos militiae natos dicas. Tana vi rapiuntur ad haec studia, ut nulla ratione possint deterreri."

[40] Erasmus, *De pueris instituendis*, as trans. by W. H. Woodward, *Desiderius Erasmus concerning the Aim and Method of Education*, pp. 206–9.

[41] Thomas Tusser, *Five Hundred Points of Good Husbandry* (London, 1573), Fol. 89 verso. These verses appear at the end of an imperfect copy.

[42] Lupset, "An Exhortacion to Young Men," ed. by John Archer Gee, *The Life and Works of Thomas Lupset* (New Haven, 1928), p. 257.

Erasmus was definite about public education: "Which brings me to claim it as a duty incumbent on statesmen and churchmen alike to provide . . . a due supply of men qualified to educate the youth of the nation. It is a public obligation in no way inferior, say, to the ordering of the army. . . . And if the community be backward in this respect, yet should every head of a household do all that he can to provide for the education of his own. . . . But the liberality of the rich can be . . . exercised here, in enabling innate powers to attain their due development by removing the hindrance imposed by poverty." [43]

In *The Instruction of a Christian Prince* also Erasmus explained that one duty of every ruler is to see that all the youth, both boys and girls, are educated in either public or private schools, since the main hope of the state lies in education. [44]

His examples of graphic devices were specific and sometimes individual. He recommended charts of genealogy and of geographical facts, tables of syntax and prosody in large type on the walls, striking quotations at the tops of exercise books, proverbs on rings and cups, and sentences on doors and windows. He suggested games of forfeits with prizes and corrections of errors, and with an advanced pupil as a judge. He considered pictures especially helpful in teaching about natural objects. He valued the plan of making biscuits in the form of letters and allowing a child to eat a biscuit when he learned a letter. He mentioned an English father whose boy aimed with bow and arrow at Greek or Latin letters painted on a target; any hit was rewarded by a cherry for the little archer. [45]

Erasmus expressed himself with clarity and power when he spoke of logic and dialectic, though again he was in agreement with Vives and other men in the More circle: "If anyone thinks that dialectic should be added, I shall not object so long as he learns it from Aristotle and not from that chattering breed of sophists, and does not, as it were, grow old (as Gellius says) on the rocks of the Sirens." [46] Erasmus used vivid comparisons, but not original ones,

---

[43] Erasmus, *De pueris instituendis*, pp. 209–10.

[44] Erasmus, *The Education of a Christian Prince*, trans. by Lester K. Born (New York, 1936), pp. 212–13.

[45] W. H. Woodward, *Desiderius Erasmus . . .* trans. of *De ratione studii*, pp. 166, 169, and *De pueris instituendis*, pp. 213, 215.

[46] Erasmus, *Opera omnia*, I, 522, B, C: "Ad haec si quis Dialecticen addendem statuet,

when he urged an early beginning of education: "Then think of the training of a colt, how early it is begun; or of the work of the husbandman, who fashions and trains the sapling. . . ." Again he said: "Handle the wax whilst it is soft; mould the clay whilst it is moist . . . dye the fleece before it gather stains." [47] (Vives, too, said that boys are naturally apes, imitating those in whom they place love and confidence, and their waxen minds receive impressions easily.) [48]

Erasmus left no doubt about his desire to have children treated as children when he said: "Wholly wrong are those masters who expect their little pupils to act as though they were but diminutive adults, who forget the meaning of *youth*, who have no standard of what can be done or be understood except that of their own minds. Such a master will upbraid, exact, punish, as though he were dealing with students as old as himself, and forgets that he was ever himself a child. Pliny warned such a one when he spoke thus to a master: "Remember that your pupil is but a youth still, and that you were once one yourself." [49]

VIVES: INDIVIDUAL IDEAS

In many areas where Vives agreed with Erasmus, he added more specific details or ideas which Erasmus did not express. For example, they agreed on the duty to provide education, but Vives suggested something like a public tax. He urged that a school be established in every township, that teachers with learning and uprightness be

---

non admodum refragabor, modo ab Aristotele eam discat, non ab isto, loquacissimo Sophistarum genere, neque rursum ibi desideat, et velut ad scopulos (ut inquit Gellius) Sirenaeos consenescat." The passage is from *De pueris instituendis.*

[47] Erasmus, *Opera omnia*, I, 494 A. "Itaque juxta Virgilianum oraculum: *Praecipuum jam inde a teneris impende laborem.* Mox tracta ceram dum mollissima est, finge argillam etiamnum udam: imbue liquoribus optimis testam, dum rudis est, tinge lanam dum a fullone nivea venit, nullisque maculis contaminata." For translation see W. H. Woodward, *Desiderius Erasmus* . . . , pp. 183, 187.

[48] Vives, *De tradendis disciplinis,* as trans. by Foster Watson, *Vives: On Education,* pp. 64, 65, 90–91; also Vives, *A very frutefull and pleasant boke called the Instruction of a Christen woman,* trans. by Rycharde Hyrd [Herde] (London, 1529?), for a general discussion of early influences.

[49] Erasmus, *Opera omnia*, I, 509 E. "Protinus instant acerbe, protinus exigunt plenam operam, protinus corrugant frontem, si minus puer expectationi respondeat, et sic moventur, quasi cum adulto rem habeant, videlicet obliti se fuisse pueros. Quanto humanius est quod Plinius admonet quendam feveriorem literatorem: *Memento,* inquit, *et illum adolescentem esse, et te fuisse.*" Or see Woodward's translation, pp. 211–12.

secured, and that salaries be paid from the public treasury. Those
who showed both goodness and a capacity for liberal training should
be provided with higher education. Vives said that at heart he
agreed with Quintilian, who deplored flogging under any conditions, and that he favored praise and rewards; but he admitted
that the pain of a beating might sometimes reclaim a boy from evil.
But he added: "I should prefer this beating to be done as amongst
free men, not harshly or as amongst slaves, unless the boy is of such
a disposition that he has to be incited to his duty by blows like a
slave." [50] Vives gave many kinds of suggestions on individual capacity, recognizing it in methods of teaching, in urging only
capable pupils to go on to higher education, and in allowing slower
pupils more time to do the same work, "for it is not expedient to
have one time for all; nothing would be more unequal than an
equality of that kind." Recognizing differences in character, he
wished to select classics for individual boys—no Ovid for a sensual
boy, no Martial for a jeering boy, no Lucretius for a boy inclined
to impiety, and little Cicero for a vainglorious boy. He made suggestions for adapting language study, nature study, dialectics,
and the investigation of natural causes to both capacity and character. He wished to train in manual and mechanical arts those
unfitted for intellectual work—those whose minds are "stupid,
very dull, rough, and distorted," those who suffer from natural
defects, those of depraved disposition who must be reformed before they are placed with other boys. Parents should not select at
random one son for future education, Vives said; he recommended
a simple, psychological inquiry to determine which minds begin
well but lose interest; which minds observe facts but go no further;
and which ones observe, reason from cause to effect, and go on to
draw conclusions. He recognized individuality enough to say that
things done against desire and under compulsion will be done
"badly and perversely." Like Erasmus, Vives quoted Horace: "say
and do nothing against your natural bent." [51]

Vives was more interested in physical exercise than Erasmus. He

[50] Vives, *De tradendis disciplinis*, pp. 72, 119. See also pp. 71, 118. Erasmus, after all
his tirades against beating, mentioned similar exceptions.
[51] *De tradendis disciplinis*, pp. 59, 124–25, 85, and *passim*.

stressed games combining honor and pleasure, long walks, and more strenuous exercises for older boys. He united nature study, appreciation of natural beauty, and walks in the woods to relieve tedium, give pleasure, strengthen the body, and train the mind in inductive reasoning.[52] He saw that the boy who learned crafts and occupations requiring manual skill was getting an education from experience by using two powers, the mind and the hands; and in combining the two powers, he said, we excel beasts. In matters of practical experience, no matter how much principles are explained, he found that one learns by applying his hands to the work. He sometimes defined experience as the personal knowledge gained by our actions or by all that we have "seen, read, heard of in others." [53]

Vives valued scientific and practical subjects and gave extended suggestions about them. He discussed the mathematical sciences—geometry, arithmetic, music, astronomy—the relation of astronomy to cosmography, the mathematical relation of all these sciences to each other, the practical relation of astronomy to agriculture and to navigation, and the instruments most useful for these studies. He emphasized many subjects as aids to daily living—clothing, housing, eating—all subjects that contribute to health and comfort in public or private life. But these things did not need to be taught in schools; let the learner visit shops and factories and watch craftsmen; let him talk to sailors, soldiers, farmers, smiths, shoemakers, and bakers, since these talks and visits would bring him the knowledge needed by every good citizen. In many connections Vives stressed the inductive approach to knowledge, but perhaps this passage is characteristic:

But I only call that knowledge which we receive when the senses are properly brought to observe things and in a methodical way to which clear reason leads us on, reason so closely connected with the nature of our mind that there is no one who does not accept its lead; or our reasoning is "probable" when it is based on our own experiences or those of others, and confirmed by a judgment, resting upon probable conjecture. The knowledge in the former case is called science, firm and indubitable, and in the latter case, belief or opinion.[54]

[52] *De tradendis disciplinis*, pp. 121–22, 167–71.
[53] *De tradendis disciplinis*, p. 228, and *passim*.
[54] *De tradendis disciplinis*, p. 22, also pp. 201–7, 209–10.

Again he said:

In teaching the arts, we shall collect many experiments and observe the experience of many teachers, so that from them general rules may be formed. If some of the experiments do not agree with the rule, then the reason why this happens must be noted. If the reason is not apparent, and there are some deviations, they must be noted down. If there are more deviations than agreements or an equal number, a dogma must not be established from that fact, but the facts must be transmitted to the astonishment of posterity, so that from astonishment—as has been the case in the past—philosophy may grow.[55]

In many things, in teaching Latin and in formulating ideas on teaching, or training boys to observe nature, Vives tended to begin with the simple, specific, and familiar, and then to proceed to the complex, the general, and the unknown. Thus he made a many-sided application of the inductive method.

When Vives spoke of teaching Latin and Greek together, his comments were penetrating. Erasmus repeated the conventional ideas, it seems, that he read in Quintilian: first, all the knowledge vital to mankind was expressed in those languages; second, the "natural affinity of the two tongues" made it profitable to study them together. He added that Quintilian advised Greek before systematic work in Latin, but proficiency in both was essential. Vives observed that Quintilian was speaking of boys whose vernacular was Latin; hence he said that boys living in countries where they first met Latin in schools should learn Latin with some exactness before they began Greek. After they had a good background in Latin, they might study the two together. Vives added, "If any one should consider the matter with close attention, he will see that my view of teaching and that of Quintilian are alike." [56]

In the teaching of Latin Vives put much emphasis on the use of the vernacular. The teacher should know the mother-tongue of the pupils exactly, so that he might make his instruction clear, easier, and more pleasant. Without this knowledge he might mislead the boys, so that errors would follow them into mature life:

Nor do boys sufficiently understand the use of their own language unless things are explained to them with the greatest clearness. . . .

[55] *De tradendis disciplinis,* pp. 87–88, 163–71.
[56] *De tradendis disciplinis,* p. 98, for his agreement with Quintilian.

The exposition of authors should be marked with ease and clearness. In the beginning it should be in the words of the vernacular and by degrees proceed to Latin. . . .

Let them [the pupils] at first speak in their own tongue, which was born in them in their home, and if they make mistakes in it, let the master correct them. From this start, gradually proceed to speaking in Latin. They will mix up in the vernacular what they have heard . . . or read . . . in Latin, so that at first the language in the school will be a mixture. . . . Let them speak their own language out of doors, so that they may not accustom themselves to speak a hotch-potch of the two languages. . . . By the gradual increase of knowledge at last they will become Latin conversationalists.[57]

If a boy refuses to speak Latin after a year, Vives added, he must be punished according to age and circumstances. Of course Vives considered Latin a living language; he praised it for its richness in words, its sweetness and power, its place in transmitting information, and its value for unity among nations and among Christians.[58] If he emphasized Greek less than Erasmus and More had done fifteen years earlier, perhaps he felt that it needed less defense, since it was established in the universities.

Vives put more emphasis upon spoken or declaimed composition than Erasmus seemed to do, with logic and rhetoric as fundamental in either spoken or written work. When the boys who began speaking in the vernacular, with corrections when necessary, proceeded to Latin (always pure and good Latin), they must never trust practice and their own judgment alone nor place them above the rules. Though Vives stressed more the practice of formal declamation, the pupils were to talk on matters which might be useful in later life; and since they were to "withdraw into a quiet nook to meditate and write orations," it seems that they were to write and to declaim the orations, being careful of pronunciation and voice. Each week the tutor was to criticize one declamation before the whole assembly, considering the subject matter, the speaker, the time, and the people to whom he was pretending to speak, as well as the words, the sentences, and the order and the quality of each argument. This criticism was difficult, Vives admitted, but so im-

[57] *De tradendis disciplinis,* pp. 103–4, 110–11.
[58] *De tradendis disciplinis,* pp. 111, 90–93.

portant that the pupils should take notes, write out the notes later, and engrave the principles in their memories for the future.[59]

Perhaps the most individual emphasis which came from Vives when he discussed the aim of education was the attention he gave to training in thinking and in finding the truth. He criticized Aristotle unfavorably because that philosopher did not always quote correctly, because he twisted the sense, and because he invented ideas of his own merely to answer opponents. Vives believed in using the arts of writing and speech, or all eloquence and all persuasion, to further truth, not to win an argument, as he said many times. He saw the search for truth as an approach to the unified source of all truth, God.

We start by observing nature; then we begin to examine the connections of things, or the "first philosophy"; then we go on to external causes; and "from the external causes we rise, provided of course that we keep the right path, to God, the Father and Author of the whole world." This view of the unity of all truth accounts for Vives' frequent mention of an ideal essence or truth, toward which we grope: in his comments on the *Civitas dei*, he speaks of the "Prince of Nature," who seems to stand for the perfect ruler; and in his *De tradendis disciplinis*, he says that "in nature there is an absolute model. . . ." All truth, he said, is incomplete:

In all natural philosophy the scholar should be told that what he hears is only thought to be true, i.e. so far as the intellect, judgment, experience, and careful study of those who have investigated the matter can ascertain, for it is very seldom that we can affirm anything as absolutely true. . . . Let them [the students] not forget that we very rarely attain actual knowledge; or rather we get none as long as so-called knowledge consists of people's views of it.[60]

Vives was more explicit in his discussion of notebooks or paper books, though Erasmus made some comments about them. Whenever the pupil read a Latin author, Erasmus said, he should notice

[59] *De tradendis disciplinis*, pp. 186–88.
[60] *De tradendis disciplinis*, pp. 172, 167, 88; and for the last two quotations, pp. 168, 214. For dialectics, see 175, 291; for philosophy of nature, 8, 87–88, 167, 172; and for Aristotle, see index.

vocabulary, grammar, ornament, and style, "the notebook being at hand to record them." Probably these notebooks took the place of individual dictionaries, at least with Vives, who complained much about the available dictionaries. In 1524, when he published *De ratione studii puerilis,* for Charles Mountjoy, Vives said that the current dictionaries were too narrow in scope, too difficult for boys, or they lacked real scholarship.[61] In 1531, writing *De tradendis disciplinis,* he suggested that each boy divide his notebook into several parts: "In one division let him put down separate and single words. In another, proper ways of speaking and turns of speech which are in daily use; and again rare expressions." [62] Good writers, he said, discuss many things which grammarians, whose aim is correctness, do not discuss. He added:

From all these authors a Latin lexicon can be collected, which can never be too full or accurate. This should be in two parts, the one containing a list of as many words as possible with a short translation of each, the other more comprehensive, with quotations bringing in each word. This will not only make the reader more certain in translating, but will also show how the word ought to be used, which he would perhaps never learn without the example.

When he described the method of building a Latin vocabulary he suggested that the master take from a dictionary, "perfect and flawless in all its parts, whatever words are needed for daily use. . . ." At first he would choose easy words such as are used in games, and gradually proceed to more difficult ones. He added that no dictionary of the kind he had described was available. In other connections he mentioned the need for Latin-vernacular and vernacular-Latin parts in a dictionary and for a good Greek dictionary.[63]

---

[61] Foster Watson, *Vives and the Renascence Education of Women* (London, 1912), Appendix, pp. 247–48, where these ideas are summarized rather than translated.

[62] Vives, *De tradendis disciplinis,* p. 108.

[63] *De tradendis disciplinis,* pp. 133–34, 144, 149. For similar methods see John Baret, *An Alvearie, or Triple Dictionary* (London, 1574). An edition of 1580 is a quadruple dictionary, adding Greek to English, Latin, and French. A preface "To the Reader," gives an interesting account of the way dictionaries were made much later in the century—if one may believe Baret. Important contemporaries of his believed him, it seems, but DeWitt T. Starnes, *Renaissance Dictionaries* (Austin, Texas, 1954), Chapter XIV, has cast doubt on the story.

ELYOT

Sir Thomas Elyot usually agreed with the other members of the More circle when he discussed theories of education in his *Governour*. He made the usual assumptions about the bases of education, man's freedom of will, and his perfectibility. In Book III, Chapter xxiii, on "Sapience," he quoted Plato (who affirmed that certain spices or seeds of things and rules of the arts and sciences are innate in man) and Socrates, who compared himself to a midwife, because in teaching young men he merely brought forth what was already in them. He became less courtly and aristocratic than usual in Book III, iii, when he said that the soul of the nobleman is made of the same substance as all other souls and that as much freedom of will is given to the poor carter or herdsman as to the mighty emperor. In Book I, iv and v, he emphasized early training, from the birth of the child, and the wise choice of nurses and servants because "often times the childe soukethe the vice of his nouryse with the milke of her pappe." [64] He wished that nurses might speak pure Latin, or at least English that is perfectly articulated, with no letter or syllable omitted. Since English children did not have either Greek or Latin as the mother tongue, they should not wait until seven years of age to begin grammar but should steal a little time from childhood and begin sooner. He compared the work of educating the child to the work of a gardener growing precious herbs—a favorite comparison with other men in the circle; a gardener looks for good soil, eliminates weeds, and guards against the dew of vice from evil custom. Elyot also stressed the power of imitation, for good or evil, in the early years.

In I, v, he praised grammar teaching in his day, implying that grammars, if wisely chosen, were easier and better than they had been in the past. He recommended that Greek and Latin grammar be taught together or that Greek be taught first because it is harder. He agreed with others who said that it is undesirable to spend too much time at first in memorizing rules; as a result, when the child comes to the real pleasure of reading the old authors his ardent

[64] Elyot, *The boke named the Gouernour* (London, 1531), Fol. 16 *verso*.

desire for learning will have been quenched, "lyke as a lyttel fyre is sone quenched with a great heape of small stickes. . . ." [65] After a few quick rules of grammar, or even along with the rules, he suggested that the teacher read to the children Aesop's fables in Greek. Of course the teacher would choose the fables that teach virtue.

Elyot frequently emphasized, as he did in I, v, the value of allurements to learning, the appeal to the senses, the child's eager response to praise, and the use of graphic devices. He would not have children forced by violence to learn but "swetely allured therto, with praises and suche praty gyftes as children delite in." [66] He spoke of the senses in learning; in I, viii, his chapter on painting and carving, he said that everything able to be expressed in portraiture "more persuadeth and stereth the beholder, and soner istructeth hym" than any statement either in writing or speaking.[67] In the same chapter he discussed the use of pictures in the teaching of sciences:

Experience we haue therof in lernynge of geometry, astronomie, and cosmographie. . . . In which studies, I dare affirme, a man shal more profite in one wike by figures and chartis, well and perfectly made, than he shall by the only reding or heryng the rules of that science by the space of halfe a yere at the lest. Wherfore the late writers deserue no small commendation, whiche added to the autors of those sciences apt and propre figures.[68]

In I, xi, he said:

It shall be . . . for refreshing the witte, a conuenient lesson to beholde the olde tables of Ptholomee, where in all the worlde is paynted, hauynge firste some introduction in to the sphere, wherof nowe of late be made very good treatises, and more playne and easie to lerne than was wonte to be.

All be it there is none so good lernynge as the demonstration of cosmographie by materiall figures and instrumentes, hauynge a good instructour.[69]

Elyot explained many views on early education in Book I, Chapters iv, v, vi. He shared the concern of the other men in the More

[65] *The Gouernour*, Fol. 30 *verso*. See I, Chapters iv, v, vi, x also.
[66] *The Gouernour*, Fol. 18 *verso*, and *passim*.
[67] *The Gouernour*, Fol. 25 *verso*.
[68] *The Gouernour*, Fol. 26.
[69] *The Gouernour*, Fol. 37.

circle about the choice of a master. He must have character; he must be a good grammarian, and as a result, he would be able to explain all good authors, their form of eloquence, their figures, sentences, words, and every person or place they name in their works; he would be familiar with poets, historians, and all other kinds of writers. He must have teaching skill which is able to use well shame and praise without cruelty or beating, and he must have sympathy with children. In I, v, he suggested that it should be no reproach to a nobleman to teach his own children or at least to examine them to test their learning; he added examples of kings who did not disdain the work of schoolmasters. In I, xiii, when he analyzed the reasons why gentlemen were not better educated, he said that parents were willing to pay more for cooks and falconers than for teachers.

Like other men in the More circle, Elyot recognized individual inclinations and aptitudes. Discussing the study of law, in I, xiv, he warned against taking up its study merely because friends advised it; we should not strive with the universal nature of man, and still we should follow our own proper natures; and though other studies may seem in theory more important, we should follow those to which our own natures incline us.

Elyot disliked idleness, gaming, and other evil occupations called pastimes. He warned against dice; in I, xxvi, he suggested chess, which would be especially good if the players thought of the moralizings about it which had been explained in English books. In I, xix-xx, he developed an elaborate moral defense of dancing, saying that the dancing together of a man and a woman suggests all the good qualities of both sexes as well as concord and marriage. In I, xiii, he refuted the enemies of poetry and comedy by saying that such literatures did not teach evil; instead, they acted as a mirror of man's life where he might discover evil and be warned against it. In I, x, he suggested that Aesop's fables might be followed by selections from Lucian or by the comedies of Aristophanes; but it would be better for a child to read no Lucian than all of Lucian. In I, vii, he said that a gentleman should be careful not to let music tempt him to wantonness and neglect of duty and that he should never perform as a professional; but he should know music in order to understand better the public weal, which is "made of an ordre of astates and degrees, and by reason therof conteineth in it a perfect harmony. . . ." [70] With all his courtliness, then, Elyot maintained the stress upon virtue, morality, and piety.

POLE AND LUPSET

In Starkey's work *A Dialogue between Reginald Pole and Thomas Lupset* these younger men were represented as expressing similar ideas on education, though education was by no means their main theme. They emphasized the basic conventions of free will, reason, and perfectibility, deplored the prevalence of bad education, suggested remedies, and mentioned the aims of education in terms like those used by the other members of the More circle. Man "far excelleth in dignity all other creatures in earth . . . seeing that by memory and wit also he conceiveth the nature of all thing." Each man has certain virtues planted within him by "the power of nature"; and these virtues are never wholly extinct, though they are diminished in evil men. They incline men to a civil life, and this inclination is a result of the law of nature. But man's diligence and labor must be used to bring these virtues to perfection. [71] The speakers were not inclined to quote Cicero, Pliny, and Quintilian as the practical teachers did; instead they used Plato, Socrates, and Aristotle to support their general theories. [72]

Both speakers in the *Dialogue* were dissatisfied with the education of noblemen and churchmen. Pole, according to Starkey, suggested a remedy for idleness and bad education—a plan for compulsory education requiring every man to send his children, when they were seven years old, to be educated either in letters or in some craft, "according as their nature requireth." Children should also have a system of supervised physical training. If children were all well trained "in tender age," idleness and other ills would vanish, especially if they had as teachers "certain of the most virtuous and

---

[70] *The Gouernour*, Fol. 24. Castiglione also recommended dancing for his courtier. See also *The Poems of Sir John Davies*, ed. by Clare Howard (New York, 1941), and the poem "Orchestra," for an amazing later analysis of the dance.

[71] Thomas Starkey, *A Dialogue between Reginald Pole and Thomas Lupset*, ed. by Kathleen M. Burton (London, 1948), pp. 29–30, 42–44, and *passim*.

[72] *A Dialogue*, see index.

wise men of the realm." Pole mentioned with approval the fact that England already had provisions in some common places and in universities and colleges for educating "in letters" the children of poor men. Of course children should be trained in virtue and learning but also in the administration of private and public justice. Pole also suggested that bishops be compelled to divide their incomes into four parts and to use one part "to maintain the poor youth in study." And since the "Latin tongue and the Greek be the ground of learning," he suggested the establishment and consolidation of schools under prudent and learned masters. Children who proved themselves competent in early schooling should receive liberal training as preachers; and they should follow the counsel of Erasmus in his treatise on the study of divinity and his book on the preacher.[73]

Pole and Lupset agreed that the educated man must be ready to serve the commonweal—they merely debated whether he should offer himself or wait to be called into public service. Pole especially said that he would ever be ready "to do service to my prince and country, to God's honor and glory. . . ." Thus the close, as well as the whole dialogue integrates the law of nature, law and government, and theories of education.

ROGER ASCHAM

Roger Ascham held ideas on education which sound so much like those of More and his friends that only his style differs. His faith in the power of education is illustrated by his quoting Cicero's opinion that a man by use may be brought to a new nature. The factors of education, he said in *Toxophilus*, are *aptness, knowledge,* and *use*. The three "make all thinges perfecte. Aptnesse is the fyrst and chyefest thinge, without whiche the other two do no good at all. Knowledge doeth encrease al maner of Aptnesse, bothe lesse and more. Vse, sayth Cicero, is farre aboue all teachinge." Aptness, he continued, is the gift of nature, knowledge is gained with the help of others, and use lies in individual diligence and labor.[74] In *Toxophilus*, too, he defended recreation and attacked idleness and

[73] *A Dialogue*, pp. 142, 145, 147, 180–81, 187–88.
[74] Roger Ascham, *Toxophilus* (London, 1545), Book A, leaf 43.

"naughty" pastimes, such as dicing, cards, and bowling, with as much zeal as he defended archery: "I am sure that good wittes, except they be let downe like a treble string, and vnbent like a good casting bowe, they wil neuer last and be able to continue in studie." [75]

On the importance of the early years Ascham said the same things as Erasmus and Vives, in almost the same language: "For we remember nothyng so well when we be olde, as those thinges which we learned when we were yong . . . new wax is best for printyng; new claie, fittest for working; new shorne woll, aptest for sone and surest dying; new fresh flesh, for good and durable salting. . . . Yong Graftes grow not onelie sonest but also fairest, and bring alwayes forth the best and sweetest frute; yong whelpes learne easilie to carie; yong Popingeis learne quicklie to speake." [76]

He waxed eloquent in favor of allurements to learning and against scolding and beating. His Preface to the *Schoolmaster* introduced the story of the boys who had run away from Eton because of beatings (as Tusser had complained of beatings at Eton); and in commenting on the situation he said that "yong children were soner allured by loue than driuen by beating to atteyne good learning." He quoted Mr. Wotton as agreeing with Socrates that "the Scholehouse should be in deede . . . the house of playe and pleasure, and not of feare and bondage"; he said also that whatever the mind learns unwillingly with fear, it quickly forgets. He cited Lady Jane Grey's tutor, who taught her gently with "faire allurementes to learning . . ."; and he contrasted that gentleness with the stern discipline of her parents. As a result of his teaching, she derived a more genuine pleasure from reading Plato than her parents found when hunting in the park. He suggested that Solomon's counsel on sparing the rod and spoiling the child was meant for fathers who needed to punish wantonness, lying, and stealing, and not for schoolmasters. [77]

As for teaching versus experience, Ascham, in the Preface to the *Schoolmaster*, deplored experience of evil. As if in the voice of

---

[75] *Toxophilus*, Book A, leaf 3; see also leaves 13 *verso*, 14, 17 *verso*, and *passim*.

[76] Ascham, *The Scholemaster*, First book, leaf 11. This idea appears frequently in both works.

[77] *The Scholemaster*, First book, Preface, also leaves 4–6, 11 *verso*, 12, and *passim*.

Erasmus, he said that learning teaches us more in one year than experience in twenty; learning teaches safely but experience alone causes misery; and he quoted Erasmus as saying that experience is the schoolhouse of fools and evil men.[78] Even if a young man is merely exposed to evil later, "the mynde shall quicklie fall seick, and sone vomet and cast vp all the holesome doctrine that he receiued in childhoode, though he were neuer so well brought vp before." [79]

On the aims of education Ascham stressed the things that the men in the More circle had stressed: virtue, piety, learning, and service to one's country (though he added what More and Erasmus did not, training to serve in war). He implied that noblemen's sons were especially to be blamed if they did not train themselves to bear the burden of important affairs; but all the youth should be so educated in learning and virtue that when they were called upon to serve their country they would be ready to act with wisdom.[80]

Ascham's discussion of subjects for instruction is somewhat limited partly by the scope of his work and partly by a difference in point of view. In *Toxophilus* he came near to agreement with Elyot when he voiced a fear that music might entice young men to naughtiness, not stir them to honesty.[81] In the *Schoolmaster* he differed from More, Vives, Linacre, and Tunstal in being suspicious of sciences (he named music, arithmetic, and geometry) because they sharpen men's wits too much, change their manners, and make them unfit to live in the world.[82]

In the *Schoolmaster* his emphasis was upon Latin and Greek, with more concern about Greek literature and details of form; and he was apparently less concerned about either Greek or Latin as a means to vital information. As his classical and Christian program for a good student, Ascham selected these books and authors: Tully, Plato, Xenophon with his books of philosophy, Isocrates, Demosthenes with his orations, and Aristotle with his

---

[78] *The Scholemaster*, First book, leaves 18–19.

[79] *The Scholemaster*, First book, leaf 13.

[80] *The Scholemaster*, First book, leaf 13 *verso*, and *passim*; also *Toxophilus*, Book A, leaf 8 *verso*, and *passim*.

[81] *Toxophilus*, Book A, leaves 9 *verso*-10.

[82] *The Scholemaster*, First book, leaf 5 *verso*.

rhetoric. Tully, he added, loved best these other five, and studied, compared, or applied and imitated them. To study them as he studied them would give a perfect knowledge of both tongues, "a readie and pithie utterance," and judgment in all learning. He added that God's holy word would be most worthy for "the louer of learning and honestie to spend his life in." Ascham had often heard Cheke say that while he liked to have a student read all Greek and Latin authors, he who read and reread thoroughly the Bible, Tully in Latin, and Plato, Aristotle, Xenophon, Isocrates, and Demosthenes in Greek "must nedes proue an excellent man." [83]

GENERAL COMPARISONS

EMPHASIS UPON GREEK

Of course the importance of the Greek language and literature was a continuing theme, but the emphasis shifted with the passage of time. More stressed the need of getting the accurate thought of the Greeks from direct reading, not from garbled translations, and the importance of secular and religious thought to the world. Erasmus expressed the same ideas many times: for example, he said in a letter of 1501 that it is "the merest madness to touch with the little finger that principal part of theology which treats of the divine mysteries, without being furnished with the apparatus of Greek. . . ." In the treatise *De ratione studii*, 1511, when he prescribed Greek and Latin from the beginning, he said that within these two literatures are contained all the knowledge which is vital for the world. Linacre supported their view when he wrote to John Claymond, the first president of Corpus Christi College, in 1516: "In the name of good learning I entreat you . . . not to abandon your plan of establishing the study of Greek in a secure home in Oxford. And as I cannot come to you . . . the only thing is for you to master the language for yourself . . . you have already made a beginning, which is half the battle . . . the true learning that you seek is acknowledged by all to be enshrined in the wisdom of the Greeks. Your toil will become light . . . and your progress sure if only you will read a little Lucian every

[83] *The Scholemaster*, Second book, leaves 51 *verso–52*.

day." [84] In the later educational treatises men spent more time explaining how to study Greek, instead of defending its study. Erasmus in *De pueris instituendis*, 1529, made little defense of its study. Vives, in *De tradendis disciplinis*, 1531, commented that the person who has joined Greek to Latin will receive the seeds of all kinds of knowledge and that knowledge of Greek deepens the knowledge of Latin; he also said once that if it were not for the knowledge contained in Latin and Greek, they would have no more value than French or Spanish. Roger Ascham, in the *Schoolmaster*, 1570, spent most of his energy on explaining which Greek classics to teach and how to teach them.

EDUCATION AND THE ATTITUDE TO WAR

The attitude to war shifted from the deep aversion of More and Erasmus, who analyzed its cause in the corruption of mankind and the result of that corruption as continued war, to acceptance. Pole, if Starkey was correct, argued that the nobility "must be constrained by lawful punishment to exercise themselves in all such things as shall be for the defence of our ream necessary" and that they should do so with the same diligence that ploughmen use in producing food.[85] Elyot, though he objected to football as "nothinge but beastly furie and exstreme violence," praised archery as "the moste excellent artillerie for warres," defensive or offensive.[86] Ascham began by saying there is nothing worse than war, yet considered it an essential civil medicine with which a prince may ward off danger from his country or recover whatever he has lost. Defining artillery as both guns and bows, Ascham continued to discuss the disadvantages of guns and the advantages of archery in war.[87]

DOUBLE TRANSLATION

The use of double or even of triple translation was an accepted method, in the More circle, of teaching a foreign language. In a

[84] P. S. Allen, *Erasmus* (Oxford, 1934), p. 153. For the views of Erasmus see Nichols, *The Epistles*, I, no. 143.

[85] Starkey, *A Dialogue*, p. 148, also p. 170.

[86] Elyot, *The Gouernour*, Fol. 99 verso.

[87] Ascham, *Toxophilus*, Book A, leaves 24–25.

letter to his school More suggested something approaching it when
he gave directions about writing letters to him. First, he suggested,
they were to write a letter in English. Second, they were to turn it
into Latin; and since they had already stated the subject matter,
they could give their whole attention to the Latin construction.
Third, they were to reread the finished version carefully, to find
and correct any solecisms. Fourth, they were to copy again the
whole letter. Fifth, they were to examine it again, to see if any
faulty construction had slipped past them. Stapleton's account
implies systematic use of double translation: "The pupils exercised
themselves in the Latin tongue almost every day, translating English into Latin and Latin into English." Speaking of More's letter
to the University of Oxford, in defense of classical learning, he
added: "I have seen another Latin version of this made by one of
his daughters, and an English version by another." [88]

Erasmus, when he was staying in Louvain, several years before
he went to Italy, "translated the *Hecuba* of Euripides for the
sake of an exercise in Greek, when there was no supply of teachers
of that tongue," as he said in his catalogue of Lucubrations. In
a letter to Archbishop Warham, he discussed his turning into
Latin two of Euripides' tragedies; he said that "the mere act of
making good Latin out of good Greek is one that requires no
ordinary artist, a person not only well provided with a copious
and ready apparatus of both languages, but also most quick-sighted
and watchful. . . ." [89] His comment on the difficulty of the
process lends meaning to his suggestion in *De ratione studii* that
the translating from Greek into Latin was one of the most useful
of the exercises before the pupil began original composition. In
this exacting task, he said, the pupil must do three distinct things:
first, analyze the construction in Greek; second, notice the peculiar
genius of each language and the principles which are common to
both; third, make an accurate translation from the Greek, a process
which requires the pupil to move freely in the resources of a Latin
vocabulary and a Latin sentence structure.[90]

[88] Stapleton, *Life,* for the letter, p. 107; for the subjects studied in the school, pp. 99–100.
[89] Nichols, *The Epistles,* I, pp. 393–95; also no. 187.
[90] Erasmus, *De ratione studii,* pp. 171–72.

Vives suggested that the pupil, as soon as he had learned syntax, should "translate from the mother-tongue into Latin, and then back again into the mother-tongue," beginning with short passages, to be increased in length from day to day. The same kind of exercise could be done in Greek, Vives said, though he thought it better for the pupil to translate from Greek authors, rather than from his own language into Greek. Though the translator must know both languages well, he would receive more practice in the language into which he was translating. Vives also suggested that translating a proverb from one language into another would be good practice.[91]

Roger Ascham quoted Cicero and Pliny with approval for recommending double translation, but he rebuked Quintilian for what he considered a perverse disagreement with Cicero. Since he cited three classic authors on double translation, it is perhaps not strange that several men in the More circle were familiar with such a system. Ascham explained his first method explicitly. First, the master took a letter of Cicero and explained it to the child, including the cause and the matter, then translated it into English as often as he needed to do, and then parsed it perfectly. Second, the child construed and parsed it perfectly. Third, the child took a paper book and without help, translated the letter into English. Fourth, the child brought his English translation, gave up his Latin copy, and after an hour had gone by, translated his English into Latin. Fifth, master and child together compared Cicero and the child's translation, with praise for the child if he had done well, but no scolding if he had done his best. By this process, the master, Ascham explained, would gradually teach all rules, and the pupil would learn without great pain.

Ascham's second plan for translation began with the master translating into English something from Cicero which the pupil did not know where to find. Then the pupil translated it into Latin. Next master and pupil compared the two. Again the master showed the pupil his faults gently, and if he could, praised him.

While Ascham considered these two ways of translating sufficient of themselves and surer than any other, he suggested a third

<hr />

[91] Vives, *De tradendis disciplinis*, pp. 113–14.

method. First, the master wrote in English some easy, natural letter, as if he were writing to the pupil's father or friend, adapting the material to the pupil's knowledge at the time, or he selected some simple narrative. Then the pupil translated this material into Latin.

Ascham also quoted Pliny on translating from Greek into Latin and from Latin into Greek, an exercise, he said, which teaches grammar, choice of words, comeliness of style for every subject and every language, invention of argument, arrangement, eloquence, good judgment—every virtue of composition. Ascham also suggested that one might attain perfection in Greek by translating Ionic Greek into Attic Greek.[92]

It seems that the method of translating from English into Latin and from Latin into English would be a rather thorough training in English composition, in addition to giving mastery of a foreign language.

IMITATION

Erasmus, Vives, and Roger Ascham had some areas of agreement when they discussed the principle of imitation. Both Erasmus and Vives considered the apelike imitation practiced by a child as either an aid or a menace to both morals and speech, depending upon the child's environment. Both stressed imitation and memory as the chief aids in learning a language. Both expected imitation in composition. Neither believed in imitating the ancient world or its paganism. Since each thought of Latin as a living language, neither believed in the rigid imitation of the Ciceronians, who would not use any word or any form of a word unless their master had used it. Each believed in using modern vocabulary, modern figures of speech, modern examples, and all possible inflectional forms of a word, whether Cicero had happened to use all the forms or not. As each said much about allowing for the child's individual nature and taste, so each believed that the road of imitation should lead finally to a new road of individuality.

Of course there was much imitation on the road to individuality,

[92] Ascham, *The Scholemaster*, First book, leaves 1–2; Second book, leaves 31–32, 33 *verso*, 35, and *passim*.

so that the student might learn balance, decorum, and judgment. When Erasmus suggested that the student practice the epistolary style in both Greek and Latin, he was suggesting imitation. First, the student was to develop an argument in the vernacular and then turn it into Latin and into Greek. He must learn, apparently by practice in composition, the style suitable for fable, moral common-place, short story, and dilemma, the art of expressing an encomium, a denunciation, a parallel, a simile, and a description. He might turn prose into poetry or the reverse, or he might take one motive to be expressed in four or five different meters, one topic for verse and prose, one for Latin and Greek, one affirmative to be proved by four or five different lines of argument. When the master re-quired an epistle, he was to point out the structure or phrasing common to each variety and the qualities which would be best in this particular letter. The master should also give exercises in formal oratory, to be treated by accepted methods. He might do well to give his pupil a kind of skeleton form, the number of propositions on a given theme, the number of arguments to be used, the number of proofs, and the sources of proof for each argument. Then the pupil was to consider the various methods of adorning his ideas, and to emphasize the exordium, the transition, the peroration. Although this study of formal oratory may seem imitative, Erasmus considered it original composition.[93]

Vives defined imitation as "the fashioning of a certain thing in accordance with a proposed model." The model was to be the best possible one, but *best* in relation to the pupil's stage of develop-ment, not the absolute best. Boys might even imitate older boys at first and then progress to the imitation of the master. For ora-tory, the boy must imitate someone enough like himself so that he could still be expressing his own individuality, or the imitation would soon become sterile. Imitation means that the art and the workmanship will in a manner be stolen, Vives said, but the pupil will not use the same material and will adapt and use those points of style which he can transfer to his own aim. That is, he will not imitate stupidly nor merely pilfer. And Vives added that imitation is a method for youth, not age; a man should grow into

[93] Erasmus, *De ratione studii*, pp. 171–73. See also pp. 169–70.

his own style: "That a boy should imitate is honorable and praise-worthy: that an old man should do so is servile and disgraceful." Since the imitation of the ancients may make us absurd because we may depart from our own strength and because our ears can-not judge fully the sound of their language, Vives said, "it would be better to write in the vernacular languages, in which the great mass of the people are themselves authorities, teachers, and judges." [94]

When Ascham discussed imitation he said many things with which the members of the More circle would probably have agreed. They would have accepted his definition: imitation is the power "to expresse liuelye and perfitelie that example which ye go about to folow," if he meant that imitation should be infused with some individuality. They would have agreed with him that imitation is an important means of learning languages, and that the litera-ture of the Greeks and Romans furnishes models, both for matter and manner. They would have agreed that it is futile to imitate merely a style. They would have agreed on the principle of dis-similar material and similar handling, or similar material with dissimilar handling, since such a principle would lead one away from slavish imitation.

Erasmus and Vives would probably not have agreed on the fact that Greek authors are best to imitate. Vives would clearly have disagreed with Ascham's principle of imitating only the absolute best, since he thought that boys might begin by imitating older boys. Probably Vives would have thought that Ascham's idea of selecting the best, chiefly one, in each field, was entirely too rigid.

Some of Ascham's ideas on imitation are outside the scope of most teaching, at least of schoolboys. For example he discussed the imitation of all types, including tragic, epic, and lyric poetry; and he suggested detailed comparisons of two authors, such as Homer and Virgil, or Tully and Demosthenes, as a basis for imitation. In his account of Watson's "Absalon" he seems to have been more concerned with mere perfection of form than More, Erasmus, or Vives.[95]

[94] Vives, *De tradendis disciplinis*, pp. 189–200, *passim*.
[95] Ascham, *The Scholemaster*, Second book, leaves 45 *verso*-48, 57, and *passim*.

APPROACH TO GRAMMAR STUDY

That More believed in making the approach to grammar easy is apparent from the epigrams he wrote for *Lac puerorum*; it seems clear, too, that John Holt shared his views. Colet left no doubt about his agreement with them when he wrote the statutes for St. Paul's School, pointing out that Latin speech existed before the rules, not the rules before Latin speech. Erasmus believed that Colet sometimes went too far in his attitude to grammar: "He could not endure that the faculty of speaking correctly should be sought from the trivial rules of grammarians. For he insisted that these were a hindrance to expressing oneself well, and that that result was only obtained by the study of the best authors. But he paid the penalty for this notion himself. For, though eloquent both by nature and training, and though he had . . . a singularly copious flow of words while speaking, yet when writing he would now and then trip in such points as critics are given to mark. And it was on this account, if I mistake not, that he refrained from writing books. . . ." [96]

But Erasmus made it quite clear that he approved of the inductive method. In 1511 when he wrote *De ratione studii*, he said: "whilst a knowledge of the rules of accidence and syntax is most necessary to every student, still they should be as few, as simple, and as carefully framed as possible. I have no patience with the stupidity of the average teacher of grammar who wastes precious years in hammering rules into children's heads. For it is not by learning rules that we acquire the power of speaking a language, but by daily intercourse with those accustomed to express themselves with exactness and refinement, and by the copious reading of the best authors." [97]

---

[96] Erasmus, *The Lives of Jehan Vitrier . . . and John Colet*, trans. by J. H. Lupton (London, 1883), pp. 38–39.

[97] Erasmus, *Opera omnia*, I, 521, C, D: "Verum ut hujusmodi praecepta fateor necessaria, ita velim esse quantum fieri possit, quam paucissima, modo sint optima. Nec umquam probavi literatorum vulgus, qui pueros in his inculcandis complures annos remorantur.

"Nam vera emendate loquendi facultas optime paratur, cum ex castigate loquentium colloquio convictuque, tum ex eloquentium auctorum assidua lectione, e equibus ii primum sunt imbibendi, quorum oratio praeterquam quod est castigatissima, argumenti quoque illecebra aliqua discentibus blandiatur."

William Lily apparently supported the easy approach and the inductive method in teaching grammar, or his grammar would not have been chosen instead of Linacre's, and he would not have been selected as Colet's headmaster.

Vives agreed upon an easy approach to the teaching of grammar: "But I wish this knowledge of grammatical science to be learned without being wearisomely troublesome, for whilst it is injurious to neglect rules, so it also injures to cling to, and to be dependent on them too much, although the evil of too much carefulness is the more tolerable course." [98] Vives recommended Linacre's grammar, which Colet had rejected for his school, but not for beginners. But when a pupil had mastered the elements of grammar and had learned to understand a number of classics, he would be ready for private study and for that advanced grammar, since Linacre "revealed many mysteries in the Latin language." [99]

Both Erasmus and Vives believed in approaching Latin or Greek by easy stages. Probably they would have agreed on a plan like this: first, teach the child the parts of speech and a few simple inflections, and then let him listen to something very simple, like a fable from Aesop, to illustrate what he has learned, and do simple reading until these first principles are fixed; second, give the child more solid reading with more grammar, but still let him fix the grammar from the reading; third, give him more advanced work in both reading and grammar, letting him use more initiative. Probably this third stage would be the one when Vives would think the pupil ready to try Linacre's grammar for himself and to write original composition.

Sir Thomas Elyot (whose opinion was discussed earlier in the chapter) and Roger Ascham agreed heartily with those who gave only a few rules at first and then taught grammar through reading. Ascham said: "For without doute *Grammatica* it selfe is sooner and surer learned by examples of good authors than by the naked rewles of Grammarians." Queen Elizabeth, Ascham's

[98] Vives, *De tradendis disciplinis*, p. 98. He is said to have spoken even more firmly in his work, *Against the Pseudo-Dialecticians*, but I have not been able to examine this work in detail.

[99] *De tradendis disciplinis*, p. 139.

prize pupil, "neuer toke yet Greeke nor Latin Grammer in her hand after the first declining of a nowne and a verb" but used double translating of Demosthenes and Isocrates and some part of Tully daily for a year or two; as a result, Ascham said, few equal her in understanding both languages and in speaking Latin well.[100]

COMPARATIVE INFLUENCES: SIR THOMAS MORE

It is difficult to say what man in the More circle exerted the greatest influence on education. In the crucial years from 1505 or 1510 to 1515, Erasmus spent some five years in England and wrote *De ratione studii,* More started his household school, and Colet established his school at St. Paul's. During these years More, Grocyn, Linacre, Colet, John Rastell, and William Lily were settled in London; and there was probably much unrecorded discussion on education. All the writers in the More circle, of course, quoted the same classic sources on education—Cicero, Pliny, Quintilian, and many others, with Quintilian perhaps the favorite.

But More exerted a large influence on practical education, besides the impetus which he and John Holt gave to the methods of teaching grammar to children. More seems to have been the first English layman who established a school in his own house and admitted to it young people outside his immediate family. According to Erasmus, More's influence changed the attitude of English noblemen toward the education of their children. Writing to Budé in 1521, Erasmus made such a statement; he added: "Although a short time ago, love of literature was considered useless in any practical life or as an ornament, now there is hardly a man who considers his children worthy of his ancestors unless they are trained in good letters. Even in monarchs themselves a great part of royal splendor is lacking when skill in literature is lacking." [101]

It seems possible, too, that More was the influence which led Sir Humphrey Wingfield to establish his household school and to ed-

---

[100] Ascham, *The Scholemaster,* Second book, leaves 42 *verso* and 35, for Queen Elizabeth.

[101] P. S. Allen, *Opus epistolarum,* IV, 1233, p. 578, Erasmus to Budé, September, 1521. "Quibus rebus factum est vt quum ante paucos dies literarum amor ad omne vitae vel praesidium vel ornamentum haberetur inutilis, nunc nemo pene sit magnatum qui liberos vt maiorum imaginibus dignos agnoscat, nisi bonis literis eruditos. Quin et monarchis ipsis bona regalium decorum pars abesse videtur, in quibus literarum peritia desideretur."

ucate Roger Ascham. Ascham called him "my singuler good mayster, Sir Humfrey Wingfelde, to whom nexte God, I ought to refer for his manifolde benefites bestowed on me. . . ." Wingfield, he said, "ever loued and used to haue many children brought up in learnynge in his house, amonges whome I my selfe was one. . . ." He trained children in the book and the bow, and he rewarded those who shot best with bows and arrows which he brought from London.[102] As Roger Ascham entered St. John's College in 1530, when he was fifteen, he was probably in Wingfield's school about 1525 to 1530.

Sir Humphrey Wingfield was a brother to Sir Richard, of whom Erasmus asked favors and to whom he wrote with affectionate greetings for his wife and children. He was a cousin to Charles Brandon, Duke of Suffolk, a chamberlain to his wife, Mary, the king's sister, and a legal and business helper of the Duke. Sir Humphrey had associations with More's father, John More, from 1515 to about 1528, the years when both men were named together on the Commission of the Peace for Essex. This John More was called Sir John from 1523; he disappeared from the commission about 1528 to 1530; and while there were other John Mores in London at this time, a check in other connections indicates that no other Sir John would fit this time pattern. Sir Humphrey and Sir Thomas More also had direct connections. A list in the state papers dated February 5, 1526, headed "Division of matters to be handled by the King's Council," with a subheading "For matter in law," includes Sir Thomas More and ends with the words, "The King's serjeants and attorney, Mr. Humfrey Wingfield." As this seems to be a mere division of work for men already on the council, it gives no indication how long Wingfield had previously been a member of that group.[103]

As Sir Humphrey's school was in a layman's household, as he took children from outside, and as he followed the principles of love and rewards for excellence, there is a reasonable probability that he was influenced by Sir Thomas More.

---

[102] Ascham, *Toxophilus*, Book B, leaf 22.

[103] *L. and P.*, II, no. 1213; IV, 1136, 2002, 5083, for connections between Sir Humphrey and Sir John More; and IV, Appendix no. 67 for the connection between Sir Humphrey and Sir Thomas More on the king's council.

It is not difficult to notice that these men were conscious of each other as influences on education. Elyot's praise of Erasmus' work on the education of a Christian prince has already been discussed.[104] Vives praised More for his keen wit and recommended the reading together of Plato's *Republic,* his discussion of laws, and More's *Utopia,* "for from them may be gathered many suggestions useful for the rule of states." Vives recommended also Linacre's six books of syntax, referred in other places to his Latin grammar, and mentioned as desirable reading Galen's *De tuenda valetudine* along with Linacre's translation of this work. He also mentioned the little book on the eight parts of speech which "passes under Erasmus' name; it was composed by Lily and revised by Erasmus"; he commented favorably on the use of Erasmus' *De copia,* his *De recta pronuntiatione in genere,* his *De matrimonio* (as he called it here), and his *Christiani principis institutio.* The order of words in the last of these titles is his own version of Erasmus' work *Institutio principis Christiani.* In other places he suggested the second book *De copia rerum* and Erasmus' translation of Gaza's Greek grammar. Sometimes he mentioned one of these works without direct comment; usually he praised or recommended. In one passage he lauded Erasmus for his fluency, his clearness, and his skill as a translator; once he named him as a contemporary who was or would be recognized as a great man.[105] Ascham, too, mentioned more than once the books or the views of Erasmus. Besides quoting his view on learning versus experience and agreeing with him, he described him as the honor and the ornament of learning in that time, mentioned his wish to have someone compare fully passages from Demosthenes and Tully, to show where one imitated the other, and criticized him for spending time pointing out the faults of other men instead of giving his own advice. He spoke with approval of Erasmus' method of noticing in his reading "All Adagies, all similitudes, and all wittie sayinges"; and thus he had left to posterity some notable books.[106] In *Toxophilus,* when Ascham was recommending exercise for students, he indicated his

---

[104] Elyot, *The Gouernour,* Book I, xi and Book III, xi.

[105] Vives, *De tradendis disciplinis,* pp. 160, 260, 131, 139, 158, 134, 135, 257, 141, 143, 157. Or see index.

[106] Ascham, *The Scholemaster,* First book, leaf 19; Second book, leaves 47 *verso,* 49 *verso,* and 51 *verso.*

interest in the habits of Erasmus at Cambridge: "This knewe Erasmus verye well when he was here in Cambrige: which when he had ben sore at his book (as Garret our bookebynder hath verye ofte tolde me) for lacke of better exercise wolde take his horse and ryde about the markette hill and come agayne." [107]

SUMMARY

The program of education explained and practiced by More, Colet, Erasmus, and other friends had breadth and completeness. It dealt with aims, methods, subjects, and masters. It included plans for the public support of education and for the training of all classes. Those pupils with the desire and the competence were to receive a liberal education in classic and Christian literature; others were to become skilled in crafts and useful occupations; all were to develop virtue, piety, and the willingness to serve the commonweal.

The program for education, like the other parts of the program which More and his friends recommended for the regeneration of society, was not original in its separate ideas. Whether Englishmen drew them from Italian educators or direct from Quintilian, Pliny, and Cicero, they had the same ideas. But the ideas as a whole program were new in England; restated and combined as they were by scholars and leaders like More and Erasmus, the drops of water became a stream. For a time the stream had power.

It seems at times that this educational program was almost entirely secular—in classic subject matter, methods, masters, and the authorities cited. But More and his friends never forgot to name religious material in the curriculum and to stress piety as well as virtue. But they did not often argue from scripture about the methods or the need for education. Erasmus and others quoted the spare-the-rod-and-spoil-the-child theory only to deny its truth for Christians in their day. Reason, man's freedom of choice, his perfectibility, and other principles of education—these they discussed as philosophers.

[107] Ascham, *Toxophilus*, Book A, leaf 13 *verso*. For Garrett Godfrey, Dutchman, host, friend, and correspondent of Erasmus, see George J. Gray, *The Earlier Cambridge Stationers and Bookbinders* . . . (Oxford, 1904); Gray and Palmer, *Abstracts from the Wills* . . . (London, 1915); Nichols, *The Epistles*, II, nos. 239, 441.

Education, as the men of the More circle evaluated it, was the basis of the ethical, moral, and secular program for improving human life. Education in virtue, piety, and learning, used for the commonweal, became the touchstone of true nobility against a false nobility based on mere wealth and lineage. Education, leading men back to a simple Christianity—an inner attitude of love for man and God expressed in worthy action—would destroy superstition and immorality among monks and priests, extravagance and the struggle for power among leaders of the church, and the practice of formalism alone among all Christians. Education, the training of men to understand Christian and classic theories of justice and the obligations of rulers and to apply Christianity to all human relations, would solve all problems of law and government. Education of women, the same liberal training men received, would lead to happy marriages and provide children with the proper environment for the early years. Hence, educational theories were like an adhesive uniting all parts of the program for reform. Divine grace and the law of nature, as the bases for education, might solve all problems.

CHAPTER **VI** *Education of women: love, marriage*

It would be a serious error to assume that no learned women existed in England or on the Continent before 1500. Abbesses, the products of feudalism and the church, were accepted in the Middle Ages as equals by the men of their own class and were valued by popes and emperors for their executive ability, their artistic creation, and their scholarship. St. Hilda, Abbess of Hartlepool first, and then founder of the double monastery at Whitby in 657, was an outstanding early example in England. Her group included the poet Caedmon and five future bishops; and ecclesiastics from the whole of England came to visit her and to honor her work.

Even the medieval romances centered around ladies of learning. In *Floris and Blanchefleur* the lover insisted that his lady learn Latin with him or he would refuse to study it himself; the wife of *Sir Bevis of Hamtoun* learned physic and surgery from great teachers at Bologna; Melior, beloved of the hero in *Partonope of Blois,* studied herbs, physic, and all the seven sciences. Heloise, no fictional character but a learned woman, was tutored by Abelard, the man who became her lover.

In fourteenth- and fifteenth-century England, few women or

none were outstanding for learning. A few were writers: Juliana of Norwich, an anchoret, wrote *Sixteen Revelations of Divine Love;* Marjorie Kemp of Norwich, perhaps in the time of Edward IV, was the reputed author of *A Short Treatise of Contemplation;* and Juliana Berners, if we may believe the stories about an unnunlike prioress, wrote treatises on sports, coats of arms, and nobility. But there is little evidence that any of these women had unusual learning, and their activities tell us little about women outside convents. In the same centuries the girl in a low- or middle-class family had little or no formal education. If her mother could read and write, she might be taught those skills in her own home and also the management of the household. Probably no grammar schools were open to girls, though the point has been disputed.[1] Girls of the higher classes were sent to the household of some great lady; examples from the Paston letters indicate that the practice was commonplace in the fifteenth century. In the early sixteenth century Anne Boleyn and her sister were sent to great households on the Continent.

Before 1500 only a few works about a girl's education were written either in English or in England, and those few had no concept of a liberal education. There were such works as the *Ancren Rule, Our Lady's Mirror, How the Good Wife Taught her Daughter,* and *The Book of the Knight of la Tour Landry,* for the instruction of his daughters, written about 1371 and translated by Caxton about 1484. The first two were concerned with the convent; the others contained conventional platitudes on a girl's dress, her honor, modesty, and obedience. None suggested that a girl should be educated in Latin and Greek or that she might take any part in public life.

Lady Margaret Beaufort, the mother of Henry VII, was perhaps the outstanding intellectual woman in fifteenth-century England; thus she was a forerunner of the sixteenth century. She was not trained in the classics. In a sermon at the "moneth mynde" for her, Bishop Fisher said that she had studied many difficult books in both French and English, that she had translated French books of

---

[1] Arthur F. Leach, *The Schools of Medieval England* (New York, 1915), pp. 88–89; Foster Watson, *The Old Grammar Schools* (Cambridge, 1916), pp. 166–67, 115–16.

devotion into English, that she understood a little Latin but regretted her lack of Latin education in her youth, and that she was as a
mother to the students of both universities and a patron of all the
learned men in England.[2] As a patron of Wynkyn de Worde and
Caxton she asked them to translate or to publish certain books.

About 1500 a great change came in the education of women in
England and in the discussions about their place in society. This
sharp change does not seem to have come entirely from the causes
usually named to explain the change in attitude to women: first,
the worship of the Virgin Mary; second, the tendency of feudalism to put some emphasis on the protection of the weak; third,
such medieval literature as troubadour poetry and medieval romances; fourth, Greek ideas expressed by Socrates and Plato on
ideal beauty or the place of women in the state; fifth, a diffused
Platonism spreading through the influence of Plotinus, Ficino,
Giovanni Pico della Mirandola, and of such creative writers as
Dante, Petrarch, Benivieni, and Cardinal Bembo.

The worship of the Virgin Mary and some developments of
feudalism may have exerted long-range influence, but they were
probably not the major causes of a change which came suddenly
in early sixteenth-century England. As for courtly romances and
troubadour poetry, perhaps this literature had done much earlier
to foster an attitude of deference to women; but the men of the
More circle would have denied hotly its influence on them, and
some would have been passionate and bitter in their denials. All of
them who mentioned love romances centering around chivalry
attacked such stories bitterly, as bitterly as they resented any
serious mention of Venus and Cupid in stories of love.

The ideas of Socrates and Plato may have had a large effect,
conscious or unconscious, on attitudes to women; for example,
More's *Utopia* seems to owe something to Plato for the status of
Utopian women. The diffused Platonism of Ficino and Pico della
Mirandola certainly influenced the ideas of men in the More circle,
though Colet turned these thoughts to religious interpretation, and
More's early poems used the language of love in the service of

---

[2] *The English Works of John Fisher*, ed. by John E. B. Mayor, *EETS*, ex. ser., XXVII
(1876, 1935), 292, 301.

religion. But great as these two influences may have been, the practical educators—More, Erasmus, and Vives—do not say much about Socrates and Plato or about contemporary Platonists when they talk of educating women. Within the limits of this study, one can only say that the education of women in England seems to have been fostered mainly by Sir Thomas More.

ACTION: THE EDUCATION OF WOMEN

TREATISES

After 1500, or more exactly between 1518 and 1540, seven important treatises dealing with the education of women were written or published. In 1518 More wrote a letter to William Gonell, presumably a new tutor in his household, making explicit suggestions on the personal character and the learning he wished his daughters to have, and defending liberal training for women. More's letter was written from the king's court. Vives published three treatises on the general topic five and six years later: *De institutione Christianae foeminae*, 1523; *De ratione studii puerilis*, for girls, in 1523; and *Satellitium animi sive symbola*, 1524.[3] In 1524 also Richard Herde wrote an Introduction for Margaret Roper's translation into English of Erasmus' *Precatio dominica*, the first discussion written in English about a liberal education for women. In 1529 Vives published another Latin work *De officio mariti;* one chapter in it dealt with the education of women. Though only two of these works were written in English, Richard Herde translated Vives' first-named work as *The Instruction of a Christian Woman.* As Herde died in Italy in 1528, while he was traveling with Fox and Gardiner as their physician, his translation was completed before that date; it was printed by Thomas Berthelet, perhaps in 1529, and before 1600 it had gone through six editions. Herde had translated the work with More's help and approval. In 1540 Sir Thomas Elyot published his English work *The Defence of Good Women,* with slightly exaggerated claims about the demonstrated ability of women in public life. More's letter,

---

[3] J. Estelrich, *Vives* (Paris, 1941), Index; or see Vives, *Opera*, 2 vols. (Basel, 1555), *passim*.

the three books by Vives, the Introduction, and the translation by Herde were all produced within ten years—from 1518 to 1528. More's letter was written five years before any other treatise on the education of women; and all the others were produced by men who had been long-time guests, intimate friends, or tutors in More's school. Erasmus, who told us explicitly that he developed a favorable attitude to the education of women because of More and his school, was making some contribution during these years through his *Colloquies*. "A Lover and Maiden," "The Uneasy Wife," "The Abbot and the Learned Woman," "The Epithalamium of Petrus Aegidius," "The Lying-In Woman," "The Unequal Marriage," and "The Parliament of Women" all deal in some way, entirely or partly, lightly or seriously, with the character, wisdom, status, and education of women. All these facts speak eloquently for More's leadership, in both practice and theory, about the liberal training of women.

MORE'S SCHOOL

More's household school, the center for the classical education of women during the early 1500's, was based on the same principles for men and women. Hence the aims and methods discussed in the previous chapter on general education are basic to this chapter also: purity and beauty in Latin style; double translation as a means to fluency; probably the easy and the inductive approach to grammar; the use of kindness, gentleness, and praise, when deserved, as incentives to further study; Greek, Latin, mathematics, astronomy, logic without a vain display of skill—the same subjects for all; modesty, humility; virtue and piety with sound learning.

More's school must have been dominantly feminine, since More had three daughters but only one son; a stepdaughter, Alice Middleton; a foster daughter, Margaret Gigs. Frances Staverton, his niece; Margaret Abarrow, who became the wife of Sir Thomas Elyot; and Anne Cresacre, who married his son John—all were said to have been pupils in the school.

It may clarify thinking to consider More's school in two distinct periods: first, a time of formal instruction, about 1510 to 1521;

second, a period of independent study, from about 1521 to the break-up of the More household.

The first period began whenever Margaret More, the oldest child, was ready for formal study. Nearly all letters from More to members of his school are dated before 1521 or in that year, and so are all references to individuals as tutors. More may himself have done some teaching at the start, when he was less involved in state business. Even Erasmus, in spite of his reluctance to do tutoring, may have given brief, informal help, about 1509 to 1511, when he spent much time with the Mores, though when Margaret Roper wrote him in 1529, she may have intended a conventional and complimentary, not a literal meaning for the word *praeceptor*. She said: "we desire nothing more ardently than to see once more our former tutor [*praeceptorem*] to whom we owe whatever culture we possess. . . ." [4] The place for this early period was the house in Bucklersbury, since Margaret was living in the parish of St. Stephen's, Walbrook, at the time of her marriage, in 1521. The end of this formal instruction is suggested by a letter from More to Margaret, reporting Pole's praise of her Latin—a letter that must be dated early in 1521 by Pole's departure for a five-year period on the Continent. More said: "I could scarce make him believe that you had not been helped by a master until I told him in all good faith that there was no master at our house, and that it would not be possible to find a man who would not need your help in composing letters rather than be able to give any assistance to you." [5]

The second period, of independent study, belongs mainly to Chelsea, since More must have moved his family there some time between 1521 and 1524. The assumption about Chelsea as the usual center has been fostered by biographers who refer to a letter of

[4] P. S. Allen, *Opus epistolarum*, 12 vols. (Oxford, 1906–1958), VIII, 2233, lines 23–26: "nihil ardentius expetentes quam vt praeceptorem nostrum, cuius eruditis laboribus quicquid bonarum litterarum imbiberimus acceptum habemus, fidelemque patris veteremque amicum, coram aliquando colloqui ac contemplari nobis liceat." For the translation see T. E. Bridgett, *Life* (London, 1891), p. 151.

[5] Elizabeth F. Rogers, *The Correspondence of Sir Thomas More* (Princeton, 1947), no. 128. "Vix etiam sibi persuaserat, praeceptoris tibi non corrogatam operam, quoad bona fide didicit neque praeceptorem quemquam esse domi nostrae. . . ." This part of the letter (and the whole seems to be two letters joined) is dated in early 1521 by Pole's departure for Italy. See Stapleton, *Life,* trans. by Philip E. Hallett (London, 1928), p. 46, for the English version.

Erasmus mentioning the location by the Thames, and who leave the vague inference that the details were in an early letter of Erasmus about More. But Erasmus made the statement about the location on the Thames in his letter to John Faber, 1532.[6] Probably this period of independent study was under the leadership of Margaret Roper, with occasional suggestions from her father.

WOMEN WHO WERE GIVEN LIBERAL TRAINING

Margaret More Roper was the outstanding woman educated in More's school; she might also be called one of the brilliant women of the sixteenth century. Besides translating Erasmus' *Precatio dominica* as the *Treatise on the Pater Noster* and writing occasional poems and letters, she wrote a treatise on the *Four Last Things* which her father considered better than his own work on the same subject; she emended successfully a corrupt passage in St. Cyprian; she wrote an oration answering one by Quintilian, and this oration was also said to have been considered equal to her father's work. She translated Eusebius from Greek, it is said, but did not have it published because John Christopherson of St. John's College had translated the same material. Contemporaries testified to her unusual ability, especially Erasmus, who treated her as a scholar and an equal, not merely as the daughter of his friend.

According to Ballard, Margaret Roper educated her three daughters, Mary, Elizabeth, and Margaret, as she had been educated. She wished to have Roger Ascham as their tutor, but since he was unwilling to leave the university, she secured a Doctor Cole (perhaps the Henry Cole who became Dean of St. Paul's in 1556); John Christopherson, later Bishop of Chichester; and a Mr. John Morwen, described as "a noted Grecian, who was preceptor to her daughter Mary in the Greek and Latin tongues." He is said to have been much pleased with Mary's learned compositions and translated into English some of her Greek and Latin compositions.[7]

Mary, who married Stephen Clarke first and later James Bas-

[6] P. S. Allen, *Opus epistolarum*, X, 2750.

[7] George Ballard, *Memoirs* (London, 1775), pp. 27, 29, 37, 43, 106, and *passim*. The 1752 edition of his work, published while he was living, is not available. It seems impossible, in the limits of this work, to vouch for all his details, but they are interesting as tradition about learned women.

sett, completed her grandfather's *Treatise on the Passion,* which he did not succeed in finishing—some say because his writing materials were taken from him in the Tower, though this statement does not seem to explain fully all the facts. The volume of More's English works, 1557, gives More's work on pages 1270 to 1349, explaining that he wrote no more in English but continued in Latin. A section follows, pages 1351 to 1404, which is described thus: "An exposition of a parte of the passion . . . made in Latine by Sir Thomas More, knight (whyle he was prisoner in the tower of London) and translated into englyshe by maystres Mary Bassett." The heading adds that she was a gentlewoman of Queen Mary's privy chamber.

Two of the queens of Henry VIII and both of his daughters were educated in classical learning. First of the queens, both in time and in eminence, was Catherine of Aragon. More had no possible influence on her education. Her mother, Queen Isabella, trained all her daughters in the plain household duties (spinning, baking, weaving); in the skills of the great lady, including genealogy, heraldry, horsemanship, and falconry; and in the classics. Catherine, as well as her sisters, was able to reply extempore to the speeches of ambassadors in Latin that was not only correct but fluent and classical. Vives dedicated to her his treatises, *De institutione Christianae foeminae,* 1523; and *De ratione studii puerilis,* 1523. The second of these two was written for the Princess Mary at the request of Catherine; *Satellitium,* in 1524, was written for Mary and dedicated to her.[8] In 1526 Erasmus wrote for Queen Catherine and dedicated to her his *Christiani matrimonii institutio.* Her request that he write such a book came to him through her chamberlain, Lord Mountjoy, his old friend and former pupil.[9]

More may have been influenced by Catherine when he was forming his own ideals for the education of his daughters. In 1501, when he was about twenty-three, he wrote to John Holt describing the formal entry of Catherine into London as the bride of Prince Arthur; he praised her beauty and added that she had all the

[8] Vives, *Opera,* I, 1; and II, 94 and 648, for these dedications.
[9] Erasmus, *Opera omnia,* 10 vols. (Lugduni Batavorum, 1703–1706), V, 613–16.

virtues which a most beautiful girl should have.[10] In 1509 when More wrote his verses of congratulation on the coronation of Henry VIII, he praised Queen Catherine for her devotion, dignity, unselfish love, unfailing judgment, beauty, eloquence, and loyalty to her husband, comparing her to Alcestis, Cornelia, and Penelope.[11] At this time More was about thirty-one, and his daughters ranged from two to four years of age. In the years that followed, More was consistently loyal to Catherine and her daughter Mary, and at his trial he told his judges that they sought his life because he refused to swerve from that loyalty.

The Princess Mary had her early education under the influence of her mother, Catherine of Aragon. In 1523 Linacre prepared for her his *Rudimenta grammatices,* and dedicated it to her mother. She is said to have followed Vives' curriculum in *De ratione studii puerilis,* for girls, with heavy emphasis upon Greek and Latin. She also studied astronomy, geography, and mathematics. When she was nine years old, she made a brief speech in Latin to the commissioners from the Low Countries. In 1527, when she was about eleven years old and her father entertained the French commissioners who came to treat about her proposed marriage to Francis I, she answered in the same languages their speeches in Italian, French, and Latin. When she was finally separated from her mother, about 1531 or 1532, the mother asked permission to correct occasionally her daughter's Latin exercises.[12]

Henry's next queen, Anne Boleyn, was no classical scholar; and no one has accused Henry of falling in love with her because of her learning. But she had acquired at least the surface of French culture. And Anne of Cleves is said to have been even less interesting to Henry because she was not educated in music and languages.

Catherine Parr, the queen who managed to survive Henry VIII, "became an accomplished scholar, as her own works remain to testify. Not only had she full command of Latin, but she was familiar with Greek . . . and had acquired facility in the use of

[10] Rogers, *The Correspondence,* no. 2.

[11] Bradner and Lynch, *The Latin Epigrams of Thomas More* (Chicago, 1953), no. 1, pp. 142–43.

[12] *L. and P.,* IV, no. 1519, a letter from Catherine to her daughter; see also *DNB* and standard biographies.

modern languages also." Ballard says that her father, "following
the example of Sir Thomas More and other great men, bestowed
on her a learned education as the most valuable addition he could
make to her other charms. . . ." She had practical ability as well
as classical training; when the king was in France she acted as
regent, as Catherine of Aragon had done earlier. Roger Ascham
addressed her as *eruditissima regina;* and if she had not been rea-
sonably learned, he would probably have chosen the superlative
of some other adjective. She published many psalms and prayers;
one edition of her *Prayers,* dated 1545, with slightly different
titles and possibly with changes, went through a number of editions by 1559. Her work called *The Lamentacion of a Sinner,* published in 1547, also went through several editions; and in 1563
it was issued with a preface by William Cecil, later Lord Burghley.
Catherine Parr may have taught handwriting to Prince Edward,
and for at least two years she had the Princess Elizabeth under
her care. In 1544 Elizabeth dedicated to her a handwritten translation into English prose of a French poem by Queen Margaret of
Navarre; she entitled her translation "The Glass of the Sinful
Soul." She began by mentioning the Queen's love and fervent zeal
for all Godly learning and her own duty to her; she also asked
her to correct the faults in her work. The *DNB* states but without giving any specific source that Catherine also urged the
Princess Mary, in a letter which is extant, to publish under her
own name her translation of Erasmus' *Paraphrase of the Gospels.*[13]

The education of the Princess Elizabeth was well publicized
by Roger Ascham, who was her tutor about 1548 and again for
several years after she became queen. Ascham liked to think of
himself as the teacher of the best scholar that was living in his
time. Attempting to rebuke young gentlemen for not doing well,
he said that they did not spend as much time for the increase of
learning and knowledge as the queen did: "Yea, I beleue, that
beside her perfit readines in Latin, Italian, French, and Spanish,
she readeth here now at Windsore more Greeke euery day, than

[13] Ballard, *Memoirs,* pp. 56–70; also *DNB* and standard biographies. The Folger Shakespeare Library has copies of the two works by Catherine. Princess Elizabeth's translation,
with its address to Queen Catherine, was reproduced in facsimile by Percy W. Ames, as
The Mirror of the Sinful Soul (London, 1897).

some Prebendarie of this Chirch doth read Latin in a whole weeke. And . . . within the walles of her priuie chamber, she hath obteyned that excellencie of learnyng, to understand, speake, and write, both wittely with head, and faire with hand, as scarce one or two rare wittes in both the Vniuersities haue in many yeares reached vnto." Ascham also used her as evidence (see Chapter V) that double translation and the indirect method of learning grammar were effective methods of teaching.[14] Other sources indicate that Queen Elizabeth, in a day's work, might answer three different ambassadors in Italian, French, and Latin. Elizabeth is said to have been taught by Sir John Cheke, as well as by Roger Ascham.

Ascham's report on Lady Jane Grey's learning is also well known. When he found her reading Plato in Greek, while her parents were hunting, she assured him that "all their sporte in the park is but a shadoe to that pleasure that I find in Plato." She contrasted her parents' strictness in discipline with the allurements to learning which her tutor, John Aylmer, used, and thus she furnished us with another example of that theory of teaching.[15] At fifteen, according to the *DNB*, Lady Jane, already accomplished in Greek, Latin, Italian, and French, was studying Hebrew. She was famous for her beauty and amiability as well as her learning. When she was nine years old, she entered the household of Queen Catherine Parr and spent much time with her until Catherine's death about two years later.

Among the women with a reputation for classical learning were Anne, Margaret, and Jane, the three daughters of Protector Edward Seymour, first Duke of Somerset, by his second wife, Anne Stanhope. Their literary reputation rested chiefly on their composing "a century of Latin distichs" on the death of Margaret of Valois. The three sisters in another family, the daughters of Henry Howard, Earl of Surrey, the poet, were praised by William Barker. He mentioned by name Lady Jane Howard, "who is of sutche marvelous towardness in learnenge as few men maye compare with her. Both greke and lattynne is vulgare vnto her—her composycion

---

[14] Ascham, *The Scholemaster* (London, 1570), First book, leaf 21; Second book, leaf 35.
[15] *The Scholemaster*, First book, leaves 11 *verso*-12.

in versis so notable that all the world dothe acknowledge hyr a worthye daughter of a moste worthy father." [16] Perhaps Barker was prejudiced in her favor, since these women were sisters of his patron, Thomas Howard, who became the fourth Duke of Norfolk. But his praise illustrates the fact that it had become the fashion to commend women for their learning.

The daughters of Henry Fitzalan, the twelfth Earl of Arundel, had some reputation for classical learning, though they did not publish any literary efforts. Joanna or Jane, married to Lord Lumley about 1552, translated the Greek of Isocrates' oration *Archidamus* into Latin; she also translated other orations of Isocrates and made an English translation from the Greek of the *Iphigenia* by Euripides. Mary was married to Thomas Howard, son of the poet, the Earl of Surrey and brother of the Howard sisters mentioned in the preceding paragraph. As Mary died in childbirth when she was sixteen, only a year after her marriage, it is not surprising that she left no published work. The manuscripts containing the work of both sisters were preserved among the royal manuscripts from Lord Lumley's library, and some or all of them are in the British Museum.[17]

The daughters of Sir Anthony Cooke, tutor of Prince Edward, had a great reputation for classical learning. Although their father was careful to have them educated in sewing, cooking, and other household arts, he himself taught them religion, obedience, modesty, all the classics, and all the other formal learning which he gave the prince, Edward VI. His maxim was that "sexes as well as souls are equal in capacity." He did not force his daughters against their natures; instead, he managed them with such "reason and sweetness that love obliged all his family." In planning marriages, "His care was that his daughters might have complete men, and that their husbands might have complete women." All these are principles which Sir Thomas More himself might have stated.

These daughters apparently justified their father's hopes. Mildred became the second wife of William Cecil, Lord Burghley. (Burgh-

[16] William Barker, *The Nobility of Women*, ed. by R. Warwick Bond (London, 1904), pp. 151, 154. Though Barker's ideas are a kind of restatement of Agrippa von Nettesheim through Domenichini's *La nobilità della donne*, he also praised Margaret Roper and many others.
[17] Ballard, *Memoirs*, pp. 87–88, also *DNB*.

ley's first wife had been Mary Cheke, sister of Sir John Cheke and perhaps a learned woman herself, though her reputation for learning seems to rest upon the fact that her brother was a classical scholar and teacher.) Anne, the second daughter, married Nicholas Bacon and became the mother of Sir Francis Bacon. Anne translated into English Bishop Jewel's *Apologia pro ecclesia Anglicana*, which he had published in 1562 and had written in Latin because it was intended to be a defense of Elizabeth on the Continent. Her work pleased Archbishop Parker so much that he had it printed for general distribution in England. She also translated from the Italian fourteen sermons by Bernardino Ochino. Katherine, the third daughter, who married Henry Killigrew, does not seem to be credited with any literary work. Elizabeth, the fourth daughter, married Sir Thomas Hoby, the translator of Castiglione's *Courtier;* after his death she married Lord John Russell. She translated from the Latin, as her title page tells us, *A Way of Reconciliation of a Good and Learned Man, touching the Truth . . . of the Body and Blood of Christ in the Sacrament;* and though the work was not published until 1605, it still shows the influence of her early training. Thomas Lodge called Elizabeth "the English Sappho," and dedicated to her with the usual high praise his "Margarite of America." It has also been said that "the inscriptions at great length in Greek, Latin, and English on the family tombs at Bisham, and on that of Lord Russell in Westminster Abbey, which were written by her, sufficiently prove her skill in the learned languages." In his will Sir Anthony Cooke remembered his daughters with three volumes each from his library, two in Latin and one in Greek. The oldest was to have first choice, and then each of the other daughters was to choose in the order of age.[18]

One example of a woman with a classical education in a rising middle-class merchant family appears by chance, though there may have been more of these middle-class women than we realize. Elizabeth Withypoll was the daughter of a merchant, and the sister of Edmund Withypoll, whom Lupset loved as if he had been a son or a brother, considered as much his son by education

[18] David Lloyd, *The States-Men and Favourites of England* (London, 1665), pp. 199–204; Ballard, *Memoirs*, pp. 127–47.

as he was Paul Withypoll's son, and the one to whom he chiefly addressed "An Exhortation to Young Men." Edmund was also a friend of Gabriel Harvey. Elizabeth married Emanuel Lucar but died in 1537, when she was not quite twenty-seven years old. Her husband erected a stone tablet as a memorial to her in the church of St. Lawrence Pountney. He praised her piety, her prudence and her other virtues, her skill in needlework and in algorism for accounts, her versatile ability as a musician—she could sing in diverse tongues and play the viol, the flute, and the virginals—her ability to write "three manner hands," and also to speak, write, and read Spanish, Italian, English, and Latin.[19]

IDEAS IN WRITINGS

John Colet made no special statement, so far as the present evidence goes, in favor of giving women a classical education. He merely interpreted St. Paul and considered any marriage a concession to human weakness.[20] Grocyn, Linacre (who is said to have become a priest in his later years), and Bishop Fisher were not inclined to comment on the problem. John Rastell, layman and married man though he was, seemed uninterested in writing on love, marriage, or the education of women—unless he was the author of *Calisto and Melebea,* and that seems unlikely. In *The Nature of the Four Elements* he used the opening speech of the Messenger to issue a blast against love stories:

> But now so it is that in our Englyshe tonge
> Many one there is that can but rede and wryte
> For his pleasure wyll oft presume amonge
> New bokys to compyle and balats [?] to indyte
> Some of loue or other matter not worth a myte.

MORE

Sir Thomas More defended as well as practiced theories of equality in classical education. His ideas in *Utopia* are an interesting approach to the discussion of his views; Utopian women were

[19] Ballard, *Memoirs,* pp. 25–26; John Archer Gee, *The Life and Works of Thomas Lupset* (New Haven, 1928), pp. 124–25, 235–36.
[20] J. H. Lupton, *The Life of John Colet* (London, 1909), pp. 77–78.

both priests and soldiers, though it does not follow that he wished to push them into these positions in sixteenth-century England. Women, he said, were less often chosen as priests and only if they were widows past the age of bearing children. But women priests and the wives of priests were honored above other women in the country. The Utopian women practiced military exercises regularly, were allowed to follow their husbands to war, in spite of the Utopian hate of war, and were placed beside their husbands in battle. These comments illustrate the free play of mind which More and his friends gave to all ideas, including equality of the sexes. It seems to be in part an influence from Plato, who said: "But the natural capacities are distributed alike among both creatures, and women naturally share in all pursuits and men in all—yet for all, the woman is weaker than the man. . . . The women and the men, then, have the same nature in respect to the guardianship of the state, save . . . as the one is weaker. . . . For the production of a female guardian, then, our education will not be one thing for men and another for women . . . since the nature . . . is the same." [21]

But these theories of equality between men and women do not seem entirely consistent with the patriarchal family government in Utopia. Farming households, with not less than forty persons and with two bondmen, seemed to have some sharing of responsibility; for all these people were under the rule of the "good man and the good wyfe, beynge both very sage and discrete persones." But religious practices had centralization of authority; on holy days, the last days of the month and the year, before going to church, wives were to "fall downe prostrat before their husbandes feete at home" and children before the feet of their parents, confessing their sins of omission and commission and achieving peace with each other. "The eldeste . . . ruleth the familie. The wyfes bee ministers to theyr husbandes, the chyldren to theyr parentes, and the yonger to theyr elders." [22] The men of More's age believed in the centralization of authority, of course, and most of them prob-

---

[21] Plato, *The Republic*, trans. by Paul Shorey, 2 vols. (London and Cambridge, Mass., 1946), I, 447–51.

[22] *Utopia*, ed. by J. H. Lupton (Oxford, 1895), pp. 121, 156–57, 291–92.

ably were sure that a monarchy was the best form of government so long as the monarch was wise and just. It seems a little uncertain whether More would have agreed with Erasmus that a woman is subject to her husband, not as a woman but as a wife; that she obeys because the man is fiercer rather than better, and that each still has some power over the other. (See the discussion of "The Lying-In Woman," by Erasmus, later in this chapter.)

More's epigram, "To Candidus: How to Choose a Wife" (Number 125 in Bradner and Lynch, *The Latin Epigrams*) is an indirect essay on the ideal marriage, written with the light touch and with some serious intention. The date of its composition is uncertain, though it was probably published first in 1518. More advised his friend, perhaps his imaginary friend, to observe the parents of the prospective wife, and thus to make certain that she had "the best of characters for her tender infant to acquire—along with mother's milk—and to imitate." She must be chaste, modest, neither garrulous nor boorishly taciturn, and agreeable. "Let her be either educated or capable of being educated," so that she may learn "from the best of ancient works the principles which confer a blessing on life." As a result, she will not become proud in prosperity nor yield to grief in distress or extreme misfortune. If she is well educated herself, "then some day she will teach your little grandsons, at an early age, to read." The husband of such a woman will enjoy leaving the company of men for her embraces, for her music as she plays and sings, for her "pleasant and intelligent conversation," for her comments in success or in sorrow. "When she speaks, it will be difficult to judge between her extraordinary ability to say what she thinks and her thoughtful understanding of all kinds of affairs." Such a woman was the wife of Orpheus; the daughter of Ovid, who rivaled her father in poetic composition; Tullia, the well-loved daughter of a famous father; the mother of the Gracchi, who was the teacher as well as the mother of her sons; and one maiden of his own period who is "the admiration and glory of the whole world" as well as of her own country, Britain. (Here he probably referred to the Princess Mary.)

More's letter to William Gonell, 1518, is both the initial pronouncement and a complete statement of principles on the education of women in sixteenth-century England. More wished Gonell to emphasize modesty and virtue with sound learning. Fame is not the object of this education, he said, though fame tends to follow virtue as the shadow follows the substance. Most people snatch at the shadow of things; he wished his children to find the realities. True wisdom is a reality because it depends on truth and justice, not on the common talk of people. Learning is not an ornament but a utility which one should apply to life on all occasions. He emphasized the elimination of pride and the cultivation of humility. He agreed with Gonell that Margaret's lofty character should not be abased, but he warned that admiration for anything vain or shallow would abase it. Pride, since it appeared early in life, should be eradicated in the earliest years by the cultivation of humility. More did not wish his daughters to admire gold and costly trappings, nor to waste their time longing for the qualities of others which they did not possess; neither did he wish them to neglect the beauty which God had given them nor to try artificial means of increasing that beauty. People with a sound education, More said, have learned to enjoy the genuine pleasures in life and to face death without horror.

More would himself grant, it seems, that these ideas apply equally to men and women. But he was conscious that he was breaking with tradition in giving women a thorough classical education:

Since erudition in women is a new thing and a reproach to the sloth of men, many will gladly assail it, and impute to literature what is really the fault of nature, thinking from the vices of the learned to get their own ignorance esteemed as virtue. On the other hand, if a woman (and this I desire and hope with you as their teacher for all my daughters) to eminent virtue should add an outwork of even moderate skill in literature, I think she will have more real profit than if she had obtained the riches of Croesus and the beauty of Helen.

He also compared the capacity of men and women for development:

Nor do I think that the harvest will be much affected whether it is a man or a woman who sows the field. They both have the same human nature,

which reason differentiates from that of beasts; both, therefore, are equally
suited for those studies by which reason is cultivated, and becomes fruitful
like a ploughed land on which the seed of good lessons has been sown. If it
be true that the soil of woman's brain be bad, and apter to bear bracken
than corn, by which saying many keep women from study, I think, on the
contrary, that a woman's wit is on that account all the more diligently to
be cultivated, that nature's defect may be redressed by industry. This was
the opinion of the ancients, of those who were most prudent as well as
most holy.[23]

More did not wish to thrust his daughters into public life. When
he wrote Margaret his hope that she would study sacred letters
and medicine, he probably expected her to minister to her family
and friends. Though he encouraged her and her husband to com-
pete with each other for excellence in learning, he also said in one
letter to her: "Content with the approbation of your conscience,
in your modesty you do not seek for the praise of the public, nor
value it over much even if you receive it, but because of the great
love you bear us you regard us—i.e. your husband and myself—
as a sufficiently large circle of readers for all that you write." [24]
But he was a proud as well as a loving father—proud of character
and of literary skill. He showed his daughters' Latin letters to
such friends as Reginald Pole and John Veysey, Bishop of Exeter,
and though he was pleased with their praise, he was annoyed by
a gift from the bishop for Margaret—because that kept him from
showing the bishop the letters of the other daughters. The bishop
had praised Margaret's letter for "its pure Latinity, its correctness,
its erudition, and its expressions of tender affection." [25] Pole had
been incredulous—surely no woman had written the letter which
More showed him. More revealed his understanding of his daughter's character and of public opinion when he wrote to her: "Mean-
while something I once said to you in joke came back to my mind,
and I realized how true it was. It was to the effect that you were
to be pitied, because the incredulity of men would rob you of the
praise you so richly deserved for your laborious vigils, as they
would never believe, when they read what you had written, that

[23] Rogers, The Correspondence, no. 63; for translation see Stapleton, Life, pp. 101–4.
[24] The Correspondence, no. 128, p. 302; see Stapleton, as cited, p. 115.
[25] The Correspondence, no. 108; Stapleton, p. 116.

you had not often availed yourself of another's help: whereas of all writers you least deserved to be thus suspected. Even when a tiny child you could never endure to be decked out in another's finery." [26]

ERASMUS

Erasmus' most interesting comments on the education of women occur in his personal letters. In a letter to Budé, about 1521, Erasmus praised the skill of the More daughters in Latin composition and their many other splendid qualities; he confessed that he had once doubted the wisdom of higher education for women but that More's experiment with his daughters had changed his mind completely. He predicted that the More plan would be imitated far and wide.[27] Writing to Margaret Roper about September, 1529, probably after receiving a copy of the picture by Holbein of the More family, Erasmus spoke of the Mores as the friends to whom he owed whatever fame and fortune he had and also the friends to whom he was glad to owe all his achievement. Then he said to Margaret: "I recognized all but no one more clearly than you. I seemed to see, through its most beautiful dwelling, your much more beautiful mind shining." [28]

In a half-dozen or more colloquies Erasmus discussed the problems of woman's education, character, and status within and outside the family. "A Lover and a Maiden" begins lightly. Pamphilus urges that his love be returned, and Mary evades him with skillful Socratic questioning, thus suggesting that she is a woman of education. There is even some light comment on Venus and Cupid. Then as the talk settles into seriousness the two emphasize these ideas: Mary has been modestly and religiously educated; the parents of both have been intimate for years; the two young people have known each other since childhood; their temperaments seem to

---

[26] *The Correspondence*, no. 128; Stapleton, pp. 114, 46.

[27] P. S. Allen, *Opus epistolarum*, IV, 1233, p. 578. "Iam neminem fere mortalium non habebat haec persuasio, sexui foeminino literas et ad castitatem et ad famam esse inutiles. Nec ipse quondam prorsus ad hac abhorrui sententia: verum hanc mihi Morus penitus excussit animo."

[28] *Opus epistolarum*, VIII, 2212. "Omnes agnoui, sed neminem magis quam te. Videre mihi videbar per pulcherrimum domicilium relucentem animum multo pulchriorem." See no. 2233 for her reply.

agree; they have equality in age, fortune, and parentage. These are the bases of a lasting, comfortable marriage—a union of minds. Pamphilus concludes that good parents develop good children and that they will educate their children in piety from the cradle. Mary encourages him to continue courting her but not to let passion rule him, since it is only temporary, but the love based on reason is permanent.[29]

"The Uneasy Wife" is a talk between two women, one being wise in solving her own matrimonial problems. She tells the younger woman, whose name is Xantippe, that a love based on beauty is only temporary. She advises the troubled young woman to be pleasant and tactful, especially in giving her husband advice to further his own welfare, to adapt food to her husband's taste, to create a happy atmosphere at home, and to make herself attractive in wifely relations. She also tells her that it is the glory of a matron to obey her husband—a piece of advice which is qualified in another colloquy, to be discussed later.[30]

In his colloquy, "The Abbot and the Learned Woman," Erasmus covered the whole problem of liberal education for women and at the same time cudgelled ignorant ecclesiastics. Magdalia is reading Greek and Latin books when a certain Abbot calls upon her and tells her that ladies should use leisure for pleasure. She defends herself by shrewd Socratic questioning, saying first that pleasure proceeds from the mind: "This is wisdom, to know that a man is only happy by the goods of the mind. That wealth, honor, and descent neither make a man happier nor better. . . . Is it not a woman's business to mind the affairs of her family and to instruct her children? . . . And do you think that so weighty an office can be executed without wisdom? . . . This wisdom I learn from books. . . . But I bless myself that I have gotten a husband . . . not like yourself. Learning both endears him to me, and me to him. . . . A woman that is truly wise does not think herself so. . . ." When the Abbot argues that custom makes it unwise for a woman to know the classics, and that learning in women is rare, Magdalia answers: "And after all it is not so great

[29] Erasmus, *The Colloquies* (London, 1878), I, 210–24.
[30] *The Colloquies*, I, 241–60.

a rarity as you think it. There are both in Spain and Italy not a few women that are able to vye with the men, and there are the Morites in England, and the Bilibald-duks and Blaureticks in Germany . . . unless you take care of yourselves it will come to that pass that we shall be divinity professors in the schools and preach in the churches and take possession of your mitres." The Abbot answers, "God forbid." Magdalia's last comment was probably intended to be a light touch in a serious discussion; but the whole colloquy summarizes competently Erasmus' position on liberal education for women of capacity.[31]

Erasmus again explained a permanent and desirable love in "The Epithalamium of Petrus Aegidius." In the latter colloquy, written for his friend, Peter Gilles, town clerk of Antwerp, student of law and the classics, and also friend of More, he discussed the ideal marriage between Peter and his Cornelia, a love based on learning and virtue, one that would increase with age and time: "Indeed Juno won't be there; she's a scolding goddess and is but seldom in a good humour with her own Jove: Nor indeed that earthly drunken Venus, but another heavenly one, which makes a union of minds." Asked whether the heavenly Venus produced anything but souls, the speaker answered: "Yes, she gives bodies to the souls, but such bodies as shall be exactly conformable to 'em, just as though you should put a choice ointment into a curious box of pearl." [32]

In the colloquy entitled "The Lying-In Woman," Fabulla, who has recently given birth to a son, is receiving congratulations from Eutrapelus, a man who is an old friend of the family. Fabulla answers that she will really deserve the congratulations if she brings her son up to be an honest man. After some asides on the evils of following custom and on the sad state of world affairs in both church and state, Fabulla accuses Eutrapelus of believing that men are stronger and more excellent than women. Fabulla then argues that men do not live longer, that they are not more free from illness, and that they are not *better* because they have more physical strength, since camels are stronger than men but

[31] *The Colloquies*, I, 376–82.
[32] *The Colloquies*, I, 383–90.

are not considered better than men. Eutrapelus says that God himself subjected woman to man. Fabulla answers that God commanded her to be obedient as a *wife*, not as a *woman*; that each still has some power over the other; that obedience does not prove weakness, since the woman is obedient because the man is fiercer, not better; that men and women, as members of one body are equal before God; and if people are made in the image of God, the likeness is not in the physical body but in the mind. Fabulla seems clearly to win the argument with these ideas. But when Fabulla admits that her child is with his nurse, Eutrapelus lectures her on the duty of an intelligent woman to care for her own child, to develop his body well so that it may not impede his mind, and by her care to develop in him more love, more obedience, and more effective training in the precepts of a good life, while he is still pliable, than any nurse can give him. Here Eutrapelus unites the principles of general education with the duty of an intelligent woman to her children, and here he clearly wins the argument.[33]

In "The Unequal Marriage," Gabriel, who has just witnessed an unhappy wedding, denounces those parents who force an attractive daughter to wed an old man who is a gambler, a drunkard, a liar, a cheat, a whoremaster, and who has the pox, merely because he has a title. Both speakers agree that marriages should produce children with sound bodies, for these reasons: physical disease not only ruins the body but also saps the mind; a ruler with wisdom and integrity is a better ruler if he has a sound, attractive body; children should be worthy of inheriting property and should be capable of becoming good rulers for the state. Thus Erasmus integrates the themes of true nobility, good government for the welfare of all, and the duties of parents to their children and to the state.[34]

In "The Parliament of Women," all ideas, serious or not, are given the light touch. Cornelia, the leader, begins by stressing the need for a congress of women, since nearly all other groups meet to discuss common problems, and since the world is in a sad state under the management of men. She suggests that women might

[33] *The Colloquies*, I, 441–64.
[34] *The Colloquies*, II, 153–66.

be able to manage it better. She admits that women have some advantages over men in the organization of society: they do not struggle to support a family, they do not go to war, and they are not punished for breaking laws in the same way that men are punished. Discussing the question of honor in relation to dress, Cornelia seems to plead for dress that will indicate both rank and character and to condemn changes in fashion. But at the close Cornelia emphasizes these more serious ideas: women are excluded from honorable jobs and are permitted to be only laundresses and cooks, while men manage everything according to their pleasure; women will concede to men the management of most public and military affairs; a woman is not treated fairly when her coat of arms, though her family may be twice as honorable as her husband's, is placed on the left side of the escutcheon; a woman's consent should be necessary for the "putting out" of children; and women might be allowed to take their turns in administering the public offices that can be managed at home without the use of weapons. These problems, Cornelia announces, will be discussed day by day with the purpose of passing an act about each one.[35] As the philosopher with a free play of mind over his topic, Erasmus is here trying to stimulate thought; he is probably not equally serious about all of these problems.

Erasmus also was positive in his condemnation of romantic tales of chivalry; and though he happened to attack them in treatises directed to boys, his statements are broad enough to apply to both boys and girls. In *De pueris instituendis* he said that a boy could learn some story from the ancient poets, a pleasant maxim, or a significant story from history, just as easily as the stupid or ridiculous stories which he learned from servants or nurses.[36] In *The*

---

[35] *The Colloquies*, II, 203–11. The complete title is "The Assembly or Parliament of Women."

[36] Erasmus, *Opera omnia*, I, 511, A, B: "Quid enim obstat quo minus eadem opera discat aut lepidam ex Poetis fabellam, aut festivam sententiam, aut insignem historiolam, aut eruditum apologum qua cantionem ineptam, plerumque et scurrilem, qua ridenda delirantium anicularum fabulamenta, qua meras muliercularum imbibunt et ediscunt nugas? Quantum somniorum, quantum inanium aenigmatum, quantum inutilium naeniarium de lemuribus, spectris . . . sylvanis et daemogorgonibus . . . etiam viri memoria tenemus, quae puelli a thattis, aviis, mammis, ac puellis colo assidentes, et inter complexus ac lusus audivimus?"

Instruction of a Christian Prince he was specific: "But today we see many who take delight in stories of Arthur and Lancelot and such tales, which are not only about tyrants but are also unlearned, silly, old wives' tales, when it would be better to spend time reading comedies or legends of the poets, instead of that sort of nonsense." [37]

AGRIPPA OF NETTESHEIM

The work of Henry Cornelius Agrippa of Nettesheim *De nobilitate et prae-excellentiae feminei sexus* seems worth a brief mention. It was probably written about 1510, published not earlier than 1529, and published in an English translation by David Clapam in 1542. About 1510 Agrippa was a guest of John Colet in his mother's home in Stepney, where he worked hard on the Epistles of St. Paul with Colet, and as a result published *An Oration . . . on the Excellence of God's Word,* a plea for simple biblical Christianity. It seems probable that he would have met More while he was Colet's guest.

Agrippa argued from the order of creation that woman is God's most honorable, perfect, and wise product. His rhapsody on woman's physical beauty is worthy of Solomon or Hollywood. But he spoke also of her dignity, honesty, and chastity—at length. "And were it not that women in our tyme ar forbydden to gyue theym to good lernynges, we shulde euen nowe haue women more excellent in wyt and lernynge than menne." Among the Romans, he said, noble women were permitted to judge, to do and to take homage and fealty, to hold court, and to administer justice. He complained that men were not giving women the education they should have; instead, a girl was usually kept at home from infancy in idleness and allowed "to know no farther than her nedle and her threede." Then she was either given to a jealous husband or put into a convent. One of Agrippa's more fascinating ideas concerns a man and a woman in danger of drowning: "she without any outwarde helpe swymmeth alofte longer than the man, whiche

[37] *Opera omnia*, IV, 587 D: "At hodie permultos videmus, Arcturis, Lanslotis, et aliis id genus fabulis delectari, non solum tyrannicis, verum etiam prorsus ineruditis, stultis, et anilibus, ut consultius sit in Comoediis, aut Poetarum fabulis horas collocare, quam ejusmodi deliramentis."

soner synketh and goth downe to the bottom." [38] Agrippa had
many of the basic ideas expressed by the men in the More circle,
but unlike them, he had an amazing ability to make them sound
unreal and fantastic.

RICHARD HERDE

As Richard Herde was both student and teacher in More's house
and as he had the help of More in his translation of Vives' *Instruction of a Christian Woman*, it is not surprising that his ideas on
the education of women are similar to More's. His treatise served
as the introduction to Margaret Roper's translation of Erasmus'
Precatio dominica in 1524. Herde did not name the translator;
she was a "young, vertuous, and well learned gentylwoman" nine-
teen years of age, but there is general agreement about her identity. He dedicated his work to a "virtuous yonge mayde Fraunces
S," saying that she had been trained with her honorable uncle's
children, that her own mother had given her a splendid example
in virtuous living, that he was much beholden to that mother himself, and that she was a kinswoman to the translator. He seemed
to have a personal interest in her, more than is usual between a
writer and the one to whom he dedicates a work. Within his work
he paid a high tribute to the character of the translator and also to
her skill and learning.

In this introduction Herde said that learning in Latin and
Greek does not cause women to be more given to vice, and that
men, though they are less moral than women, judge women more
harshly. Latin and Greek do not contain more evil than books
in French and English; they do include the writings of many
holy doctors. It is not true that women who know Latin and
Greek are likely to misbehave with priests and friars, for evil
priests themselves shun good learning. If a woman is disposed to
goodness, learning will make her better; most learned women are
good and most evil women are unlearned. Good learning is a
jewel which will adorn all the other gifts of grace, or its lack will
be a blemish. It has an influence on the love between husband and

---

[38] Agrippa von Nettesheim, *A treatise of the nobilitie and excellencye of women kynde*
(London, 1542), trans. by David Clapam. In the photostatic copy I have used, few pages
are numbered; thus exact reference is impossible.

wife: "And surely the beauty of it, though ye had none other, shall get you both greater love, more faithful and longer to continue of all good folks than shall the beauty of the body, be it never so excellent, whose love decayeth together with it that was the cause of it, and most commonly before, as by daily experience we may see them, that go together for the love of the bodily beauty, within a small while, when their appetite is satisfied, repent themselves. But the love that cometh by the means of virtue and goodness, shall ever be fresh and increase, right as doth the virtue itself." [39]

Herde began his dedication to his translation of Vives' *Instruction of a Christian Woman* with humility, he said, not only because he was addressing the queen and offering a translation of an eloquent work but also because he knew the importance of the topic: "For what is more frutefull than the good education and ordre of women, the one halfe of all mankynd, and that halfe also, whose good behauour or euyll tatchis, gyueth, or bereueth the other halfe almoste all the holle pleasure and commoditie of this present lyfe, byside the furtherance or hynderance forther growyng there upon concernyng the lyfe to come." Herde said that no better treatise than Vives' had been written on the education of women, and the book had caused him to do much speculating: "I wisshed in my mynde that eyther in euery countre women were lerned in the latin tonge or the boke out of latin translated in to euery tonge; and moche I marueiled, as I often do, of the unreasonable ouer sight of men, whiche neuer ceace to complayne of womens conditions. And yet hauyng the education and order of them in theyr owne handes nat only do litell diligence to teache them and bryng them up better but also purposely with drawe them fro lernynge, by whiche they mighte haue occasyons to waxe better by them selfe." So he planned to translate the work into English "for the commoditie and profite of our owne countre." When he had finished the work he showed it to his "syngular good mayster and brynger uppe, Syr Thomas More, to whose iugement and correction I use to submyt what so euer I do or go about that I set any store by." More was glad that Herde had made the translation, though he had meant some time to do it himself, but press of business would delay him. So Herde "besoughte hym to take the labour to rede hit ouer and correcte hit. Whiche he ryght gladlye dyd." [40]

Herde's translation, checked by More, probably gives a more exact picture of English thinking than Vives' Latin version; but it is interesting to compare the two in some particulars. Herde made some changes in the lists of romances which were not to be read. For Spain, Herde named the same unholy books except *Splandianus,* which he omitted. In naming Celestine, he added only, "the baude mother of naughtynes"; Vives had described her as "Coelestina laena nequitiarum parens, carcer amorum." In naming books of France, Herde omitted *Petrus Prouincialis & Maguelona* and the phrase *domina inexorabilis,* which Vives had added after *Melusina.* He followed Vives' list of books in Flanders. He made this complete addition: "In England, Parthenope, Genarides, Hippomadon, William and Melyour, Libius and Arthur, Guye, Beuis, and many other." In the group of those translated from Latin into the vernaculars, he added the works of Aeneas Silvius and omitted the hundred tales of Boccaccio.[41] Omissions may of course be accidental. But the additions, especially the entire list of English works, seem to indicate that More and Herde were in complete agreement with Vives on the general principle but wished to add warnings against similar English works which may have been unfamiliar to Vives. (The complete passage is quoted in the discussion of Vives further on in this chapter.)

[40] Vives, *A very frutefull and pleasant boke called the Instruction of a Christen woman,* trans. by Rycharde Hyrd [Herde] (London, 1529?), leaves Aii *verso,* Aiiii *verso.* Hereafter cited as *Instruction of a Christen woman.*

[41] *Instruction of a Christen woman,* Eiiii; compare Vives, *Opera* (Basel, 1555), II, 657–58, under heading "Qui non legendi scriptores, qui legendi." Vives said: "Tum et de pestiferis libris, cuiusmodi sunt in Hispania Amadisus, Splandianus, Florisandus, Tirantus, Tristanus: quarū ineptiarū nullus est finis, quotidie prodeūt nouae, Coelestina laena nequitiarum parens, carcer amorum. In Gallia Lancilotus à lacu, Paris et Vienna, Ponthus & Sydonia, Petrus Prouincialis & Maguelona, Melusina, domina inexorabilis; in hac Belgica Florius & Albus flos, Leonella, & Cana morus, Curias & Floreta, Pyramus and Thisbe." [Here Herde inserted his English list.] "Sunt in uernaculas linguas transfusi, ex Latino . . . Poggii, Euryalus et Lucretia, Centū fabule Boccatii, quos omnes libros conscripserunt homines ociosi. . . ."

ELYOT

Sir Thomas Elyot supported More, Erasmus, Herde, Vives, and others in opposing "carnal" romances and in praising women for their good qualities. Though he was mainly concerned with the education of men to be rulers in the *Governour*, he sometimes praised women for their wisdom. One example, in Book II, vii, was Livia, whose wise counsel enabled her husband to save both himself and his people.[42] In Book I, vii, he mentioned with approval the choice of Alexander, when he refused to see the harp of Paris, the ravisher of Helen, and preferred the harp of Achilles "wherto he sang, nat the illecebrous dilectations of Venus, but the valiaunt actes and noble affaires of excellent princis." In Book I, x, he granted that the information in Ovid's *Metamorphoses* and *De fastis* might be necessary to understanding other poets, but since there was little in them about virtuous manners or policies, he suggested that the information be given the students without having them read the works. In Book I, xix, he agreed with St. Augustine in condemning any dancing tinged with idolatry, superstition, and immorality. He added: "Also in those daunces were enterlased dities of wanton loue or ribaudry, with frequent remembrance of the moste vile idolis, Venus and Bacchus . . . whiche most of all abhorred from Christes religion . . . I wolde to god those names were nat at this day vsed in balades and ditties, in the courtes of princes and noble men, where many good wittes be corrupted with semblable fantasies, whiche in better wise employed mought haue bene more necessary to the public weale and their princes honour." [43] In the chapter on continence (III, xviii) Elyot attacked "carnall affection," which its followers call love.[44] In the same chapter Elyot described the temptation which Valerian, Emperor of Rome, devised for a young Christian. He put him in a beautiful garden with a "fayre tender yonge woman . . . all naked. . . ." The details have a certain likeness to romantic medieval stories, in which the hero enjoyed himself. But Elyot's

---

[42] Elyot, *The boke named the Gouernour* (London, 1531), Fol. 127.

[43] *The Gouernour*, Fol. 22 *verso* and Fol. 75 *verso*.

[44] *The Gouernour*, Fol. 218 *verso*. In the 1531 edition, Book III, two chapters are numbered xvi.

hero was made of sterner stuff. With Elyot's approval he chewed out his own tongue, so that pain would overcome his sensual desire.[45] In Book III, xx, Elyot defined a continent man as one who "no thinge will do for bodely pleasure, whiche shall stande agayne reason." [46]

In his *Image of Governance,* a translation of Greek sayings from Severus, Elyot recorded without comment the way in which public officials directed education. The maidens were "brought up in shamefastnes, humblenesse, and occupation necessary for a housewyfe." They were not seen outside their fathers' houses except when they went to the temples which were set aside for women only, "in the company of their mothers, or such other as were in their places." [47]

But in his *Defence of Good Women,* published first in 1540, Elyot made extreme statements about the ability of women to take part in public work. Candidus, the defender of women, argued that men and women both have reason, that the most desirable part of reason is prudence, and that women, who have more prudence, consequently excel men. Zenobia, presented as the ideal woman, well trained in Greek, Latin, and Egyptian, explained that she really felt justified in postponing her marriage until she had reached the age of twenty, since she was thus enabled to learn moral philosophy—prudence, constancy, fortitude, temperance—qualities which were both an honor to her husband and an advantage to herself. As a result of her education, she had been able to please her husband during his lifetime, to train her children well, and when it became necessary, to govern the realm and to enlarge it by counsel, by the plan and execution of good laws, and by the choice of good officials. Zenobia had been first of all a good wife and mother, but when she found public work necessary, she was perfectly competent. As a character, then, she lacked none of the learning and ability required for the ideal man. Thus Elyot, in the *Defence of Good Women,* gave women high praise, with emphasis on classic learning and classic virtues.[48]

---

[45] *The Gouernour,* Fol. 219 *verso*-220.
[46] *The Gouernour,* Fol. 226 *verso*, misnumbered and placed between 223–224.
[47] Elyot, *The Image of Governance* (London, 1541), Chapter XIX, 34 *verso*.
[48] Elyot, *The Defence of Good Women* (London, 1540), *passim*.

Sir Thomas Elyot's publication of *A Defence of Good Women* in 1540 has at least a time relationship to three works on the same topic: an attack on their claims to importance *Here begynneth . . . the Schole house of Women,* which was perhaps first printed in 1541; Robert Vaughan, *A Dyalogue defensyue for Women,* 1542; and Edward Gosynhill, *The prayse of all women called Mulierum pean,* about 1542.[49] These works have no known connection with the More circle, and their ideas have no independent importance here. Whether they were triggered by Elyot's book is merely an interesting speculation.

THOMAS BECON

The ideas of Thomas Becon, a Protestant who had "proceeded B.A. at St. John's College" by 1530, are interesting and perhaps not irrelevant here, since they resemble the ideas expressed by the men in the More circle. In *The Catechism,* a dialogue between father and son, the speakers suggested that education be used as a means of reducing the number of idle and evil women; that schools for girls be set up in every Christian community by public authority, with honest, wise, discreet, and learned matrons in charge; that the schoolmistresses be paid liberal salaries. The father supplied other basic reasons for their education: woman is God's creature also and as dear to God as man; the woman is a necessary member of the commonweal; we all have our beginning in her; and children usually are like their mothers.[50]

LUIS VIVES

Vives had much to say about the education and the conduct of women. Of course he repeated many of the general principles of

---

[49] See also Beatrice White, "Three Rare Books about Women," *HEH Library Bulletin,* no. 2 (1931), pp. 165–72. Miss White's contention that there was a 1541 edition of the *Schole house of Women* makes possible the order indicated here. I examined the material in the works themselves at the Huntington Library.

[50] Thomas Becon, *The Catechism,* or vol. II of *The Works,* ed. by John Ayre for the Parker Society (Cambridge, 1844), pp. 376–78. Richard Mulcaster's ideas in *Positions* (London, 1888), pp. 166–73 are interesting but published too late in the century to be pertinent here. The opposition of Sir Thomas Smith, *De republica Anglorum,* to participation of women in public affairs, is an interesting contrast if the views were Smith's, as the book was first published six years after his death. Smith had been an associate of Cheke at Cambridge.

education which he and his friends shared, especially in the work he prepared for the Princess Mary, *De ratione studii puerilis*, a plan of study for girls. He emphasized differences in capacity, the need to encourage slower pupils, the importance of the early years, the influence of mothers and nurses, the evils of idleness, dice, and cards, and the value of praise. He discussed pronunciation, style and subject matter, Latin composition, and the great importance of Latin conversation. It might be taken for granted that methods he mentioned in his general work *De tradendis disciplinis* would be applied in the formal teaching of girls wherever they were appropriate.

Writing his *Instruction of a Christian Woman*, Vives advocated training in the duties of a housewife even for a queen or a princess. When the girl is old enough to learn anything, he said, let her begin "with that whiche perteyneth unto the ornament of her soule and the kepyng and ordryng of an house." This age may vary according to the child; Aristotle and others suggest seven years but Quintilian mentions five years: "Therfore lette her bothe lerne her boke and beside that to handle wolle and flaxe; whiche are two craftes yet lefte of that olde innocent worlde, bothe profitable and kepers of temperance, whiche thynge speciallye women ought to haue in price. . . . But I wolde in no wyse that a woman shulde be ignorant in those feates that muste be done by hande, no, nat though she be a princes or a quene." In the same chapter he said: "Let the maide also lerne cookery, nat that slubberyng and excesse in meates to serue a great meyny, full of delicious pleasures and glotony . . . but sobre and measurable, that she maye lerne to dresse meate for her father and mother and bretherne while she is a mayde, and for her husbande and chyldren whan she is a wyfe. . . . But her selfe prepare suche thynges as shall be more pleasant . . . than if they were dressed by seruants. And that the more pleasant if they were seke." [51]

In other areas it is hard to be fair to Vives by quotations because he said so many different things and because his almost fanatical zeal about a woman's chastity led him to many prohibitions. He advised women against jewelry, other adornments, cos-

---

[51] *Instruction of a Christen woman*, Book I, Chapter III, Ciii *verso*, D *verso*.

metics, perfumes; he warned them against highly seasoned foods
or any wine; he believed that girls should avoid plays, public en-
tertainments, feats of arms, talks with men, casual association
with priests and friars, and hearing or reading songs or romances
or any other literature to stir unseemly thoughts; and a small girl
should be trained to avoid any unseemly gestures even before she
could know their meaning. He was not content with a mere
chastity of body: he demanded an unsullied mind and emotions
which had not been kindled by lewdness or by too much association
with men. The teacher of a girl should be either a holy and a
learned woman or a man in love with an attractive wife, to safe-
guard the girl's chastity. His use of the term chastity included
soberness, modesty, and piety; it might be said that he applied to
a woman's chastity the test of inner attitudes, instead of outer
forms, and that he was concerned with educating every woman
to be a holy woman.[52]

Vives was a little afraid of the emotions that might develop between husbands and wives. Citing many examples of couples who
lived together with little or no "carnall dealyng" he added: "For
these holy folkes understode well inough that thyng whiche is
writen of wyse men, that the bodely pleasure is unworthy this
excellent nature of ours whiche we haue of the soule. And therfore
euery bodye dispiseth it the more and casteth it away, the more that
he hath of that excellentnes of the soule and the nigher that he is
to god. . . ."[53]

In *The Office and Duty of a Husband* he expressed similar
views:

Pansanias in platose Simpose doth put two Venus and two loues, a
heauenly and an earthly. The earthly is blind, abiect, vyle, fyithye [sic],
and occupyed aboute vile and filthye thinges, neuer lokynge up to thinges
of more worthines. But that celestiall and heauenly loue doth see most
clearelye, folowyng vertue and those thynges whiche are mooste beautifull
and moost lyke unto heauenlye thinges. Those husbandes that loue the
beautye or the ryches of their wiues are blynde and subiecte to that earthly
loue, not perceauinge the reason nor yet the measure therof. But thei whiche

[52] *Instruction of a Christen woman*, Book I, Chapter XII, "How the mayde shall be-
haue . . . abrode," also VI and VII, on virginity and chastity.
[53] *Instruction of a Christen woman*, Second book, Chapter VI, eiiii *verso*.

are true husbandes loue the soule and vertue and haue a iudgemente in loue. . . . The wise husbande doth loue his wyfe feruentlye, but yet as the father loueth his sonne; the head, the body; the soule, the fleshe; and as Christe dothe loue his churche. . . .[54]

Vives expressed strict prohibitions about a girl's conduct in public places:

Let her nat suffre to be plucked at or to be touched wantonly; let her chaunge her place or go away and nede be; let her gyue nothyng to no man nor take ought of any man. The wyse man sayth: He that taketh a benefyt selleth his libertie. And ther is in France and Spayne a good sayeng: A woman that gyueth a gyft gyueth her selfe; a woman that taketh a gyfte selleth her selfe.[55]

He condemned dancing, calling it a kindling of lechery and kissing: "Wherto serueth all that bassynge, as hit were pydgyns, the byrdes of Venus"; he deplored the fact that kissing, formerly used among kinfolks, had become common in England and France.[56] Again he said:

Loue is bredde by reason of company and communycation with men; for amonge pleasures, feastis, laughynge, daunsyng, and volupties is the kyngedome of Venus and Cupide. And with these thynges folkes myndes be entysed and snared, and specially the womens, on whom pleasure hath sorest dominion. . . . After thopinion of Aristotel and Plutarche Loue of the beautie is a forgettyng of reason and the nexte thynge unto fransy, a foule vice . . . it troubleth all the wyttis, hit breaketh and abateth hygh and noble stomackes and draweth them downe from the studye and thynkyng of high and excellent thynges unto lowe and vile and causeth them to be full of gronyng and complaynyng, to be angry, hasty, foole-hardy, strayte in rulynge, full of vile and seruile flaterynge, unmete for euery thynge, and at the laste unmete for the loue hit selfe.[57]

He advised the maiden:

Gyue none ear unto the louer, no more thanne thou woldeste do unto an inchauntoure or a sorcerer. For he cometh pleasantly and flaterynge, fyrst praysynge the mayde, shewynge her howe he is taken with the loue of her beautie and that he must be deed for her loue. . . . He calleth the fayre,

[54] Vives, *The office and duetie of an husband,* trans. by Thomas Paynell (London, 1553), "Of the accesse and goynge into Mariage," Mvii *verso*-Mviii.

[55] *Instruction of a Christen woman,* Book I, Chapter XII, leaf O.

[56] *Instruction of a Christen woman,* Book I, Chapter XIII, Piii *verso.*

[57] *Instruction of a Christen woman,* Book I, Chapter XIV, Q.

propre, wytty, welspoken, and of gentyll bloode, wherof parauenture thou
arte nothynge at all, and thou lyke a foole arte glad to here those lyes.
. . . If he had loued thy good vertues and mynde, as longe as thou haddest
lyued he wolde neuer haue ben full or wery of the. But nowe bycause he
loued but only thy body and the shorte pleasure therof . . . his loue also
vanisheth away, and he, fylled and saciate with pleasure, lotheth the
plente.[58]

In the chapter on how a maiden ought to love, Vives became
positive and said that mankind is shaped for love, "to thentent
they may be coupled to gether in charite, and nat with this carnall
and fylthy erthly Cupide and Venus, but the heuenly and spirituall,
whiche causeth holy loue." [59]

In the preface to the *Instruction of a Christian Woman* Vives
sharply prohibited a certain type of reading:

Some wryte fylthye and baudye rymes. Whiche men I can nat se what
honeste excuse they can ley for them selfe. . . . But they call them selfe
louers, and I beleue they be so in dede, ye and blinde and madde. . . . In
my mynde no man was euer banysshed more ryghtfully than was Ouide,
at lest wise if he was banisshed for writyng the crafte of loue. For other
write wanton and noughty balades, but this worshipful artificer must make
rules in goddis name and preceptes of his unthriftines, a schole maister of
baudry and a common corrupter of vertue. Nowe I doubt nat but some
wyll thynke my preceptes ouer sore and sharpe.[60]

In Book I, the fifth chapter, he expressed himself about chivalric
tournaments and named specific reading to be avoided. The passage as translated by Herde, with More's help, reads:

I haue herde tell that in some places gentyl women behold marueilous
busily the playes and iustynges of armed men and gyue sentence and
iudgement of them, and that the men feare and set more by theyr
iugementes than the mennes. . . . Therfore whan I can nat tell whether
it be mete for a Christian man to handle armur howe shulde it be lefull for
a woman to loke upon them, yea though she handle them nat, yet to be
conuersant amonge them with herte and mynde, whiche is worse. . . .
And this [the use of songs full of filth and ribaldry] the lawes ought to
take hede of; and of those ungratious bokes suche as be in my countre in

---

[58] *Instruction of a Christen woman*, Book I, Chapter XIV, Qiii *verso*-Qiv.
[59] *Instruction of a Christen woman*, Book I, Chapter XV, Rii *verso*.
[60] *Instruction of a Christen woman*, Preface by Vives, Bii.

Spayne: Amadise, Florisande, Tirante, Tristane, and Celestina the baude mother of noughtynes. In France Lancilot du Lake, Paris and Vienna, Ponthus and Sidonia, and Melucyne. In Flanders Flori and Whiteflowre, Leonell and Canamour, Curias and Floret, Pyramus and Thysbe. In Englande Parthenope, Genarides, Hippomadon, William and Melyour, Libius and Arthur, Guye, Beuis, and many other. And some translated out of latine into vulgare speches, as the unsauery conceytes of Pogius, and of Aeneas Siluius, Eurialus and Lucretia: whiche bokes but idell menne wrote unlerned, and sette all upon fylthe and vitiousnes. . . .

Recommending good reading as a contrast, in the same chapter, Vives indicated the preference for Stoical writers which he shared with More and Erasmus:

And as for those that preyse them, as I knowe some that do, I wyll beleue them if they preyse them after that they haue redde Cicero and Senec or saynt Hieronyme or holy scripture and haue mended theyr lyuyng better.[61]

In *The Office and Duty of a Husband,* in the chapter dealing with the instruction of a woman Vives added other reading which he considered undesirable:

The workes of Poetes, the Fables of Milesii, as that of the golden asse, and in a maner all Lucianes workes and manye other whiche are written in the vulgar tonge, as of Trystram, Launcelote, Ogier, Amasus, and of Artur the whiche were written and made by suche as were ydle and knew nothinge. These bokes do hurt both man and woman, for they . . . kyndle . . . all beastly and filthy desyre.[62]

Like the other men of the More circle who wrote on the education of women, Vives believed that women were capable of development by education: "The woman is euen as man is a reasonable creature, and hath a flexible witte both to good and euill, the whiche with use and counsell maye be altered and turned." He continued arguing that learned women are better in character than unlearned women and that men would not be far different from beasts if they were left to their own nature: "understande that the womans witte is no lesse apte to al thinges then the mans is; she wanteth but counsell and strengthe. . . ." He quoted Seneca's

[61] *Instruction of a Christen woman,* Book I, Chapter V, Eiii *verso*-F.
[62] Vives, *The office and duetie of an husband,* "Of the discipline and instruction of women," Ovii.

opinion that a woman, no matter how rich or honorable she may be, is "a very impudent creature, and without erudition unchaste." [63]

A woman should obey her husband, Vives thought, but he also recognized a need for some division of authority. A woman had no right to receive strangers or to arrange the marriage of her daughter, but the husband might give her the right to manage affairs in the kitchen, rule her maidens, and if she had wit and fidelity, to buy and sell certain necessary things. He added, "There be women of whom I woulde take counsell and suffer them to doe great maters, euen after their owne industry and iudgement." [64]

But Vives had also a knowledge of human relations which was deeper than mere surface rules:

A womanne well broughte uppe is frutefull and profitable unto her husbande, for so shall his house be wisely gouerned, his children vertuouslye instructed, the affections lesse insued and followed, so that they shall liue in tranquillitie and pleasure. Nor thou shalt not haue her as a seruaunt . . . but also as a most faythful secretary of thy cares and thoughtes, and in doubtfull matters a wise and a harty counseler. This is the true societie and felowship of man. . . .[65]

In the *Instruction of a Christian Woman* he explained a wise and good marriage:

But they that wolde kepe the nature of thynges holle and pure, neyther corrupte them with wronge understandyng, shulde reken that wedlocke is a bande and couplyng of loue, benyuolence, frendshippe, and charite, comprehendynge with in hit all names of goodnes, swetnes, and amyte.[66]

When a woman has lived well, is "past the pleasure of the body," and has finished bearing and bringing up children:

than in dede a vertuous woman shall rule her husbande by obeysaunce and shall brynge to passe that her husbande shal haue her in great auctorite, whiche afore tymes hath lyued euer under her husbandes rule.[67]

In *An Introduction to Wisdom* he said in words that express the views of other members of the More circle:

[63] *The office and duetie,* Pi *verso*-Piii *verso,* and *passim.*
[64] *The office and duetie,* Ui, and *passim.*
[65] *The office and duetie,* Svi.
[66] *Instruction of a Christen woman,* Book I, Chapter XVI, Tiii.
[67] *Instruction of a Christen woman,* Book II, Chapter XV, p *verso.*

Trewe loue, sure and stable frendshyppe resteth in them onely that be good and vertuouse, amonge whom loue lyghtely encreaseth.

Euyll men are so farre frome louynge the good that they can nat one loue an other. . . .

Loue is gotten also by Vertue, whiche of her selfe is so amiable that ofte tymes she inuiteth and in maner constrayneth men to loue her which neuer knewe her.[68]

At times Vives praised learned women with great feeling. In the *Instruction of a Christian Woman,* where he discussed the mother's influence on the innate "fire" or "seeds" of goodness in children he identified learning and goodness. As he continued calling the roll of noble women in the classic world he mentioned Hortentia, daughter of Hortentius the orator, whose skill in speech was like her father's and who "made an oration unto the iuges of the cite for the women, whiche oration the successours of that tyme dyd rede, nat only as a laude and preyse of womens eloquence but also to lerne counnyng of it as well as of Cicero or Demosthenes orations."[69] In the same chapter he mentioned the four daughters of Queen Isabella as outstanding learned women and praised them for their skill in extempore Latin orations. Then he mentioned by name the three daughters of Sir Thomas More and their kinswoman, Margaret Gigs, as examples of girls who had been trained in chastity, other goodness, and learning. Though Herde's English translation uses only initials for all of them, including More, Vives had used the full names of the entire group in his Latin version.[70]

So Vives left no doubt about his desire to see women educated, his admiration for the woman who has some skill in public work, his belief that learning fosters virtue, helps to create the highest type of love between husband and wife, and is essential for the proper training of children in the early years. If he has, in certain passages, a curious dualism, the attitude comes from his fanatical zeal about chastity and the fear that its bloom may be blighted by public appearances of women and perhaps from his consciousness

---

[68] Vives, *An Introduction to wysedome,* trans. by Richard Morysine (London, 1540), "Of Charity," I *verso.*

[69] *Instruction of a Christen woman,* Book I, Chapter IV, Diii, Diiii, and *passim.*

[70] *Instruction of a Christen woman,* Book I, Chapter IV, E; Vives, *Opera,* II, 656.

that middle and lower class women should not be urged to imitate the public work of queens.

The influence of Vives in England did not die after his last visit there in November, 1528. It is estimated that he had a large influence on studies at Oxford; that his friendships with eminent men—Linacre, Tunstal, Bishop Fisher, John Longland (who became Bishop of Lincoln in 1521), William Latimer, William Blount (Lord Mountjoy), Sir John Wollop, and others besides More—served to diffuse his ideas; and that some of his prayers translated into English became a part of Queen Elizabeth's prayer book and thus were used into the reign of the Stuarts. His greatest influence perhaps came from translations of his Latin works into English and the many editions of these translations, though Latin versions seem occasionally to have been reprinted. Richard Herde's translation of the *Instruction of a Christian Woman* appeared in eight editions: 1529(?), 1540(?), 1541, 1547 (or 1541), 1557, 1557, 1585, 1592. Richard Morison's translation of *Introductio ad sapientiam, An Introduction to Wisdom,* was issued five times: 1540, 1544, 1550, 1550(?), 1564; and some version entitled *Ad sapientiam introductio* was printed in 1623. Thomas Paynell's translation of *De officio mariti, The Office and Duty of a Husband,* was printed only once, possibly in 1553. Though Vives' treatises *De disciplinis,* of which *De tradendis disciplinis* is a part, seem not to have been printed in sixteenth-century England, *De disciplinis* was printed again in 1612; and a work under the title *Linguae Latinae exercitatio* was issued in Edinburgh in 1623.[71] After nearly a hundred years, then, Vives' works were not forgotten.

ROGER ASCHAM

Roger Ascham's accounts of Lady Jane Grey and of Queen Elizabeth as classical scholars show his interest in the education of women; though he wrote no treatises about women, many of his methods of teaching would be as applicable to women as men. His comments on medieval romances show a kinship of feeling with More, Erasmus, and Vives, though a lack of historical perspective

---

[71] *STC;* Henry de Vocht, *Monumenta humanistica Lovaniensia . . .* (Louvain, 1934), pp. 1–43.

led him to correlate such romances with papistry. In the prefatory statement of *Toxophilus* he said:

In our fathers tyme nothing was red but bookes of fayned cheualrie, wherin a man by redinge, shuld be led to none other ende, but onely to manslaughter and baudrye. Yf any man suppose they were good ynough to passe the time with al, he is deceyued. For surelye vayne woordes doo woorke no smal thinge in vayne, ignoraunt, and younge mindes, specially yf they be gyuen any thynge thervnto of theyr owne nature.[72]

In *The Schoolmaster* he said:

In our forefathers tyme, whan Papistrie, as a standyng poole, couered and ouerflowed all England, fewe bookes were read in our tong, sauyng certaine bookes of Cheualrie, as they sayd, for pastime and pleasure . . . as one, for example, Morte Arthure, the whole pleasure of which booke standeth in two speciall poyntes, in open mans slaughter and bold bawdrye: In whiche booke those be counted the noblest Knightes that do kill most men without any quarell, and commit fowlest aduoulteres by sutlest shiftes, as Sir Launcelote, with the wife of king Arthure his master; Syr Tristram with the wife of kyng Marke his uncle; Syr Lamerocke with the wife of king Lote, that was his own aunte. . . . What toyes the dayly readyng of such a booke may worke in the will of a yong ientleman or a yong mayde, that liueth welthelie and idlelie, wise men can iudge and honest men do pitie.[73]

INFLUENCE OF SIR THOMAS MORE

To a candid mind influences are seldom absolutes. But it seems highly probable that More was the major influence on the education of women in England, just as he had been one of the pioneers in adapting Latin grammar to the minds of children and in establishing a school in the household of a layman. His letter to Gonell in 1518 was the first of the treatises dealing with the education of women, and all the other treatises were written by men closely connected with him. So far as we know, More carried on the first practical experiment in giving girls a sound literary education, and that experiment had probably been going on for some years when he wrote his letter to Gonell. More was conscious himself that he was going against tradition.

[72] Ascham, *Toxophilus* (London, 1545), Preface, Book A, leaf i.
[73] Ascham, *The Scholemaster*, First book, leaf 27.

Erasmus was completely changed from disbelief to a firm belief in the education of women by his association with More's
household, as he told us in his 1521 letter to Budé. Possibly
Henry VIII was influenced by More, though one must recognize
the influence of Catherine of Aragon on the education of the
Princess Mary. But the king used to do much conferring with
More, as Roper told us: after the king had finished his devo-
tions on holy days he used to send for More and discuss with him
not only matters of state but astronomy, geometry, divinity, and
the motions of the stars and the planets. The king once paid More
a surprise visit in Chelsea, as Roper told us; and on one occasion
at least More's daughters disputed on philosophy before the king.
Hence the king must have been familiar with More's school several years before the birth of the Princess Elizabeth.

All the other women who became famous for classic learning in
sixteenth-century England had their education some time after
More's experiment; and though it is a fallacy to argue *post hoc,
ergo propter hoc,* there is still a strong probability of More's influence. Perhaps the outstanding example is that of Sir Anthony
Cooke. Born in 1505, Sir Anthony was a young man of twenty or
twenty-five when More's daughters disputed before the king. But
since Cooke seems to have held no court positions until he was appointed with Sir John Cheke as a tutor to the young Edward, there
is no evidence of direct contact between him and Sir Thomas More.
But Cooke followed many of More's principles.

The statement of Erasmus that More had completely changed
the thinking of English noblemen about the education of their
children may have an important bearing on the education of
women as well as men. Significant also is the testimony of Ballard
years later, when he said that the father of Queen Catherine
Parr "following the example of Sir Thomas More and other great
men, bestowed on her a learned education as the most valuable addition he could make to her other charms . . . that she soon became celebrated for her learning and good sense . . . employing
it to the best purposes through every stage of her life." [74] In his

[74] Ballard, *Memoirs,* p. 57.

discussion of the daughters of Sir Anthony Cooke he mentioned the number of educated women and the number of great women who appeared in England between 1500 and 1600 and raised questions about the reasons. A reason given by Strype, he said, was the influence of Henry VIII in educating his daughters. Ballard himself chose to attribute it either to the invention of printing or to "the example of Sir Thomas More, whose daughters were celebrated, even in foreign countries . . . before the daughters of Henry the eighth were born." [75]

CONTRASTS

Perhaps the ideas of love expressed by the men in the More circle will be emphasized by contrasting them with neo-Platonic and courtly views, for example, those explained in Castiglione's *Courtier*. The soul, Castiglione said, has three modes of perceiving: by sense, by reason, and by intellect; sense leads to appetite, which we share with the brutes; reason leads to choice, which is peculiar to man; from the intellect springs will. As a result, there are quite different types of love, one founded upon the senses and another founded upon reason. Those who follow the senses and wish to enjoy beauty by possessing the body are misguided and are most unhappy in love; they are pale, melancholy, in continual tears and sighs, and they wish to die. But those who control the desire of the senses with the bridle of reason are the ones who really possess beauty, and their possession of it brings them good, because true love of beauty is holy. Though Cardinal Bembo granted that the young courtier might be somewhat excused for a sensual love, the mature courtier should use reason to rise to a perception of spiritual beauty and finally to an ecstasy of heavenly beauty: "Whiche is the origion of all other beawtye . . . all other beawtifull thinges be beawtifull bicause they be partners of the beawtie of it." [76] Other neo-Platonists analyzed this ascent a little more definitely than Castiglione, as the seven stages in ascending the ladder of love: first, the perception of a beautiful face; second, love

[75] *Memoirs*, pp. 126–27. His statement could apply only to Elizabeth.

[76] Castiglione, *The Courtyer*, trans. by Thomas Hoby (London, 1561), Book IV, Xxiii, and *passim*.

for an idealized portrait of it framed by the imagination; third, the formation of an idealized abstraction of all beautiful faces; fourth, the realization that this abstraction has come from one's own soul, not from outside the self; fifth, an aspiration to pattern oneself after the ideals which exist in one's own soul; sixth, a desire for the true beauty which is in God; seventh, the attainment of a oneness with God which is ecstasy.[77]

More, Erasmus, and others were familiar with Platonic concepts but they turned them to religion or treated them lightly, and then went on to more serious ideas, as Erasmus did when he wrote the epithalamium for Peter Gilles. Ascham was perhaps giving Platonism the same light treatment when his Toxophilus said he had been reading in Plato's *Phedro* that "some soules being well fethered, flewe alwayes about heauen and heauenlie matters, other some hauinge their fethers mowted awaye, and droupinge, sanke downe into earthlie thinges." [78] More and his friends had a concept of love which grew from daily life on this earth. It was idealistic only as their whole program was idealistic in reaching for perfection of character.

SUMMARY

More and his friends did have much to say about two kinds of love: first, a love of the senses, which they called a disease, a frenzy, a physical appetite based only on beauty, a superficial, irrational, impermanent emotion; second, a love directed by reason, based on wisdom and character, a permanent love which could exist and grow only between equals. Hence the truly educated man could love only a woman equally trained in virtue, piety, and learning. They said nothing about a woman's right to develop her individuality for herself, but they did not assume that a man developed his powers for his personal enjoyment. Education for men and women was based on equality—the same methods, and the same liberal subjects, with some training in the management of home and children for women and some training in a profession for men.

[77] Giovanni Pico della Mirandola, *A Platonick Discourse upon Love,* ed. by Edmund C. Gardner (London, 1914), pp. 73–74, written to explain a sonnet of Benivieni.

[78] *Toxophilus,* Book A, first leaf *verso. Phedro* is, of course, Ascham's spelling.

The results were to be almost the same, with sometimes a greater emphasis on obedience, modesty, and chastity for girls. Medieval romances, for example, were bad for all because they glorified irrational, adulterous love—especially bad for boys because they exalted the corruption of war and the false nobility of chivalry, especially bad for girls because they destroyed modesty and chastity. But all women needed wisdom, they said, to manage households, to train their children from their earliest years, to counsel their husbands, to be partners in the good life, and in cases of necessity or inherited power, to perform public duties and to rule kingdoms. The education of both men and women was necessary for the good life of wisdom and virtue, necessary for the commonweal. Hence, the education of women was a logical outgrowth of their whole program—both premise and completion.

These ideas, it seems evident, could not have come from St. Paul or from Christian doctrine only, though the writers sometimes argued that men and women as members of one body were equal before God. The ideas owed something to the classics (perhaps to Plato's idea that education for men and women should be the same since their nature is the same) for the ideas of well-rounded development, liberal training in the classics, and participation in public life. Again the classics were combined with Christian literature; again the emphasis was upon virtue, piety, and learning.

CONCLUSIONS

Neither More nor his friends had any desire to "revive classical antiquity." They were able to comprehend four worlds: first, their real world of so-called Christian civilization with its political, ecclesiastical, and economic evils; second, a world that might develop if people really shaped their lives by the essentials of Christianity—love of God, love of fellow men, and worthy action; third, a world that could grow from the practice of the best classical philosophy; fourth, an ideal world that might evolve from educating youth in both classic and Christian literature—in the refinement of liberal studies with virtue, piety, and a desire to take action for the good of the commonweal. They were trying to make this last world a reality, not to bring to life classical antiquity. They were not interested in paganism or in any moral and religious deviations as a result of their concern with the literature of Greece and Rome; they never exalted classic literature above Christian literature. They were not interested in classical painting, sculpture, or architecture—unless William Lily, who studied classical antiquities in Italy, or the silent William Latimer harbored such interests without revealing them. They expressed no aesthetic theories. Though they knew classic theories of decorum and the five-act play, and though they appreciated beauty of style, they exalted beauty of character and placed duty above beauty. They had no admiration for excessive individualism, or personal development for its own sake, in either men or women. Since the teachings of the great classical philosophers and the teachings of Christ were similar, to be a philosopher was to be a Christian.

They were not aristocrats, either in their theories of education, of true nobility, or of anything else. They believed that poor but competent young men should have a chance to receive a good education and to rise in both church and state. It was the duty of rulers, wealthy men, and educated men to help these poor boys and others to secure an education. Those without the desire or the ability to secure a liberal education should be trained in crafts and useful occupations and in piety, to give them reasonable incomes, to eliminate idleness and crime, and thus to further their good and that of the commonweal. Men and women were to be educated alike, without any aristocratic assumption that men were better able to take an education. In discussing true nobility More and others stressed the right of the poor boy to rise through character, and intellect, and education, and the obligation of others to give him a chance to so rise. Passages in *Utopia* which contrast the imaginary commonwealth with the European and English reality, and thus reflect More's views, attack the false ideas of rank and honor because of mere wealth and point up economic injustices: a public weal, More said, is unjust when it fails to make provision for the old age and sickness of such men as plowmen, colliers, laborers, carters, ironsmiths, and carpenters; it is unjust when it permits rich men to take from these poor men part of their wages, either by fraud or by unjust laws. Erasmus, too, protested against honoring the idle rich more than the shoemaker or the farmer, who do essential work for the common good. Vives, in attacking the idleness and sin of titled persons, praised farmers and sailors for their practical knowledge and the contribution in their labor. John Rastell, chiefly in his plays or in the introductions to them (to be discussed in Part II) strongly emphasized the contribution and the rights of uneducated laborers, since all wealth is either a gift from God or comes from "the labour of poor men's hands." These are not aristocratic ideas.

More and his friends had no great originality in an absolute sense, so far as single ideas were concerned. But they brought fresh insights and fresh ideas into sixteenth-century England. They made contributions to mathematics and medicine. They, more specifically Vives, pointed out the errors of Aristotle, the need of observation and more observation until one might deduce general principles, and thus approach a truth which is incomplete but cannot be completed so long as one considers his view of the truth as final. Vives also gave a fresh if not an entirely original emphasis to the observation of nature as recreation and as enjoyment of beauty. In discussing true nobility several of these men gave a new slanting to old theories by stressing the right of the poor boy to rise through education to high positions in church and state. In education, though some of their ideas were stirring into action before the sixteenth century, they expressed in treatises the whole body of classical theories on the aims, methods, and results of education; then they firmly united these ideas with religious materials and religious results, in an education for virtue, piety, wisdom, and service for the commonweal. Discussing the education of women, they suggested the same liberal education for competent women as for competent men; they realized the influence of the mother on her child in the early years, and the need for men of wisdom and virtue to marry women with the same qualities, since, they said, an enduring love based upon reason and similar ideals is possible only between equals. Neither More nor any of his friends was looking for original ideas. Their aim and their achievement was a synthesis, a critical selection of ideas best suited to the regeneration of Christian civilization. Of course they drew their ideas from a broad knowledge of Christian and classical literature, from the teachings of Christ and the greatest classical philosophers.

In style also, they did not strive for great originality nor did they achieve it by some happy chance, as far as one can discover. They sought a classic Latin style—correctness, clarity, and eloquence. Largely through the influence of Lucian, they achieved some larger qualities of style which were not common in England at that time. They used imagination and fantasy for moral and religious ideas. They were masters of the light touch with the serious intention. Erasmus developed a kind of dialogue in which a wise fool, or a character who begins as a naïve innocent, gradually leads his opponent and uses his questions to bring out wisdom.

More and his friends built upon the great foundations of their past, of course, not through any conscious planning or choosing to do so, but because these ideas were as natural to them as breathing. They built upon the essential doctrines of the Catholic church. They built upon the medieval philosophy of law—eternal law, the law of nature, and the relation to these of divine and human law. They built upon the belief in man's perfectibility, his ability to develop by education because of innate seeds of goodness and wisdom, and the freedom of his will. If they were more optimistic about the potentials of human development than their predecessors or many of their successors, perhaps a cause for that optimism was their breadth of classical reading and their discovery that the classic philosophers had found many great truths which were like the ideas of Christianity.

But they also opposed much that we now call medieval, though they did not know that modern term for their aversions; and sometimes when they spoke of a former "barbarous" age, they may really have had in mind the intellectual decay and the abuses of the fifteenth century. But they were specific about the things they disliked. First, they objected to abuses which had attached themselves to the elaborate structure of the medieval church and the monastic orders, or to the mere elaborateness of the structure; but they reverenced good bishops, the episcopal system, and monastic ideals. Second, they disliked feudalism and chivalry, with the emphasis upon fighting, chivalry, false nobility, and irrational or illicit love. Third, they abhorred medieval romances for the same reasons. Fourth, they disliked the extremes of dialectical hair-splitting, the use of logic merely to win an argument rather than to find the truth; and with some exceptions they rejected the "mountains" of glosses on scripture which the Schoolmen had accumulated. Fifth, they did not approve the medieval encylopedias which included scientific principles and explained them by theology; and they scorned summaries of the classics as a substitute for whole units in the original languages. Sixth, they were suspicious of those interpretations of canon law which had become complex and cloudy, and which, they thought, were being used for injustice and extortion. Seventh, some of them hated with equal fervor and for the same reasons the elaborate complexities of the English common law. All law, they believed, should be simple, clear, known to all, used to give justice and prevent wrongdoing. Eighth, they had a belief—whether they were right or wrong— that the Latin used in the centuries immediately preceding them was not "classic," that it lacked eloquence and beauty, and that law French was "barbarous." Ninth, they believed that even the greatest men in the same centuries had been handicapped by their lack of Greek, the lack of skill in reading the language, and the lack of complete, accurate translations in Latin.

The men of the More circle opposed the blind following of custom without a critical examination of the custom and its consequences. They approved of custom when it helped to establish habits of virtue and piety. They hotly opposed custom whenever it was ignorant, irrational, or immoral, or whenever it led to anything less than the best in any area of human life. Thus the discussion of custom often appears in the discussion of every other topic, from the mothers who turn over their infants to ignorant nurses for suckling or for other care, to the rulers who enforce "moth-eaten" laws or govern in other ways by unexamined custom. Human beings had themselves created evil in social, economic, political, and ecclesiastical affairs and in their own hearts. These conditions were not immutable and they were not sent upon us as God's punishment for sin. So human beings could and should bring about change, instead of following custom blindly. Of course the passionate belief in the power of sound education to change individuals and thus to reform society was closely connected with the faith in change.

More and his friends were optimists and they were pessimists. They were realists and they were idealists. They were optimists when they considered human possibilities: man's reason, his ability to find truth by reason and also to use the truth as revealed by authority, his freedom of will, and his perfectibility. Thus they were often optimists when they discussed the law of nature and man's ability to rise from the level of beasts to that of the angels or to a status near to that of God himself. But they were pessimists when they looked at human actions and human achievements— when they saw diplomacy and international treaties used in a great game of power, and when they saw Henry VIII turn from his promising youth to his ruthless and despotic maturity. They were realists and idealists. Perhaps More was one of the great realists of Western civilization if knowing the social, economic, political, and ecclesiastical evils in his own time, knowing their causes and their cures, is evidence that one is a realist. Erasmus, too, had seen many courts and known many rulers; he was no innocent about political games even if he chose not to play these games on a large scale. They and their friends were also idealists if an idealist is one who wishes to regenerate society, has a complete program for this regeneration, believes that he and other men of knowledge and good will can bring about some change for the better, and that it is his duty to try.

More, some of his English friends, Erasmus, and Vives were also realists in their clear view about authority; accepting it, they knew exactly where it ended and where critical thinking might begin. They made a clear separation of the physical and the natural from the spiritual and the supernatural. As a result they rejected superstition (according to their own definition of it, not a modern agnostic's definition), astrology in the sense of foretelling human events by the stars, all forms of magic, and mystic interpretations of scripture. In all things their feet had a habit of touching earth. They relished the speculative philosophy which was the free play of mind among friends; but they valued more the philosophy which came from critical thinking based on available knowledge and which led to action.

Several of these men were much concerned with the Stoic philosophers, Seneca, Plutarch, and Cicero. More's estimate of Greek and Roman thought in his summary of the books Hythlodaye took to Utopia; Erasmus' concern with editions of Seneca and Cicero, and his references to Stoical thought, for example, in *The Praise of Folly;* the books in Grocyn's library at his death; and many other facts indicate this influence. Of course they valued these and other philosophers for the resemblances they found in their thought and in the essentials of Christianity.

They were naturally concerned with the question what is the good life. They defined it as *knowing* the good and *doing* the good in all areas of human life and in all human relationships. The good life was the life of wisdom, virtue, piety, and service for the public good. Thus they separated themselves sharply from any philosophers who taught the duty of individual perfection as an end in itself or any who suggested that the individual should withdraw from participation in economic or political affairs.

With their comprehensive view of life and its regeneration, More and his friends also seemed to think of all human life as one— not fragmented into life for men and for women, life for certain classes and not other classes, or sacred areas and secular areas of life. Hence, they did not have one kind of education for men and another for women; they did not prescribe an education for certain classes and not for other classes, though they did wish to adjust the kind of education to the ability and desire of the individual. Education was to be an unfolding of innate powers, a growth from within, not a mere pouring in of information nor a conforming to ideas of the teacher; and all normal people, even those of small intellectual power, might develop through education. Their program was so integrated that whenever they discussed one phase, such as true nobility, reform in religion, law and government, or education, they were likely to touch upon any or all other phases of their program. Of course they saw all truth as one, but they recognized two great sources for this truth: the law of nature and revelation through authority. From classic literature, they drew scientific ideas as a basis for further development in medicine and in other sciences, political and educational ideas, and much great philosophy. In a consistent assumption that human life is not made up of rigidly separated secular and sacred areas, they assumed the same causes and cures for all human evils. The basic causes were hate, greed, and strife. The cure lay in removing these corruptions from human hearts. The method which they were most hopeful about was a sound education from the earliest years, a development of innate seeds of goodness and wisdom into virtue, piety, and a desire to serve the commonweal. It might be said, then, that their whole program for the regeneration of society, not merely for law and government, was based upon a breadth of view and a refining influence from the classics and upon applying the essentials of Christianity.

PART II *The impact of their ideas on secular drama*

INTRODUCTION

The record of drama in the More circle began in the household of John Morton, Archbishop, Chancellor, and later Cardinal Morton. There Henry Medwall lived from 1490 to 1500, and there his *Nature* and *Fulgens and Lucres* were probably performed. There More, as a boy, about 1490 to 1492, used to step in among the players and delight Morton and others with his extempore speeches, and there, perhaps, More wrote plays and acted in the little comedies which Erasmus mentioned.

More perhaps carried on his dramatic interests in other places. In his letter of 1501 to John Holt, he spoke of a comedy called *Solomon*, which "we" wrote, probably to help teach boys their Latin. Probably More kept up his connections with Lincoln's Inn, since it was usual for gentlemen to do so; he may have been the person meant in an item of 1528–29: "Master of the Revels: Arnold. If not, More." [1]

More's skill in presenting "the inward disposition of the mind" and in writing dialogue—also the skill of Margaret Roper, Lady Alington, and William Rastell—has been pointed out. It is of course possible that some anonymous plays printed by the Rastells

[1] *Records of Lincoln's Inn: the Black Books,* ed. by W. P. Baildon, 4 vols. (London, 1897–1902), I, 222.

were written by members of the More household, for example, *Calisto and Melebea*, in preparation for John Rastell's stage.

The semidramatic interest which More and Erasmus had in the dialogue of Lucian seems worth mentioning in connection with drama. More translated four of Lucian's works; Erasmus translated thirty-six works, including declamations as well as dialogues.

As one might expect, More and his literary friends knew Plautus and Terence well. More, Erasmus, and Vives quoted from the two casually in all sorts of connections. Erasmus superintended editions of Plautus and Terence with special attention to the meters; he apparently began an edition of Seneca's plays but turned his notes over to the printer Bade, who used his material along with that of other editors. More and Erasmus also knew some classic theories of drama and the five-act play, as well as theories of non-dramatic classic style, though perhaps they knew far less than Italian humanists knew earlier. Erasmus translated the Greek plays of *Hecuba* and *Iphigenia* into Latin verse, having begun *Hecuba* to teach himself Greek when it was hard to find a good teacher of that language.

But of all the men in the More group, the most enterprising undertaker of drama was John Rastell, who not only printed plays (as his son William also did), and wrote plays, but concerned himself with staging plays. Rastell's interest in dramatic productions of some kind may possibly have begun in Coventry. There he had a chance to see plays given in 1493 and 1500, for Henry VII and his queen, and there he may have had some connection himself with a pageant of nine hierarchies of angels and a "goodly stage" play given in 1510 for Henry VIII and his queen. In 1520 he worked with Sir Edward Belknap and Sir Nicholas Vaux in making and decorating the roofs of the banquet hall at the Field of the Cloth of Gold. In 1522 he was employed to arrange a pageant at the Little Conduit in Cheapside, to honor Charles V. He built a place like heaven, with clouds, orbs, stars, and hierarchies of angels. In the summer of 1527, when French ambassadors came to arrange a marriage with the Princess Mary, Rastell presented the "Father of Heaven," and received pay for writing the dialogue and making Latin and English rhymes. For the same occasion, he was paid, according to Guildford's accounts, for designing the roof of the pageant hall; he used the whole earth surrounded by sea, like a map or chart, the twelve signs of the zodiac, the five circles or girdles, the two poles, and the seven planets, "every one in their proper houses, made according to their properties." [2]

But John Rastell's outstanding contribution to drama was his public stage in Finsbury Field. In 1524 he leased one and three-quarter acres of ground and built both a house and a stage. Most of our information comes from testimony in a lawsuit brought by Rastell against a man named Walton, who "occupied at his pleasure" the "stuff and the goods" for a half year or more while Rastell was in France. We learn that the stage was built of "board, timber, lath, nail, sprig, and daubing" at a cost of fifty shillings; that ten or fifteen garments were involved, one for a priest and one for a woman; that some garments used fur, colored silk, and satin; that there were curtains, pieces of linen cloth, and a piece of red buckram. Rastell estimated the value of the supplies at twenty marks. The garments were well made: some tailors had been employed, and Mistress Rastell (More's sister) had helped. Rastell complained that Walton had let them out to hire, since the "praisement," at twenty nobles or more; that they had been lent to "stage plays in the summer and interludes in the winter . . . twenty times a year in interludes." Some of them, also, had been used for the king's banquet at Greenwich. There is specific mention of the fact that the public had resorted to the stage.[3]

Though no one knows what plays Rastell presented to the public on his stage, it seems probable that he used the ones which came from his printing press or the press of his son William. About 1525 to 1530 John Rastell printed three plays without an author's name definitely attached. The three were *Gentleness and Nobility, The Nature of the Four Elements,* and *Calisto and*

[2] *Letters and Papers of . . . Henry VIII,* under the years indicated; see also A. W. Reed, *Early Tudor Drama* (London, 1926), Chapter I.

[3] A. W. Pollard, *An English Garner: Fifteenth-Century Prose and Verse* (Westminster, 1903), pp. 307–21, for reprint of an article by H. R. Plomer, "Pleadings in a Theatrical Lawsuit, from . . . the Court of Requests." The material was summarized by A. W. Reed, *Early Tudor Drama,* Appendix VIII.

Melebea. At some time he printed a play on Lucretia, also anonymous, but only a fragment of it remains. About 1512–16 he printed *Fulgens and Lucres,* by Henry Medwall; and about 1530, he was probably the printer of Skelton's *Magnificence.*

About 1530 to 1534 William Rastell, who had set up his own press, printed *Nature,* by Henry Medwall, and *The Play of Love,* and *The Play of the Weather,* by John Heywood. He also issued without an author's name two other plays which were probably by Heywood: *The Pardoner and the Friar;* and *John John, the Husband, Tyb, his Wife, and Sir John, the Priest.*

Another play, *Witty and Witless,* undoubtedly the work of John Heywood, was not printed during Heywood's life, but it survived as a manuscript in the British Museum. A play by John Redford, who was associated with Heywood both as musician and dramatist, and who put into dramatic form outstanding educational theories advocated by the men of the More group, also belongs to the total dramatic output. It is *Wit and Science,* which survived in manuscript form to be printed in the nineteenth century.

CHAPTER **VII** *Nature and the law of nature*

The drama which members of the More group wrote, printed, or staged tends to echo the ideas which they stressed in non-dramatic writing—ideas selected as a program of social reform, a means to the good life of wisdom, virtue, and piety. The growing concern with the study of the physical world and the continued unconscious emphasis upon the law of nature are reflected to some extent in two plays: *Nature* by Henry Medwall; and *A New Interlude and a Merry of the Nature of the Four Elements*, probably by John Rastell. *A Play of Witty and Witless* by John Heywood will be mentioned briefly also, but its ideas are conventional.

Medwall's *Nature* was printed without date, probably by William Rastell about 1530 to 1534, when he worked as an independent printer. He said that the play was "compiled" by Henry Medwall, chaplain to Cardinal Morton. Since Morton died in 1500 and the last definite record of Medwall is dated 1501, the play was doubtless written before 1500. It was probably performed in Morton's episcopal palace, perhaps while More was a boy in the service of Morton; its authorship may have been established for the printer by his uncle, Sir Thomas More.

Medwall's *Nature*, like many medieval works, is a struggle between reason and sensuality for the control of man, and a brief summary of the plot sounds like any other medieval morality.

Part I may be said to have three parts, though there are no formal divisions: first, man is committed by Nature to the control of reason; he recognizes his true destiny and makes noble promises; second, he yields to sensuality; third, he repents and returns to reason. Part II also seems to have three parts without any formal divisions: first, man vows to continue his obedience to reason; second, he again yields to sensuality; third, he repents, because of old age this time, and prepares himself for eternal salvation. At the beginning of Part II man's life is conventionally compared to the siege of a castle; he struggles against the world, the flesh, and the enemy; he is plagued by the seven deadly sins—pride, wrath, envy, sloth, covetousness, gluttony, and bodily lust; he combats them with their opposites—meekness, patience, charity, good occupation, liberality, abstinence, and chastity. Long before the sixteenth century these ideas, of course, were thoroughly conventional.

Medwall's *Nature* has other conventional ideas emphasized by More and his friends but also by other philosophical writers for generations before them. Chief among these are the dignity of man, his freedom to make choices, his reason which lifts him above beasts, and his perfectibility. Among other conventional ideas the play mentions the importance of inner piety instead of outer forms alone, a dislike for rank without virtue and character, a protest against the blind following of custom, a cynical comment on some nuns and priests, connected with loyal piety, and a specific analysis of the place sensuality should have in life. The dislike for rank without character is implied when an unsympathetic character, Pride, whose ancestors are wealthy nobles, complains because he has not been properly welcomed.[1] A cynical tone about nuns and priests appears when Man makes his first effort to return to reason and, as a result, Margery, a prostitute, becomes so unhappy that she enters a religious place at the "green friars"; and when

[1] Alois Brandl, *Quellen des Weltlichen Dramas in England vor Shakespeare* (Strassburg, 1898), Part I, lines 732–35. All line numbers in the footnotes which follow refer to this edition. For the entire play see pages 75–158. In this and other passages I am copying wording and spelling faithfully, with these exceptions: adding an *m*, an *n*, or any other letter which is clearly indicated by a mark in the text, and transcribing a sign for *and* or for *es* into letters, to make easier printing and easier reading.

Sensuality is told that Covetousness has been dwelling with a priest, as he and men of the church are fond of each other.[2] Three characters, Sensuality, Pride, and the World, furnish satirical comment on following custom, in sensual appetite, dress, and general conformity.[3] Reason and Sensuality debate as they had done in the preceding centuries: Sensuality suggests that he and Reason should merely be "good fellows together" instead of deciding which should rule; Reason concedes that without any Sensuality man can have no living but argues that Sensuality unrestrained makes man bestial and that man can dignify himself by making choices (*libertas specificationis*) and can even approach excellence. Without being asked, Nature suggests that some Sensuality was granted to man in his first creation.[4]

These ideas, whether major or minor, have little in Medwall's *Nature* to distinguish them from their expression in the Middle Ages. Probably no educated man could have written a page without some implications about the major ones. Medwall, however, does not write of them with the optimistic enthusiasm which More and his friends expressed when they contemplated human possibilities. He does not express faith about the power of education in Christian and classic literature nor in early training for the service of the commonweal to win man away from sensuality. As his main character has good intentions but keeps returning to sensuality, his view is comparatively pessimistic.

Perhaps only two ideas in the play have a certain originality in a religious play. The first is a freshness in the appreciation of natural beauty; the second is the characterization of Nature.

Some human beings in all ages have appreciated the beauty of the world, of course, and have occasionally expressed this appreciation in literature. But English morality plays such as *Everyman* and *The Castle of Perseverance* lack the freshness of detail in these lines from Medwall's *Nature*:

> Who taught the cok hys watche howres to obserue
> And syng of corage wyth shryll throte on hye,

[2] Henry Medwall, *Nature*, Part II, lines 114–45, 996–98.
[3] Part I, lines 197–200, 449–55, 582–88, 1024–32.
[4] Part I, lines 282–88, 162–68, 173–81.

> Who taught the pellycan her tender hart to carue
> For she nolde suffer her byrdys to dye.
> who taught the nyghtyngall to recorde besyly
> Her straunge entunys in sylence of the nyght?
> Certes I nature and none other wyght. (I, 43–49)

For this discussion perhaps the most significant element in Medwall's play is his character called Nature. She is a goddess, but she has none of the romantic trappings associated with Nature in the *Roman de la Rose,* Chaucer's *Parlement of Foules,* or Lydgate's *Reason and Sensuality.* Though Lydgate's Nature rules over stars, planets, and the whole firmament, unites or severs the elements, and wishes man to choose virtue, she is a glamorous figure. She appears in spring, in a garden, where birds and flowers are conventionally described at length. She is herself dazzlingly beautiful; it seems easy for the author to progress from her to the choice of the fairest, where Pallas, Juno, and Venus are rivals in the beauty contest. Then Lydgate's main character disdains the advice of Diana, preferring Venus; soon he finds himself in the garden of pleasure, and Cupid asks him to play a chess game with a beautiful maiden, for her love. Even the chess pieces are made of precious stones; and the whole tapestry of the gardens, the odors, the beauty of attendants and chess pieces are a glorification of love and pleasure. Man puts up little if any struggle—he enjoys. Sensuality is made attractive, and reason by contrast seems unattractive. How different from the crude tavern scenes which represent sensuality in Medwall's *Nature!* Lydgate, too, assumes that there are two separate ways: an Eastern gate leads to heavenly things, and a Western gate leads to earthly, temporal things, or sensuality; and Nature herself, before she leaves the author to enjoy himself, advises him to choose heavenly, rather than transitory earthly things.

In Lydgate's poem, too, the main character has a belief that he should choose virtue. He says that he has free will and that he wishes to know natural causes. But in the lush atmosphere there is little time to brood over perfectibility; virtue is soon forgotten; and though the poem is unfinished, free will is used in the choice of sensual pleasure.[5]

[5] John Lydgate, *Reason and Sensuality,* ed. by Ernst Sieper, *EETS,* ex. ser., LXXXIV (1901).

Compared with this background, Medwall's character called Nature is dignified, almost austere. She is the benevolent minister of God. She describes herself as a "wordly" goddess, meaning probably a "worldly" goddess, or one in charge of this world. She names her functions: to continue life by "natural engendure"; to assuage the former strife between the elements; to appoint Diana as lady of the sea and of every fresh fountain that responds to the tides and as princess of every town or isle that is surrounded by the sea; to cause flames or so-called falling stars to appear in the sky; to care for stones, herbs, trees, animal life:

> I do prouyde for euery beste lyuynge
> Of naturall foode alway suffycence,
> And geue theym also a maner of prudence
> Wherby they may naturally ensew
> Thyng that ys delectable and thother exchew. (I, 38–42)

She recommends to man that he study nature (lines 37–63) but in Aristotle, "my philosopher elect." She stresses man's dignity, perfectibility, and his freedom to choose—old ideas but somewhat newer in drama and in relation to a goddess:

> Namely, thow man, I speke to the alone
> Byfor all other as chyef of hys creance,
> Thynke how he hath made the to thys semblance;
> Pluck vp thyn harte and hold thyn hed vpryght,
> And euer more haue heuen in thy syght.
>
> Ouyde in hys boke cleped the transformacyon
> among all other hys fables and poesyes
> Maketh specyall mensyon of thy creacyon,
> Shewyng how god wonderously gan deuyse
> whan he the made and gaue to the thempryse
> Of all thys world, and feoffed the wyth all
> as chyef possessyoner of thyngys mortuall. . . . (I, 73–84)

As Medwall's Nature is a goddess but connected with Diana and not with Venus and Cupid, and as she is kept carefully separated from the lush beauty of gardens and handsome maidens, she is at least a new combination of elements in religious drama. She seems to owe something to the classic views of Cicero and the Stoics.

The play entitled *A New Interlude and a Merry of the Nature of the Four Elements,* usually called *The Nature of the Four Elements,* is the work of John Rastell, though the acceptance of his authorship is not unanimous. Rastell began an ill-starred venture at exploring the New World in 1517; he was stranded in Ireland, where he remained until about 1519. The best assumption is that he wrote the play soon after his return to England. He also printed the play, without author or date, between 1519 and 1529, perhaps between 1526 and 1527.[6]

The Nature of the Four Elements is a strange play, so undramatic that one wonders how a popular audience ever sat through it; it is also a strange mixture of conventional ideas, Rastellian views, and the general philosophy of the More group with some Rastellian slanting. Although the play has no formal divisions but only occasional directions for the entrance or exit of characters, it may be broken down into these parts for convenience in discussing it:

The author lists the characters.
He lists the natural science to be taught in the play.
A messenger speaks the prologue.

Humanity, urged on by Nature, expresses a desire for knowledge.
Humanity is further instructed by Studious Desire.
Humanity is tempted by Sensuality; Studious Desire leaves him.
Humanity receives the Taverner, who will provide food, drink, and "proper wenches."
Humanity returns and joins Studious Desire and Experience while they discuss cosmography and the new-found lands.
Humanity wishes to go out with Sensuality and the Taverner, but when they leave, he continues to listen to Experience.
(Leaves of the play are missing at this point.)
Humanity succumbs again to both Sensuality and Ignorance, listens to songs and dances; Ignorance sings of Robin Hood.
Humanity is rebuked by Nature, who returns. (The play breaks off.)

Unlike the struggle for the soul of man in *The Castle of Perseverance, Everyman,* and Medwall's *Nature,* the conflict in *The Nature of the Four Elements* is secular. In the part of the play that

---

[6] W. W. Greg, *A Bibliography of the English Printed Drama to the Restoration,* 2 vols. (London, 1939), I; A. W. Reed, *Early Tudor Drama* (London, 1926), Appendix I.

remains, Sensuality and Ignorance fight against Studious Desire to determine whether Humanity will satisfy his appetite for sensual indulgence or for knowledge.

The basis of the conflict is the conventional assumption, perhaps unconscious on the part of the author, that Humanity has reason, freedom of choice, educability, and perfectibility. Minor conventional ideas appear, more conventional because they are not joined with a plea for classical education—such ideas as service to the commonweal, recreation as a preparation for return to work, and a dislike of love stories. Rastell says that service to the commonweal includes relieving the material needs of the poor, persuading people to turn away from vicious living, and educating the ignorant; and there is nothing individual in these bare statements. His dislike of love stories, in the undeveloped form of his wording, might have been the utterance of any member of the More group. This dislike is emphasized in the Prologue spoken by the Messenger, when the writer is pleading for significant books written in English.[7]

Besides these conventionalities the play has some ideas which belong to Rastell and not to other members of the More circle. These center around the New World. Rastell had a burning desire to see that world explored because reports of it had stirred his imagination and because his own voyage had been stopped; he wished to have Englishmen make some of these discoveries; he was interested in material products such as minerals, fish, timber, and its by-products; and he was concerned with spreading Christian civilization.

The passage on actual exploring of the New World, in the speech of Experience to Studious Desire while Humanity is out reveling at the tavern, seems related to Rastell's own expedition:

> But yet not longe ago
> Some men of this contrey went,
> By the kynges noble consent,
> It for to serche to that entent,
> And coude not be brought therto;

---

[7] *The Interlude of the Four Elements*, ed. by James O. Halliwell (1848), for the Percy Society, p. 4. It does not have numbered lines; neither does any other available edition, including Farmer's Students' Facsimile Edition.

> But they that were they venteres [th' adventurers]
> Have cause to curse their maryners,
> Fals of promys, and dissemblers,
> That falsly them betrayed,
> Which wold take no paine to saile farther
> Than their owne lyst and pleasure;
> Wherfore that vyage and dyvers other
> Suche kaytyffes have distroyed.
> O what a thynge had be than,
> Yf that they that be Englyshemen
> Myght have ben the furst of all
> That there shulde have take possessyon,
> And made furst buildynge and habytacion,
> A memory perpetuall. (p. 29)

As the speech continues, the writer shows his knowledge of the exploring that had been done earlier by John Cabot, with Sebastian and his other sons, in 1497 and 1498:

> And also what an honorable thynge,
> Bothe to the realme and to the kynge,
> To have had his domynyon extendynge
> There into so farre a grounde,
> Whiche the noble kynge of late memory,
> The moste wyse prynce the vij Herry
> Causyd furst for to be founde. (p. 29)

Besides these individual comments on the New World—individual as compared with comments by the More group or by other Englishmen at this time—Rastell also developed other ideas similar to those expressed by other men in the More group but he tended to give them his individual slanting. In his concept of Nature, he created a character even farther removed than Medwall's Nature from the medieval romantic figure associated with Venus and Cupid. He made Nature masculine. After the opening discourse of Nature, when Humanity finally gets a chance to speak, he says, "O excellent prynce, and great lorde Nature!" Again after Nature's second speech, when it seems clear that Humanity is addressing the character who is present with him on the stage, he says, "O gloryous lorde and prynce moste plesant." Later Studious

Desire mentions Lord Nature.[8] Although there is little emphasis upon the sex in the rest of the play, the character of Nature never becomes feminine.

Like Medwall's Nature, though, Rastell's Lord Nature is benign and educative. He is the minister of God in charge of the preservation of life and the cause of generation and corruption; he is responsible for both ethereal and lower regions, both of which he shows on his "fygure," whatever it may be. He explains that the movements of the bodies in the ethereal region—apparently the planets, stars, and spheres, which he had mentioned earlier— cause or have an influence on corruption and generation in the lower region. He explains at length the indestructibility of matter. He tells Humanity that he is in charge of all these things.

Nature makes clear that he believes also in the conventional ideas on the dignity and perfectibility of man, and by implication, at least, in man's freedom of choice. Man is like inanimate things in being made of the elements and like brute beasts in having "memory and wits five"; but he is superior to the beasts when he uses his reason. Nature closes his second speech with this passage:

> So every thynge is made to do his nature:
> So lykewyse reason, wit, and understondyng,
> Ys gyven to the, man, for that thou sholdyst indede
> Knowe thy Maker and cause of thyne owne beynge,
> And what the worlde is, and wherof thou doest procede;
> Wherfore it behovyth the of verey nede,
> The cause of thynges furst for to lerne,
> And than to knowe and laude the hye God eterne. (pp. 12–13)

Two speeches later, Studious Desire promises to quicken Humanity's wit:

> His courage and desyre I shall also inhaunce,
> So that his felycyté shall be most of all
> To study and to serche for causys naturall. (p. 13)

Thus the benign educative function of Nature is fully clarified. But Rastell's use of the terms *Nature Naturate* and *Natura*

---

[8] *The Interlude*, pp. 10, 13, 19.

Naturata seems strange. In the Greek view, chiefly of the Stoics, the universe included four things: a first cause, a causal agent, matter unformed, and matter formed by the agent into earth with its inanimate, animate, and human creatures. According to this philosophic concept, Rastell's Nature is the causal agent, an educative agent described as *Nature naturans;* but the terms Rastell uses are applied to the things Nature has created, not to the agent. But if John Rastell had a certain vagueness about his philosophic concepts, he was after all a practical man, not a philosopher.

When he spoke of natural philosophy Rastell apparently knew some views related to the great chain of being as they were expressed by Pico della Mirandola, More, Erasmus, Vives, and others. But his approach was different. He began with the lowest forms of existence and the education of the common man. He wrote as one might expect him to write if he had just been quarreling with his brother-in-law, Sir Thomas More, because More emphasized astronomy as well as Greek and Latin and assumed that the members of his school were approaching the knowledge of heavenly things. Through his Messenger in the prologue Rastell said:

> But man to knowe God is a dyffyculté,
> Except by a meane he hymselfe inure,
> Whiche is to knowe Goddes creaturys that be;
> As furst them that be of the grosyst nature,
> And than to know them that be more pure,
> And so by lytyll and lytyll ascendynge,
> To know Goddes creaturys and mervelous werkinge,
> And this wyse man at the last shall come to
> The knowlege of God and hys hye mageste,
> And so to lerne to do his dewté, and also
> To deserve of his goodnes partener to be: (pp. 5–6)

So he meant to begin with the nature of the elements and to teach this information to unlearned men because nothing is more necessary for them. He continued:

> How dare men presume to be callyd clerkes,
> Dysputynge of hye creaturis celestyall,

As thyngys invysyble and Goddes hye warkys,
And know not these vysyble thyngys inferyall? (p. 6)

With these views on natural philosophy Rastell expressed additional attitudes to the common man and to education. When he
introduced his theme of natural philosophy he put himself on a
level with the common man:

But though the matter be not so well declaryd
As a great clerke coude do, nor so substancyall,
Yet the auctour hereof requiryth you all,
Though he be yngnorant, and can lytyll skyll,
To regarde his only intent and good wyll. . . . (p. 3)

Of course an apology by the author of a play is conventional but
not an apology for lack of scientific information; and one cannot
imagine More, Erasmus, or Vives pleading his ignorance in this
manner.

Rastell emphasized the common man also when he discussed
his economic contribution to the world:

Yet all the ryches in the worlde that is,
Rysyth of the grounde by Goddys sendynge,
And by the labour of pore mennys handys;
And tho thou, ryche man, have therof the kepynge,
Yet is not this ryches of thy gettynge,
Nor oughtyst not in reason to be preysed the more,
For by other mennys labour it is got before. (p. 5)

More, Colet, and Erasmus had much sympathy for the common
man; they wished to give him legal and economic justice but they
did not indicate the same concern about teaching him scientific
facts.

Again Rastell emphasized education for the common man when
he complained because books on natural science and other matters
of gravity were not written in English nor more often translated
into English. Greek and Roman writers, he said, used their mother
tongues; and the English language had become sufficient for explaining any difficult matter. Then there were many "pregnant
wits," both noblemen and men of mean estate, who understood no
language but English. In this plea for English Rastell differed

from More and Erasmus only in the subject matter emphasized; for instead of being concerned about science for the common man, they spoke for the English Bible, under the usual approval of the bishops.

Rastell disagreed in his approach to another educational idea when he apparently valued experience more than formal teaching. He emphasized it in the geography lesson which Experience gave to Studious Desire, and in a later talk of the two with Humanity— the only time when Humanity showed much intellectual curiosity. Studious Desire said of Experience:

> But this is the man with whome ye shall
> I trust be well content with all,
> And glad of his commynge;
> For he hath expownyd connyngly
> Dyvers poyntes of cosmogryfy,
> In fewe wordes and shorte clause.

Humanity answered:

> So I understande he hath gode science,
> And that he hath by playne experience
> Lernyd many a straunge cause.

Studious Desire continued:

> Ye, syr, and I say for my parte,
> He is the connyngest man in that arte
> That ever I coude fynde;
> For aske what questyon ye wyll do,
> Howe the yerth is rounde, or other mo,
> He wyll satysfye your mynde. (pp. 38–39)

In natural philosophy Rastell's chief concern was geography, as one might guess from his own abortive voyage. Other members of the More group had some of the same interest. Grocyn owned copies of Ptolemy and Pomponius Mela. Linacre translated *Proclus de sphaera*, combined astronomy and geography, from Greek into Latin. Erasmus recommended the use of a hanging globe and wall maps, but he tended at times to speak of geography as if it were a mere help to understanding the classics. Young John More translated *The legacy or embassate of prester John unto Emanuell, Kynge of Portyngale,* by Damian à Goes, and William Rastell printed it in 1533. Young John Rastell, following his father's taste in practical exploring, was with an expedition which reached Labrador in 1536. Elyot recommended all graphic devices, including the old tables of Ptolemy, but he tended to think of geography as a help to teaching history. Even if More's *Utopia* "could perhaps have been written exactly as well if there had been no discoveries since Plato," and even if More had not heard the name America when he wrote it, he was conscious of new continents and the voyages of Vespucci.[9] And More did some imaginative thinking quite different from Pliny when he deduced the nature and civilization of the tropical and south-temperate zones from the known features of the northern zone.[10] Vives spoke of measuring the height, decline, and relative distance of the constellations by an astrolabe, and he recommended the maps which indicated the new Spanish discoveries. So Vives, the Spaniard, and John Rastell, the practical explorer, were the two men of the More group who turned to the future and the new world in geography.

In discussing John Rastell's geographical information there has been a tendency to search for his exact sources, to overlook his real aims, and to belittle his knowledge. It does not seem necessary to crawl out on any limb here about his sources. Enough people have done so already, and limbs have been sawed off. Even some of his comparisons which sound individual—for example, the hills and mountains like "pricks on a gall," and the air and fire about the earth like the white about the yolk of an egg—came from sources which were already time-worn.[11] One writer on the problem has wisely summed it up in this way: "the culling and 'plagiarism' practiced by Renaissance writers on cosmology, cosmography, natural history, and kindred sciences make it perilous to assign such

---

[9] George B. Parks, *Richard Hakluyt and the English Voyages* (New York, 1928), p. 7. This is Special Publication No. 10, American Geographical Society.

[10] George B. Parks, "More's *Utopia* and Geography," *JEGP*, XXXVII (1938), 224–36.

[11] Johnstone Parr, "More Sources of Rastell's *Interlude of the Four Elements*," *PMLA*, LX (1945), 48–58. See also these articles: Murray E. Borish, "Source and Intention of *The Four Elements*," *SP*, XXXV (1938), 149–63; George B. Parks, "The Geography of *The Interlude of the Four Elements*," *PQ*, XVII (1938), 251–62; Elizabeth M. Nugent, "Sources of John Rastell's *The Nature of the Four Elements*," *PMLA*, LVII (1942), 74–88; George B. Parks, "Rastell and Waldseemüller's Map," *PMLA*, LVIII (1943), 572–74.

works as definite sources on the basis of parallel passages alone—even verbatim ones." [12]

His aims, besides giving scientific information to the men who knew no Greek or Latin, were to stir men to voyages of discovery and also to persuade them that they could sail about the whole earth and come home again, safe and sound. As for the mere roundness of the earth, that idea was a commonplace to educated men. Aristotle had stated the case and argued by pointing out that matter falls toward a common center, that the stars appear and disappear as one travels from north to south, and that the moon in eclipse has a circular shadow. Ptolemy summed up all the Greek theories, Sacrobosco in the thirteenth century estimated the circumference of the earth with an astrolabe, and both geographers were accepted sources in the Middle Ages. Mandeville argued in the fourteenth century that we and those who live on the opposite side of the earth from us "be feet against feet," and that any men with the shipping and the company could "environ all the earth of all the world, as well underneath as above," and then return home again.[13]

But the question still is what did the common man in 1519 actually believe—the man who knew no Greek or Latin, the Englishman who was reluctant to go on voyages of discovery. Probably he was doubtful about these facts, since even the educated Englishmen knew little geography and since Magellan's men did not complete their circumnavigation of the globe until 1522, about three years after the time when we think Rastell wrote *The Nature of the Four Elements*. At least Rastell, writing for the common man, used the conventional proofs for the roundness of the earth but he also emphasized man's ability to sail around it:

> But from those new landes men may sayle playne
> Eastwarde, and cum to Englande againe,
> Where we began ere whyle. (p. 32)

Rastell's knowledge of geography, too, even if it was practical rather than theoretical, was not bad compared with that of other

---

[12] Johnstone Parr, "More Sources of Rastell's *Interlude* . . . ," p. 58.

[13] Sir John Mandeville, *Travels*, ed. by P. Hamelius, EETS, v. 153 (1916), 118, Part II, Chapter XXI, "The Earth Is a Sphere." In some editions the chapter numbers are quite different.

Englishmen about 1517 to 1519. He knew that the Cabots had made voyages, he accepted Vespucci as the discoverer of the New World, he had some exact information about the products of the New World, and he realized that explorers had found a fourth continent, not a mere group of islands. Probably, according to geographers, he had been using navigators' charts, rather than regular maps. His "figure" which Studious Desire carried when he entered, may have been a rare experience for a London audience of common men. A geographer suggests that it was "either a polar projection of the northern hemisphere in plano, or a half-sphere," [14] since the words indicate that he is showing a complete circuit from England and back and that he is not showing the southern hemisphere:

> But the South parte on the other syde
> Ys as large as this full, and as wyde,
> Whiche we knowe nothynge at all,
> Nor whether the moste parte be lande or see. . . . (pp. 32–35) [15]

Perhaps those who belittle Rastell's knowledge of geography do so because they estimate him by all the new developments and discoveries before 1525 and not by the knowledge which other Englishmen actually had by 1525.

The new developments were impressive, and they had come during the life of Rastell. In 1492 Columbus had reached a new world. In 1497 Vespucci was alleged to have reached the mainland of that world and Cabot really reached it. In 1522 Magellan's survivors completed their circumnavigation of the globe. In the same years globes and maps were developing. In 1492 the Behaim globe, the "Erdapfel," was first used at Nuremberg. In 1507 Waldseemüller issued a wall map with the name America, a small globe using the same name, and a textbook, *Cosmographiae introductio,* to be used with the globe and map. In 1508 John Ruysch published at Rome a new map of the world in a reissue of a Latin Ptolemy. This map, *Nova et universalior orbis cogniti tabuli,* included the Spanish and Portuguese discoveries. [16]

---

[14] E. G. R. Taylor, *Tudor Geography, 1485–1583* (London, 1930), p. 8.

[15] For other mention of the figure or the instruments, see pp. 12, 13–14, 16–17, 26–27, 41.

[16] For the main facts see *Encyclopaedia Britannica* (11th edition) under "Globes," "Geography," and individual explorers; *Catholic Encyclopedia* (New York, 1907–1914);

It might be assumed that new textbooks in geography appeared at once, but they were slow in coming, at least in England. Ptolemy and Sacrobosco continued to be popular. Ptolemy "concentrated in his writings all Greek geographical knowledge," and editions of his work continued—Latin translations from the Greek in the first half of the fifteenth century, and vernacular editions in both Italy and England from the middle of the sixteenth century. In 1566 Sir Thomas Smith, whom Richard Eden revered as his tutor, owned half a dozen other classic works on geography, editions of Ptolemy in Greek, Latin, and Italian, but only three books on modern geography dealing with the New World.[17] "Printed maps of the late fifteenth century and a large part of the sixteenth as well . . . were all under the dominance of Ptolemy's *Geography*"; and that influence continued until 1570, when Ortelius' *Theatrum orbis terrarum* appeared.[18] The influence of the *Tractatus de sphera* by Joannes de Sacrobosco was as great as that of Ptolemy in England, perhaps greater. Sacrobosco has been described as "the clearest, most elementary, and most used textbook in astronomy and geography from the thirteenth to the seventeenth centuries." In 1409 the work was required for the B.A. degree at Oxford; and two and a half centuries later the English astronomer, Flamsteed (1646–1719), shifted his interest from history to astronomy because he read Sacrobosco.[19] In 1570 John Dee, the eminent mathematician, considered it "still the best work for elementary instruction" in geography.[20] As a historian of science has said, human inertia has often been stronger than any religious opposition in delaying the spread of new scientific discoveries.

If Englishmen were conservative in clinging to classic textbooks on geography, they were even more conservative about the printing of new books. In 1511 John of Doesborowe printed three

Boies Penrose, *Travel and Discovery in the Renaissance* (Cambridge, Mass., 1952); Henry Vignaud, *Toscanelli and Columbus* (London, 1902); Joseph Fischer and Franz von Wieser, *Die Älteste Karte . . . 1507 . . .* (London, 1903); and *Cosmographiae introductio* (New York, 1907).

[17] Taylor, *Tudor Geography*, pp. 35–36.

[18] Penrose, *Travel and Discovery*, pp. 255, 261.

[19] Lynn Thorndike, *The Sphere of Sacrobosco and its Commentators* (Chicago, 1949), pp. 1, 43, 42.

[20] Taylor, *Tudor Geography*, pp. 2–3.

tracts, the first being *Of the newe lands and of the people founde by the messengers of the kynge of Portyngale named Emanuel.* This tract, described as a sheet of paper rather than a book, had one paragraph on the discovery of America and nine paragraphs on the passage to India. When Richard Eden found it more than forty years later, it was still, "amazing though it may seem, the only English work on the revelation of a Fourth Continent." [21]

The geographical lag in England appeared even in plans for practical voyages. After Rastell's venture was stopped in 1517, Wolsey planned an expedition in 1521. The men of Bristol had promised two ships, but the London merchants, approached through the great Companies, were reluctant. There was, they said, no rutter—a marine guide indicating courses and tides—and there were no English-born mariners to take charge.[22] Apparently the new lands did not quite seem real to them. Thus the new geographical knowledge moved slowly into English minds; and this is true whether we consider changes in globes, maps, and textbooks, or action in the discovery of new lands.

Against this background, John Rastell's interest in geography seems bold and daring. One geographer, E. G. R. Taylor, says that his play "may be accepted as the first work on modern geography of English authorship." [23] Another geographer says, "England came late into the picture, both with respect to exploration and travel literature. The first work of even passing geographical interest to be written by a Tudor Englishman was . . . a lecture in verse disguised as a play, on natural science, by John Rastell. . . . It is to Rastell's credit that even at that early date he realized the continental nature of North America, and it is a fair implication that through his interlude he was trying to provoke support for a further American voyage." [24] Still another writer on geography says that Rastell was the one Englishman "with an immediate intellectual interest in the new age," and that his play is "the only publication under either of the Henrys that

[21] *Tudor Georgraphy*, p. 7.
[22] *Tudor Geography*, pp. 9–10.
[23] *Tudor Geography*, p. 9.
[24] Penrose, *Travel and Discovery*, p. 313.

reveals a more than casual interest in the new geography." [25]
Though we have no evidence that Rastell made further efforts to
explore the New World or to write about it himself after 1519, it
is possible that the plans for a voyage which did not materialize
in 1521, the presence of a fishing fleet in the waters around the
"New found Island" in 1522,[26] and the plans for another voyage
of 1527 which failed were results of his propaganda.

A *Play of Witty and Witless*, by John Heywood, has the main
theme of reason, which lifts man above the beasts. The play was
probably composed about 1520 to 1525; it was not printed until
the middle of the nineteenth century, and it survives as Harleian
MS. 367 in the British Museum. Since this manuscript has Heywood's signature at the close, "Amen qd. John Heywood," his
authorship has not been challenged.[27]

The play is a double debate involving three characters. In the
first part James convinces John that it is better to be witless than
witty: first, the witty and the witless suffer the same pains of
body; second, the witty suffer more pains of the mind; third, the
witless, being unaccountable for their conduct, are sure of happiness in eternal life.

In the second part of the debate, Jerome starts his Socratic work,
James withdraws, and Jerome leads John to a new attitude. Jerome
begins his verbal attack by analyzing the difference between wit
and wisdom:

> No and man may have gret wytt and wysdom nowght.
> Wytt ys the wurker of all perseyvyng
> And indyfert to good or yll wurkyng,
> And as muche wytt may be in thyngs of most yll
> As in the best thyngs wytt can aspyr vntyll,
> In vertu or vys I meane, and wytt hath receyght
> Off non yll where vppon wysdom doth weyght.
> Wysdome governth wytt alwey vertu to vse
> And all kynds of vys alway to refewse. (p. 132)

---

[25] Parks, *Richard Hakluyt and the English Voyages*, p. 8.

[26] *L. and P.*, III, no. 2458, has the somewhat doubtful mention in a letter from Fitz-
william to Henry VIII.

[27] R. de la Bère, *John Heywood, Entertainer* (London, 1937), pp. 115, 143. For the
text of the play see pp. 117–43.

The substance of the debate or Socratic dialogue which follows runs like this:

> Question by Jerome: Which would you rather be, a reasonable man or an unreasonable beast?
> Answer: The simplest man, rather than the best beast.
> Q. Why?
> A. Two reasons: the beast, for example, the mill horse, must endure pains at his master's pleasure; the beast can never have man's pleasure in using his imagination and his reason and in enjoying recreation.
> Q. What is the real cause of this difference in man and beast?
> A. Reason, in man.
> Q. Is there any advantage, then, in being an unreasoning man?
> A. None in this life. None in a future life, since we shall differ there. Our future reward depends on ourselves, on our own wills, since God does not will any to sin and since he remits sin at the call of the penitent.
> Q. Now which would you rather be?
> A. Witty, and the more wit the better.

After this debate, it is easy to turn a compliment to the king as one who has the wit to give his subjects good government and to further God's glory.

A Play of Witty and Witless is a young man's work, as *Love's Labour's Lost* was the work of a young Shakespeare—a young man fresh from contact with formal education, unsure about the emotions of individual characters, interested in cleverness and word play, affected alliteration, cumulative lines with parallel structure, proverbs and catch phrases, and general play on words. Heywood used such terms as *schoolman, prime proposition, degree positive* or *comparative* or *superlative*—terms which the other members of the More group did not tend to use in their published work unless they wished to poke fun at the extremes of logic.

It has been said, perhaps with good reason, that Heywood's play resembles Erasmus' *The Praise of Folly* and a French *Dyalogue du fol et du sage*. It has been said also that the "latter part . . . in which wisdom is reinstated by Jerome," could be due to neither *Encomium moriae* nor the French *Dyalogue*. This original addition of Heywood's illustrates the freedom with which he handled all his sources and may perhaps be accounted for by his grasping an opportunity to display his dialectical cleverness, or better still, by his desire to pay a compliment to Henry VIII.[28]

What is the relation between Heywood's play, *Witty and Witless*, and the program of reform developed by More and his friends? Probably there is no conscious relationship at all. Certainly this writer does not have the delusion that Heywood wrote the play to bring about reforms. Neither the theme of reason nor the theme of reason joined with free will and perfectibility proves any such relation, since these were time-honored religious ideas. Neither does Heywood develop the theme with any of the optimism that More and his friends felt when they thought that the law of nature was operating in the philosophy of those without Christianity and when they wrote of a classical education with virtue and piety. Probably the influence of Erasmus contributed, with his work *The Praise of Folly;* and possibly More and Erasmus with their interest in the classics and in Lucian contributed to the style of Heywood's play. But since the play is connected with the More circle, it seems well to examine it even if the results are negative.

And what of the three plays discussed here in relation to the ideas of the More circle? Medwall's *Nature,* the earliest of the plays to be written, is almost entirely medieval, with possibly fresh touches of nature which had not been appearing in religious plays and a benign, educative character called Nature, carefully separated from the trappings of Venus and Cupid.

Rastell's play *The Nature of the Four Elements* takes ideas of education similar to those of More, Erasmus, and Vives, but gives them an individual slanting. The author wishes to begin with the lowliest parts of the great chain of being and thus to lead the common man up to the knowledge of God; to educate capable men, noble or common, who did not know Greek or Latin; to make scientific ideas available in English; and to educate by experience more than by formal teaching. In his concern with natural

---

[28] Karl Young, "The Influence of French Farce upon the Plays of John Heywood," *MP,* II (1904–1905), 114.

science he chose to emphasize geography; in his efforts to teach it and to interest men in exploring he surpassed most Englishmen of his day. In the More group he stood above all the others, unless it be Vives, in his practical knowledge of geography and in his efforts to teach it to the common man.

CHAPTER **VIII** *The bases of true nobility*

Two plays connected with members of the More circle use the question of true nobility as a major theme: *Fulgens and Lucres* by Henry Medwall and the debate *Of Gentleness and Nobility* probably written by John Rastell. Of course the question who really has a right to be called noble did not originate in the sixteenth century; it has roots in the Christian religion, with its doctrine of equality before God, and in such classical philosophers as Aristotle, Plato, and Seneca. But More and his friends made certain ideas about nobility a part of their program for the reform of society. In the play of *Fulgens and Lucres* neither the question who is truly noble nor the character and status of Lucres was original with the group of writers in England. A source of the English play was Buonaccorsi's work *Declamatio de vera nobilitate;* his ideas were restated by John Tiptoft, Earl of Worcester, as the *Declamacyon de noblesse,* printed by Caxton in 1481, and used by Henry Medwall.

Fulgens and Lucres, according to the title page, was "compyled" by Henry Medwall, "late chapelayne to the ryght reuerent fader in god, Johan Morton, cardynall and Archebysshop of Caunterbury." As its editors, F. S. Boas and A. W. Reed, pointed out, it may have been given at Lambeth Palace during the Christmas season of 1497, when Morton probably entertained the Flemish and Spanish ambassadors. The Spanish dance of the mummers and the line of Flemish spoken by B to the musicians support this view.[1] Though More had left Morton's household some years before 1497, the free and easy appeals of A and B to the audience suggest the atmosphere in which he may have moved some years earlier. As the colophon states, the play was printed by John Rastell while he lived on the south side of Paul's church beside Paul's "cheyne," and thus about 1513 to 1519.[2] Hence by authorship, place of performance, and printing, it belongs to the More circle.

In its major theme, the question what is true nobility and why men should be honored, *Fulgens and Lucres* establishes the definite pattern of ideas which was emphasized by the More circle in non-dramatic literature about 1500 to 1530. The man of rank without virtue competes with the man of virtue without rank, and the latter wins. Publius Cornelius, asking for the hand of Lucres, urges the nobility of his ancestors and his own inherited wealth. He offers Lucres idleness, hawking, hunting, dancing, minstrelsy, and fine clothing. He is extravagant and wasteful; the servant B gives a vivid account of the way he squanders his money daily, as if he never thought of the future, and of his extravagant garments—his striped hose, his enormous codpiece, his gowns into which he puts seven yards of material, with big sleeves and pleats so that he seems to have wings ready to fly. His life is one of sin and lust. Gayus refutes Publius by saying that the nobility of his ancestors is unimportant compared with his own bestial life, that both he and Publius came of Adam and Eve; that he himself avoids sensuality and idleness; that he has sufficient means to support Lucres; and that he has acted often for the good of others and for the commonweal. Lucres, after listening to both, suggests that she will inquire what "common fame" says of each one and then she will make a decision; but for some reason she makes her decision as soon as they have gone out—in favor of Gayus Flaminius.

While this sentence by Lucres is very definite, it is still handled

---

[1] Henry Medwall, *Fulgens and Lucres,* ed. by F. S. Boas and A. W. Reed (Oxford, 1926), Introduction, p. xx, also pp. 67–68. As a balance for the strong emphasis here on Flemish influence see C. R. Baskervill, "Conventional Features of Medwall's *Fulgens and Lucres,*" *MP,* XXIV (1927), 419–42.

[2] *Fulgens and Lucres,* p. 86, at the close of the play, and Introduction, p. ix.

with much tact or even with apologies. In the beginning of the
play, when B summarizes the plot for A, saying that the senate
gave a decision in favor of Gayus, A expresses his surprise:

> what, wyll they afferme that a chorles son
> Sholde be more noble than a gentilman born?
> Nay beware for men wyll haue therof grete scorn,
> It may not be spoken in no maner of case. (I, 130–33) [3]

B thinks that they will not fail to follow the original story (though
the definite decision is not in the original story), but he adds:

> I trow here is no man of the kyn or sede
> Of either partie, for why they were bore
> In the cytie of Rome as I sayd before. (I, 178–80)

Lucres is careful to say, long before she makes her decision, that
her own fantasy may not be considered as a general precedent;
and when she chooses the man of virtue without noble ancestors,
she is tactful:

> For in this case I do hym commend
> As the more noble man sith he thys wyse
> By meane of hys vertue to honoure doth aryse.
> And for all that I wyll not dispise
> The blode of cornelius, I pray you thinke not so:
> God forbede that ye sholde note me that wyse,
> For truely I shall honoure them wheresoeuer I go
> And all other that be of lyke blode also,
> But vnto the blode I wyll haue lytyl respect
> where tho condicyons be synfull and abiect.
> I pray you all syrs as meny as be here
> Take not my wordis by a sinistre way. (II, 756–67)

Then B, the servant of the patrician, Publius Cornelius, enters, surprised at what he has heard:

> yes, by my trouth, I shall witnes bere,
> wheresoeuer I becom another day,
> How suche a gentylwoman did opynly say
> That by a chorles son she wolde set more
> Than she wolde do by a gentylman bore. (II, 768–72)

[3] Line numbers refer to the edition cited above.

Lucres further defends her position:

> I say euyn as I saide whan I began—
> That for vertue excellent I will honoure a man
> Rather than for hys blode, if it so fall
> That gentil condicyons agre not withall. (II, 776–79)

Answering B's question about a gentleman born who has goodly manners, she says:

> Suche one is worthy more lawde and praysyng
> Than many of them that hath their begynnyng
> Of low kynred, ellis god forbede! . . . (II, 783–85)
> But neuerthelesse I said this before
> That a man of excellent vertuouse condicions,
> Allthough he be of a pore stoke bore,
> yet I wyll honour and commende hym more
> Than one that is descendide of ryght noble kyn
> whose lyffe is all dissolute and rotyde in syn. (II, 788–93)

After she goes out, A and B continue to beat their brains about her decision. A, who did not hear her, remains skeptical, to give dramatic emphasis to the idea of true nobility:

> B. By my fayth she saide, I tell the true,
>   That she wolde nedis haue hym for his vertue
>   And for none other thynge.
> A. Uertue, what the deuyll is that? (II, 839–42)

A asks the women in the audience whether they are going to choose their husbands in this fashion; and B, in the closing speech, says:

> Is not the question
> Of noblenes now fully defynde,
> As it may be so by a womans mynde? (II, 883–85)

Then he points out that the play was given to provide entertainment and to persuade gentlemen to avoid sin, since sin in them is worse than in men of low birth.

All this tact, as the editors suggest, may have been used to soften the decision because the play was planned for the entertainment of the Flemish and Spanish ambassadors. But human nature being what it is, the tactful presentation would make the idea more acceptable to almost any audience in a society with class distinctions.

Another interesting difference appears in Tiptoft's translation and Medwall's play. Tiptoft's version put a much greater emphasis on the details of a classical education.[4] But in Medwall's play Gayus Flaminius merely points out that he spends time in study, though he also describes himself to Lucres as being "a man accordyng To youre owne condicions in euery thing." In Tiptoft's version the same character is specific about his training in philosophy, Latin, and Greek, and also about the effects of his education on his own character—his virtue, piety, and service to the commonweal. He is also more specific about the previous study of Lucres in liberal philosophy and about her future study; he says that Lucres will desire to know the "marvelous causes of things, of the moving of the planets," and that he will help her in her study of Greek, Latin, and philosophy.

When Medwall had a definite decision made by a woman who seems educated, why did he not transfer this specific emphasis to the play? Perhaps one cannot say with finality, but there are several possibilities. Medwall was writing early, before More had stressed the teaching of the same liberal studies for men and women; and in England, More seems to have been the chief or at least the first exponent of liberal training for women. Then Medwall had various problems in adapting material to the stage: he brought in a satirical subplot of the servingmen contesting for the hand of Ancilla, to add mirth to the matter; he had the problem of length, since his play was to be given in a great hall; he apparently chose to emphasize the question of true nobility and to subordinate all other things to this one theme.

But even without these details, Medwall's play does bring out clearly the wisdom, virtue, and piety of the ideal woman; the family relationships which develop when people have wisdom and virtue; the distaste for immoral, emotional medieval romances. In treating the question of true nobility also Medwall puts his emphasis not on the aristocrat but on the commoner who is moving

---

[4] *Tulle of Old Age, Tullius de amicicia, Declamacyon de noblesse* (1481), printed by Caxton. I used the copy at the J. Pierpont Morgan Library.

toward true nobility—who has virtue, piety, and learning but continues to spend time in study, not idleness; who has the freedom of choice and struggles toward perfectibility; who not only leads the good life of wisdom and virtue but who serves the commonweal.

The play *Gentleness and Nobility* is certainly centered around the question of true nobility and the rights of the common man. But there is no definite evidence about the date of its composition, its printing, or even its authorship. Probably it was written about 1523 to 1526 and printed about 1529, and there seems to be little reason for doubting that its author was John Rastell. John Rastell certainly printed the play, though some details in the style of printing suggest the influence of William Rastell, who was working with his father about 1527 to 1530. The colophon of the play reads "Johannes Rastell me fieri fecit." Some argue that the words refer to the printing; others, to authorship; and one scholar has said: "we can hardly doubt that the word 'fieri' refers to performance, if not to composition," and he implied that it probably meant both.[5] Some scholars have argued for Heywood's authorship, others have argued well for that of John Rastell.[6] Any argument for individual authorship on the basis of parallel passages alone has its pitfalls when one is dealing with a group of men who were looking for universal truth and who held so many ideas in common. In this discussion of ideas which the members of the More group shared, the question of authorship is relatively unimportant; but it will be assumed that the author was John Rastell.

The author of the play seems to have had serious intentions. Also he followed his intention as he stated it at the beginning of the play: to dispute who is a noble man and how men should come

[5] Charles Mill Gayley, *Representative English Comedies*, 3 vols. (New York, 1916), I, 8–9, "Critical Essay," by A. W. Pollard; W. W. Greg, *A Bibliography of English Printed Drama before the Restoration*, 2 vols. (London, 1939), I.

[6] C. F. Tucker Brooke, "*Gentleness and Nobility*: the Authorship and Source," *MLR*, VI (1911), 458–61; Esther C. Dunn, "John Rastell and 'Gentleness and Nobility,'" *MLR*, XII (1917), 266–78; A. W. Reed, *Early Tudor Drama* (London, 1926); Kenneth W. Cameron, *Authorship and Sources of "Gentleness and Nobility"* (Raleigh, N.C., 1941).

to authority. He added that it was compiled in the manner of an interlude, with toys and jests added to make merry pastime and disport. The only remarkable thing, after this promise, is how little space is given to toys and jests compared with other serious plays of the period—such plays as *Nature, The Nature of the Four Elements,* and *Fulgens and Lucres.* Of course the Plowman might seem amusing at moments, or to a Tudor audience he might seem only shocking. For he is a Plowman who outargues both the Knight and the Merchant, quotes Latin to illustrate the different views held by philosophers and by churchmen, threatens physical violence against the Knight, and rather freely calls his opponents fool or knave. But his argument is close-knit; and the author emphasizes his views by space, terminal position, and general force and power.

A summary of the argument, in the form of question and answer, will serve perhaps to bring out the integration of ideas: What have our ancestors done that we may claim as an honor? What have we done that we may claim as an honor? These are the answers: Lineage does not give us the right to claim honor, or nobleness; property does not give the right to claim nobleness; sufficiency gives us some right to claim nobleness. Part II gets under way with the Plowman's proposition: a nobleman who departs from virtue should be "dispraised" more than a man of low birth who does the same; a man of humble ancestry who does good deeds should be praised more than the nobleman who does good deeds.

Then other questions are raised: Why do men desire praise for lineage? Why do they boast of descent from bad men, if the men are kings and emperors? The Plowman answers: They lack learning; they lack virtue for which they can themselves be praised; they do not love virtue. He asks: Why do men desire praise for property, and how did private property develop from a condition where, we know, all things were held in common? The Knight answers: It developed as people increased and complexity grew, to reward those who made good laws and waged defensive war for the public good. But the Plowman contends: It developed as tyranny and extortion, followed by the laws of inheritance.

The disputants raise another question: Is inheritance a good or a bad thing? The Knight answers: It is good; it causes a man to develop and care for his property. The Plowman argues: It is bad; though the result may be good, the intention is evil.

Finally they reach this question: Who are really worthy to have possessions? The Plowman answers: Those who are virtuous and apt at serving the commonweal. The Knight objects: All men, the Bible says, may pass on property to their seed. Then the Plowman attacks him for shifting from reason to authority. The Merchant proposes a return to the original question: What really makes a gentleman. The Plowman says that gentle conditions are the principal cause. When the Merchant agrees, the Plowman adds this definition: Gentle conditions come from avoiding pride, wrath, envy, covetousness, gluttony, sloth, lechery, and from practicing meekness, patience, charity, liberality, abstinence, good business, and chastity. The Knight agrees. Then the Plowman draws his conclusion: I am more of a gentleman than either of you. The Knight and the Merchant refuse to agree, and they leave the stage.

When the Plowman is left to comment, the order and the emphasis upon ideas are of great importance in realizing the author's purpose. The Plowman says with complete seriousness: Men will not yield to reason; evil men will remain in authority for a time, in spite of our exhortations, teaching, preaching, and "gesting"; finally our governors will take up reform and correction with authority.

Then the Knight and the Merchant return. It has not been observed, I believe, that they argue superficially, using authority and custom to support them. The Merchant says it is necessary for rulers to have possessions, so that they may drive the people to labor, instead of idleness. The Knight says that rulers should come to their positions by inheritance rather than election; for election is often accompanied by "drede, mede, and affeccyon"; the proof of this is in old chronicles. Elected men will be proud and will refuse to take advice. Men who come to authority by inheritance are better:

> But thy [sic] that by enherytaunce rulers be,
> Though they haue no grete lernyng yet we see
> yet makyth them more ferefull and better content
> To folow wyse mens councell and aduysement. (II, 1049–52) [7]

[7] *Gentleness and Nobility,* Malone Society Reprints (Oxford, 1950).

Surely that is a tongue-in-cheek argument—but the author's tongue, not the Knight's or the Merchant's, since these lines may belong to either one. Then the Knight argues from long continuance, or what the men of the More circle called *custom* when they argued so hotly against following unwise custom. Yes, the Merchant says solemnly, that is good reasoning. The Knight argues that men of gentle blood are usually the ones who show courtesy; but he illustrates by the superficial instance that when gentlemen are in company together they are glad to pay for each other and to show each other such pleasures as they can.

The Merchant agrees that poor wretches, unlike noblemen, cannot show liberality; the Knight insists that gentlemen born to lands are the ones who have sufficiency, of material property, of course. The Merchant agrees that only the rich can afford liberality and gentleness. Of course they are distorting the Plowman's argument about self-sufficiency. The Merchant adds that it is necessary for some to live in wealth and some in misery, no matter what churls say; it has been so in the past; it will be so in the future. It is also, the Merchant concludes, the plan of Almighty God for wise men to have the rule over the fools. So they close the argument, to their satisfaction, by arguing from custom, authority, and the will of God.[8]

Then the Philosopher in an epilogue states the final conclusions: virtue and gentle conditions make the true gentleman; and these qualities are often seen in poor men. Sufficiency is important when joined with goodness, since God is noble not for his sufficiency alone but for his goodness. Heads, rulers, and governors should come to office because of their virtue and should continue in office only so long as they use virtue. The author of the play has brought in reasons on both sides for the one aim of rebuking sin; he has tried to appeal to reason, hoping that a "grudging" of conscience, then compunction, and then amendment might follow. If any "blind beasts" refuse to change their ways, they should have sharp correction and punishment; and if necessary, the "princes and governors" should make new laws to curb them. As a final result, we shall have men in office who are good, just, and impartial.

[8] Lines 1027–1112.

The writer of the play not only had serious intentions but he also worked out a close integration of ideas through the whole. In the two parts of the dialogue, in the Plowman's comment after the two others leave him toward the close, in the final talk between the Knight and the Merchant where they cling to custom, authority, and the will of God and refuse to hear new reasons, and in the didactic explanation of the philosopher at the close there is a close-knit progression of ideas.

Again, these general ideas were not entirely original with John Rastell or any other member of the More group. It has been suggested that the stress on sufficiency was an individual comment by Rastell, but others expressed somewhat similar opinions. The concept of holding all things in common, with its origin in the practice of the early church and with implications about inheritance, was discussed by More, Colet, Vives, and other members of the group. The election of rulers, discussed in Chapter IV under law and government, had been given a new emphasis from the growing interest in the classics. The extreme concern with the common man, like the concern about his education in *The Nature of the Four Elements*, may be a Rastellian touch, though it cannot be soundly argued that More and other friends were not interested in the common man; and Rastellian perhaps is the earthy realism in the Plowman's reminder that all men alike are conceived and born in uncleanness, that the blood of all men is the same color, and that all alike are subject to wounds and illness. The emphasis upon natural reason and philosophy in the play has been called "a very advanced position for the early Tudor mind." [9] But such a view seems hardly sound when one remembers that the emphasis upon reason has strong roots in the Middle Ages, that Erasmus had turned reason wrong side out in *The Praise of Folly*, and that More had based his Utopian civilization upon natural reason. But the emphasis may be newer in secular drama. Then Rastell, who emphasized his concern for the common man in his dramatic propaganda about natural science, may again be slightly individual in using reason to teach the nobility of a plowman, and in objecting to the shift from reason to biblical authority.

[9] Reed, *Early Tudor Drama*, p. 109.

Remembering Chaucer and the long series of comments in the Middle Ages on true nobility and the religious origins of the idea of equality before God, one may still say that More and his friends gave a new emphasis in the discussion of true nobility. Instead of stressing the need of the man with lineage and wealth to act nobly, they emphasized the power of the humble man to rise to nobility by education in virtue, piety, and classical learning. Thus they added an important idea to their whole program of social reform and infused it with dynamic optimism.

CHAPTER IX *Religious reform*

In this section we are concerned briefly with three plays, probably all of them by John Heywood. They are *The Play Called the Four PP's; A Merry Play between John John, the Husband, Tyb, his Wife, and Sir John, the Priest;* and *The Pardoner and the Friar.*

The Four PP's was no doubt written by Heywood, probably about 1521 to 1525, and certainly within the first of Heywood's two periods of favor at court, 1519–28. It was printed first by John Middleton, about 1544 or 1545, with the evidence of authorship on the title page, "Made by John Heywood." It was reprinted perhaps about 1555, and again in 1569. The colophon of the third edition closes with the words, "Qd. John Heywood," as if it had been set up from manuscript.[1]

The Four PP's is said to have its source in a French *sottie,* the farce called *D'un pardonneur, d'un triacleur, et d'une taverniere,* and to owe something to Chaucer for the character of the Pardoner. It has also been described as the debate form with the farce spirit. Because of the farce spirit readers too readily conclude that the play is merely a contest to see who can tell the biggest lie and that women are chiefly the butt of the satire. It is true that the Pedlar's wares lead to a satirical discussion of women's

[1] W. W. Greg, *A Bibliography of the English Printed Drama before the Restoration,* 2 vols. (London, 1939), I.

dress, that the devils find women troublesome in hell, and that the prize lie is the Palmer's quiet remark that he has never seen a woman out of patience. But the farce spirit has perhaps tended to obscure the essential unity of the play and its serious ideas on religion.

The real question of the play is not merely the wonder who can tell the biggest lie, but which man excels? Which one should have the rule over the others? At first the question takes this form: Which one excels in getting souls into heaven? The Palmer advances his claim by telling of the shrines he has visited in many countries to get his own soul into heaven. The Pardoner contends that he can get souls into heaven without all this wandering about: give him a penny or two and when the soul leaves the body

> In halfe an houre—or thre quarters at moste—
> The soule is in heuen with the Holy Ghost! (ll. 149–50) [2]

The Potycary challenges their superiority by describing the help he gives with his drugs in separating soul from body; for even if a man has a thousand pardons around his neck he can't reach heaven until he has died. The Pedlar enters, commends them so far, but suggests a contest in lying. In this he is sure they all have some skill, and it is necessary that one, the winner, be the head, whom the others obey. He himself knows enough about lying to make a good judge.

The Pardoner begins to prove his skill by showing his relics: the blessed jawbone of All-Hallows; the great toe of the Trinity, which will cure toothache; the buttock-bone of Pentecost; an eye-tooth of the Great Turk; a box of the humble-bees that stung Eve while she was tasting the forbidden fruit; a glass of the liquid served at the wedding of Adam and Eve. It is worth noticing that these relics have all been reduced to such complete absurdity that they cannot be compared with any that the believer would call genuine; the purpose is perhaps twofold. First, a contest in lying calls for absurd exaggeration. Second, such exaggeration prepares the way for the Pedlar's serious analysis of religious truth at the close of the play.

[2] J. Q. Adams, *Chief Pre-Shakespearean Dramas* (Cambridge, Mass., 1924), pp. 367–84. Line numbers refer to this edition.

Then the Potycary recommends his wares: a rhubarb that will keep a man from living to be hanged, an ointment good for a fistula or a canker, an "alkakengy" good for mangy dogs or for people, and so on. The Potycary tries a bribe and other devious means to get a decision. But there is no decision.

Continuing to act as a master of ceremonies, the Pedlar decides that there has been no real test of skill and that each is to tell a tall tale of some kind. The Potycary spins his yarn about the wanton whom he cured of the falling sickness. The Pardoner tells of his descent into hell to rescue an old friend, Margery Corson, whom the devil is glad to release because women make so much trouble in hell.

It is in this trip to hell that the material comes nearest to the spirit of Lucian in *Menippus* (which More had translated), not merely because it is a trip to the underworld, but because of the satirical details, the imagination and fantasy which Heywood uses. The Pardoner first tries Purgatory, but Margery is not there; he does not try Heaven because he is too well acquainted with her life to consider her sainted. But while he is in Purgatory he happens to sneeze; a soul says "Christ help!" He promptly uses all his pardons and that soul flies straight to heaven. The narrative continues with many delightful imaginative details. The porter at the gate of hell happens to be an old friend who used to "play the devil" in the Corpus Christi play at Coventry; this porter gets him a safe-conduct from Lucifer on condition that he check his pardons at the gate. It happens to be a festival day in hell, the anniversary of the fall of Lucifer, and the devils are in holiday trim:

> Theyr hornes well gylt, theyr clowes full clene,
> Theyr taylles well kempt, and, as I wene,
> With sothery butter theyr bodyes anoynted—
> I neuer sawe deuyls so well appoynted.
> The mayster deuyll sat in his iacket,
> And all the soules were playnge at racket.
> None other rackettes they hadde in hande
> Saue euery soule a good fyre-brande;
> Wherwith they played so pretely

> That Lucyfer laughed merely,
> And all the resedew of the fendes
> Dyd laugh full well togytther lyke frendes. (ll. 877–88)

The chief, Lucifer, is described with imaginative vividness:

> He smyled on me well-fauoredly,
> Bendynge hys browes, as brode as barne-durres,
> Shakynge hys eares, as ruged as burres,
> Rolynge hys yes [eyes], as rounde as two bushels,
> Flastynge [flashing?] the fyre out of his nose-thryls,
> Gnashynge hys teeth so vaynglorousely
> That me thought tyme to fall to flatery. (ll. 896–902)

After Lucifer had gladly released Margery, the Pardoner brought her back to New Market Heath, he says, and there they may find her if they wish.

Then the Palmer, who says he has known well all sorts and conditions of women, quietly makes his comment:

> Of all the women that I haue sene,
> I neuer sawe, nor knewe, in my consyens,
> Any one woman out of paciens. (ll. 1002–4)

In their first rush of admiration his opponents agree that his is the biggest lie; the Pedlar says that it is excellent—it can be tested by relating it to known and tangible things; the Palmer has won. But recovering, the Pardoner and the Potycary object to another knave having the mastery over them. The Pedlar, still master of ceremonies, advises the Palmer to release them; he does so.

Then the Pedlar begins estimating the actions and the ideas of the play in terms of religion, as if he is an authority. His ideas seem to represent the author, John Heywood; they might have been spoken by More, Erasmus, or any others of the group, though perhaps none of the others would have combined fantasy, imagination, satire, and scorn of absurd relics with these firm beliefs. The Palmer has done well, says the Pedlar, to go on a pilgrimage if he has done so for the real love of Christ; the Pardoner has done well if he has procured indulgences for his neighbors "charitably" and only for love of them and God. Every kind of virtue is worthy;

their fault has been that each has been despising the virtue of the other:

> And so for all that do pretende,
> By ayde of Goddes grace, to ensewe
> Any maner kynde of vertue:
> As, some great alymse for to gyue,
> Some in wyllfull pouertie to lyue,
> Some to make hye-wayes and suche other warkes,
> And some to mayntayne prestes and clarkes
> To synge and praye for soule departed—
> These, with all other vertues well marked,
> All-though they be of sondry kyndes,
> Yet be they nat vsed with sondry myndes;
> But, as God only doth all those moue,
> So euery man, onely for His loue,
> With loue and dred obediently
> Worketh in these vertues vnyformely.
> Thus euery vertue, yf we lyste to scan,
> Is pleasaunt to God and thankfull to man. . . .
> One kynde of vertue to dyspyse another
> Is lyke as the syster myght hange the brother.
> (ll. 1158–74, 1187–88)

The Potycary pertly says, much in the spirit of Lucian:

> For fere leste suche parels to me myght fall,
> I thanke God I vse no vertue at all! (ll. 1189–90)

The Pedlar rebukes him; he tries to defend himself by insisting that all the pardons and relics which have been shown here are counterfeit. The Pedlar continues, with ideas similar to those of Erasmus in "The Child's Piety" and "The Religious Pilgrimage":

> For his, and all other that ye knowe fayned,
> Ye be nother counceled nor constrayned
> To any suche thynge in any suche case
> To gyue any reuerence in any suche place;
> But where ye dout the truthe, nat knowynge,
> Beleuynge the beste, good may be growynge.
> In iudgynge the beste, no harme at the leste,
> In iudgynge the worste, no good at the beste.
> But beste in these thynges, it semeth to me,

> To take no iudgment vpon ye;
> But, as the Churche doth iudge or take them,
> So do ye receyue or forsake them;
> And so, be sure, ye can nat erre,
> But may be a frutfull folower. (ll. 1205–18)

The Potycary, the Pardoner, and the Palmer all hasten to agree with the Pedlar; the Pardoner declares that "Reason wolde we shulde folowe hys counsell." The play comes to a close with the wish that all may prosper "In the fayth of hys Churche Vniuersall."

So *The Play Called the Four PP's* has qualities of Lucian—imagination, fantasy, satire, other humorous details, and lively dialogue. It has also the combination of an attack on abuses with an expression of genuine piety, love of God and of man, which More and Erasmus were able to approve or to use; it has, that is, a largeness both of thought and of style. The play, of course, is not original. But in developing it John Heywood wrote in the spirit of Lucian, and thus his play has a kinship to the imaginative work of More and to the style of Erasmus in *The Praise of Folly.*

A Merry Play between John John, the Husband, Tyb, his Wife, and Sir John, the Priest was probably written by John Heywood, but evidence in the documents is lacking. It was printed by William Rastell, February 12, 1533. Since he and John Heywood had been brothers-in-law, possibly for ten years, at this date, he must have known whether Heywood was the author. If Heywood was the author, Rastell must have chosen, for some reason which might be connected with the unsettled times, not to use the author's name. Some have argued that the play was written by Sir Thomas More, and that he did not wish to be known in 1533 as one who pictured immorality in priests. There is a lack of convincing evidence for More's authorship.[3]

The play has little definite connection with the ideas advocated by members of the More group as a part of the reforming program. Of course More and Erasmus commented seriously or satirically on corrupt churchmen, but they usually joined adverse criticism with positive loyalty. Instead, this play represents the attitude

---

[3] Adams, *Chief Pre-Shakespearean Dramas,* pp. 385–96; W. W. Greg, *A Bibliography . . . ,* I.

of mere enjoyment without any concern for reform. Sir John, the priest, is described as a known whoremonger and a haunter of stews; the actions of the priest and wife, as well as their conversation, leave no great doubt about the nature of their interest in each other; and if any doubt still lingers, it is removed at the close by the exchange of epithets and the departure of wife and priest. All this emphasis upon a priest as a wife's lover is typical of medieval farce and fabliau.

The play is believed to have a French source *De Pernet qui va au vin,* and certain resemblances between the two have already been thoroughly analyzed. In each the plot concerns a wife, her husband, who is a henpecked cuckold, and her lover; the husband is sent to get drink for the hated guest; the lover and the wife eat the pie without giving any to the husband; the husband is given the task of softening wax before the fire; the wife and the lover show enough familiarity to make an audience believe in their misconduct. There are also interesting differences: in the French farce the husband is sent for wine; the lover is a cousin, alias Amoureaux, instead of Sir John the priest; the wife talks to her husband about a kinsman instead of a good friend; the ending of the French farce is uncertain.[4] Heywood's play, then, changes material to stress the immoral priest; but many medieval farces gave the same emphasis.

The Pardoner and the Friar is usually believed to have been written by John Heywood.[5] Sir Thomas More and William Cornish have been suggested as possible authors, but the evidence for them is not overwhelming. The play was printed by William Rastell, April 5, 1533; again Rastell must have known if either his uncle or his brother-in-law wrote the play; but he may have had reasons for omitting the author's name. There was no other printing of the play in the sixteenth century. Of course the play may have been written some years before it was printed in 1533.

The play is a good example of a distinctive attitude of some

---

[4] Karl Young, "The Influence of French Farce upon the Plays of John Heywood," *MP,* II (1904–1905), 101–3, and *passim;* Ian Maxwell, *French Farce and John Heywood* (Melbourne and London, 1946), Chapter V.

[5] See R. de la Bère, *John Heywood, Entertainer* (London, 1930), pp. 147–82, for the play.

members of the More circle—More, Erasmus, and Heywood—on religion: it has the largeness which combines attack on abuses with positive belief in the church. Again the plot is simple. A Friar enters a church and begins asking for money, promising to bless those who give and to curse those who refuse. A few minutes later a Pardoner comes in, offering a pardon which is "the greatest under the sun," is granted by the Pope's bulls, and is available for groats or pence. There is no mention of confession, contrition, inner attitudes, worthy action—no assumption that pardon will lead to better lives. The Pardoner offers many relics; but as in *The Four PP's,* all of them are complete absurdities: a bone of a holy Jew's sheep, warranted to cure diseases of animals, to increase flocks, and to cure a husband's distrust of his wife even if she has been taken in adultery with two or three friars; a mitten which will cause grain to increase—if one offers pence or groats; the arm of "sweet Saint Sunday," which brings good fortune to travelers by sea or land and "high promotion" to those who are blessed by it; the toe of Holy Trinity (as in *The Four PP's*) which will cure toothache, canker, or the pox—for a price; the "bongrace of our Lady's French hood," helpful to pregnant women; the blessed jawbone of All-Hallows, a charm against poison; and the brainpan of St. Michael, which wards off headache, even after one has died or his head has been cut off with a sword. The Pardoner offers these with repeated emphasis on the money which one must give.

Finally the Friar and the Pardoner become so excited that neither will permit the other to say more than a line at a time. The good Parson of the church decides to intervene; he calls on the constable, Neighbor Pratt, to help him. But the two rascals together are stronger than honest religion; they finally escape. Thus we have what might be called a stimulating, artistic ending to a farce which again combines the satirical spirit of Lucian with positive attitudes in religion.

Again a French farce, *D'un pardonneur, d'un triacleur, et d'une taverniere,* or a similar farce now lost, is said to be the source of Heywood's *Pardoner and the Friar.* If this be true—and most assumptions about one definite source in medieval literature are to be taken with grains of salt—Heywood's changes are again interesting. The action of the French farce is described as follows: A pardonneur, laden with relics, begins his bombastic appeal in a public place. A triacleur, or traveling apothecary, enters and starts selling his wares. The two fakirs carry on in alternate short speeches, mixing comments on their own wares with curses and ridicule of each other. Finally they become reconciled to each other long enough to visit the tavern together. They leave a precious relic as a payment to the bar maid.[6]

If this is Heywood's source, he has deepened both his satirical and his serious concern about religion. He has both his rascals connected with religion, where the French source had only one; and the two contend for the privilege of saving souls. Then he has introduced the defenders of serious religion, using a church as the setting. His Parson wishes to keep the church unpolluted; but he and the constable, Neighbor Pratt, are forced to let the rascals escape. Thus Heywood combines and also intensifies the satirical attack on abuses and the devotion to serious religion and the church.

How much of the material in these three plays contributes to the program of reform which the More group supported? *John John, the Husband* has nothing at all to differentiate it from the medieval fabliaux which roused cynical laughter. In *The Pardoner and the Friar* corrupt churchmen are satirized; the Friar and the Pardoner are greedy for money; the latter uses absurd relics which cannot be mistaken for genuine; and of course the efforts of the Parson and Neighbor Pratt add the genuine respect for true religion. While this combination of satire and seriousness was not new in the sixteenth century, as one may learn from Chaucer and from G. R. Owst's book, *Literature and Pulpit in Medieval England*, it was used by More and Erasmus as well as John Heywood. All found it effective in pointing up the need for religious reform. *The Four PP's* not only combines satire of abuses with serious concern for religion but it also uses the imaginative fantasy of a trip to the underworld, with the details and the spirit of Lucian's *Menippus*. About 1506 or earlier More had translated

---

[6] Young, "The Influence of French Farce . . . ," pp. 107–8.

Menippus; about 1530 John Rastell printed an English metrical version which he probably wrote himself, basing it on More's Latin version. *The Four PP's,* then, has perhaps some slight relation to the whole program of religious reform discussed in the More circle; and it reflects the spirit of Lucian.

CHAPTER X *Law and government*

Though the men of the More group were intensely interested in government and the good of the commonweal, this concern, when expressed in their manner, does not appear as the major theme of any play. Instead, it appears as a minor theme in connection with education, the basis of true nobility, or the education and status of women. But we do find much indirect comment on government and the commonweal in *Fulgens and Lucres, The Nature of the Four Elements, Gentleness and Nobility,* and also in *Godly Queen Hester,* although the latter play has no known connection with More and his friends except that it indirectly defended Catherine of Aragon. *The Play of the Weather* by John Heywood also uses government and the common good as a main theme.

The play of *Fulgens and Lucres,* discussed earlier for its dominant idea, the basis of true nobility, has much comment on a man's contribution to the commonweal as a test of his nobility. For example, Publius Cornelius pleads his case by saying that his ancestors have served their country:

How ofte haue myne auncetours in tymes of necessite
Delyuerd this cyte from dedely parell
As well by theyr manhode as by theyr police!
what ieopardi and paine they haue suffred in the quarell
Thempire to encrece and for the comune wele! (II, 465–69) [1]

---

[1] Henry Medwall, *Fulgens and Lucres,* ed. by F. S. Boas and A. W. Reed (Oxford, 1926).

They have often been named the fathers of their country; and when their country was in need, it has called upon them as a child turns to its father.

Gayus Flaminius points out that his opponent has talked only of his ancestors' deeds, not his own, and that his own life is dissolute. Then Gayus pleads his own virtues and finally comes to his service to the commonweal:

> Another tyme my contrey manly I deffend,
> And for the victoryes that I haue done therin
> ye haue sene yourselfe, syr, that I haue come in
> To this noble cytee twyse or thryse
> Crownyd with lawryel as it is the gyse. (II, 681–85)

It is Gayus Flaminius who is finally chosen by Lucres as her husband, because of his other virtues and because of his service to the commonweal.

Rastell's *Nature of the Four Elements* or *Interlude of the Four Elements* has much emphasis upon the good of the commonwealth. The messenger who speaks the prologue is concerned with refuting the common opinion that a man should be valued for his wealth and defending the better opinion that he should be valued for his service to the commonweal:

> Yet amonge moste folke that man is holdyn
> Moste wyse, whiche to be ryche studyeth only;
> But he that for a commyn welth bysyly
> Studyeth and laboryth, and lyvyth by Goddes law,
> Except he wax ryche, men count hym but a daw!
> So he that is ryche is ever honouryd,
> Allthough he have got it never so falsely,
> The pore beynge never so wyse is reprovyd;
> This is the oppynyon moste commynly
> Thorowe out the worlde, and yet no reason why. . . . (p. 4) [2]

> For every man in reason thus ought to do,
> To labour for his owne necessary lyvynge,
> And than for the welth of his neyghbour also;
> But what dyvylish mynd have they, which musing

---

[2] John Rastell, *The Nature of the Four Elements*, ed. by James O. Halliwell (London, 1848), p. 4. Other page numbers refer to this edition.

And labouryng all their lyffes, do no other thyng
But bringe ryches to their owne possessyon
Nothyng regardinge their neyghbours distruccion.
Yet all the ryches in the worlde that is,
Rysyth of the grounde by Goddys sendynge,
And by the labour of pore mennys handys;
And though thou, ryche man, have therof the kepynge,
Yet is not this ryches of thy gettynge,
Nor oughtyst not in reason to be preysyd the more,
For by other mennys labour it is got before . . .

For all clerkes afferme that that man presysely,
Whiche studyeth for his owne welth pryncypally,
Of God shall deserve but lytyll rewarde,
Except he the commyn welth somwhat regarde;
So they sey that that man occupyed is
For a commyn welth, whiche is ever laborynge
To releve pore people with temporall goodys,
And that it is a commyn good act to brynge
People from vyce and to use good lyvynge;
Lyke wyse for a commyn welth occupyd is he
That bryngyth them to knowledge that yngnorant be. (p. 5)

Later the character called Experience delivers to Studious Desire a didactic speech which centers on the good of the commonweal, so far as that commonweal is England.[3] The whole prologue is a didactic essay, with strong emphasis upon working for the good of a whole people.

The play called *Of Gentleness and Nobility,* discussed in Chapter II of Part II because of its main theme, has also a close relationship to the good of the commonweal.[4] The idea of sharing with others appears in an early speech by the Merchant:

For I call hym a gentylman that gentilly
Doth gyf unto other men louyngly
Such thing as he hath of hys own proper,
But he that takith ought a way from a nother

[3] Pages 29–30.
[4] *Gentleness and Nobility,* Malone Society Reprints (Oxford, 1950). All line references are to this edition.

> And doth gyf hym no thyng agayn therfore
> Owght to be callyd a chorll euermore. (ll. 47–52)

The Knight argues that his ancestors have aided the commonweal by doing many things that the Merchant's ancestors were completely incapable of doing:

> For in the contrey at sessyons and syse
> They haue be electe to be Justyce,
> And for theyer wyt and grete dyscressyon
> They haue Juggyd and donne correccyon
> Uppon thyne auncestors . . .
> But because myn auncestours haue euer be
> Dyscrete and wyse they haue had auctoryte. (ll. 129–33, 147–48)

The Merchant also argues on the basis of the good of the commonweal:

> I say the comyn well of euery land
> In fete of marchauntdyse doth pryncypally stand. (ll. 249–50)
> And I spende my studi and labour contynually
> And cause such thyngis to come hyder dayly
> For the comfort of thys land and commen welth,
> And to all the people grete proffet and helth. (ll. 273–76)

After the Knight, the Merchant, and the Plowman have argued the theories of self-sufficiency and of reason in man lifting him above the beasts, they argue the origin of property. The Knight contends that property came to his ancestors as a reward they earned by their good deeds. The Plowman hotly answers:

> So possessyons began by extorcyon,
> And when such extorsyoners had oppressyd
> The labouryng people than they ordeynyd
> And made laws meruelous strayte and hard
> That theyr heyres (?) myght injoy it afterward.
> So the law of inherytaunce was furst begon,
> whych is a thyng agayns all good reason
> That any inherytaunce in the world shuld be. (ll. 616–23)

Though there are some good merchants, the Plowman admits, many of them do not make good officers for the commonweal:

> And yet more ouer when any of them be
> Promotyd to rule or auctoryte

> They dysdayn all lernyng law and reason
> And Jugge all by wyll and affeccyon. (ll. 681–84)

The Plowman continues:

> But such men as haue gret rentes (?) and landes (?)
> And no estate but terme of theyr lyuys
> And euery thyng theron wyll norysh and saue
> For the grete zele and loue that they only haue
> To the commyn welth of theyr contrey,
> And for god sake, lo, these people be they
> That be worthy to haue possessyons,
> And such people of vertuouse condycyons
> And no nother shuld be chosyn gouernours,
> And thei shuld haue landes (?) to maintain their honours
> Terme of theyr lyuys as long as they take payn
> For the commyn welth, thys is good reason playn. (ll. 780–91)

After the Plowman has proved—to his own satisfaction at least—that he has more gentle conditions or more virtues than the others, he addresses the audience on the subject of reforms:

> Therfore no remedy is that I can see
> For yuell men that be in auctoryte
> But let them alone tyll god wyll send
> A tyme tyll our gouernours may intend
> Of all enormytees the reformacyon
> And bryng in theyr handis the rod of coreccyon. (ll. 1006–11)

After all the speakers have given up the argument, the Philosopher delivers a formal epilogue emphasizing the need of virtue in all rulers, the ability of the rulers to persuade the people by natural reason first and then by sharp correction if that is necessary, and the possible need of new laws that these things may be done:

> So vertue is euer the thyng pryncypall
> That gentylnes and noblenes doth insue.
> Then these hedys, rulers and gouernours all,
> Shuld come therto be cause of theyr vertue,
> And in auctoryte they ought not contynue
> Except they be good men, dyscrete and wyse,
> And haue a loue and zele unto Justyce. (ll. 1136–42)
>
> For the best wey that is for one to be gyn
> To conuert the people by exortacyon,

Ys to perswade them by naturall reason. (ll. 1147–49)
But such blynd bestes that wyl not inteud
To here no good councell nor reason
Ought by the law to have sharp coreccyon.
But then yf the laws be not suffycyent,
whych haue be made and ordeynyd before
To gyfe ther fore condygne ponyshment,
The pryncys and gouernours be bound euermore
To cause new laws to be made therfore
And to put such men in auctoryte
That good men, Just and indyfferent be. (ll. 1154–63)

The Philosopher continues, saying that human nature is frail; even the governors will not always be impartial and just unless they are controlled; and the punishment of a judge or an officer does more good than the punishment of a thousand other men.

Thus the author of the play is concerned not only with his main theme, what makes true nobility, but also with the good of the commonweal, the kind of men who make good rulers and officers, the origin of property—whether it was a reward of merit or a result of tyranny—the punishment of evil men who are officers, and the making of new laws to bring about necessary reforms. This concern for the commonweal, with good rulers and officers, and with new laws wherever needed, is a minor theme which is woven through the whole fabric of the play *Of Gentleness and Nobility*.

Godly Queen Hester, which will be mentioned in Chapter XII for its presentation of the ideal queen, has no known connection in authorship or printing with the members of the More group. It came from the press of William Pickering and Thomas Hacket in 1561, after being entered on the Stationers' Register in 1560–61. Because of its implications about Wolsey and Catherine of Aragon, the play was probably written about 1525 to 1529. Conjectures about authorship, including Skelton, William Roy (a friar observant of the Franciscan house at Greenwich), and William Hunnis, have no connection with the More circle.[5] The prologue

---

[5] Anonymous, *A New Enterlude of Godly Queene Hester*, ed. by W. W. Greg (Louvain, Leipzig, London, 1904). Line numbers refer to this edition.

raises the question whether honor should be given for wealth and noble blood or for virtue:

> Diuers Philosophers auncient and sage,
> Their clargy and cunnynge to put in practise
> Oft haue disputed by learniug and language
> To whome greatest honour men ought to demise,
> Or for what cause, hie reuerence shoulde aryse,
> And amonges manye, some were there doubtlesse,
> That concluded honour due vnto ryches.
>
> Some also to noble bloude, and high parayge
> Affirmed honour dewly to pertayne
> And some to policie and wysedome sage
> And some to power and superiall raigne,
> Eche man his reason sayde in certayne.
> Ouer this some said, that vertuous demenoure
> To be excellent, and of moste honour. (ll. 1–14)

Following the prologue, the king, Assuerus, guides a debate among his counselors. The first and second counselors insist that honor should be paid to virtue; the third one raises the question which is the most important princely virtue, and all agree that it is justice. Aman is then appointed chancellor. When Aman plans to destroy the Jews he uses the argument that they are not good for the commonweal; and when the king finally takes action against Aman, he makes it clear that he is concerned about the common good. But these ideas and the fact that a ruler should avoid negligence are unimportant conventions with little direct relation to the program of More and his friends.

The Play of the Weather was undoubtedly written by John Heywood; the title page names him as the author. It was printed by William Rastell in 1533, when the two men had been brothers-in-law for perhaps ten years. The play was reprinted two or three times in the sixteenth century.

A passage from Lucian's *Icaromenippus* is generally recognized as the source of *The Play of the Weather*. While Menippus was a guest of Zeus he went along with Zeus to listen to the prayers which came from all over the world through a row of openings like the mouths of wells. "From every quarter of earth were coming the most various and contradictory petitions. . . . Of those at sea, one prayed for a north, another for a south wind; the farmer asked for rain, the fuller for sun. Zeus listened, and gave each prayer careful consideration, but without promising to grant them all. . . . Righteous prayers he allowed to come up through the hole . . . while he sent the unholy ones packing with a downward puff of breath. . . . In one case I saw him puzzled; two men praying for opposite things and promising the same sacrifices, he could not tell which of them to favour, and experienced a truly Academic suspense of judgment, showing a reserve and equilibrium worthy of Pyrrho himself." [6]

If Lucian was Heywood's source, and there seems no reasonable doubt that he was, the fact furnishes further evidence of similar tastes in More, Erasmus, and Heywood. Erasmus published a translation of the *Icaromenippus* about 1512; and from 1509 to 1514, when he was spending most of his time in England, he was working on other translations of Lucian. More's translations of Lucian were apparently completed about 1505 or 1506; but the work of both men continued to come out in new editions. Heywood, born about 1497, was probably fifteen years old when Erasmus published his translation of *Icaromenippus;* and as Heywood married Joan Rastell, he had family ties with the Mores and Rastells and was being helped to various positions by More. Probably, then, *The Play of the Weather* was written because of associations between the three men and also because More and Erasmus were translating Lucian.

The play shows considerable dramatic skill. The boy Dick, who wishes to have snowballs and is spokesman for a hundred other boys, seems more human and boyish than Shakespeare's precocious little boys—like a fresh breeze blowing through the generalities. Merry Report helps give unity to the play as well as humor. A reader is not surprised, then, to find that such ideas on government as may appear are woven subtly into the whole play, instead of being declaimed in prologue and epilogue.

[6] *The Works of Lucian of Samosata*, trans. by H. W. Fowler and F. G. Fowler, 4 vols. (Oxford, 1905), II, 140–41; J. Q. Adams, "The Play of the Weather," *MLN*, XXII (1907), 262.

The main theme of the play concerns the good of the common-weal. Its plan is simple: Jupiter, concerned about quarrels among the gods and complaints among mortals because of the weather, takes over its control and starts hearing the complaints of people, so that he can remedy the situation. Jupiter is powerful, wise, generous, and has lofty aims, as he tells us himself; he starts as if he expects to achieve perfection. Merry Report, a sort of Puck or Robin Goodfellow, acts as a crier, receives each complainer, and presents him to Jupiter. The Gentleman, the Merchant, the Ranger, the Water Miller, the Wind Miller, the Gentlewoman, the Laundress, and the Boy, "the lest who can play," enter in the order named, and each explains his difficulties and his desires. Finally Jupiter asks Merry Report to reassemble the company, and in the presence of all the complainers he gives this judgment: the power to decide the weather is to remain perpetually in his hands; and he will send such a variety that each shall have his wish some-time. Each thanks Jupiter effusively, as if he were the only favored one; and Merry Report rounds off the play with the Puckish comment:

> God thanke your lordshyp. Lo, how this is brought to pas!
> Syrs, now shall ye have the wether even as yt was. (ll. 1239–40) [7]

Jupiter is conscious of his obligations to those whom he rules and he emphasizes those obligations in his opening speech:

> we evermore beynge,
> Besyde our puysaunt power of deite,
> Of wysedome and nature so noble and so fre,
> From all extremytees the meane devydynge,
> To pease and plente eche thynge attemperynge—
>
> They [the other gods] have, in conclusyon, holly surrendryd
> Into our handes, as mych as concernynge
> All maner wethers by them engendryd,
> The full of theyr powrs, for terme everlastynge,
> To set suche order as standyth wyth our pleasynge . . . (ll. 66–75)
>
> We have clerely fynyshed our foresayd parleament,
> To your great welth, whyche shall be fyrme and stable. (ll. 80–81)

[7] J. Q. Adams, *Chief Pre-Shakespearean Dramas* (Cambridge, Mass., 1924), pp. 397–419.

Citizens who make requests about the weather often plead that they are serving the commonweal, but sometimes the pleas are mere sophistry. The Gentleman, who introduces himself as a man of noble and ancient stock, asks good weather for hunting; he says that he needs recreation because he is one of the heads of the commonweal. The Merchant also pleads for his desire about the weather because he brings wealth to the commonweal. The Ranger is thoroughly self-centered. The Water Miller and the Wind Miller both stress their concern for the common good of all people. Though the Laundress has provided herself with work as a bulwark against idleness and vice, and though she scorns the Gentlewoman, who does no work and asks an absence of sunshine to preserve her complexion, she makes no mention of any service to the commonweal. Neither does the Gentlewoman, who seems concerned with self only.

At the close when Jupiter gives his final judgment, he emphasizes his concern with the good of all people:

> There is no one craft can preserve man so,
> But by other craftes, of necessyte,
> He muste have myche parte of his commodyte.
>
> All to serve at ones, and one destroy a nother,
> Or ellys to serve one and destroy all the rest—
> Nother wyll we do the tone nor the tother,
> But serve as many, or as few, as we thynke best. (ll. 1194–1200)

Again, in *The Play of the Weather,* we find a serious idea developed with imagination and fantasy, with the contrast between Jupiter and the complainers who step from the English life of the time, and with a largeness of attitude which leads to a many-sided irony. First, Jupiter tells us that he is wise, lofty, generous, and also all-powerful; but in the end he finds that he is unable to change the weather. Second, each person clamoring for relief declares himself satisfied. Jupiter has won all hearts—yet Jupiter has done nothing. Third, Jupiter's final comment has the double edge of ironic difference between his initial promise and his performance:

> We nede no whyte our selfe any farther to bost,
> For our dedes declare us apparauntly. . . . (ll. 1241–42)

The Play of the Weather by John Heywood is not only from a classic source, *Icaromenippus,* which Erasmus translated, but it is evidence of a taste for style which Heywood shared with Erasmus and More and perhaps learned from them and their translations of Lucian: the development of a serious idea with satire, imagination, and fantasy. He also shared their concern about the good of the commonweal, as this play indicates. But John Heywood was also an individual and a dramatist, not a mere propagandist. He did not bring in any discussion of a liberal education, the study of Greek and philosophy, or the need of clear and simple laws. But consciously or unconsciously, he approached the serious ideas of More, Erasmus, Rastell, and Vives, when he stressed the contributions which common men like the Wind Miller make to the commonweal and the difficulties a ruler meets when he tries to give justice to all. Again, as in his use of religious themes for drama, he achieved the light touch with the serious intention, in the spirit of Lucian.

Certain other plays of this period or a little later deal with the theme of government: *A Satire of the Three Estates* by Sir David Lindsay; *Respublica,* perhaps by Nicholas Udall; and the anonymous plays *Wealth and Health, Albion Knight, Impatient Poverty, Gorbuduc,* and *Cambises.* But these plays seem to have no relation to the program of reform advocated by More and his friends. They do not stress education as a means of reform, nor the classics and Christian literature, nor any of the other principles which were important in this program. Hence they need no discussion here. Another interesting later play, *The Queen's Majesty's Entertainment at Woodstock,* deals with rank, love, and renunciation for the good of the commonweal.[8] But it is late for the limits of this work, and it is doubtfully and distantly related to the program of social reform advocated by the members of the More group.

Skelton's *Magnificence,* another play on rulers and government, was printed about 1530 to 1533. The printing is usually assigned to John Rastell, for though the type belonged to Peter Treveris, it was used in several other books with the Rastell imprint. *Mag-*

[8] See the reprint of the play edited by J. W. Cunliffe, *PMLA,* XXVI (1911), 92–141.

nificence was probably written between 1515 and 1518. Skelton had few friendly relations with the men of the More circle. He was not master of a Latin style they approved, he opposed the textual work of Erasmus, he disliked the emphasis which Erasmus and others placed upon the teaching of Greek and Latin together, and he quarreled with William Lily over methods of teaching grammar. His play *Magnificence* has some interesting contrasts to their dominant ideas.

Magnificence is like a fifteenth-century morality play, though the play is a secular struggle between prudence and folly. The vices cloak themselves under virtuous names; and Despair and Mischief, as an editor of the play points out, have the functions of the devil. Adversity and Poverty are not vices but agents of redemption. Good Hope, Measure, Circumspection, Redress, and Perseverance are virtues. Magnificence is the neutral figure; Felicity and Liberty are semineutrals; and Felicity is the object of the whole struggle. Thus the characters are all vices and virtues, personified abstractions.[9]

The main theme of *Magnificence* is the Aristotelian mean: rulers must use measure in handling material possessions, though they may use more liberty than common men. *Liberty* means man's freedom of will, his power to choose; when abused, this freedom becomes appetite, wantonness, irrational impulse, and fancy, or excess. Reason and sensuality, then, are in conflict. In the sixteenth century there was nothing new about the theory of the mean; it had appeared in versions of the *Secreta Secretorum*, in the *Roman de la Rose*, in Hoccleve and Lydgate; it continued to be mentioned in the work of Pico della Mirandola, Erasmus, More, and others.

The sources of *Magnificence*, as analyzed by Robert L. Ramsay, an editor of the play, are Hoccleve's *Regiment of Princes*, versions of the *Secreta Secretorum*, and perhaps Barclay's *Ship of Fools* through Skelton's own earlier poem "The Bowge of Court," instead of the classic philosophers and historians with whom More, Erasmus, and their friends were concerning themselves at this time.[10]

---

[9] John Skelton, *Magnyfycence*, ed. by Robert L. Ramsay, *EETS*, ex. ser., XCVIII (1906, 1925), xxvi–xxviii and *passim*.

[10] *Magnyfycence*, pp. lxxi–lxxxix, for sources.

The ideas of *Magnificence* do not resemble those expressed by the men of the More circle. Skelton exalts fear, prudence, and personal happiness. As a character, Magnificence is not struggling for wisdom and virtue but merely for his own worldly welfare. The use of the *ubi sunt* lament is a conventional element in the play; and the action stresses the conventional fall of princes theme, the insecurity of worldly glory, and the fickleness of fortune, though fortune cannot justly be called fickle when the main character has chosen the action which caused his downfall. There is little or no emphasis upon the duties and obligations of a ruler to his people, the good life of wisdom and virtue as the path to happiness, an education in virtue and piety, or training in Christian and classic literature as a means to regenerating society.

But the thought of *Magnificence* has some resemblance to the thought in Elyot's *Governour*. Elyot began, in Book II, Chapter x, by saying that philosophers have applied "Magnificence to the substaunce and astate of princes, and to priuate persones Beneficence and Liberalitie," yet he did not wish to take from the latter qualities any part of their due praise:

For if vertue be an election annexed vnto our nature, and consisteth in a meane, which is determined by reason: and that meane is the verye myddes of two thynges viciouse, the one in surplusage, the other in lacke. Than nedes must beneficence and liberalitie be capitall vertues, and magnificence procedeth from them, approchinge to the extreme partes. And may be tourned in to vice if he lacke the bridle of reason. But beneficence can by no menes be vicious, and retaine still his name. Semblably liberalite (as Aristotle saith) is a measure, as well in gyuing as in takyng of money and goodes. And he is only liberall, whiche distributeth accordyng to his substance, and where it is expedient. Therfore he ought to consider to whom he shulde gyue, howe moche, and whan. For liberalitie . . . resteth nat in the quantite or qualitie of thynges that be gyuen but in the naturall disposition of the gyuer.[11]

He that is liberal does not neglect his substance or goods, nor does he give to all men but considers carefully the time, place, and person to whom he gives: "for the employment of money is nat liberalitie if it be nat for a good ende or purpose." After praising those who make their contributions by labor, study, and diligence,

[11] Elyot, *The boke named the Gouernour* (London, 1531), Fol. 139.

and calling upon Tully to help him reprove those who waste their money on extravagant feasts and banquets, Elyot returned to the idea which suggests magnificence:

Natwithstandinge that liberalitie in a noble man specially is commended all though it somwhat do excede the termes of measure; yet if it be well and duely emploied it acquireth parpetuall honour to the giuer, and moche frute and singuler commoditie therby encreaseth.[12]

When Elyot said that the employment of money is not liberality unless it is used for a good end or purpose, and that the gentleness which consists of labor, study, and diligence is more commendable than the gentleness which concerns itself with mere rewards and expenses, he was taking a position like that of More and his friends.

Castiglione also related magnificence to material spending; he advised a prince to use magnificence:

he ought to be full of liberality and sumptuous, and giue unto euerye manne without stint, for God (as they say) is the treasurer of freharted princis: make gorgious bankettes, feastes, games, people pleasinge showes, kepe a great number of faire horses for profit in war, and for pleasure in peace, Haukes, Houndes, and all other matters that beelong to the contentation of great Princis and the people.[13]

The author added that a prince should erect great buildings, to win honor in his lifetime and to leave a memorial of himself for posterity. All this magnificence was the antithesis of views expressed by More and Erasmus and by Vives. In discussing the two aims of practical wisdom, Vives made sharp distinctions:

One part has regard to that "prudence" which brings everything into the service of the lust of the body and its affections, whatsoever either the judgment or experience of affairs has contrived for ingeniously converting into pleasures, honors, wealth, power. This employment of "prudence" is craftiness and astuteness. It is called by our sacred scriptures carnal wisdom, because it is bent on what the flesh lusts after. The second aim is with regard to those things which belong to the improvement of the mind, and the helping of all the actions and thoughts of others, i.e., the consideration how to better our own minds as well as those of others.[14]

---

[12] *The Gouernour*, Fol. 139 *verso*-140 *verso*.
[13] Castiglione, *The Courtyer*, trans. by Thomas Hoby (London, 1561), Book IV, Qqiiii–Rrii.
[14] Vives, *De tradendis disciplinis*, trans. by Foster Watson, *Vives: On Education* (Cambridge, 1913), p. 229.

In the explanation just quoted, Vives brings out the real difference between Skelton and the humanists of the More circle: Skelton dealt with that prudence which is concerned with material things, or with crafty astuteness. Vives and the other friends of More, in dozens of passages where they talked of inner attitudes and of wisdom and virtue, showed that they were concerned with measure as it led to the development of mind and spirit. They believed that happiness comes, not from material wealth, but from wisdom, virtue, and piety, developed by education.

Skelton, in his *Magnificence,* then, is appealing to fear and prudence; his prudence is connected with honor, wealth, power, personal enjoyment which is self-centered, or with "carnal wisdom"; his definition of felicity is based on material things. The basic ideas of the More group—happiness as a development of the mind related to reason, piety, virtue; the study of Latin and Greek classics to get ideas for practical life, and the study of moral and natural philosophy; a belief in the philosopher-king with associated views on law and government—do not appear in Skelton's *Magnificence.*

CHAPTER XI *Education in general*

The program of education discussed by Erasmus, More, Herde, Vivès, and others of the More group is reflected more or less in three early sixteenth-century plays. They are *Wit and Science* by John Redford, and two anonymous plays, *The Marriage of Wit and Science* and *The Marriage of Wit and Wisdom*. Of the three the play by John Redford is outstanding in importance for its dramatic qualities, its authorship, and its ideas.

John Redford, author of *Wit and Science*, was almoner and master of the singing boys at St. Paul's. He probably began work in this position some time between 1531 and 1534, and he died in 1547. In 1568 William Whytbroke, a minor canon and subdean of St. Paul's, asked to be buried in the cloister "near the grave where the body of Mr. Redford, late master of the choristers and almoner of St. Paul's Church" had been buried. Redford was an intimate friend also of Sebastian Westcott, who became his successor, at first informally and then by formal appointment, and who was the executor of his will.[1] It has also been suggested that Redford, not Westcott, in collaboration with John Heywood, started the children of Paul's on their dramatic career.[2]

---

[1] A. W. Reed, *Early Tudor Drama* (London, 1926), p. 56, and *passim*.

[2] Arthur Brown, "Two Notes on John Redford," *MLR*, 43 (1948), 508–10; "Three Notes on Sebastian Westcott," *MLR*, 44 (1949), 229–32.

Redford was a composer of music but probably not of all the works attributed to him; some of his poems, some of Heywood's and of others were included in the manuscript with *Wit and Science* and a dramatic fragment *Will and Power*. Thomas Tusser's complimentary reference to Redford in his autobiographical verses and his derogatory comment on Nicholas Udall emphasized Redford's skill in teaching.[3]

Redford's play *Wit and Science* was probably written about 1530, and it was probably performed by his singing boys. Since the colophon says that the play was "made by Master John Redford," the authorship is beyond dispute. But the material remained in manuscript until it was edited in 1848 by James O. Halliwell.

Though the play has no formal divisions, perhaps a summary of the plot by stages will simplify the discussion of its ideas and its dramatic qualities:

Stage I. Wit, wooing Lady Science, wins the approval of her Father Reason and his gift of a glass of reason; Wit sends her his picture and hopes for a token from her.

Stage II. Wit fails: he refuses the help of Instruction, uses only Study and Diligence, and is overcome by Tediousness. He is revived by Honest Recreation, along with Quickness, Comfort, and Strength; but he dallies until he is enamored of Idleness, who blacks his face and puts on him the coat and fool's cap of Ignorance.

Stage III. Wit's servant, Confidence, comes with a sword of comfort from Lady Science but does not recognize Wit. Wit is to be greeted by Lady Science (who talks with her mother Experience, and dismisses Fame, Favor, Worship, and Riches); but when the changed Wit tries to kiss Lady Science, he is repulsed. As they leave, Confidence takes away the sword of comfort.

Stage IV. Wit looks at himself in the glass of reason, is beaten by the whips of Shame, and receives Instruction again, along with Study and Diligence. Confidence comes back with the sword of comfort and takes a gold heart as a token from Wit to Lady Science.

Stage V. Wit climbs Mt. Parnassus, and with the help of Instruction, Study, and Diligence, kills the giant Tediousness, and wins Lady Science.[4]

[3] Thomas Tusser, *Five Hundred Points of Good Husbandry* (London, 1573), Fol. 89 verso.

[4] J. Q. Adams, *Chief Pre-Shakespearean Dramas* (Cambridge, Mass., 1924), pp. 325–42.

For those who like drawings to represent plots, this plot might be pictured by a capital V, with a decline in the middle to the bottom of the V, when Wit is repulsed by Lady Science. Then Wit, using the glass of reason, climbs gradually to success again and to union with Lady Science. Redford's plot also rises organically out of his material and illustrates his ideas. He does not explain his meaning in general prefaces or overuse moralizing conclusions, to exhort readers to virtue. He uses action and leaves us to make the application.

Wit and Science, like many other plays connected with the More circle, is a secular morality; man's life is the center of the conflict, though the reward, instead of eternal life, is the blessing of an education. The characters, of course, represent abstract qualities, ideas in education, not theological vices and virtues. But the whole play is made dramatic and interesting, considering the material, by tangible objects, action, and songs. For instance, Wit fights with a giant Tediousness, who comes in "with a vyser over hys hed" and a club in his hand. Ignorance has a fool's coat and cap, big ears, and a coxcomb. The scene of Wit's downfall is also a good example of tangible action: Wit throws off the garment of Science, dances a galliard with Honest Recreation, but dallies and falls into the lap of Idleness; Honest Recreation quarrels with Idleness, calling her strumpet and harlot; Idleness blackens the face of the sleeping Wit, whistles to Ignorance to enter, teaches him to say his own name, and then puts his coat and cap on Wit. Another good example of tangible action is the last fight with Tediousness: using the advice of Instruction, Study and Diligence give ground a little, Tediousness pursues them and while he is thus occupied is attacked by Wit; Wit pursues the giant off the stage, and returns with his head; Confidence comes running with the gown of Knowledge from Science; Instruction and others help Wit put it on. Then we are ready for the final song. By details like these the whole play is made a spectacle to be watched, not a mere set of ideas.

Line references are to this edition of the play. The source of the play is Add. MS. 15, 233, at the British Museum. Brandl's dating of the play as 1541 by the use of *galliard* is unsound, since Elyot used the word in 1531. Stephen Hawes, *Pastime of Pleasure,* 1506–1509, is an interesting forerunner of the play with theories of education.

Throughout the play, as well as at the close, music and song enhance the dramatic quality of Redford's *Wit and Science*. Three songs are used in the play. The first of these, "When travelles grete in matters thycke," is used by Honest Recreation, with the help of Quickness, Comfort, and Strength, when all are trying to revive Wit after he has been overcome by Tediousness; and throughout, action is integrated with the song.

The second song, "Exceedyng Mesure," is less closely connected with the main conflict. Fame, Favor, Riches, and Worship, sent by the World to pay tribute to Lady Science, praise a beauty and truth which they wish to serve, although they know that they may never attain it themselves. Experience asks her daughter why she does not join in the song. But Lady Science thanks them and then dismisses them:

> I thank the World; but cheefly God be praysed,
> That in the World such love to Science hath raysed!
> But yet, to tell you playne, ye iiij ar suche
> As Science lookth for lytell nor muche;
> For beyng, as I am, a lone wooman,
> Neede of your servyce I nether have nor can.
> But, thankyng the World, and you for your payn,
> I send ye to the World evyn now agayne. (ll. 654–61)

The third song, "Wellcum, myne owne," is used in the closing scene, when Wit is told that Lady Science is coming and he must bid her welcome. The stage direction indicates that Wit, Instruction, Study, and Diligence sing the first stanza; and that Science, Experience, Reason, and Confidence come in at the left and "answer evre second verse" sung by the first group. Thus Wit and his company sing:

> O ladye deere,
> Be ye so neere
>   To be knowne?
> My hart yow cheere
> Your voyce to here.
>   Wellcum, myne owne!

Science and her group answer:

> As ye rejoyse
> To here my voyce
>   Fro me thus blowne,
> So in my choyce
> I show my voyce
>   To be your owne. (ll. 986–97)

After one more six-line stanza sung by each group, each follows with a three-line stanza; Wit and his company sing the single line, "Wellcum, myne owne!" and then all sing together, "Wellcum, myne owne!" This song not only has a pleasing pattern, but it also rounds off the real action of the play. It is followed by speeches in which the characters, especially Science, Experience, and Wit, generalize about the use of an education for the glory of God and the profit of other people, but these ideas will be mentioned later.

How is Redford's *Wit and Science* related to the program of ideas on education discussed by More, Erasmus, and Vives? First, the play has a positive quality which has already been mentioned; the hero comes to success in the end and not to failure, and the means by which he achieves this success stand out in the play. Second, the play uses a comparison to a romantic wooing, but it keeps that comparison entirely free from beautiful gardens, Venus and Cupid, the physical beauty of maidens, and irrational terms for lovers' emotions, such as burning in love's fire. Third, Wit himself is a character who has capacity, along with the will and the desire to learn. Lady Science, grieving over Wit's fall, says that she had expected much of him because he was a son to "Dame Nature." Here we meet again the concept of nature as God's agent, like the character in Medwall's play called *Nature,* and like the masculine being in Rastell's play, *The Nature of the Four Elements.* And Father Reason, in his first soliloquy says that Wit has the right gifts, that he is "Yoong, paynefull, tractable, and capax." Fourth, Father Reason considers character more important than material things in estimating a suitor for his daughter:

> Wherfore, syns they both be so meete matches
> To love ech other, strawe for the patches

Of worldly mucke! Syence hath inowghe
For them both to lyve. (ll. 23–26)

His worldly muck probably includes both wealth and titles, or any
trappings of rank.

Fifth, the play has the same attitude to Reason, to the importance of Instruction, to Honest Recreation as a means to avoiding Tediousness, and also the same dislike for Idleness and Ignorance. In emphasizing the connection between idleness and actual
wrongdoing, Father Reason includes the dislike of swearing, which
Elyot and other men of the More circle often expressed, when he
reads an indictment before Wit kneels to receive the lashes of
Shame:

Forthlye, he hath folowed Idellnes scoole
Tyll she hath made him a verye stark foole;
Lastlye, offendyng both God and man,
Sweryng grete othes as any man can,
He hathe abused himselfe, to the grete shame
Of all his kynred and los of his good name. (ll. 850–55)

Lady Science had also rebuked Wit sharply a little earlier in the
play for letting Idleness make him into a fool of the worst kind:

I take ye for no naturall foole,
Browght up among the innocentes scoole,
But for a nawgty vycious foole,
Browght up wyth Idellnes in her schoole.
Of all arrogant fooles thow art one! (ll. 784–88)

Sixth, Reason and Instruction are emphasized, but Experience is
subordinated in the action of the play. Though Experience is the
mother of Lady Science, she does little except listen to her daughter's ideas; and her daughter, so to speak, sets her right. Her sub-
ordination stands out most clearly in the scene where Fame, Favor,
Riches, and Worship, sent by the World, come to honor Lady
Science; Lady Science acts on her own initiative in sending them
away and merely explains to her mother why she has done so. But
Experience is allowed a slight bit of initiative when she states first
that Wit has set his love another way.

Seventh, the play has no suggestion whatever of beating or driving a child to learning. Wit is apparently responsible for himself; his parents do not enter the play; and by implication he seems to have freedom to choose, dignity or worth, and the power of perfectibility. Wit is given the glass of reason, and many characters hope that he will choose wisely; but he has freedom to make his own choice.

Eighth, the aims or the results of education are emphasized according to the same pattern. When Fame, Favor, Riches, and Worship offer themselves to Lady Science but are sent back to the World again, the action implies a rejection of material values as main values. The positive aims of education are stated by Experience and accepted by Science and Wit in the close, the most didactic part of the play. Wit is told that Science is God's gift, and well used, will be a joy and comfort to him; but he must so use her as to honor God and serve mankind.

The personified abstractions in Redford's play have some interesting parallels in discussions of education by Elyot and Ascham. In the *Governour* Elyot included under idleness not only the condition in which the body or mind ceases from labor but also the omission of all honest exercise, saying that there is no plainer figure of idleness than playing at dice:

The firste occasion to playe is tediousnes of vertuous occupation. Immediately succedeth couaiting of an other mans goodes, whiche they calle playinge; therto is annected auarice and straite kepynge, whiche they call wynnyng; sone after cometh sweryng in rentyng the membres of god, whiche they name noblenesse (for they wyll say he that swereth depe, swereth like a lorde); than folowethe furye or rage, whiche they calle courage; amonge them cometh inordinate watche, whiche they name paynfulnesse; he bringethe in glotonie, and that is good fellowshippe; and after cometh slepe superfluous, called amonge them naturall reste; and he some tyme bringeth in lechery, whiche is nowe named daliance. The name of this Tresorie is verily idlenesse, the dore wherof is lefte wyde open to dise plaiers; but if they happe to bringe in their company, lerninge, vertuouse busines, liberalitie, pacience, charitie, temperance, good diete, or shamefastnes, they muste leue them without the gates. For Euill custome, which is the porter, will nat suffre them to entre.[5]

_____

[5] Elyot, *The boke named the Gouernour* (London, 1531), Fol. 96. Or see Book I, Chapter xxvi.

In the same chapter, Book I, xxvi, Elyot recommended games which were battles between vice and virtue; books were available in English, he added, which described the moralization of chess.

Though More did not personify idleness, he expressed similar ideas about it. According to Stapleton's *Life*, he kept his servants from wasting their time in "sloth or improper pastimes"; and servants who escorted him when he went abroad were kept busy at other times by being assigned to look after a certain part of the garden. He would allow no one in his home, "not even if he were of noble rank, to play at dice or cards." His Utopians, according to details in pages 141–45 of Lupton's edition, also opposed idleness; almost the only office of the syphogrants was "to see and take hede that no man sytte ydle." They allowed no one to misuse his time in riot, slothfulness, dice playing, or similar games. Instead they had games which resembled chess: one, a game of numbers; another, a conflict between vices and virtues, with emphasis upon the means by which the virtues conquer.

Ascham said, through his character called Toxophilus: "The Nource of dise and cardes, is werisom Ydlenesse, enemy of vertue, ye drowner of youthe . . . and as Chauser doth saye verie well in the Parsons tale, the greene path waye to hel. . . . Agayne, shooting hath two Tutours to looke vpon it . . . the one called Daye light, ye other Open Place, whyche ii. kepe shooting from euyl companye. . . . Lykewyse, dysinge and cardynge haue ii. Tutours, the one named Solitariousenes, whyche lurketh in holes and corners, the other called Night, an ungratiouse couer of noughtynesse. . . ." [6] So Ascham, like Elyot, but unlike More, personified idleness and linked it with evil action.

Another type of play sometimes called the prodigal-son play presents interesting contrasts to the theories of More, Erasmus, and Vives and to the educational ideas in the play by John Redford. Described in general, this play has less emphasis on the classics and Greek literature; it stresses practical and personal reasons for education; it develops the spare-the-rod-and-spoil-the-child theme, with emphasis on the responsibility of parents; it generally leads to an unhappy ending. Often this play grew from a desire to

[6] Ascham, *Toxophilus* (London, 1545), Book A, leaf 17 *verso*.

substitute the story of the prodigal son for pictures of alleged evil in Plautus and Terence.[7] In non-dramatic literature ideas emphasized in this type of play may be illustrated by a book written by Hermann von Wied, Elector, and also Archbishop of Cologne. An English translation of the work, with a section called "Of Schools for Children," was printed in 1547 and again in 1548. The author emphasizes religion, admits those liberal sciences which contribute to the common life and civil administration, names some classics recommended by Erasmus but often for later use in a boy's life, suggests Erasmus' dialogues for the second form, and *De copia rerum* for use in the more advanced divinity school. But he shows no concern about honest recreation, allurements to learning, or the adaptation of material to young and tender minds. Instead, pupils are to know "Donate" without book and then to learn some common grammar "without book in order word by word." The teacher, to use the phrasing of the translator, is to "beat in the same with convenient interrogations and answers"; and in the fourth form he is to "beat in the catechism." The author warns against the "preposterous" method of hastening to Tully and the poets because they are more pleasant for teacher and pupil.[8]

In drama the prodigal-son type may be illustrated by the play called *Nice Wanton*, an anonymous work of uncertain date, probably written in the reign of Henry VIII or Edward VI, printed first about 1560 and again about 1565. The plot is simple:

Xantippe has three children, the pious Barnabas and the naughty Ismael and Dalilah. She coddles the naughty ones and complains if the schoolmaster whips them even moderately. They play truant, cast dice, become immoral, and follow Iniquity. The naughty ones come to a bad end: Dalilah returns to be nobly forgiven and offered care by Barnabas before she dies of the pox, which she caught in the stews; Ismael is tried for theft, murder, and other crimes, by a just judge who will not be bribed, and is condemned to death. Xantippe meets Worldly Shame and tries suicide, but she is saved by the pious Barnabas.

---

[7] Charles H. Herford, *Studies in the Literary Relations of England and Germany in the Sixteenth Century* (Cambridge, 1886), pp. 84–88, 150–60, and *passim*.

[8] V. Herman, *A Simple and Religious Consultation* (London, 1547). See the section "Of Schools for Children," Mnii. The author, really Hermann von Wied, was deposed and excommunicated in 1547.

The spare-the-rod-and-spoil-the-child theme is announced by the
Messenger in the opening lines:

> The prudent prince, Salomon, doth say,
>> "He that spareth the rod, the chyld doth hate";
> He wold youth shuld be kept in awe alwaye
>> By correction in tyme at reasonable rate.[9]

The theme is again stressed by Eulalia, a neighbor, who tries to
warn Xantippe about her folly, but she is rewarded with a tongue-
lashing. It is repeated by the dying Dalilah, who tells us that she has
come to an evil end because she was petted and spoiled instead of
corrected. It is emphasized many times by Barnabas: in his opening
speeches he complains of his naughty brother and sister but says
that they are indulged too much for their own good; again in his
closing speech to his mother he says that she is to blame since she
winked at their faults and let them do as they wished; and again
in his closing lecture he advises the audience:

> But chastice them before they be sore infect;
> Accept their well-doing, in yll them reiect.
> A yonge plant ye may platte and bowe as ye wyll;
> Where it groweth strong, there wyll it abyde styll:
>
> Euen so by chyldren—in theyr tender age
>> Ye may worke them like waxe to your own entent. . . .[10]

As a model of virtue, Barnabas is eager for learning, of course; he
appreciates the fact that his parents send their children to school
at "their cost"; but his idea of education is that it brings a knowledge of God and trains one to make an honest living.

Other plays of the same general type as *Nice Wanton* are the
Disobedient Child, Lusty Iuventus, Jacob and Esau, and a fragment called *The Prodigal Son*, printed by one of the Rastells about
1530.[11] Somewhat similar plays are *Hyckescorner, Mundus et In-
fans, Thersites,* and the *Interlude of Youth.* About 1540 John Palsgrave published a translation of *Acolastus*, a prodigal-son story
written in Latin by a Dutch author; but as he explained his de-

---

[9] For *Nice Wanton*, see J. M. Manly, *Specimens of the Pre-Shakespearean Drama*, 2
vols. (Boston, 1897), I, 457–79.

[10] *Nice Wanton*, p. 478.

[11] *Collections*, for the Malone Society, ed. by W. W. Greg (London, 1908), I, 27–30.

sire to help teachers and his plan to set forth in the margin information about any form of speech used in Latin but not in English, he seems to have been more concerned with teaching language than with the subject matter of *Acolastus*.[12] George Gascoigne's play, *The Glass of Government*, printed in 1575, is outside the limits of this study, but it is interesting because it continues to use some ideas of Erasmus and his friends but combines with them elements from the prodigal-son plays.[13] None of these plays, with the exception of *Acolastus*, have any known connection with any member of the More group.

The play called *The Marriage of Wit and Science* was first printed without date by Thomas Marsh after it had been entered for him on the Stationers' Register in 1569–70. But it is usually assumed that it was first written and perhaps performed about 1530, and the assumption seems reasonable. There are no clues to the authorship. Like Redford's play, it dramatizes theories of education; but it seems natural for certain reasons to assume that Redford was the originator. First, his play appeared with his name attached; second, his play has far more dramatic skill, including balance, proportion, use of songs for dramatic effect, and tangible objects and actions which emphasize the ideas on education; third, Redford's position as chorister of St. Paul's and associate of John Heywood seems to indicate that he was the originator. But while these assumptions are natural, they are by no means inevitable.

This brief summary of *The Marriage of Wit and Science* serves to bring out its similarity to Redford's play:

Wit desires to win Lady Science, the daughter of Father Reason and Mother Experience. He sends her his picture and receives word of her encouragement. Reason gives Wit as aids Instruction, with his two helpers, Study and Diligence. Wit and Will become impatient and quarrel with Instruction. Wit is overcome by the giant Tediousness; he is revived by Recreation, with Idleness; but he dallies too long, and while he sleeps, Idleness dresses him in the garments of her son, Ignorance. When he meets Reason and Science, they fail to recognize him; but when he uses the glass which

---

[12] John Palsgrave, *The Comedy of Acolastus*, ed. by P. L. Carver, *EETS*, v. 202 (1937). For the Dutch author of the Latin original see *Biographie Universelle*, under *Foulon, Guillaume le*.

[13] George Gascoigne, *The Glasse of Governement*, in the *Complete Works*, ed. by John Cunliffe, 2 vols. (Cambridge, 1907–1910), II, 1–90; Charles H. Herford, *Studies . . .*, pp. 159–63.

Reason gave him, he knows Shame. Science pleads for him. In a second trial, Wit uses the advice of Instruction, the help of Study and Diligence, and the special help of Will. He slays Tediousness and wins Science.[14]

The Marriage of Wit and Science is a less dramatic play than Redford's *Wit and Science*. Two songs are well used: "Give a leg, give an arm, arise, arise," is sung by Will and Recreation to the prostrate Wit while he recovers and gets up; and "Come, come, lie down," is sung by Idleness as Wit succumbs to her charm.[15] But many scenes have much talk and little tension. The language of the play also is often artificial; the long lines rhymed in couplets are mechanical and too facile; the laments in balanced parallel lines are empty rhetoric:

> O hap of haps, O rueful chance to me!
> O Idleness, woe-worth the time that I was ruled
>   by thee . . .
> On me, you furies all, on me have poured out your spite,
> Come now and slay me at the last, and rid my sorrows
>   quite . . .
> This same is he that fought and fell in open field:
> This same is he that in the song of Idleness did
>   yield.[16]

Wit often uses language, too, which members of the More group might dislike because it is used in irrational, romantic love stories. For example, Wit wishes to woo Science although he is not yet able "to show her sport in bed"; and "pleasure pricketh forth my youth to feel a greater fire." Will reports that his "noble child doth feel the force of Cupid's flame," and "at this pinch he burneth." Of course these details are allegorical, not literal.

A minor difference in this play and Redford's is the mention of the exact number of years that Wit must study. Will tells Science in II, 2, that his master Wit is about seventeen; in IV, 1, Wit is overcome by the idea that he must spend three or four years more before he can win Science.[17] These details happen to correspond

---

[14] Anonymous, *The Marriage of Wit and Science*, in *A Select Collection of Old English Plays*, ed. by W. Carew Hazlitt, 15 vols. (London, 1874), II, 325–94. Page references are to this edition.

[15] Pages 368, 374.

[16] Page 382.

[17] Pages 345, 355.

with Elyot's comment in the *Governour* that a young man should study liberal subjects until he is twenty-one before he turns to law.

The aims of education in the two plays are much the same, though Redford perhaps gives the noble aims more emphasis and presents them more consistently. In *The Marriage of Wit and Wisdom* Will says that his master is not moved by "fantasies," "vain and idle toys," or any desire to win wealth and noble blood; he is concerned with the virtue, grace, and other noble gifts of Science. Father Reason tells his daughter Science that she must marry to help the commonweal and to give her knowledge to the world. But in the closing speeches of the play, Science herself plays down these noble aims by her talk of honor and everlasting fame.[18]

The character called Will, probably representing "untutored desire," is an interesting addition to the play. He resents the fact that he or his master must come under the control of Reason or Science; he is uneasy when his master takes Instruction, with Study and Diligence, home to live with him; and he is always impatient. But when he and Wit together use the guidance of Instruction and other helpers, it is Will who succeeds in tripping Tediousness.

Nature and Wit as characters are like the characters by the same names in plays already discussed. Wit is the young man who has capacity, is willing to use instruction, and develops his skill by his own efforts, as Erasmus implied in discussing *nature, instruction,* and *use.* He has the power of all normal human beings to develop his reason; and he has the special individual capacity and desire which make him worth educating.

Nature is like the feminine character in Medwall's *Nature* and the masculine lord or prince in Rastell's *Nature of the Four Elements.* She is benign, educative, and she acts as the agent of God. She introduces herself in these words:

> Grand lady, mother of every mortal thing:
> Nurse of the world, conservative of kind:
> Cause of increase, of life and soul the spring;

[18] Pages 343–44, 341, 394.

At whose instinct the noble heaven doth wind,
To whose award all creatures are assigned,
I come in place to treat with this my son . . .
Come, tender child, unripe and green for age,
In whom the parent sets her chief delight,
Wit is thy name, but far from wisdom sage,
Till tract of time shall work and frame aright
This peerless brain, not yet in perfect plight:
But when it shall be wrought, methinks I see,
As in a glass beforehand with my sight,
A certain perfect piece of work in thee. . . .[19]

When Wit, in explaining his desire to win Science, asks Nature
to "settle this unsettled head in some assured place" and to bring
about his wish without disturbing his "great ease" she tells him that
such a feat is beyond her. Wit reminds her that she called herself
the lady of this world and asks her if anything can be too hard for
her; she makes clear in her answer that she is the agent of God:

My power it is not absolute in jurisdiction,
For I cognise another lord above,
That hath received unto his disposition
The soul of man, which he of special love
To gifts of grace and learning eke doth move.

Wit is also characterized or explained in this opening scene where
he is talking with Nature, partly through the comments of Nature:

To thee, son Wit, he [God] will'd me to inspire
The love of knowledge and certain seeds divine . . .
The massy gold the cunning hand makes fine;
Good grounds are till'd as well as are the worst,
The rankest flower will ask a springing time;
So is man's wit unperfit at the first.

Wit challenges her with the question why he was not given
cunning also. Nature answers that virtue would "lose her price,
and learning would abound" and that the man "not born to land
should lack to live upon" if cunning were passed out to all; she
says that there are also five thousand other reasons. Wit, she makes

[19] Page 325, and *passim*.

quite clear, must struggle to achieve his own skill. But she helps him by leaving him a servant, Will, "A bird of mine, some kin to thee," and she tells Will to obey Wit in all things.[20]

As a parallel to some of these ideas, Vives also explained why diligence and industry are necessary to an education, when he discussed the knowledge of music, poetry, prose, and oratory:

These matters have been thought out in the human mind by industry, in accordance with the mind received from the great Artificer God, the gift we receive through Nature. This special favour bestowed by God surpasses all others which can be compared with it. But since God has not allowed us on account of the magnitude of our sins to have this imparted as a gift, for all the details of experience, we have to apply diligence so as to seek out what is useful, whilst we are lighted by that Lamp, which He has bequeathed to the human race.[21]

The anonymous play called *The Marriage of Wit and Science,* then, is another allegorical and didactic play which develops theories of education. Like Redford's *Wit and Science,* it is addressed to youth rather than to parents; instead of showing the evil results of no education and no chastisement, it deals with positive achieve-ment. Nature, a benign agent of God, is anxious to further educa-tion; but though she has given her son capacity, a love of knowl-edge, "certain seeds divine," the will to have an education, the power of perfectibility, and freedom to make his choices, he can-not win with these helps alone. Its major theme is that youth must secure an education by long-continued toil and by the help of in-struction and study.

Another anonymous play, *The Marriage of Wit and Wisdom,* may have been written about 1530 also, by a certain Fr. or Francis Merbury; or he may have been merely the scribe, who said "Amen" at the close of the play. The source is a manuscript at the British Museum (Add. MS. 26, 782), dated 1570, but it has been conjectured that the extant copy is "a transcript from a man-uscript which the scribe had difficulty in deciphering." Thus we are left without evidence about the date of the original manuscript.

---

[20] Pages 328–34.

[21] Vives, *De tradendis disciplinis,* trans. by Foster Watson, *Vives: On Education* (Cam-bridge, 1913), p. 40.

It has been argued that the same man wrote this play and *The Marriage of Wit and Science*, but there is little evidence for this theory.[22] In printed editions this play also is divided into acts and scenes; but there are only two acts. The first act has three scenes properly numbered; the second, six scenes numbered four, five, six, seven, eight, and ten, instead of nine. Perhaps a summary will show that it is a strange play with some theories of education like those developed by Redford, but the theories have been watered down:

I. 1. Father Severity and Mother Indulgence discuss with Wit his wooing of Wisdom. Severity tells his son to follow religion, virtue, and learning, and to avoid Idleness and Irksomeness. He tells Indulgence that she is mother of only the outer man; if Wit wins Wisdom he will be his father's heir; if not, he will not get a groat.

   2. Idleness, posing as Honest Recreation, and Wantonness as Mistress Modest Mirth, cozen Wit, lull him to sleep, put a fool's bauble on his head, and blacken his face; and Idleness takes his purse. Good Nurture rescues him and turns him over to Honest Recreation.

   3. After Idleness has been robbed by Snatch and Catch, Wit, coming in with Honest Recreation, believes that Idleness is Due Disport. He lets Idleness lead him to the den of Irksomeness, who beats him down. Wisdom rescues him and gives him the sword of perseverance. He cuts off the head of Irksomeness.

II. 4. The scene is mere byplay between Idleness, and Search, who robs him.

   5. Fancy, pretending to be a messenger for Wisdom, captures Wit.

   6. Idleness steals a porridge pot.

   7. Lob and Doll are reproved by Mother Bee; Inquisition brings in Idleness, with his pot, and promises to take him before a justice.

   8. Good Nurture finds Wit, releases him from captivity, and promises him that he will wed Wisdom next day. Idleness, disguised as a priest, comments on his rejection when the two are wed; but some, especially women, will still listen to him.

   10. Severity plans to give Wit to Wisdom; Wit comes in with Good Nurture, and the nuptials are planned.[23]

[22] Samuel A. Tannenbaum, "Comments on *The Marriage of Wit and Wisdom*," PQ, IX (1930), 338–40.

[23] Anonymous, *The Marriage of Wit and Wisdom*, ed. by James O. Halliwell for the Shakespeare Society (London, 1846). Page references are to this edition.

The play has several curious differences from the other two plays which deal with theories of education. First, three of the nine scenes in the play are mere byplay between Idleness and other characters, instead of having any real connection with the plan to win Wisdom. Second, there are fewer and vaguer ideas on education; those which appear are so obvious that they need little discussion. Third, we have a different set of parents for Wit—Father Severity and Mother Indulgence—instead of Reason and Experience, as if the play might be a cross between the so-called "prodigal-son" play and the other plays which have been discussed. Father Severity is concerned with the inner condition of his son, but Mother Indulgence tells him to lie and to buy his sweetheart with beautiful presents. But Mother Indulgence appears only in the first scene, and in the final scene Father Severity acts as if he is the only parent.

One character in *The Marriage of Wit and Wisdom* called Fancy is different from the characters in the other plays and seems to contribute to the ideas on education. Fancy introduces herself:

> So likewise I, which commonly
>   Dame Fancy haue to name,
> Amongest the wise am huted [hated] much,
>   And suffer mickle blame,
> Because that, wauing heare and there,
>   I neuer stidfast stand,
> Whereby the depth of learnings lore
>   I cannot vnderstand.[24]

As a character, Fancy certainly opposes the ideal of sound learning. It is possible, too, that she has affiliations with the non-Platonic love of the senses only, a superficial, impermanent love which "dies in the cradle where it lies"; at least she tries to persuade Wit to marry her instead of Wisdom.

The conventional prologue and epilogue do little for the play; the prologue points out the fact that virtue depends on the union of wit and wisdom, and the epilogue enjoins listeners to escape their foes as Wit did:

[24] Page 46.

Thus if you follow fast,
[You] will be quite from thrall,
[And] eke in joye an heuenly blisse;
The which God graunt vs all.[25]

Of the plays which have been discussed in this chapter, *Nice Wanton* is a strong contrast to the theories of education held by men in the More circle. In this play a mother protects and coddles two of her children; they refuse to get an education and they also come to miserable ends. Thus we are told what we should not do. Three plays—John Redford's *Wit and Science,* and two anonymous plays, *The Marriage of Wit and Science* and *The Marriage of Wit and Wisdom*—have some relation to the theories of education which More and his friends were expressing in non-dramatic writing. Of these, *The Marriage of Wit and Wisdom* seems like a feeble imitation, with much extraneous material; *The Marriage of Wit and Science* follows some major ideas of John Redford's play but adds some concepts which he did not have and it is less dramatic than Redford's work. Neither of the two, so far as we know, had any connection with the More group in authorship or in printing. But Redford's *Wit and Science,* written by an associate of John Heywood, uses in a fresh, original, and effective way the theories of education expressed by Erasmus and Vives and by some of their friends. The likeness to some theories of Elyot and Ascham and to many ideas of More, Erasmus, and Vives is not a mere accident. The play was written by a man well acquainted with their theories and one who may have used them in his training of boys at St. Paul's School.

[25] Page 63.

CHAPTER **XII** *Education of women: love,*
marriage

Of all the ideas which More and his friends emphasized in their
program of social reform perhaps the newest ones (in English
literature, not on the Continent) concerned the character and
status of women educated in the classics and the associated ideas
of love and marriage. Two plays connected with the group, *Fulgens and Lucres,* and *Calisto and Melebea,* emphasize such women;
and two others, *Godly Queen Hester* and *The Play of Love,* by
John Heywood will be examined briefly.[1]

Fulgens and Lucres, written by Henry Medwall and printed by
John Rastell, was discussed in Chapter VIII for its major theme
of true nobility. Its chief woman character, Lucres, handles with
competence the problem of wealth and rank without character,
against learning, virtue, and service to the commonweal without
rank and wealth, when she chooses a husband. Her father trusts
her to make her own choice. The author of the play transfers to
her the definite decision which his source had first assigned to the
senate but had finally left for the audience to decide. The char-

---

[1] Two other plays about women have been carefully examined: *Apius and Virginia,*
entered on the Stationers' Register in 1567 and printed in 1575; and John Phillips,
Patient Grissil, entered in 1566 and 1569 and printed perhaps about 1569. Each is thoroughly conventional and neither has any known connection with the More group.

acter of Lucres is first explained to us by Fulgens, who describes his daughter as a paragon of virtue, wisdom, and beauty, even though she does resemble him in visage:

> Nature hath wrought in my lucres so
> That to speke of beaute and clere vnderstanding
> I can not thinke in here what shold be lakking. (I, 262–64) [2]

> She is so discrete and sad in all demeanyng
> And therto full of honest and verteous counsell
> Of here owne mynd that wonder is to tell
> The giftes of nature and of especiall grace. (I, 267–70)

Gayus Flaminius, the suitor who has virtue and learning, characterizes her and suggests his own standards of marriage when he describes himself as a man who is like her own conditions in everything.

The relationship between Fulgens and his daughter not only characterizes Lucres but contributes to an ideal family pattern like that stressed by More and his friends in non-dramatic literature. Fulgens trusts his daughter's wisdom; he thinks that she needs no counsel, though he will give her advice if she wishes; but he is quite willing to let her make the choice. Lucres, on the other hand, offers to let her father decide, in spite of her belief that he inclines to Publius Cornelius. Fulgens makes only one suggestion, that she entertain them both impartially until she is sure of her preference. Fulgens also mentions his relationship with his wife in his introductory speech; she is a wife of good condition who is conformable to his wishes in everything.

The play also contrasts the two kinds of love discussed by More and his friends—the irrational impermanent love which is physical, and the love which is based on character and wisdom and promises permanency. Cornelius, the nobleman who has wealth also but is extravagant and sinful, burns in love's fire, and is sure that nothing except possessing Lucres will ease his pain. Gayus Flaminius refuses to woo with romantic methods:

> And to say that I will folow the gise
> Of wanton louers nowaday

[2] Henry Medwall, *Fulgens and Lucres,* ed. by F. S. Boas and A. W. Reed (Oxford, 1926). Line numbers refer to this edition.

> whiche doth many flatering wordis deuise
> with gyftis of ringis and broches gay
> Theyr lemmans hartis for to betray,
> ye must haue me therin excusid
> For it is the thing that I neuer vsid.
> Therefore I will be short and playne,
> And I pray you hartely, feyre lucres,
> That ye wyll be so to me agayne. (I, 519–28)

Lucres declares that she will have no fighting or violence over her, she has bound both of them to keep the peace, and she forbids them to use any words that will lead to brawling or to any other ungodly condition.

All these attitudes about family relationships, the character of Lucres, and the irrational love versus the love which is based on character agree with the ideas expressed by More, Erasmus, Vives, and other friends in non-dramatic literature. Though the play does not stress the fact that Lucres had a classical education, she acts like a woman of education. She possesses virtue, wisdom, and initiative.

Godly Queen Hester has no known connection with the More circle either in authorship or in printing. But the date of composition was between 1525 and 1529 if the intent was to defend Catherine of Aragon and to attack Wolsey; such an intent has been discussed by W. Bang and ably defended by W. W. Greg.[3]

The play follows the general outline of the Bible story with some additions and omissions. A satirical addition is the group of abstractions—Pride, Adulation, Ambition, and Hardydardy, who help push Aman to his destruction. Interesting omissions are the king's displeasure with Vashti, his putting her away, and his trial of many virgins in a period of concubinage. Instead, the king in the play hears a debate about who should be honored and what quality is most important for a ruler. Then he announces suddenly that he is all comfortless for lack of a queen. A pursuivant assembles a company of maidens, Hester joins them, the king looks at them and selects Hester at once, puts her through a verbal examination

---

[3] Anonymous, *A New Enterlude of Godly Queene Hester,* ed. by W. W. Greg (Louvain, Leipzig, London, 1904), Introduction, xi–xii.

on her wisdom, and announces, apparently without leaving the stage after the maidens were brought in, that his queen is to be Hester. This emphasis upon chastity and wisdom agrees with the ideas of More and Vives, and it protects the name of Catherine of Aragon, if the writer had her in mind.

The character of Hester has some other interesting qualities. When Mardocheus, known in the King James version as Mordecai, instructs her and prepares her for her appearance before the king, he emphasizes the noble qualities of goodness, bounty, grace, obedience, true love, kindness, loyalty to the prince, justice, and consideration for the commons. Assuerus, surveying the group of maidens before him, says:

> In theym shoulde be kyndnes, myrth, and dalyaunce,
> wysedome, sadnes, and in loue perseueraunce,
> Constauncie knit wyth comliness, ioy to increase,
> Vertue with good demenour, pleasure to put in presse. (ll. 223–26)[4]

After Assuerus has centered his attention upon Hester and has asked about her, Mardocheus answers:

>   she is a virgin puer,
> A pearle vndefiled and of conscience cleare,
> Sober, sad, ientill, meke, and demure,
> In learninge and litterature, profoundely seene,
> In wisdome, eke semblante to Saba the Quene,
> Fytt for any prince to haue in marriage,
> If his pleasure agree to her personage. (ll. 255–61)

The king tests Hester further:

> ye say ryghte well, then we thynke it expedient
> Some what to proue by communication
> Her lernynge and her language eloquent,
> And by some probleme of hye dubitation
> To knowe her aunswere and consultation.
> Howe saye you, Hester, haue you ought reade or seene
> Of vertues that be best and fittest for a queene? (ll. 262–68)

Hester replies tactfully that the queen, like all else in a country, is under the jurisdiction of the king:

[4] Line numbers refer to the edition by W. W. Greg.

Albeit, sometyme, more for loue than for awe
The king is content to bee counselled by the queene,
In many sundrye causes, as ofte hath been seene. (ll. 277–79)

But eftsons it may chaunce at sundrye season
The kynge wyth hys councell most parte of all
From this realme to be absente, when warr doth call.
Then the Quenes wysdome, sadly muste deale,
By her greate vertue, to rewle the common weale. (ll. 282–86) [5]

Wherfore as many vertues be there muste,
Euen in the Quene as in the prynce,
For feare lest in warre, sume treason vniust,
The realme shoulde subdewe, and falsely conuince.
The Quene muste sauegarde all the hole prouince,
And so as muche goodnes aye muste be seene,
As in the kynge to be in the Quene,
And how many vertues longe to a kynge,
Lyke unto youre grace I cannot make recknynge. (ll. 287–95)

The king answers:

Then I doute not, but the wysdome of vs two
Knytte both to gether in parfytte charyte
All thynges in thys realme shall cumpas so,
By truth and Justice, law and equitye,
That we shall quenche all vice and deformitie. (ll. 296–300)

Hester then continues with advice on providing for all in the
country:

There maye be wealth in places two or three
But I assure you the most part in generall,
Neither haue meate nor money, nor streugth substancial
Fytte to doe you seruice, when ye haue nede,
whiche is no good order, me thynkes in very dede. (ll. 313–17)

In the closing part of the play Hester acts with wisdom, poise,
and assurance; and when she makes her charge against Aman, she
supports her view with spirit and with wisdom—as the ideal woman
of the More group should act but also, it must be admitted, as
the biblical Esther did act. But some things that are not in the

---

[5] Catherine of Aragon had acted as regent during Henry's absence in the French Wars,
1513, and had carried the burden of the Scottish revolt. Catherine Parr also acted as
regent later.

Bible story have entered the picture; the learning, language, and the skill in speech which the king finds in Hester. Even Vives, in spite of his great zeal about protecting the chastity of a woman, might approve of Hester, as he approved of Catherine of Aragon.

The debate about who should be honored and what quality is most essential in a ruler sounds like an echo of More, Erasmus, and their friends, especially in the prologue, cited in Chapter X. But this beginning must be discounted, for in the end of the play Aman, who has come from lowly stock, like Wolsey, is condemned; and Mardocheus, who is honored, is introduced as a gentleman of the stock of Benjamin. Thus the play tends to reverse the idea usually expressed by the men of the More group.

The Play of Love was "made by John Heywood," as the title page tells us, and was printed by William Rastell in 1533.[6] The play is a debate on the question who suffers the most pleasure and the most pain. It is begun by characters called "Lover not Beloved," and "Woman Beloved not Loving"; they are joined by the "Lover Beloved," who enters singing, and then by a fourth character, "Neither Loved nor Loving." Two ideas in the play might have been given the stronger emphasis we expect from friends of More. One idea is the use of reason in the argument about the horse or the tree. But Heywood uses it in a medieval or conventional way, not with happy optimism and classical slanting. The other is the concept of love. The Lover Beloved is concerned only with the physical perfections of his lady and his own pleasure. The character called Neither Lover nor Loved had once been charmed by a woman's physical beauty—her white skin, blue veins, golden hair, rosy lips, small round breasts, and beautiful legs; but she had been false, and she and her new lover were now laughing at him. None of the ideas in *The Play of Love*, then, are related to the good life of wisdom and virtue, to classical education, or the good of the commonweal.

The play which seems most closely related to the ideas of the More group on "the beauty and good properties of women" is the

---

[6] Alois Brandl, *Quellen des Weltlichen Dramas in England vor Shakespeare* (Strassburg, 1898), pp. 161–209.

English play usually called *The Interlude of Calisto and Melebea* or merely *Calisto and Melebea*. It was printed without date about 1526 to 1530, more probably about 1530. Bibliographers find some influence of John Skot and William Rastell, but the colophon says that John Rastell "me imprimi fecit." [7] There is no definite evidence of authorship, but some argue from Rastell's phrasing that he not only printed but also wrote and staged the play. But such conclusions seem doubtful.

In discussing *Calisto and Melebea* we are concerned with a Spanish original; with James Mabbe's translation, published in 1631 and usually considered an excellent translation; and with the English interlude. Mabbe's translation will be used as the basis for comparing the source with the English play. The Spanish work, a long dialogue which was probably not intended for the stage, was published first at Burgos, in 1499, in sixteen acts, as the *Comedia de Calisto y Melibea,* and again at Seville in 1502 as a *Tragicomedia . . .* in twenty-one acts. Its author, in spite of other contenders for the honor, was probably a converted Jew, Fernando de Rojas. His change in religions may help account for the fact that his work has no religious feeling; but he was "a humanist, well read in the Latin classics and in Greek philosophy." [8] But his ideas were not like those of the "humanists" in the More circle.

There are many differences between the Spanish work as translated by Mabbe and the English play. First, the Spanish work is much longer. In H. Warner Allen's edition of the two, the translation from the Spanish covers 263 pages; the English play covers 24 pages, and has only 1,099 lines.[9] Second, in the Spanish *Celestina,* the old procuress herself is the center of interest, as Mr. Brenan points out. He calls her "one of the most vivid and splendid creations of all literature"—an intelligent, libidinous old bawd

---

[7] Anonymous, *The Interlude of Calisto and Melebea,* ed. by W. W. Greg for the Malone Society (Chiswick, 1908); W. W. Greg, *A Bibliography of the English Printed Drama to the Restoration,* 2 vols. (London, 1939), I, for bibliographical details.

[8] Gerald Brenan, *The Literature of the Spanish People . . .* (Cambridge, 1951), pp. 131–32, 137. Mr. Brenan doubts whether the parts added to the later editions, many of them less artistic, were by Rojas.

[9] H. Warner Allen, *Celestina, or the Tragi-Comedy of Calisto and Melebea . . .* trans. from the Spanish by James Mabbe . . . 1631 (London, 1923).

who consistently uses a hedonistic philosophy without hate, envy, or violence, and who is skillful in manipulating people. She is great, somewhat as Falstaff is great.[10] Third, the Spanish story and the English interlude are quite different in depicting the passion of love. The Spanish story is sensual; the lovers are self-centered, never rising above self in their concern for each other; the love is truly illicit since the lovers seek neither the blessing of parents nor of the church; and the lovers seem to be unmotivated in meeting secretly. There is no feud to separate them, as there is in *Romeo and Juliet,* for example; and though Calisto admires Melebea both for her beauty and for her position in life, it does not seem to occur to either that they might marry.

But the Spanish *Celestina* has power—"an inhuman violence which makes it completely transcend the nature and identity of the person loved"; and the love has "a violent compulsory nature. . . ." Calisto and his Melebea are not individuals, for personal traits have been overshadowed by passion. The lovers, Mr. Brenan says, are under the control of a force that has deprived them of their reason; and the story "purges by pity and terror . . . we see the daemonic power of love bringing destruction on every one connected with it." Though he says that Calisto's urgency is due to "amour propre," not lust, he adds that the Spanish story lacks the "charm and sweetness" of *Romeo and Juliet*.[11]

Fourth, many other events in the Spanish story are omitted from the English play, especially other illicit loves and murders. Some of these are the illicit loves of Sempronio and Parmeno for Areusa and Elicia, as well as the month of meetings between Calisto and Melebea. Celestina is murdered by two servants because she refuses to give them part of her fee; the servants commit suicide to escape arrest; Areusa and Elicia plan to take revenge because their men have been killed; Calisto is killed by accident on a visit to Melebea, and Melebea commits suicide.

Fifth, the main plots of the Spanish *Celestina* and the English *Calisto and Melebea* are quite different. The Spanish plot may be summarized thus: Calisto tries to seduce Melebea but fails; he and

[10] Brenan, pp. 133–34.
[11] Brenan, pp. 135–36.

his servants call upon the wily bawd, Celestina, to help them; Celestina succeeds in enticing Melebea to receive Calisto; the seduction is speedily accomplished; for nearly a month she continues to receive him and they live in a "delightful error of love"; on one visit, when an alarm is sounded, Calisto hurries to descend the ladder, and is killed; Melebea, after explaining her story to her father from the top of a tower, commits suicide, leaving her parents to grieve and to moralize about her fate.

Only the first two of these seven events in the Spanish story are carried over to the English interlude. With the third step, the direction changes completely: Celestina, who remains a shrewd woman, sees that she is failing; but at last she moves Melebea to compassion for Calisto's toothache. Melebea sends him her girdle, which has had contact with holy relics, and she promises to send him a prayer of St. Appoline. When Celestina is alone again, she congratulates herself upon her ultimate success. But just then Danio, the father of Melebea, with a new name in the English interlude, rushes in. He tells his daughter of a dream he has had about her: she was on her way to a wholesome hot bath in a beautiful orchard, but a foul bitch fawned upon her, so that she stepped to the edge of a vile-smelling pit nearby. Just then her father woke up from his dream. Melebea immediately recognizes her danger, repents, and confesses the truth to her father.

The English interlude has many other details which differ from the Spanish story. Many of these seem to be deliberate changes to teach virtue, morality, and religion. For example, a biblical character is substituted for a pagan goddess; at one point Melebea is going to mass instead of merely going abroad; a Cumean charm becomes a prayer of St. Appoline; and Melebea's girdle has touched many holy relics. Celestina, too, though she has lost her amoral greatness, remains shrewd enough to realize the character of the English Melebea and to base her appeals to her on religion.

The English play also has a large amount of moralizing. The didactic tone begins with the full title describing an interlude "wherein is shewd and dyscrybyd as well the bewte and good propertes of women as theyr vycys and euyll condicions, with a morall conclusion and exhortacyon to vertew." The play has these parts, though they are not indicated by any formal divisions:

Lines   1– 43. Generalizations by Melebea.
          44– 929. Conflict: Melebea vs. Calisto, Sempronio, Celestina.
        930–1043. Father Danio's dream; Melebea's confession and repentance.
       1044–1099. Danio's sermon to the audience.[12]

Even lines 44 to 929 are not highly dramatic, though they have more tension than any other part of the play; and lines 930 to 1043 are mostly noble platitudes rather than drama. The closing speech of Danio to the audience is a lecture imploring parents and rulers to educate children in virtue and thus to eliminate the main causes of crime—idleness and lack of training in useful work. Danio says, by implication or direct statement, that a practical education is a chief means of reforming society.

The characters in the English play have been changed where necessary or not changed to further the moral impact of the play. Calisto and Sempronio remain much the same, but both are intended to be unsympathetic characters. Calisto's disease of love is irrational; he looks for a remedy for his sickness; he has his servant bring his lute (which is found to be out-of-tune) and his chair, because his love-sickness has made him weak; there are sharp needles in his breast; he is in a turmoil of peace, war, truth, hate, injury, hope, and suspicion. Celestina emphasizes Calisto's lineage and his physical beauty in pleading his cause, but never his education, piety, and virtue. Calisto praises Melebea's nobleness, ancient lineage, great patrimony, excellent wit, and resplendent virtue; but he is more enamored of her physical beauty—her eyes, her hair, and her breasts have not escaped his notice. She is worthy to have the apple which Paris gave to Venus, he says; he rejoices more to see her than he would rejoice to see the saints in heaven; it would mean more to him to declare his grief in her presence than to win heaven by good works.[13] Calisto is a victim of something like Eros' malady,

---

[12] *Calisto and Melebea,* ed. by W. W. Greg. All references by lines are based on this edition.
[13] Lines 44–61; 80–250.

whether the writer of the English interlude knew that term or not.[14] His love is based mainly on physical beauty; it is impermanent and unconnected with virtue, piety, and learning.

In the English play also Sempronio is an ultrarealistic character, a cynic who despises women, thinks men are more noble, and is sure that any woman will yield to Calisto when she is persuaded by Celestina. His "anti-humanistic" attitudes are developed to fit his function as a pander for Calisto; they should not be a cause for wonder.[15]

In the English play Melebea is the ideal maiden, or nearly so. At the beginning of the play, where she quotes Petrarch and "Eraclito" on nature, "the mother of all things," and on the strife which belongs to creation and to lovers, she knows philosophy and the concept of nature as the agent of God. She realizes, too, that Calisto's behavior is irrational, and that her own beauty gives her an even greater obligation to behave well; when she first repulses Calisto, she resolves that she will never satisfy his voluptuous appetite. Even her wavering, in the scene where Celestina makes her shrewd approach, is based on appeals to her compassion for Celestina's age and for Calisto's toothache, and on her religious feeling. Thus the wavering is not entirely irrational, not motivated by a real response to seduction. Her intelligence in seeing the implication of her father's dream, her frankness, her quick contrition, her prayer for forgiveness, as well as her love for her father, might satisfy almost any member of the More circle. Even Vives might concede that her inner feeling of chastity had been scarcely touched.

Danio, the father, who replaces the Spanish parents of Melebea, in the English play, is the ideal father who has educated his daughter in virtue, is concerned about her chastity, believes that even a slight yielding in her mind is wrong, but meets her confession and contrition with forgiveness and love.

[14] John Livingstone Lowes, "The Loveres Maladye of Hereos," MP, XI (1913–1914), 491–546. See also Lawrence Babb, The Elizabethan Malady (East Lansing, Mich., 1951), Chapter VII, "The Lover's Malady in Elizabethan Literature."

[15] R. Warwick Bond, in his introduction to The Nobility of Women, by William Barker (London, 1904), implied surprise at Sempronio's sentiments. Barker flourished about 1540 to 1572.

Calisto and Melebea, when compared with its source and with the comments of More, Erasmus, and Vives on women, love, and marriage, seems a deliberate piece of propaganda for the beauty and the good properties of women. One cannot escape the belief, which has been stated before, that the presence of Vives in England during the 1520's had an influence on the composition of the play. While More and his friends agreed in condemning stories of illicit, irrational love, it was Vives who mentioned, as a specific example of the ungracious books in his own country, "Celestina, the bawd, mother of naughtiness," in 1523. It was Vives who said: "A woman that giveth a gift giveth herself; a woman that taketh a gift selleth herself. Therefore an honest woman shall neither give nor take." It was Vives who said that the sensual lover "is vexed both day and night with the firebrand of Cupid," so that he is able "neither to take meat nor to sleep, nor see nor rest. . . ." It was he also who said to the maiden: "Give none ear unto the lover, no more than thou wouldst do unto an enchanter or a sorcerer. . . . He calleth thee fair, proper, witty . . . and of gentle blood . . . and thou, like a fool, art glad to hear those lies. . . ." It was Vives also whose emphasis on chastity, including a complete chastity of mind and emotions, was almost fanatical.[16]

On Vives' first visit to England, in 1523–24, More supplied his personal needs, gave him understanding and sympathy, and used his influence for him at court. On the second visit Vives was a guest in More's home the whole month of April, 1525, on terms of intimate personal friendship.[17] Undoubtedly More helped him secure the readership which he was given by Wolsey, since More had mentioned this position earlier to Erasmus as a possibility for him. In 1523 Vives had written his work *De institutione Christianae foeminae* and had dedicated it to Catherine of Aragon. In it he had mentioned "Celestina the bawd, mother of naughtiness." Richard Herde had translated that work some time before his death in 1529 as *The Instruction of a Christian Woman.* The devotion

---

[16] Vives, *The Instruction of a Christen woman,* trans. by Rycharde Hyrd [Herde] (London, 1529?), Book I, Chapters XII–XV. For detailed references see Part I, Chapter VI.

[17] Henry de Vocht, *Monumenta humanistica Lovaniensia: Texts and Studies about Louvain Humanists* (Louvain, 1934), pp. 1–43.

of Vives for the More household was indicated by an instance mentioned in Chapter V. Using More as one example of proper salutations in letters, he suggested that his reader should greet More first
and then his children, but especially Margaret Roper, whom, he
added, he had loved as if she had been his own sister.[18]

John Rastell had constructed his public stage about 1524; he also
printed the English interlude *Calisto and Melebea* some time between 1526 and 1530.

What bearing, if any, do these facts have on the author of the
play? Was it written by Luis Vives, by John Rastell, by John
Heywood, by a pupil or friend of Vives, or by members of More's
household school?[19] John Rastell gave no indication in his known
works that he had any interest in the "beauty and good properties"
of women. Neither did John Heywood. Vives had no known interest in drama; and surely the members of More's household
could have done a more consistently dramatic job than the whole
interlude indicates. The letters written between More, Margaret,
and Alice Alington when More was in prison have more skill in
dialogue than most of the play *Calisto and Melebea*.

Possibly the English interlude was really written by three different hands. First, someone who knew a little Spanish may have
written the dialogue up to line 930, since this part uses more details from the Spanish source and since it is slightly better drama;
but he did not know enough Spanish to keep him from changing
the Tarpeian rock into a maiden loved by Nero:

> Behold nero in the loue of tapaya oprest,
> Rome how he brent, old and yong wept. (ll. 121–22)

Second, one without benefit of Spanish or dramatic skill wrote the
talk between Melebea and her father, lines 930 to 1043. Third,
someone else with even less dramatic skill, probably John Rastell,
wrote the sermon to the audience, from line 1,044 to the close of
the play. This part, if one grants that Rastell wrote either *Of
Gentleness and Nobility* or *The Nature of the Four Elements—*

---

[18] Vives, *De conscribendis epistolis* (Basel, 1536), leaf 40a.
[19] A. W. Reed, *Early Tudor Drama* (London, 1926), pp. 112–16, for a defense of
Rastell's authorship; H. Warner Allen, *Celestina*, for the suggestion that the author
was a friend or pupil of Vives.

and it seems probable that he wrote both of them—is more like Rastell's manner of expressing himself. But the ideas of Calisto and Melebea, the English interlude, so far as they relate a story of a young woman who remains chaste, might have been developed by More, Erasmus, Vives, Herde, or any teacher or student in More's school.

Three plays, then, have some relation to the ideas on women which were expressed by members of the More group, though the degree of the relationship varies. *Godly Queen Hester* has only one idea to connect it with the More group—the emphasis on eloquence, literature, and language in the accomplishments of the queen. *Fulgens and Lucres* characterizes a young woman of beauty, wisdom, virtue, and initiative who makes a choice in marriage based on true, not false nobility. The play was connected with members of the More group by authorship, place of performance, and printing. But *Calisto and Melebea,* with the change from its sources to teach morality and its emphasis on the beauty, learning, and chastity of Melebea, reflects the ideas of More, Erasmus, Herde, and especially the ideas of Vives on the character and status of women. Very probably it had a connection with the visits of Vives to England in the 1520's, with his disapproval of Celestina in the Spanish source and his mention of that disapproval in *The Instruction of a Christian Woman,* which was translated by Herde, a member of More's household. Whoever wrote the play, the person was probably connected with the More group. And the play was printed by John Rastell.

CONCLUSION

It seems a sound conclusion to say that secular drama in England was largely developed by men who were connected with the More circle. But much of this drama was propaganda turned into dialogue; and as compared with Marlowe or Shakespeare, it was without power, passion, or flesh-and-blood characters.

Of the anonymous plays *Godly Queen Hester* probably owed

more to a learned Catherine of Aragon and to hate of Wolsey than to any member of the More group. The two anonymous plays on education, *The Marriage of Wit and Science* and *The Marriage of Wit and Wisdom,* have no known connection with the More group, but they have at least a distant connection with the theories of education expressed by Erasmus, Vives, and other friends of theirs. Most important of all the anonymous plays is *Calisto and Melebea,* which probably owes its existence to the presence of Vives in England, and which seems to represent his individual slanting and also the general ideas of his friends. It was probably not written by Vives himself, since he showed little interest in the dramatic form; the more dramatic parts were probably not written by John Rastell, since he had little interest in the "beauty and good properties of women," but the closing lecture by Danio might have been his; it may well have been the work of several authors, perhaps members of More's school.

The men who made the greatest contribution to this drama, at least the known ones, are Henry Medwall, John Rastell (assuming his authorship of two plays, his stage, and his printing of plays), John Heywood, and John Redford.

In all this drama the outstanding themes are education in general; the education, character, and status of women, and theories of true nobility. In the area of religious reform there are no striking ideas; but the spirit of Lucian lends fantasy and imagination to some plays, especially to *The Four PP's,* with its visit to the kingdom of Satan. In the area of law and government there is no play clearly connected with the More circle which uses law and government as a major theme; but many plays echo and re-echo the phrase, the good of the commonweal, and education is often related to the welfare of the whole country. But good government is often the subject of sermons at the beginning and the ending of plays, or the idea of government is closely woven into the main theme, for example, in *Fulgens and Lucres.* Only one play, *The Nature of the Four Elements,* and one author, presumably Rastell, emphasized natural science—a desire to teach science to the common man and to further the exploration of the New World. One play, perhaps connected with the More group by its printing, John

Skelton's *Magnificence,* used the theme of government; but instead of stressing the ideas of the More group this play exalted fear, prudence, personal success, and a magnificence which is worldly prudence. Thus the play is more closely related to the aristocratic courtliness of Castiglione and to the more courtly passages in Elyot.

In printing, writing, and perhaps in staging plays, then, the men of the More group exerted influence on the development of secular drama about 1500 to 1535. Some of this influence may have had no conscious relation to their program of social reform; but in such plays as *The Nature of the Four Elements, Fulgens and Lucres, Of Gentleness and Nobility, Calisto and Melebea,* and *Wit and Science,* there was probably a conscious desire to further the good life of piety, virtue, and wisdom, classical and Christian education, and training for the commonweal, and thus to bring about the regeneration of society in the Christian world.

INDEX

As Erasmus and More are named on many pages, it seemed best not to list all pages where their names appear.

Erasmus, Colet, Linacre, Sir Thomas Elyot, Vives, Roger Bacon, John Clement, Lupset, Pole, Ascham, Starkey, John Rastell, Heywood, Medwall, Redford. These are among the many names that highlight this smoothly written and thoroughly documented contribution to the knowledge of Sir Thomas More and his circle and to the history of sixteenth-century ideas.

Sir Thomas More and his friends were in close agreement on a body of ideas which cover the important phases of human life. Though their ideas were not highly original when considered separately, these men had a complete program for the reform of society, based upon a breadth of view and a refining influence from the classics and upon applying the principles of Christianity.

Part One of this study analyzes and documents the main ideas which More and his friends wished to use for the reform of society. These ideas dealt with nature and the law of nature, the bases of true nobility, religious reforms, education in general, and the education of women apropos love and marriage. Part Two is concerned with the expression of these same ideas in the drama connected with the More circle, either by printing or writing, and possibly by staging.

Using the conventional ideas about the law of nature, the unity of all law, free will, and human perfectibility with a new vigor, Sir Thomas More and his friends developed natural science, especially medicine; they stressed a true nobility which might be achieved by virtue, character, and learning; they sought religious reform by a return to the essentials of early Christianity resulting in worthy action motivated by a love of man and God; they urged changes in law and government to give justice and equality of opportunity for common men; they proposed